"Enemies of the People"
Under the Soviets

ALSO BY PETER JULICHER

Renegades, Rebels and Rogues Under the Tsars
(McFarland, 2003)

"Enemies of the People" Under the Soviets

A History of Repression and Its Consequences

PETER JULICHER

McFarland & Company, Inc., Publishers
Jefferson, North Carolina

LIBRARY OF CONGRESS CATALOGUING-IN-PUBLICATION DATA

Julicher, Peter, 1946–
    "Enemies of the people" under the Soviets : a history of repression and its consequences / Peter Julicher.
        p.   cm.
    Includes bibliographical references and index.

    ISBN 978-0-7864-9671-6 (softcover : alkaline paper) ∞
    ISBN 978-1-4766-1855-5 (ebook)

    1. Soviet Union—Politics and government—1936–1953.
    2. Soviet Union—Politics and government—1917–1936.
    3. Political persecution—Soviet Union—History.   4. Political persecution—Social aspects—Soviet Union—History.
    5. Political prisoners—Soviet Union—History.   6. Enemies—Soviet Union—History.   7. Stalin, Joseph, 1879–1953.
    8. Glavnoe upravlenie ispravitel'no-trudovykh lagerei OGPU—History.   9. Soviet Union. Narodnyi komissariat vnutrennikh del—History.   I. Title.
    DK268.4.J85 2015
    323.4'909470904—dc23   2015003777

BRITISH LIBRARY CATALOGUING DATA ARE AVAILABLE

© 2015 Peter Julicher. All rights reserved

No part of this book may be reproduced or transmitted in any form or by any means, electronic or mechanical, including photocopying or recording, or by any information storage and retrieval system, without permission in writing from the publisher.

Cover image: Group of men declared "enemies of the people" in 1933 for "wrecking" while employed in food production (Russian State Archives of Film and Photo Documents, Krasnogorsk, Russia)

Printed in the United States of America

McFarland & Company, Inc., Publishers
  Box 611, Jefferson, North Carolina 28640
  www.mcfarlandpub.com

For two friends of the people:
Vladimir and Henry

Table of Contents

Acknowledgments	ix
Preface	1
A Note About Russian Names, Words, and Dates	2
Introduction	3
I. Capitalists, the Bourgeoisie, Landlords and the Romanovs	11
II. Socialist Revolutionaries, Anarchists and Civil War	33
III. Russian Orthodoxy and the Soviet State	48
IV. Trotsky and Trotskyism	70
V. Wreckers and Kulaks	96
VI. Old Bolsheviks, Ordinary People and the NKVD	119
VII. The Military, Foreign Communists and Repatriated POWs	150
VIII. The Creative Intelligentsia, Cosmopolitans and Jews	176
IX. The Secret Speech and Its Aftermath	201
Epilogue	210
Chapter Notes	245
Bibliography	258
Index	261

Acknowledgments

"*Enemies of the People" Under the Soviets* is intended to be a follow up to my previous book, *Renegades, Rebels and Rogues Under the Tsars*. It has been a difficult but fascinating undertaking. Fortunately, I have been able to rely on many colleagues and friends who have helped and supported me along the way.

The most important of these has been professor emeritus at Temple University Roderick E. McGrew, who has been my teacher, mentor and friend for many years. His vast knowledge of Russian and Soviet history and his constructive criticism have guided me through many challenges and difficulties. Another source of inspiration and wisdom at Temple was the late Ernst L. Presseisen, whose area of specialty was German history, but who also had a keen interest in Russia. He inspired me to achieve more than I ever thought I could. More recently, I have enjoyed the friendship of Leonid Neville and Maria Barash, both of whom were born and raised in the USSR. Together they have deeply broadened my knowledge and understanding of Russian history, language, music, art and especially humor.

Another source of help and inspiration was many old friends who share many of my academic interests. One of these is Mark Reber, who encouraged my interest in Russia while we were students at Lower Merion High School in Ardmore, Pennsylvania. I am also grateful to the late Elena Alexandrovna Shatagin, who was my first teacher of Russian. Mrs. Shatagin was born in Imperial Russia and came to America in 1922; she eventually took a position at Swarthmore College to teach Russian. Also at Swarthmore are my longtime friends Tom, Ann and Manya Bradley, who proofread parts of my manuscript and offered many useful comments and suggestions. Two other erudite friends, Geoff Levitt and Karen Collias, went to Moscow with me in 1978 to study at the Puskhin Institute in Moscow. This duo has been helpful over many years by sharing their thoughts and insights about all things Russian and Soviet. Doug Gaston of Temple University also did some proofreading and found mistakes that I otherwise would not have noticed. Finally, I must pay homage to my tenth grade world history teacher, Don Anderson, whose broad knowledge and skill as a teacher helped me enjoy the study of history, encouraged me to consider a career in education and then gave me my first teaching job as principal of Swarthmore High School.

Central to my entire academic life has been my more than three decades at Cranbrook Kingswood School in Bloomfield Hills, Michigan. The school's policy of encouragement and support for faculty professional development has enriched the lives of its faculty. This policy includes the Elizabeth Bennett Fund, which provided support for me to travel to Russia so that I could study at the Lenin Library in Moscow and speak with those who lived through the Great Terror of the 1930s. I have also been fortunate to work with colleagues like Eric Linder, Chip Wiswall and Bill Hancock, whose stellar academic examples and moral support encouraged me when I most needed it. Special mention must also be made of our dedicated and resourceful library staff including Linda Stone, Gail Thomas and Mary Peterson. These amazing women have helped me and others in so many ways over the years. They have made our school library a wonderful and exciting place to be.

Finally, I am deeply indebted to my dear wife Olga, who found, and obtained official permission for me to use, the photos in this book. She also helped me to cite these sources properly so the Russian organizations that offered their assistance could be properly recognized and thanked.

Preface

FOR MOST OF MY THIRTY-TWO YEARS as a history teacher at Cranbrook Kingswood School in Bloomfield Hills, Michigan, I taught a junior-senior elective entitled "Russia and Eastern Europe." This allowed me to share with my students my interest in and enthusiasm for Russian and Soviet history. The course covered most of the tsarist period and the entire seventy-four years of Soviet rule in the twentieth century.

The Soviet period in particular was a time of profound social and economic upheaval as Soviet leaders strove to create a socialist utopia based on the communist theories of Karl Marx. Central to this endeavor was the twenty-five-year dictatorship of Josef Stalin, whose ruthless determination to make the Soviet Union a world-class industrial and military power created misery on a grand scale and caused the deaths of millions of people. To achieve complete domination over his Soviet subjects, Stalin invoked the specter of "enemies of the people" on a regular basis. This allowed the regime to arbitrarily abuse and destroy anyone who opposed, or in some way impeded, the building of the new socialist order.

The "enemies of the people" concept has existed in various forms throughout history and in many societies. My experience as a teacher, however, has persuaded me that this label, especially as it was applied in the USSR, needs to be examined in some depth in order to fully understand how it fatally distorted the Soviet mission to create the world's first socialist society. Thus, it is my hope that this book will explain how this came to be and serve as a warning to those who think it can't happen again.

A Note About Russian Names, Words, and Dates

ALL RUSSIANS HAVE A FIRST NAME and a patronymic or middle name, which is derived from their father's first name. However, the feminine forms of the names usually end in the letter "a." Thus Nicholas II, who was the last tsar of Russia, was called Nicholas Alexandrovich Romanov. His only son was called Alexei Nicholaevich Romanov, and his youngest daughter was called Anastasia Nicholaevna Romanov. The transliterations of these names have many variations, but I have tried to adhere to a system that will be easiest for the reader. Russian words used in the narrative can also be a problem to the reader; I have italicized and defined those that I believe are not familiar to most people.

Another source of confusion that requires explanation is the calendar. Until the time of Peter the Great, the Russians had always counted time from the beginning of the world. Thus, the year 1700 in Western Europe was the year 7208 for people living in Russia. In that year, however, Tsar Peter decreed that his subjects adopt the Julian calendar, even though it was eleven days behind the more accurate Gregorian calendar. By the twentieth century, dates of the Julian calendar had fallen thirteen days behind those of the Gregorian calendar. In February 1918, the new Bolshevik regime imposed the Gregorian calendar to bring the new Soviet state in line with most other countries around the world. To avoid confusion, I have cited dates prior to 1918 according to both the Julian and Gregorian calendars. Thus the date for the Bolshevik coup that overthrew the Provisional Government, which began the Communist Revolution in Russia, is October 25 (November 7), 1917.

Introduction

ON NOVEMBER 12 (24), 1917, ORDINARY RUSSIANS went to the polls for the first time in history to participate in a nationwide democratic election. Their task was to elect delegates to a soon-to-be convened Constituent Assembly. The event was hailed around the world as a major turning point for a country that only nine months earlier had been ruled by a tsar-autocrat. The atmosphere, however, which should have been celebratory, was decidedly tense. Not only was the country at war with Germany and the Central Powers, but less than three weeks earlier, the radical Bolshevik Party had overthrown the Provisional Government, which had formed the previous March after the tsar's abdication. The members of this interim body had scheduled the elections and intended to supervise them. But the Bolsheviks, having taken power by force, feared they could not win at the ballot box. It was only with the greatest reluctance that they allowed the elections to take place. In fact, their concerns proved to be well founded. The big winners were the Socialist Revolutionaries and the Mensheviks, who combined to capture sixty-two percent of the vote. Far behind them were the Bolsheviks, who won a mere twenty-five percent. Least successful were the Constitutional Democrats or Kadets, which, with all other parties combined, totaled only thirteen percent.

The Bolsheviks' most influential leader, Vladimir Ilich Lenin, had anticipated such an outcome. After the election, he began to openly deny the validity of any results that did not recognize the recently formed Petrograd Soviet of Soldiers and Workers as the ultimate authority in the land. Now, as chairman of the Council of People's Commissars, he endeavored to protect Soviet power by postponing the scheduled opening of the Constituent Assembly from November 28 to January 5. This was protested by members of the former

Provisional Government, who were in hiding to avoid arrest. Using newspapers that belonged to the Constitutional Democrats or Kadets, they defiantly called for the elected members of the Constituent Assembly to meet in the Tauride Palace as originally scheduled. Lenin reacted swiftly and angrily to this affront. He shut down the Kadets' newspapers and arrested their leaders, denouncing them as "enemies of the people."[1]

The term had originally been employed by the Jacobins and their fanatical leader, Maximillian Robespierre, during the French Revolution. In the spring of 1793, many were so alarmed by the activities of counterrevolutionaries and by the threat of foreign invasion that they created the Revolutionary Tribunal and the Committee of Public Safety—the former to judge those accused of crimes against the state, and the latter to root out enemies of the revolution. But things soon got out of hand, as food shortages, wild rumors, and the defection of a high-ranking general to the Austrians created panic among the common people. The Committee, which originally had been intended only to serve as a link between the deputies and the Executive Council of the National Convention, expanded its power to replace ministers and suppress rebellion in the countryside. And still the crisis intensified, allegedly because the opponents of the Revolution were undermining all that had been achieved in the name of liberty, justice, and equality. Thus, in the fall of 1793, the country was engulfed in a reign of terror that prompted the Revolutionary Tribunal to divide itself into four courts operating day and night. In their determination to "purify" the Revolution, the Jacobins had thousands arrested, tried, and convicted on unfounded accusations or the mere suspicion of wrongdoing. Many of these, like the poet Andrea Chenier and the chemist Antoine Lavoisier, were sent to the guillotine even though they were loyal to the revolution and had committed no crime.

Lenin, a keen student of history, had long believed that revolution by its very nature demanded force and terror. He was particularly fascinated by the example of the Jacobins in eliminating their enemies, and in an article for the Bolsheviks' newspaper, *Pravda,* on June 20, 1917, he praised and recommended their courage and ruthlessness. Initially, however, he identified only landowners and capitalists as the implacable "enemies of the people."[2] Later, he and others expanded the list to include monarchists, former nobles and tsarist officials, petty merchants, bankers, speculators, kulaks, intellectuals, priests, believers, political opponents, and ordinary street hooligans and bandits. Such people were so classified not necessarily for what they had done, but for who they were. They were outside the law, had no rights, and were beyond redemption.

This, coupled with the Bolsheviks' belief in their own infallibility as scientific socialists and in the inevitability of class warfare, prepared the way for an enormous social and economic calamity that few could have foreseen or even imagined.

Lenin and Robespierre had much in common: both were dedicated to the creation of a new kind of society, and both were prepared to exploit their enemies to achieve this end. The innate malevolence of those who opposed the Revolution made it easy for them to be demonized, and this allowed revolutionary leaders to rationalize failures and setbacks. It also inspired ordinary people to overcome hardships and to fight in defense of the new order. The problem was that the eradication of these "enemies of the people" encouraged a level of savagery that engulfed even those who supported the Revolution and who were innocent of any wrongdoing.

In France, this process in its most intense form lasted about nine months, from November 1793 to July 1794. Eventually, the man who instigated the terror, Robespierre, was himself denounced and sent to the guillotine. This was the beginning of the end of the French Revolution. A new conservative government known as the Directory was established and lasted for several years. This was followed by followed by a coup d'etat in 1789 in which a general, Napoleon Bonaparte, became the country's most prominent leader. In 1802, the general went to Rome to crown himself Emperor of France in a ceremony sanctioned and attended by the Pope.

To be sure, Lenin's own ideas about how to protect the Revolution and construct socialism changed dramatically within a relatively short time. In *The State and Revolution,* written during the summer of 1917, he prophesied that a socialist society would have no need for a police force. Ordinary citizens would themselves confront potential exploiters and counterrevolutionaries and administer summary justice. But the intractability of the problems he faced once in power all but overwhelmed him. These included food shortages, street crime, and "wine pogroms"—orgies of public drunkenness that tore at the very fabric of the new social order. Still, Lenin did not act decisively until he learned of an impending strike by all state employees set for December 20. On that very day, and at Lenin's behest, the Council of People's Commissars created the All-Russian Extraordinary Commission for Combating Counterrevolution and Sabotage, better known as the Cheka. This was the first of many security agencies created under Soviet power.

The man chosen to head this new force was a Pole who had spent eleven of his forty years in tsarist prisons. Felix Dzerzhinsky (Dzierzynsky) was a man of intense revolutionary fervor with a high sense of honor who was prepared to dedicate himself completely to the task of hunting down opponents of the new order and avenging past wrongs. In his chilling acceptance speech to the council of People's Commissars, Dzerzhinsky left no doubt about his intention to employ terror as a tool to rid the country of enemies, real and potential:

> Do not think I seek forms of revolutionary justice; we are not now in need of justice. It is war now ... face to face, a fight to the finish. Life or death! I propose, I demand an organ for the revolutionary settlement of accounts with counter-revolutionaries.[3]

Dzerzhinsky's rhetoric notwithstanding, the Cheka was intended primarily as an investigatory institution and was allotted only a small staff and modest offices in the Smolny Institute in Petrograd. Though it had the right to arrest suspects almost from the beginning, it was required to hand them over to the newly created Revolutionary Tribunals. Moreover, its powers of punishment were harsh, but not necessarily lethal: it could confiscate wealth, deprive people of their ration cards, and publish lists of the people's enemies. But this changed dramatically in February 1918, when peace negotiations with the Germans at Brest Litovsk stalled. The situation was unbearably tense, and when Lenin learned that the German army was advancing on Petrograd, he promptly wrote a decree entitled "The Socialist Fatherland in Danger." In it he called for a number of emergency measures, including work brigades made up of members of the bourgeoisie, who were forced to dig trenches at gunpoint. He also demanded the summary execution of enemy agents, speculators, burglars, hooligans, counterrevolutionary agitators, and German spies." How these individuals were to be identified and judged was not explained. Near anarchy reigned, because the laws of the old regime had been annulled. Thus, the Cheka made up its own rules about who would be shot and who would be spared.

In March of 1918, Lenin ordered the capital moved from Petrograd to Moscow. The Cheka was assigned the imposing former headquarters of the Lloyd's Insurance Company in Lubyanka Square. By now, Dzerzhinsky's organization had roughly 600 employees, as a network of Chekas began to form at the provincial and district level. Throughout the spring and summer, the agents of this vast security apparatus acted with increasing abandon against the perceived enemies of the new order. At the same time, the regime was threatened by a number of crises; these included the Allied intervention, civil war, an armed uprising of the Socialist Revolutionaries against the Bolsheviks in July, assassinations, and an attempt on the life of Lenin. This final event was followed by The Council of People's Commissars' Decree on the Red Terror on September 5, 1918. The Cheka was authorized to incarcerate all class enemies in concentration camps and shoot "all persons involved in anti-revolutionary White Guard organizations, plots and insurrections."

It is not known how many people were executed during the first year of the revolution, although Martyn Latsis, a deputy to Dzerzhinsky, estimated the number to be in excess of 6,000. The true figure can only be guessed at, since the local soviets and Revolutionary Tribunals also carried out executions without documentation. But the most dispiriting aspect of the carnage was not only the high number of victims and the essential indifference of the perpetrators to their guilt or innocence, but that anyone could become an "enemy of the people" for any reason and without warning. Consider the case of Bim-Bom the clown of the Moscow Circus, who sometimes entertained his audience by telling jokes about the regime. The Cheka saw something threatening in his impertinence and came to arrest him while he was performing his act. As Bim-Bom tried to escape, the audience laughed, thinking it was all part of the show. But the Cheka agents were not amused and, to the horror of all, shot the actor dead in the back.[4]

Lenin himself was never known to indulge in personal cruelty and at times could be quite solicitous to those who had been wrongly abused. Still, he was absolutely insistent that terror was necessary if the revolution were to succeed. The only way to deal with the people's enemies was to exterminate them. Nor did he think it necessary to worry much about the fate of innocent victims. Such mistakes could not be avoided and, in any case, were a necessary part of what terror was supposed to be. It was for these reasons that he was violently opposed to any attempt to abolish the death penalty and was enraged when the Second Soviet Congress actually did so on October 26, 1917. As he put it at the time: "How can you make a revolution without firing squads?"[5]

Actually, Lenin's attitude regarding the issues of terror and capital punishment was not only ideological; it was also personal. Though he approved of systematic mass terror, he had always opposed such acts when performed individually. The latter he thought ineffective as a revolutionary tool, possibly because his own brother, Alexander Ulianov, had been executed after a failed attempt to assassinate Tsar Alexander III in 1887. Not only had this resulted in his family's abuse and ostracization by longtime friends and neighbors, but it played a large part in his own expulsion from the University of Kazan in 1889, after he participated in a student demonstration. Eventually, Lenin did get a degree in law from the University of St. Petersburg, but by this time he had developed a seething hatred of the old order and had resolved to destroy it. To this end, he became a Marxist and joined the Social Democratic Labor Party, only to be arrested for inciting strikes. He spent three years in Siberia and left Russia for western Europe upon completion of his term in 1900. Once abroad, he continued the seemingly futile struggle to promote the cause until the outbreak of the First World War offered a ray of hope. After two and a half years of fighting, the tsar was forced to abdicate because of military defeats and chaos on the domestic front. This allowed Lenin to return to Russia one month later to agitate against the newly formed Provisional Government. More than any other individual, it was Lenin who made the Bolshevik Revolution happen by demanding that his comrades seize power in October 1917.

Once in power, Lenin had no intention of turning back or stopping short. He envisioned not only the creation of socialist society in Russia, but also a world revolution. At the same time, he was determined to obliterate those enemies of the people who threatened or even passively opposed the new order. But this involved a danger that he never fully recognized. Indeed, the extreme fluidity of the designation itself became a serious problem. If anyone could be defined as an "enemy of the people," how could loyal comrades express their differences and doubts without fear of retribution? In *The State and Revolution,* Lenin seemed to have an answer. He called for a government of the "dictatorship of the proletariat" consisting of Bolshevik party members, which would serve until the perfect communist society was achieved. By that time, he prophesized, the state itself would have withered away and people would live and work together peacefully and cooperatively. In the meantime, however, the party would deal with the practical realities of daily government according to the principle of democratic centralism, a term that emphasized the strictest party discipline. Thus, problems could be discussed and voted upon, but in the end, the minority had to submit to the will of the majority. This also meant that all decisions of higher authorities were to be binding on lower ones.

But things did not go quite as Lenin planned. The Red Terror and the civil war devastated Russia, causing as many as four million deaths. The country was far too exhausted to create a state based on socialism, so Lenin, at the Tenth Party Congress, in a very unpopular move, urged the New Economic Policy on his doubting comrades. This allowed the return of the market economy and a certain amount of free enterprise until the country recovered. But Lenin died in January 1924 without having designated a successor. Gradually,

Josef Stalin, who held the posts of Commissar of Nationalities and General Secretary of the Communist Party, began to establish control. It was an ominous development. Stalin had every intention of ruling despotically, and he used his position as General Secretary to pack the bureaucracy with people loyal to him. This included such agencies as the Cheka and its successor, the GPU. In time, Stalin began to apply the term "enemy of the people" to anyone who opposed him, actively or passively.

The most prominent of his early victims, in 1927, was Lev Davidovich Trotsky, who had previously served as Commissar of Foreign Affairs and Commissar of War. Despite Trotsky's heroic leadership of the Red Army during the civil war, Stalin succeeded in having him expelled from the Party, sent into exile, and eventually murdered. The "enemy of the people" label became especially widespread during the mid–1930s during the Great Terror, when millions of Soviet citizens were arrested and sent to concentration camps or shot. At one point, a secret letter was sent out by the Central Committee to Party organizations all over the country, warning citizens to be vigilant: "enemies of the people" might seem "tame and inoffensive," but their goal was to infiltrate the socialist system for the most sinister reasons. Lavrenty Beria, who for many years headed various organs of the Soviet secret police, went even further. He defined an "enemy of the people" as not necessarily a saboteur, but merely "one who doubts the rightness of the Party line."[6] Ironically, Beria himself would eventually be declared an "enemy of the people" and executed.

The term "enemy of the people" remained active in the Soviet vocabulary for nearly four decades. It gradually slipped into disuse after Nikita Khrushchev's secret speech to the Twentieth Party Congress in February 1956, in which he denounced the crimes of his predecessor, Josef Stalin. This highly controversial act was followed by the release of thousands of political prisoners and the creation of a freer intellectual atmosphere in the Soviet Union. With this came some minor improvements in the area of human rights: Now, people who challenged the system tended to be persecuted for what they did rather than who they were. Still considered outside the law, such individuals were generally not referred to as "enemies of the people," but "dissidents or *inakomyclyashchii*." (The latter term in Russian roughly translates as "one who thinks otherwise.") Most were sent to the Gulag, although in the more serious cases the death penalty continued to be applied. Still others were confined to mental institutions and "treated" as patients, which might suggest that they were no longer considered beyond redemption.

As significant as these developments were, fundamental change to the

Soviet system proved impossible, even though most in the ruling elite recognized its need. Thus, when the Soviet Union's last General Secretary of the Communist Party, Mikhail Gorbachev, offered *glasnost* (openness), *perestroika* (restructuring), and *demokratizatsiya* (democratization) as a means to reform in the late 1980s, it was already too late. The people, long alienated from and distrustful of their government, did not know what to make of these initiatives. Many feared an eventual return to the mentality that allowed those who opposed Marxist-Leninism to be branded "enemies of the people." Indeed, this seemed about to happen in August 1991 when hardline Communists attempted to remove Gorbachev and end his reforms. In the end, the coup failed, although the Soviet Union was mortally wounded and officially disbanded in December of that year. Today the Russian Federation struggles with many of the same problems that beset the tsars and soviets, and those who long for a civil society remain disappointed.

Still, the Bolsheviks made a profound contribution to the 20th century's revolutionary culture, especially by their revival and development of the concept "enemies of the people." Their example was copied in Castro's Cuba, radicalized in Mao's China, and taken to insane lengths in Pol Pot's Cambodia. The "enemies" concept has also been applied, perhaps less obviously, by Muslim clerics in Iran, by Baathists in Iraq, and by Shining Path terrorists in Peru.

Chapter I

Capitalists, the Bourgeoisie, Landlords and the Romanovs

THE DEEPLY HELD CONVICTION of many Bolsheviks that certain kinds of people would always be enemies of socialism had profound and long-lasting consequences. Not only did it block the growth of democracy and retard economic prosperity in the new Soviet state, it led to the abuse, incarceration, and deaths of tens of millions of citizens, most of whom were innocent of any wrongdoing. That this process could have been initiated and carried out virtually unchallenged over many decades can partially be explained by the passivity of a Russia traumatized and exhausted by war and revolution. In addition, the new regime's extreme Marxist view of history with its "scientific" explanation for the existence of economic injustice and class enemies proved remarkably durable. At its simplest, this interpretation identified the landowning nobility as the earliest such class enemy, which, having claimed ownership of the land from time immemorial, had exploited and abused the peasants who worked it. By the late 1890s, however, a far more lethal culprit had emerged: the bourgeoisie. This term included a wide variety of entrepreneurial types, such as industrial capitalists, small business owners, merchants, and various kinds of professionals such as doctors, lawyers, and engineers. The wealthiest and most powerful of these were the big industrial capitalists who owned the means of production (i.e., factories, farms, and mines). The technological developments of the Industrial Revolution had allowed them to amass fantastic fortunes. However, in their determination to increase profits and drive their competitors out of business, they had reduced their own workers to the most degrading poverty and squalor.

The new system of production, or industrial capitalism, had other consequences as well. It created a need for raw materials and new markets, which encouraged the acquisition of colonial empires by the industrial powers. Countries such as Britain, France, the United States, Italy, and Japan built large militaries and competed with each other for colonies around the world. In the process, they subdued the native populations by force and subjected them to various forms of abuse and exploitation. Attempts by these peoples to gain redress through peaceful protest or outright rebellion generally proved fruitless and often led to savage repression. The conquerors had scant regard for their captive peoples and few second thoughts about the morality of what they were doing. Most imperialists smugly embraced the illusion that by bringing civilization and Christianity to the "primitive" peoples of the world, they were actually engaged in a noble enterprise.

To many nineteenth-century socialists, and especially those who adhered to the theories of Karl Marx (1819–1883), these developments aroused dismay and indignation.[1] Never had wealth of the privileged been more plentiful or the poverty of the toiling masses more abject. For all its marvelous productive potential, the capitalist system in the industrial age had produced armies of underpaid and unemployed workers, vast urban slums, cesspools of toxic pollution, and a culture of vice and violence that seemed destined only to become worse. Still, the most determined socialists took heart. Surely capitalism could not long survive its many contradictions and self-destructive nature. At some point it was doomed to collapse from its own rottenness, helped along, undoubtedly, by war and revolution.

Belief in this apocalyptic end found adherents not only in the advanced industrial states, but also in Russia, where industrial capitalism was still in its infancy. Its most fervent proponent was Vladimir Lenin, who, in 1903, split the Social Democratic Labor Party into two factions[2] to aggressively promote the destruction of capitalism in Russia and to build an industrial state based on socialist ideals. But Lenin was not content to limit his vision to Russia. He believed the destruction of capitalism in Russia would spark socialist revolutions in other industrialized countries, and this would lead to the establishment of a new world economic and social order. The new socialist states that emerged would feature collective ownership of the means of production and an end to the market economy with its business cycles and stock-market speculation. Careful economic planning would result in a nearly unlimited supply of goods and services and an equitable and fair system of distribution. Poverty and all forms of economic and social injustice would vanish. Workers and peasants would contribute "according to their ability and receive according to their needs," and humanity would at last be free to fulfill its true creative potential.

In the Russia of October 1917, however, this idyllic scenario could hardly be imagined, let alone realized. The country was at war for its very existence with Germany and the Central Powers, its economy had collapsed, and near anarchy reigned in the streets. Under such conditions, the newly empowered Bolsheviks, who enjoyed little popular support, seemed on the verge of being overwhelmed by the many problems and enemies they faced. Even so, Lenin pushed forward, determined to impose his socialist "dictatorship of the proletariat," which he defined as a "system of organized violence" against the bourgeoisie.[3] Acting through the newly created Council of People's Commissars (Sovnarkom), he was determined to eradicate the capitalist basis of society and everything that was connected to tsarist rule. Thus, one of the Council's first decrees was to abolish the Table of Ranks—the system of social, political, and military advancement that had been established by Peter the Great in 1722. This was followed by the elimination of all titles, ranks, and social estates. Henceforth people were to address one another either as *grazhdanin* (citizen) or *tovarishch* (comrade), and all rights of inheritance were declared null and void. The stock market was abolished, banking was made a state monopoly, savings accounts were expropriated, and the private ownership of land was declared illegal. Many factories were nationalized, with ordinary workers being urged to take control. What had once been considered ordinary business activity was now a crime.[4]

For the so-called "former people" or *byvshchie liudi,* who had previously enjoyed almost unlimited social and economic privilege, the world had turned upside down. By December 1917, the new regime had authorized the confiscation of all mansions and large houses, many of which were divided up and turned into apartments for needy workers. If the original owners were fortunate, they were allowed to inhabit one room of what had once been their family home. In some cases, however, they were evicted altogether and had their furniture and most of what they owned confiscated. Such people were now reduced to selling their family heirlooms and jewelry in the street to buy bread. Others sold pies, knitwear, and matches at bazaars and flea markets. To the Bolsheviks, all this was fair and just, and it soon became enshrined in law that "he who does not work, neither shall he eat." To enforce this dictum, municipal soviets began organizing work brigades of idle bourgeoisie to shovel snow and clean the streets. Commissar of War Lev Trotsky adopted the same practice for the Red Army and took pride in the fact that former members of the leisured classes were being forced to dig ditches and clean up filth in the barracks. As he put it: "We must make life so uncomfortable for them that they will lose the desire to remain bourgeois."[5]

Many aristocrats fled to their estates in the countryside, hoping to find some refuge from the upheavals of the cities. But even in isolated and distant rural areas, the Revolution was making itself felt. The Bolsheviks' October Decree on Land had encouraged the peasants, most of whom lived in communes, to divide up the land, tools, and livestock among themselves. This proved to be no easy task due to the lack of maps and measuring implements. Arguments and fighting were not uncommon. Still, the commune elders generally tried to be fair and based the amount of land that each peasant household received on the number of mouths each had to feed. They also allowed members of the gentry to retain small portions of their former estates in the belief that all people should be given a chance to live by the fruits of their own labor.

Indeed, some former landlords were determined to make the best of the situation. One such family, the Rudnevs, actually turned over most of their land to the local peasant commune and sold their tools and livestock at artificially low prices. They also hired destitute peasants to work on what remained of their farm, paying them in vodka and fruit liquors. Nor did they resist when the commune demanded that the Rudnevs sell their surplus grain to poor peasants at fixed prices. Unfortunately, all this goodwill and exemplary behavior came to naught in the summer of 1918, when they were driven off their farm by a detachment of Red Guards, who denounced them as class enemies. The situation became increasingly volatile as more and more demobilized soldiers returned from the front. In some cases, these angry young men organized into paramilitary units and pressured the local soviets to take revenge on the former landlords. One such victim was a poor widow, who had once been prosperous. She, too, tried her best to adjust to new order by turning over most of her land and livestock to the commune. Even so, the soldiers drove her to suicide when they shot her only horse and pet dog.[6]

In the new Soviet state, many thought such vindictiveness not only proper, but necessary to avenge past wrongs. The goal of the Bolshevik regime was to create a "republic of equals" based on the notion that property was theft, surplus wealth was immoral, and that labor was the only real source of value. This necessitated an outright war on privilege in order to "loot the looters." After all, had not the nobility and the bourgeoisie accumulated their wealth at the expense of the toiling masses? Had not the proletariat and the peasantry been denied their fair share of what they had produced? Now with their positions reversed, socialist justice could finally be done.

To this end, the old legal system was abolished and replaced with another that featured two new types of courts. The first of these were the People's Courts, which dealt with cases involving crimes against individuals. They were composed of twelve elected judges, most of whom had no knowledge of the law and very little education in general. Trials in the People's Courts often resembled little more than mob justice since they lacked formal legal procedures and rules of evidence and relied instead on denunciation and slander. And because the judges were officially encouraged to act according to their own revolutionary consciences, spectators often tried to influence them by shouting their opinions from the gallery. A defendant's class origin was often the deciding factor in determining his or her guilt or innocence.[7]

Another kind of court, the Revolutionary Tribunal, was created on November 9 (22), 1917, to deal specifically with crimes against the state. These bodies were composed of a president and some combination of six peasants, workers, and soldiers. As with the People's Courts, the only prerequisite to serve was an ability to read and write. Initially, these tribunals were denied the power to impose capital punishment and were instructed to render decisions based on the "circumstances of the case and the dictates of revolutionary conscience." However, Lenin's desire to make these bodies an instrument of terror led to a new resolution on June 18, 1918, which not only gave the tribunals the freedom to impose any penalty, but actually required them to condemn criminals to death when so ordered by the government. Even so, these Bolshevik-dominated Tribunals, to Lenin's disgust, refused to live up to their potential. Of the thousands of capitalists, property owners, speculators, and small shopkeepers who died violently during the first year of the Revolution, only fourteen were executed on the basis of verdicts rendered by the Tribunals.[8]

Lenin's fervor on this issue was not due to any particular lust for blood on his part, but rather to his relentlessly "scientific" interpretation of history and the laws of human behavior. People, as he insisted again and again, could not help but act in accordance with their basic class interests. Thus the "bourgeois elements" who were still at large in society could never be trusted to support the Revolution and were bound either consciously or unconsciously to undermine its most fundamental goals. He was inclined to apply the same harsh logic to his declared political opponents, whom he denounced as "agents of the bourgeoisie," "agents of imperialism," and "socialist traitors." Herein lies the seed that later grew to such monstrous proportions and claimed so many innocent victims: That a person might be *subjectively* honest and believe himself devoted to the socialist cause meant nothing. What mattered most were the positions he or she *objectively* or involuntarily supported. In Lenin's view it followed that anyone who opposed Bolshevism helped the bourgeoisie and jeopardized the Revolution. Therefore there was some logic in exterminating such people before they could harm the socialist cause.[9]

In the immediate aftermath of the Bolshevik takeover, such a draconian solution was neither practical nor feasible. The regime needed bourgeois specialists to help build socialism, and it needed the cooperation of other less extreme political groups to keep the revolution on track. It was this predicament that drove Lenin to extremes as he attempted to deal with the new regime's many problems. He often lashed out at those who opposed him, calling them "harmful insects, scoundrels, bloodsuckers, fleas, bedbugs, spiders and leeches." In December 1917 he went so far as to call for a "war to the death against the rich, the idlers and the parasites." He urged each village and town to come up with its own solutions for dealing with their enemies. Incarceration, forced labor, and the death penalty should all be considered. "The more variety the better," said Lenin "for only practice can devise the best methods of struggle."[10]

Probably his most irresponsible outburst was that of February 1918, when peace negotiations with the Germans at Brest Litovsk temporarily broke down. Fearful that the Bolsheviks might be swept from power by a German invasion, Lenin submitted a proposal to the Council of People's Commissars entitled "The Socialist Fatherland in Danger," in which he urged ordinary people to save the Revolution by summarily executing anyone who might be enemies of the regime. One man who opposed this initiative was Minister of Justice Isaac Sternberg, who had previously tried (and failed) to curb the excesses of the Cheka. Now he appealed to Lenin directly, asking, "Why do we bother with a Commissariat of Justice at all? Let's call it frankly the 'Commissariat for Social Extermination' and be done with it?" Lenin actually seemed to like the suggestion and replied, "Well put, that's exactly what it should be; but we can't say that."[11]

Lenin's motivation in singling out the bourgeoisie as "enemies of the people" was derived in large part from the belief that Russia needed a civil war to destroy the enemies of the working class in order to complete the Revolution. Still, it is doubtful that he imagined how destructive the process would become and how difficult it would be to contain. Ordinary workers and peasants, having been officially encouraged to abuse their class enemies, hardly understood what the word bourgeoisie meant. The official Marxist definition had explained the term to include members of the ruling class in the capitalist mode of production, who engaged in business, banking, and/or stock speculation. Such people were easy to demonize because they made their living by exploiting the labor of others. After the Bolshevik takeover, however, the Russian word *burzhui* was often applied to people whose class identity was in doubt or, at best, mixed. These included "officers, landowners, priests, merchants, Jews, students, professionals or anyone else well dressed, foreign looking or seemingly well-to-do." Even a peasant might be denounced as a *burzhui* if he or she was suspected of hoarding food. As the economic situation deteriorated and the country slipped into terror and civil war, this became a serious matter. Soon the term became synonymous with "enemy of the people," which brought on the most severe forms of abuse and sometimes death.[12]

This is exactly what happened in Nizhni Novgorod when the local Bolsheviks adopted the practice of taking hostages among the petite bourgeoisie to enforce compliance with various rules and regulations, especially the payment of taxes. In this instance, the local Soviet imposed a twenty-two-million-ruble levy on those suspected of being wealthy. When the money could not be collected, the Cheka imprisoned 105 alleged *burzhuii* to frighten them and others into compliance. Among them were "petty traders, half-impoverished teachers, doctors and clerks," most of whom had never had much in savings or owned anything of great value. Still, as long as the money was not forthcoming, they remained incarcerated. Soon more arrests were made, and when this didn't work, the Cheka began shooting the inmates.[13] As hideous as this seems in retrospect, it aroused little concern among Bolsheviks at the time. True, the victims posed little or no threat to the Revolution, but neither could they be expected to actively assist in the development of socialism. Hence, they were of no use to the state.

Logically, it should have followed that Lenin's attitude toward Russia's wealthiest entrepreneurs, who were, in Marxist parlance, the archenemies of the laboring class, should have been far more hostile than to the petite bourgeoisie. But Lenin could be surprisingly pragmatic when confronted with the realities of building socialism. With economic collapse looming, and mindful that the capitalists knew how to create wealth, he considered doing the unthinkable. Having written about the virtues of state capitalism, he now began to look for practical ways to involve Russia's big industrialists in the building of socialism. Accordingly, he approached an influential iron and steel magnate named Alexei Pavlovich Mershcherski in March 1918 and urged him to put together a plan to develop the country's heavy industry. The proposal required Mershcherski to recruit other capitalists in return for joint ownership with the Soviet government of whatever enterprises were created. Mershcherski, for his part, gave the idea serious consideration, although most of the Party's left wing was adamantly opposed. The deal fell through because Lenin lacked the authority to impose such a controversial initiative on his doubting comrades.[14]

Lenin might also have been tempted to entice some of Moscow's merchant entrepreneurs to cooperate with the Bolsheviks. The ability of these arch- "enemies of the people" to create wealth clearly suggested that they understood something about economics and finance worth knowing. Among the most interesting of these was the senior member of a very devout Old Believer[15] family, Pavel Pavlovich Riabushinsky, who had inherited his father's textile business in 1899. Born in 1871, he demonstrated his unique abilities by rebuilding the family business after a fire destroyed its textile mills in 1900. To restore and expand his family's fortunes, Riabushinsky, helped by his five brothers, invested in several banks and eventually gained control of Russia's third-largest mortgage bank. In 1912, the family converted this enterprise into a joint stock bank, which they renamed the Moscow Commercial Bank. By 1914, the family business employed some 4,500 workers and produced an estimated eight million rubles of wealth annually. Too, the Riabushinskys were model citizens who gave to charities, engaged in philanthropy, and patronized the arts.[16]

But the Riabushinsky brothers, and Pavel in particular, were in many ways troubled men. As they looked westward toward a dynamic and increasingly militant Germany, they feared for the very survival of Russia. Moreover, the revolutionary upheaval of 1905, which had grown out of the country's disastrous war with Japan and the Bloody Sunday massacre of January 1905 convinced the Riabushinskys and many others that the tsar's regime could not possibly be expected to manage the challenges of the modern world. Almost in exasperation, Pavel developed his own utopian vision of Russia's future, which he propagated by publishing a daily newspaper called *Utro Rossii* or the Morn of Russia. This vision consisted of a parliamentary democracy based on the rule of law and free from autocratic interference. He also offered a vigorous defense of capitalism and extolled what he called his "bourgeois idea." Membership in Russia's entrepreneurial elite was "a special calling from God." And if such a status conferred certain privileges, it also imposed serious responsibilities. In Riabushinky's view, Russia's entrepreneurs would be enjoined to "constrain all predatory instincts and exploitive behaviors" as they harnessed the "protean power" of free capitalism for the good of society. Not only would this result in the production of more wealth and a better standard of living for the people, but the citizenry would be united by a noble and patriotic purpose: Russians would once again "share the same piety, the same rituals, the same ethos that they had in ages gone by, yet both would now be dedicated to the common task of building a new Russia."[17]

That this dream was never realized was only partly due to the outbreak of war in 1914. In fact, well before the assassination of Archduke Franz Ferdinand in Sarajevo, the tsar and his ministers were becoming increasingly reactionary and took little interest in Riabushinsky's "bourgeois idea." The problem was that those entrepreneurs who believed in capitalism as a dynamic force for Russia were too divided and too timid to act decisively. Thus, by 1911, Riabushinsky and other members of his circle began meeting secretly with certain Bolsheviks and other radicals to discuss a possible "superorganic," or revolutionary, solution as a way of moving forward. When this failed, Riabushinsky fell into deep despair and worried about the "dark forces" at work in the land. "We are at the limits of the possible. What can we do?"[18]

As it turned out, not much. When the Great War came, Russia was woefully unprepared. One disaster followed another, which culminated in the tsar's abdication in March 1917. The Bolsheviks came to power the following November and immediately set out to make peace with Germany and construct the new socialist order. By the spring of 1918, with civil war looming, the new regime started dealing with their hated enemies among the bourgeoisie in earnest. Many were arrested or shot; others were driven out of their homes and forced to wander the streets or to emigrate. Most did the latter, including the six Riabushinsky brothers, who went to France. The lone exception was Dmitri, who hoped to find a place in the new order. In addition to his business activities, Dmitri was the creator in 1904 of an aerodynamic laboratory and the world's first wind tunnel on his estate just outside Moscow. Thus began the Russian scientific study of flight and the beginning of the Russian aerospace industry. Since he could not bear to part with what had become his life's work, in April 1918 he persuaded the Soviet government to nationalize his laboratory. This done, he became part of the Academy of Sciences, which for a time protected him from the revolutionary tumult swirling around him.[19]

This sensible arrangement, however, came to an abrupt end early that summer when a gang of young Bolshevik activists came to Kuchino looking for Dmitri. As it happened, he had gone to Moscow to attend to some Academy business. The intruders, not finding him, decided to amuse themselves by vandalizing his estate. They tore down drapes, smashed furniture, and threw grenades into the river to kill fish. They even terrified the French nanny by firing shots at the horse-drawn cart that was bringing her home. This went on for many hours. Only late in the afternoon did the young men tire of their fun and leave. They promised to return soon to finish the job and arrest the *burzhui*.[20]

Upon his return, Dmitri learned of the visit later that evening and resolved to send his family to a safer place. He had them dress in working-class clothes and sent them south to stay with some relatives. Being so well known, he did not dare to go with them. Instead, he waited for several weeks before traveling to Petrograd. His plan was to go abroad by pretending to be on assignment for the Academy of Sciences. In Petrograd he was detained and brought before the head of the Cheka, Moisei Uritsky, who placed him under house arrest in the Hotel Evropa until his story could be confirmed. But the very next day, August 30, 1918, Socialist Revolutionary opponents of the Bolsheviks assassinated Uritsky and seriously wounded Lenin. Dmitri was arrested in his hotel and taken to prison, where he languished for two months. During this time, the Cheka compiled a list of five hundred enemies to be executed in retaliation for Uritsky's murder and an attempted assassination of Lenin. Fortunately for Dmitri he was not included on this list. In fact, upon his release from jail, he was deported to Denmark, where he continued to pursue his interest in aerodynamics.[21]

For a time, the Bolsheviks seemed determined either to destroy or to drive away Russia's most talented people. But with the end of the civil war, Lenin began to reconsider this policy. The country was in dire straits after seven years of war and upheaval (see Chapter II). As economic productivity in every sector sank to new lows, the country was beset by a famine in which millions died. As Lenin well understood, the Bolsheviks could not begin the construction of socialism until peace was assured and the economy recovered. Once again he turned to the private sector for a solution, although this time without trying to involve the big industrialists. He sought to win over the peasantry by allowing them to sell their grain and other products on the free market in return for the payment of a tax in kind. This would encourage them to grow more and create surpluses, which could be sold abroad to fund industrialization. Finally, almost as an afterthought, Lenin called for the revival of some business activity at the local level to satisfy the country's pent-up demand for consumer goods. The individuals who responded to this call were part of the regime's New Economic Policy and known as Nepmen.[22]

All this made good sense, but Lenin had to work hard to sell it to the

Party. He pointed out that real communists were few and their opponents many. The only way the Party could hope to rebuild the economy was with bourgeois hands. Not only would this get the job done, it would enable the communists to learn from those who really knew what they were doing. As he said in a speech made in October 1921: "Let them (the capitalists) make a fortune, but learn from them how to run a business. Only then will you be able to build a communist republic."[23] But Lenin's determined rhetoric won only grudging acceptance from the Party rank and file. Most could not forget that the Revolution had been waged against the very people who were now being enlisted to help. Even so, a decree was promulgated on May 24, 1921, from the Sovnarkom that allowed peasants to sell their surplus food on the open market. The same law also allowed free traders to sell goods produced by small private manufacturers almost anywhere. Two months later, another decree stipulated that those who wanted to participate in this activity needed to purchase a license. In this way, the Soviet state hoped to be able to regulate and control the same activity that they intended eventually to eliminate.[24]

At first, many potential traders and entrepreneurs were afraid to touch what had so recently been against the law. But another decree from Sovnarkom on August 9 broke the ice when it ordered state agencies to implement more rapidly the earlier directives that had established the NEP. *Pravda* likewise did its part by urging people to understand the situation. Given the current economic crisis, it was imperative that free trade and some private enterprise be allowed to flourish in order to further strengthen the economy so that the Revolution could continue. Thus, the new laws kept coming. One passed on August 8 allowed individuals to buy, sell, and own non-public buildings to establish private publishing houses, hospitals, and clinics. Private trade in medicines was also allowed, as well as in agricultural tools and equipment. The following year it became legal for private citizens to own foreign currency, precious stones, gold, and silver. People were allowed to inherit up to 10,000 gold rubles at a low tax rate and could pass on wealth to their heirs. This encouraged people to reinvest their profits in the economy rather than spending it wildly to keep it from going over to the state when they died.[25]

Incredibly, the Sovnarkom, with Lenin's encouragement, seemed to be conducting a counterrevolution as it restricted needless regulation and formalism to create a more business-friendly climate. Small-scale factories, previously nationalized, were allowed to resume their commercial activities. Another law provided that individuals eighteen or over were free to set up small-scale manufacturing enterprises and engage in handicrafts, provided they did not employ more than twenty workers. Nepmen and cooperatives were also allowed to lease factories from the state. State factories were being directed to buy the materials they needed on the open market. On January 1, 1923, the Civil Code of the USSR was issued, containing a compilation of all the primary laws that defined the New Economic Policy.[26] All this empowered the Nepmen and worried doctrinaire Bolsheviks that the gains of the Revolution were in the process of being lost.

This fear became even more palpable when the Nepmen and their wives began to prosper and spend money. Conspicuous consumption became a popular pastime as the "new bourgeoisie" strolled about town showing off their jewels and stylish apparel. Expensive restaurants, nightclubs, and hotels became popular haunts for these erstwhile enemies of the socialist order, as did casinos, racetracks, gambling parlors, and brothels. Even bootleg liquor, heroin, and cocaine were readily available for those with the right connections and enough money. All this clashed shamefully with the squalor of the real soviet world. According to Victor Serge, a postman making fifty rubles per month could barely make ends meet. But at least *he* could put some food on his modest table. In contrast, there were hordes of beggars and abandoned children who wandered the streets in perpetual search of shelter and bread.[27]

If the Nepmen epitomized what an "enemy of the people" was supposed to be, most in the Party nevertheless were agreed that, at least for the time being, they had to be tolerated. But the Soviet government was determined to keep the Nepmen in their place by taxation and regulation. In July 1921 a business tax was assessed, which consisted of a license fee and a leveling fee. The former increased with the size of the business and was to be paid every six months; the latter was three percent of production and sales and paid monthly. In November 1922, a tax for luxury goods was imposed. These included items made from precious metals and stones, various silk, wool, and linen fabrics, foreign tobacco and cigarettes, art objects, furniture, caviar, sturgeon, mayonnaise, pastries and candies, live flowers, perfumes, cosmetics, and many more. That same month an income tax was levied on town dwellers who made money from business activity and /or securities and/or who derived income from the countryside. Likewise, people living in the countryside were taxed if their source of income was in a city or town. The Nepmen were also charged a substantial fee for the use of business facilities such as shops and market stalls. There were also various ad hoc taxes such as for famine relief, which was collected from the producers and traders of luxury goods.[28]

The year 1923 seemed to presage the end for the Nepmen. In January, the Sovnarkom raised the cost of renting business space. Two months later, it called for a new campaign to get all private businessmen to register with provincial economic councils and to purchase licenses. Moreover, those who had registered previously were scrutinized to ensure they had not violated any laws. Also, the Nepmen were being pressured to buy government bonds and insurance for their businesses and employees. All this, plus the onset of winter reduced the number of private traders in the country by forty percent during the first quarter. The anti-business atmosphere continued into 1924, when state banks were ordered to cut back dramatically on credit to the Nepmen. So draconian were these measures that a visiting German correspondent wrote of a "second Revolution" taking place in the country. He estimated that some 300,000 private enterprises had been shut down in a matter of months and noted that "a general attack was being made on all remnants of bourgeois Russia. To this end, churches were being closed and "the children of the bourgeoisie were being driven with merciless fanaticism from schools and universities."[29]

The effect of all this anti-free-trader sentiment on the economy was disastrous because the regime still needed the private sector to restore the consumer market. This dilemma reflected a larger ideological struggle in the party between the supporters of Trotsky, Zinoviev, and Kamenev, who were impatient to end private trade and eliminate the NEP, and supporters of Bukharin and Rykov, who wanted to extend the NEP indefinitely. The former were particularly concerned that the vital alliance, or *smychka*, between the proletariat and the peasantry remain based on the simple commodity exchange that Lenin intended. That is, the state would supply the peasants with manufactured goods, and the peasants would turn over their surplus grain to the state. The surplus grain would be sold abroad for hard currency to finance industrialization. Many in the Party, however, feared that if the Nepmen sold manufactured goods that were of better quality and cheaper, the peasants would forge an alliance with them. This would jeopardize the program for industrialization that was the very cornerstone of the Bolshevik program.[30]

But Bukharin, Rykov, and to a lesser extent Stalin (whose motives since Lenin's death in 1924 became increasingly political) argued that the Nepmen posed no danger to the regime. Bukharin was especially compelling, as he lauded the "the strength and durability of Soviet power" and called for a more deliberate, gradual approach to building socialism. His argument was this: the NEP had to be continued in order to develop the consumer market. The state-run stores and cooperatives were too few in number and too inefficiently run to satisfy the needs of workers and peasants. But if government enterprises were forced to compete with the Nepmen, they would improve and eventually drive the free traders out of business. By then the peasant would have come to understand that trade in a socialist society was indeed a public service, "not an endeavor to extort the highest prices possible according to the laws of supply and demand."[31]

The Nepmen reached the pinnacle of their political strength at the Fourteenth Party Congress in December 1925. The Left Opposition, which had favored more state regulation and higher taxation, could not prevail despite the fact that Stalin himself had warned about the increase in private capital and the danger of the Nepmen developing trade links with the wealthier peasants or kulaks. Even so, the Sovnarkom's policies throughout 1925–26 continued to favor the free traders. Not only did their taxes go down, but some taxes were eliminated altogether. Some were able to trade without buying a license, while others received a tax break if they used no hired help. In early 1926, the government removed the limit on the amount of property that individuals could bequeath to their heirs. Even though one was still obliged to pay a tax on gifts and inheritances, the state's avowed purpose in imposing them was practical rather than ideological. Thus, it was "to make it easier to continue the existence of industrial and trading enterprises after the death of their owners, and also to create more favorable conditions for the circulation of material and financial resources in the country."[32]

The year 1926 marks the high point of prosperity achieved by the "new bourgeoisie." By now other voices were growing louder and more hostile. Rank-and-file Bolsheviks who had never been at ease with the notion that "socialism could be built with capitalist hands" were demanding to be heard. Even Bukharin had misgivings about the growing influence and power of the Nepmen and urged higher taxes and called for more regulation lest they undermine state planning. But the most threatening assault on the free traders came from Stalin late in 1927. Having just defeated the Left Opposition, he had switched sides and begun to criticize the Right (namely Bukharin and Rykov) for its continuing support of the NEP. At the Fifteenth Party Congress in December of that year, Stalin warned ominously of the danger the Nepmen posed to the construction of socialism and of the need to eliminate them sooner rather than later.[33]

In fact, the ultimate demise of the Nepmen was never in doubt despite their usefulness to the regime in satisfying the country's consumer needs and in paying taxes. Ideological purity simply counted for too much as the Bolsheviks relentlessly propagandized against the private traders as greedy, vulgar, parasitic, and, most damningly, Jewish. Most people saw them somewhat ambiguously as outlaws and symbols of scorn on the one hand and as necessary providers of the very items that they needed to live on the other. But as the 1920s drew to a close, the regime began to clamp down more aggressively on their activities, as it raised taxes, restricted sources of credit, and redefined the term "speculation" to include almost any kind of private trade. As talk about the need to "liquidate the new bourgeoisie" rose in volume, the private traders became fewer and fewer. "A Nepman is like a splinter of an abolished way of life," said Boris Lavrenyov, "something contemptible, not quite a man— an ape, only one burdened with obligations."[34] Their extinction, however, which was proceeding apace by 1928, was usually not attended by arrest and imprisonment or execution. Instead, the Nepmen themselves, seeing the inevitable, chose to move into other kinds of livelihoods. Some took up small-scale handicraft work or drifted to the countryside to become agricultural workers. Others found employment in the vast Soviet bureaucracy or became active on the black market. For the most part, the Nepmen were allowed to simply fade away.[35]

In stark contrast to the regime's mostly pragmatic treatment of the Nepmen was its lethal hostility toward the Romanovs and other members of the high nobility. Almost as soon as the Bolsheviks came to power in November 1918, they made their intention clear. Unlike the private traders, there was no obvious reason to tolerate these enemies as a necessary evil; the sooner they were wiped off the face of the earth, the better. And where Lenin was concerned, the reasons were personal, ideological, and highly compelling. The execution of his older brother, Alexander Ilich Ulianov, after a failed attempt to assassinate Tsar Alexander III in 1887, made the younger brother a marked man. It was largely his relationship to a would-be assassin that prompted his expulsion from the University of Kazan that same year. However, it was the monarchy's long history of abuse of the workers and peasants that did far more to provoke all revolutionaries' anger and hostility. Indeed, the dynasty's worst crimes had followed in the wake of Tsar Alexander II's abolition of serfdom in 1861, which had left the former serfs with too few rights, too little land, and high redemption payments.[36] Many peasants, unable to afford their own freedom, left the countryside to take factory jobs with low wages amid squalid living conditions. Their labor was ruthlessly exploited by a new generation of aggressive entrepreneurs, who were generously aided by protectionist legislation and direct intervention by the government. The official support provided to these fledgling capitalists created a new class of privileged elite, who were uncritically loyal to the tsar and his policies. Most had little concern for the well-being of the workers and scorned any activism on their behalf.

Organized support for poor workers and peasants was, however, promoted by Russia's increasingly radical intelligentsia in the years following the Emancipation Edict. This occurred at the very time when Tsar Alexander II was introducing other reforms that affected nearly every aspect of Russian life. The most important of these eased censorship, promoted education, and reformed local and municipal government, the judiciary, and the military. But these measures did little to impress those who had long been dissatisfied with the old order. This new generation of revolutionaries was dedicated to the creation of a society based on agrarian socialism. To this end, they were prepared to assassinate the tsar in order to destroy autocracy once and for all. It took nearly twenty years and many attempts, but on the morning of March 1, 1881, a new revolutionary group, the People's Will, murdered Tsar Alexander II by throwing bombs made of dynamite at his carriage during his Sunday outing. The immediate effect of this action was to derail a tentative plan for a representative assembly and a form of cabinet government that the tsar had approved just hours before his death.[37]

The last two Romanov tsars were confirmed reactionaries. The terrorism continued, but the throne offered no concessions for the sake of domestic tranquility. Indeed, Alexander III, who succeeded his slain father, issued a new law for the security of the realm, which made it much easier for local authorities to impose martial law, make arbitrary arrests, issue fines, close down factories and shops, deport undesirables, and dismiss elected officials. His son, Nicholas II, who ascended the throne in 1894, was arguably even more retrograde in his attitudes and policies. Not only did he steadfastly resist any initiative that even minutely encroached on his autocratic prerogatives, he allowed his troops to apply deadly force against unarmed demonstrators on more than one occasion. Not surprisingly, revolutionary activity rose sharply during his reign, and a number of important officials were assassinated. Among them was a minister of the interior, Vyacheslav Plehve, in 1902, a governor general of Moscow, Grand Duke Sergei,[38] in 1907, and a prime minister of the Imperial Duma, Piotr Stolypin, in 1911. Nicholas also involved the country in two disastrous wars: one against Japan in 1904–1905 that sacrificed the lives of some 300,000 men, and the other against Germany and the Central Powers, in which at least three million men perished between 1914 and 1917. This latter debacle led to the overthrow of the monarchy and the incarceration of the imperial family by the Provisional Government in their home at Tsarskoe Selo just outside Petrograd. Both the tsar and Empress Alexandra were accused of having treasonously aided the Germans in the Great War. There was no substance to these charges, but the Romanovs remained in captivity until the Bolsheviks came to power the following November and annihilated them as "enemies of the people."

Actually, the Prime Minister of the Provisional Government, Alexander Kerensky, had tried to protect the Romanovs from their most lethal enemies. After interviewing the tsar and empress at their palace at Tsarskoe Tselo about some of the more controversial aspects of their reign, Kerensky concluded that they were essentially clueless about almost anything that mattered. He hoped to be able to send the family to England, but King George V, the tsar's cousin, refused to grant them asylum. Later that summer, however, he was able to move the Romanovs to the town of Tobolsk in western Siberia, far from the revolutionary madness of Petrograd. Thus, it seemed like the family would be able to ride out the turmoil until some measure of peace and tranquility was restored to the country. But this hope was dashed when the Bolsheviks overthrew the Provisional Government on November 7, 1917.

At first the new regime was too busy constructing the socialist order to bother much about the Romanovs. But by the spring of 1918, Lenin and all the leading Bolsheviks were agreed that Tsar Nicholas should stand trial in Moscow for the crimes he had committed against the Russian people. Thus the family was forced to make the long journey from Tobolsk only to be detained in Yekaterinburg by the fiercely anti-monarchical Ural Regional Soviet, which wanted to impose its own brand of revolutionary justice on the captives. The Romanovs spent the last two months of their lives incarcerated in the Ipatiev House[39] in Yekaterinburg. The royal inmates consisted of Tsar Nicholas (49) and Empress Alexandra (45); their four daughters, the grand duchesses Olga (22), Tatiana (20), Marie (18), Anastasia (17); and the Tsarevich Alexei (13). The latter, a hemophiliac, was the object of great concern on the part of his parents because he was in constant need of medical care. He was frequently treated by the family doctor, Evgenii Botkin, and served by the family's three other retainers, Anna Demidova, the maid; Alexei Trupp, the footman; and Ivan Kharitonov, the family's kitchen boy, all of whom were incarcerated with the imperial family.

The eleven captives lived their final days in stifling heat and great boredom. They were hoping to be rescued, but time passed and nothing happened. In fact, a feeble attempt had been made by some monarchist officers who had

The Romanov family circa 1914: (from left) Olga Nicholaevna, Tatiana Nicholaevna, Tsar Nicholas, Empress Alexandra Feodorovna, Anastasia Nicholaevna, Tsarevich Alexei Nicholaevich, and Maria Nicholaevna. The family was arrested and held captive for eighteen months before being executed in July 1918 for their crimes against the Russian people. Photographer unknown (courtesy Memorial International Photo Archives).

arrived in the city for just that purpose, but this had been easily foiled. In late June, however, with the civil war heating up, the White Army and the Czech Legion began to close in on Yekaterinburg. This prompted one of the leaders of the Ural Regional Soviet, Filip Goloshchekin, to travel to Moscow to get permission to execute the family to prevent their rescue by the Whites. Goloshchekin picked a bad time to go to the capital. The city was in turmoil. The Left Socialist Revolutionaries were in full rebellion against Lenin's domestic policies and the Treaty of Brest Litovsk. They had taken up arms, assassinated the German ambassador, arrested the head of the Cheka, Felix Dzerzhinsky, and were assaulting the Kremlin. Under the circumstances, Goloshchekin had no one to talk to. He finally did confer with an old friend, Jakob Sverdlov, but did not receive the affirmative answer he wanted. According to Sverdlov, Lenin was insistent that Nicholas not be executed without a formal trial, and he was categorically against harming the rest of the family for fear that it would discredit the Soviet regime both at home and abroad.

This last point is controversial to say the least, since it has long been believed that Lenin had approved of the death penalty for all the prisoners, not just Nicholas. There is, however, good reason to question whether this was actually the case. At the time of the Revolution, there were fifty-two members of the Romanov family living in Russia. Of these, seventeen would die at the hands of the Bolsheviks at various times and in differing circumstances. Lenin is not known to have personally ordered any of these executions, and he had good reason to keep at least some of the Romanovs alive. For one thing, the German Kaiser, Wilhelm II, who was related to both Nicholas and Alexandra, had repeatedly expressed interest in their well-being. He had even urged the Bolsheviks to move them from Tobolsk to Moscow, where he thought they would be safe. Thus the safety of the royal hostages gave Lenin a potential bargaining chip that he could possibly at some point exploit.[40]

Also intriguing is Lenin's treatment of Grand Duke Michael, who was the brother of Tsar Nicholas and the first Romanov to be put to death after the Revolution. Michael was by most accounts a weak-willed, hapless fellow of dubious intellect and no personal ambition. Previously, he had tried to move to England, where he owned property, but had been denied a visa by the British. Later he sent a petition to Lenin to be allowed to change his name to Michael Brassov[41] and to leave the country. Lenin scornfully refused to involve himself in either matter, and the grand duke never received an answer. In 1918, however, Lenin had Michael sent to the city of Perm, 100 miles east of the Ural Mountains, to keep him from falling into the hands of reactionary forces, who might try to use him to restore the monarchy. However, he did not order his incarceration or stipulate that he be executed should a rescue attempt be made. In retrospect, it is curious that Lenin, who was always urging his comrades to destroy the enemies of the revolution, did not order Michael to be shot if only as a precaution due to the increasingly tense military situation. In June 1918, however, the members of the Perm Soviet were prepared to do just that in order to keep a potential claimant to the throne from falling into the hands of the nearby, fiercely anti–Bolshevik Czech Legion.[42]

The man who organized this effort was a Chekist named Gabriel Myasnikov, who recruited five members of the Soviet to assassinate the grand duke. Late on the night of June 12, the conspirators entered Michael's room in the Korolev Hotel with their guns drawn and awoke him and his English secretary, Nicholas Johnson. At first they pretended to be enforcing an evacuation order, although subsequently one of the men confided to Johnson that they were really monarchists, who had come to rescue the grand duke. Soon the prisoners and their abductors were riding out of the city in horse-drawn carriages. When they reached a wooded area near the Motovilikhia factory, Michael and his secretary were ordered to alight from the carriage and walk into the woods. There they were shot dead and buried. Interestingly, Myasnikov concealed what he had done from the Bolshevik leadership in Moscow. In a telegram sent just hours after the murder, he claimed that Grand Duke Michael and Nicholas Johnson had been kidnapped by unknown agents. He promised to conduct a thorough search.[43]

Whatever the truth about Lenin's role in the murders, the Ural Regional Soviet, with some trepidation, decided to eliminate all the Romanovs and their retainers. The Bolshevik chosen to perform the deed was the commandant of the Ipatiev House, Jakov Yurovsky, who resolved to carry out the murders without approval from Moscow in a small cellar room, which had previously been used as a dormitory for the guards. He selected ten men to help him do the shooting, assigning each man a specific target so that the execution could be carried out expeditiously and in a manner that would minimize the suffering of the victims. Yurovsky himself claimed the right of killing the tsar.

Thus, at 1:30 on the morning of July 17, Yurovsky awoke the prisoners, ostensibly to warn them that there was "trouble in the city." He ordered them to dress and, for their own safety, to go down into the cellar until they could be moved to a new and safer location. At 2:10 a.m. the family and the four retainers started downstairs, the tsar carrying Alexei, followed by the empress, the grand duchesses, and the family's four retainers. None of the condemned suspected anything sinister, and Tatiana, Marie, and Anastasia actually smiled at their executioners as they passed them in the corridor. Once the family was assembled in the murder room, Yurovsky read from a paper the following statement to Nicholas II: "In view of the fact your relatives continue their offensive against Soviet Russia, the Presidium of the Ural Regional Soviet has decided to sentence you to death." Nicholas was remembered to have said "Lord, oh, my God! Oh, my God! What is this? He turned to look at the others, who made similar exclamations. The tsar then turned to Yurovsky and asked him to read the death sentence again. Annoyed, the commandant complied, but Nicholas was still uncomprehending. "What? What?" said the tsar, to which Yurovsky replied, "This!" as he shot Nicholas in the chest.

What followed was pandemonium. The executioners ignored their instructions and repeatedly shot the tsar, even though he was clearly already dead. It was as if everyone wanted to claim credit for killing Nicholas II. But the situation became chaotic, with bullets flying everywhere amid the deafening roar of the gunfire and the screams of the victims. Soon Yurovsky had to order a halt because the air had become so thick with plaster dust and smoke that it was impossible to tell the dead from the wounded. In the meantime, the executioners, some wounded by ricocheting bullets, some suffering from powder burns, and some splattered by the blood of their victims, needed time to collect themselves. A few were physically ill, and one man actually vomited. Even so, within minutes they were ordered back to the murder room to finish the job. But the task proved no easier the second time around, because, as it was later learned, the clothing of the victims had acted as bullet-proof vests because of jewels and precious stones that had been sewn into the fabric. One of the executioners, Piotr Ermakov, a man notorious for his sadism and savagery, finished off some of them with his bayonet.[44]

Now that the victims were all dead, there were difficulties that the murderers did not expect. It fell to Alexander Beloborov, the chairman of the Ural Regional Soviet, to inform Moscow that the deed had been done. At 4:00 a.m. on July 17, he sent a telegram to Lenin and Sverdlov announcing the execution of Nicholas and falsely claiming that the rest of the family had been "evacuated to a place of greater safety."[45] The need to lie was obvious: the commissars in Moscow had not given permission to execute all the prisoners, and Beloborov feared their wrath. It didn't take long for him to realize that this clumsy deception could not be maintained, and later that evening he sent a second telegram in which he admitted that the "entire family suffered the same fate as the head."[46] To the great relief of the Ural Regional Soviet, however, Moscow apparently was prepared to accept what could not be changed.

Far more challenging for all involved was the task of disposing of the corpses. The original plan had been to entrust this task to Ermakov, but Yurovsky doubted his reliability and took over the job himself. What followed was a cascade of unexpected problems and circumstances that made it devilishly difficult to find a suitable location to bury the victims.[47] Over the course of the next two days, these difficulties compelled him to make the nearly forty-mile round trip to the Kopyaki Forest outside Yekaterinburg no less than five times. He had almost no sleep during this period and had to appear a number of times before the Ural Regional Soviet and the Cheka to explain what was going wrong and why. In the end, the task was accomplished, and the Romanovs seemed to have disappeared from the face of the earth for the next six decades.

In retrospect, it is easy to see in the fate of the Romanovs a chilling prelude of what was to follow. By the mid-1930s, summary justice and murder had returned to Russia on a grand scale, only now the war on "enemies of the people" was mostly fought against those who were almost surely not guilty of what they were accused of. Loyal citizens, accused of sabotage, anti-Soviet activity, or treason, were arrested, often in the middle of the night, tortured, and forced to confess their guilt. By this time, however, the murder of the imperial family and its servants had become a source of official pride. After lying about the fate of the empress, children, and retainers, the Bolsheviks attempted to glorify the massacre by turning the Ipatiev House into a kind of patriotic shrine. It was now known as the House of the People's Revenge.[48] Important visitors were invited to descend into the murder room to have their pictures taken against the bullet-riddled wall.[49] But truth and time eventually worked against the regime, and by the 1970s, more people were coming to the Ipatiev House to mourn than to exult. By 1977, this had become a serious embarrassment, and the head of the KGB, Yuri Andropov, ordered the house torn down.[50]

During the last years of the Brezhnev era, it seems there were at least a few Soviet officials in high places who actually wanted the truth to come out. Accordingly, some of them gave help and encouragement to two independent researchers, Alexander Avdonin and Yuri Ryabov, to search for the remains of the Romanovs and their servants. It took nearly three years, but on May 31, 1979, they located the gravesite and unearthed some of the bones. The two men were tempted to make their find public immediately so that the site could be properly excavated, but feared doing so because the prevailing political climate in the Soviet Union was still far too communist. Thus Avdonin and Ryabov waited ten long years until Mikhail Gorbachev's campaign for *glasnost*, or openness, convinced them that the time was right. In an article that appeared in the *Moscow News* on April 10, 1989, entitled "The Earth Yields Up Its Secrets," Ryabov explained in some detail how the gravesite had been discovered and thereby created a sensation both in the Soviet Union and around the world. It also may have prompted many Soviet citizens to revisit the horrors of the past in order to confront the truth and rehabilitate those who had been unjustly condemned and punished.

CHAPTER II

Socialist Revolutionaries, Anarchists and Civil War

THE SPRING AND SUMMER OF 1918 were in many ways the low point of the Revolution for the Bolsheviks. Not only were their domestic enemies resolute and gaining in strength, but just days after the Bolsheviks concluded the peace treaty of Brest Litovsk with Germany, the British landed troops at Murmansk. The Japanese did the same at Vladivostok on April 12. This was the beginning of the foreign intervention, which eventually included more than a dozen nations and lasted about a year and a half. Officially, these foreign soldiers had been sent to keep supplies intended for the Provisional Government from falling into the hands of the Bolsheviks or the Germans. Though they did little fighting, their presence was an unnerving reminder of the hostility of the outside world to the regime.

The Bolsheviks were dealt another blow in June when the Czech Legion, helped by the Whites, captured the city of Samara on the Volga River. This prompted five White Army officers, all former members of the defunct Constituent Assembly, to establish the Committee of Members of the Constituent Assembly. Komuch, as it came to be known, was declared by its members to be the sole legitimate government in Russia. Soon eighty-five other former members of the disbanded Assembly were on their way to Saratov to assume their places in the new government. It nullified all the edicts that had been issued by the Bolsheviks and recruited an army of several thousand men to fight against the Soviet regime. It also restored the zemstvos (local units of self government) and municipal dumas,[1] allowed professional unions, factory councils, and peasant congresses, called for an eight-hour workday, and offered compensation to those who had lost land to the Bolsheviks.[2]

A more immediate threat to the regime, however, was the growing hostility of Russia's impoverished proletariat due to food and fuel shortages. Those who had originally cheered the Bolshevik takeover now retaliated by voting themselves pay raises, skipping work, stealing tools and materials, and by abusing factory bosses and managers. Angry workers also participated in strikes and demonstrations and formed the Extraordinary Assemblies of Factory and Plant Representatives. These assemblies soon grew to a membership of several hundred thousand and attracted the support of the Mensheviks and Socialist Revolutionaries and a significant part of the general public. People not only blamed the Bolsheviks for the country's economic and social woes, but also for stifling political opposition, shutting down the Constituent Assembly, and for the shameful Treaty of Brest-Litovsk with Germany.[3]

Lenin initially reacted cautiously to these provocations, but when it was learned that a general strike had been planned for Petrograd on July 1, he promulgated the Decree of Nationalization. This shifted power from the factory committees and trade unions to the newly created All-Russian Council for the Economy. The Extraordinary Assemblies were abolished, strike leaders and agitators arrested or executed, and the SRs and Mensheviks expelled from the Soviets for counterrevolutionary activity. Lenin also made an important change of policy to restore discipline in the workplace and boost production. Factory managers were henceforth to be chosen for their ability and without regard to class origin.[4]

The most intractable problem the Bolsheviks faced during the civil war was that of supplying food to the cities and towns. Years of war and revolution had severely disrupted the country's normal agricultural productivity. The crisis was further aggravated by the dilapidated state of the transportation system and by the peasants' reluctance to accept paper currency as a means of exchange. Soon, people in urban areas were fleeing to the countryside to be closer to the food supply. Many became "bagmen," traveling back and forth from city to farm with clothes, household goods, and other items of value to exchange for food. As shortages became increasingly acute, Lenin declared grain a state monopoly on May 9, 1918.[5] This required the peasants to turn over all surplus grain to the state. When they resisted, food brigades were sent into the countryside to take their quota at gunpoint. When these proved inadequate, the government organized the Committees of the Poor, or Kombedy, to assist in the effort. These were gangs of the poorest peasants, who were also encouraged to abuse the more wealthy peasants or kulaks. In this manner, the Kombedy were to serve two purposes: to help provide food for the cities and to inflame the civil war in the countryside by splitting the peasants along class lines.[6]

In the end, these tactics achieved very little. For one thing, those labeled kulaks were generally neither rich nor exploitive. In most cases, they were merely village leaders, who perhaps owned an extra horse or cow, or lived in a house of brick rather than wood. They were not viewed with any special hostility by other members of their community and certainly not as enemies of the people. Instead, it was the Bolsheviks whom the peasants really came to loathe. Sensing this, Lenin abolished the Kombedy in December only to impose new initiatives that were even more draconian and equally self-defeating. One of these was the Food Levy (*podrazverstka*) of January 1919, which applied not only to grain, but to foods of all kinds, including livestock. Lenin also authorized the creation of Flying Brigades (*zagranitel'nye otriady*) in order to stamp out the bag trade. These paramilitary units were charged with confiscating excess food from anyone coming to town by rail or by road. But the government was soon forced to relent when it was realized that the cities and towns would starve if the bagmen stopped bringing in food from the countryside.[7]

The month of July 1918 was a major turning point for the Bolsheviks and the revolution. Having disposed of the imperial family, the regime now had to contend with the White Army and the Czech Legion, both of which were steadily growing stronger. To this was added a new enemy, the Left Socialist Revolutionaries, who had originally been part of the Socialist Revolutionary Party.[8] The Left SRs had sided with the Bolsheviks after the overthrow of the tsar in opposing the Provisional Government. They had also participated in the October coup and had subsequently headed several commissariats in the new government. But the relationship was not an easy one because the Left SRs, like the Socialist Revolutionaries, were ideologically committed to redistributing the land to the peasants. The Bolsheviks, on the other hand, planned to eventually nationalize agriculture and force the peasants to join collective farms. In any case, cooperation between the two parties soon disintegrated over other issues such as the power of the Cheka, the Treaty of Brest Litovsk, and the practice of food requisitioning in the countryside.

By early summer, many Left SRs had come to view the Bolsheviks as their mortal enemies. On June 20, 1918, one of their members assassinated Commissar of Press, Propaganda and Agitation Moisei Volodarsky. The immediate effect of this action was minimal, but two weeks later, a group of Left SRs led by the head of the Cheka's counter-espionage section, Jakob Bliumkin, and prodded by the fierce SR activist Maria Alexandrovna Spiridonova resolved to do something much more drastic. On the afternoon of July 6,

Bliumkin and a single co-assassin, Nikolai Andreev, appeared at the German Embassy in Moscow with a forged note from Felix Dzerzhinsky authorizing them to enter into immediate discussions with the German Ambassador, Count Wilhelm Mirbach, on an undisclosed topic. When the ambassador appeared, he was shot twice and riddled with shrapnel from a hand grenade. The assassins made their getaway confident that the Germans would react by annulling the Treaty of Brest Litovsk and by declaring war on the Bolshevik regime.[9]

But the German reaction was less than expected, thanks to some quick damage control by the Bolsheviks. Later that afternoon, a group of them went to the German Embassy to offer their condolences. Lenin sought to avoid this nasty chore by remaining in the Kremlin, but when the acting German ambassador, Kurt Riezler, demanded his presence, he complied. According to one witness, Lenin expressed his regret in a tone that was "as cold as a dog's snout."[10] Even so, he managed to convince German officials that the assassins would be punished and ordered the Cheka to arrest the perpetrators. What followed was a series of mishaps that must surely have left him in a state of consternation. The first of these occurred when the head of the Cheka, Felix Dzerzhinsky, became a hostage of the very people he was supposed to take into custody. Lenin, aghast at the loss of his chief of security, tried to improvise a new security force under the command of Martyn Latsis. But Latsis, too, was arrested when he went to the main Cheka headquarters at the Lubianka. He had apparently been unaware that the Left SRs had already taken control of the building.[11]

The Bolsheviks were saved during the early morning hours of July 7, when the regime's Latvian riflemen, who had been temporarily out of the city, returned. They attacked and defeated the Left SR rebels in a ferocious battle that lasted seven hours. They also rescued Dzerzhinsky and arrested the Left SR's Central Committee. This fortunate turn of events, however, was nearly wasted the next day when Lenin came under attack trying to investigate the former headquarters of the Left SRs. Traveling alone with his driver, his car was fired upon and forced to halt by a Bolshevik watch group, which apparently took him for a wealthy *burzhui*. Badly shaken, Lenin could do little except admonish the men to be more careful.[12] Somewhat later, his car was stopped again by a team of Bolshevik youths on patrol, who, after checking the chief commissar's identification papers, decided they were suspicious. This time he had to submit to being taken to a local police station so he could be properly identified. Lenin actually chuckled about his predicament with the policeman on duty, but he was not yet out of danger. Not long after leaving the station, his car was again fired upon by unknown gunmen. This time his driver pressed his foot on the pedal and kept going.[13]

Curiously, the Bolsheviks' response to the treachery of the Left SRs was relatively mild. Despite acting German Ambassador Riezler's shrill demand that the assassins and their accomplices be executed, few were. Not even the Left SR's most prominent member, Maria Spiridonova,[14] who proudly claimed responsibility for the assassination, was seriously punished. Sentenced to one year in prison, she soon escaped to resume her subversive activities. The Bolsheviks' leniency on this occasion is difficult to explain. Possibly they hoped to avoid complete political isolation by luring their former allies back into the fold. In any case it was not to be. Soon a new crisis made the split between the two parties irreconcilable.

On the afternoon of August 30, 1918, news reached Moscow that the head of the Petrograd Cheka, M. S. Uritsky, had been murdered by a member of the SRs, Leonid Kannegiser. The assassin had acted alone and in retaliation for the execution of a friend. Even so, some of Lenin's family and close advisers, fearing that this might signal a new campaign of terror, urged him to avoid appearing in public for a time. But the head commissar ignored this advice and made two speaking appearances that very day—first at the Grain Commodity Exchange and then at the Mikhelson factory in the southern part of Moscow. At the latter event, he lectured the workers about how democracy promotes economic injustice and how the abolition of the private ownership of land had created a "vital unification of the proletariat of town and country." Finally, he ended his talk by urging everyone to destroy the enemies of the revolution, calling for "victory or death."[15]

Lenin's address was reasonably well received, but minutes later as he was climbing into his car, he was fired at three times by a member of the Socialist Revolutionary Party, Fanya Kaplan.[16] Two of the bullets found their mark: one in the arm, the other in the neck. Lenin, bleeding profusely, soon lapsed into a semi-conscious state. Though his recovery was swift, one of the bullets would remain permanently lodged in his body. In the meantime, the alleged assassin was caught, taken to the Lubyanka, and interrogated by the Cheka. Far from denying her guilt, she justified her deed by declaring that Lenin was a traitor who was preventing the establishment of a truly socialist state. Later, Kaplan was moved to a basement cell in the Kremlin, where she was pronounced guilty by Cheka agents and sentenced to death. On September 3, Kaplan was shot by a single executioner in a courtyard somewhere in the Kremlin.[17]

Uritsky's assassination and the attempt on Lenin's life had an immediate and profound effect on the revolution and the civil war. On September 2, the All-Russian Central Executive Committee published a resolution calling for mass terror against those true "enemies of the people," the bourgeoisie and its agents. The Committee seemed to have forgotten that the attackers of Uritsky and Lenin were both Socialist Revolutionaries. Two days later the People's Commissar for Internal Affairs, Grigorii Petrovsky, directed his agents to inflict terror on any and all enemies "without any hesitation or indecision." He also encouraged the taking of hostages among the bourgeoisie and military officers. On September 5, the Sovnarkom issued yet another resolution calling for the execution of "anyone involved with White Guard organizations, plots and conspiracies."[18] Within days more than 500 people were summarily shot in Petrograd. Some of these were former tsarist officials, who were either in jail or living in poverty. Other prisoners in Moscow's Butyrka prison were executed despite the lack of any evidence linking them to the terror.

The Bolsheviks' assault on the country's non-socialist middle class coincided with the Red Army's first great victory of the civil war, when it retook the city of Kazan on September 10, 1918. This triumph was followed by more at Samara on October 7 and at Omsk on November 10. With momentum now on their side, the Bolsheviks formally nullified the treaty of Brest Litovsk and ordered the Red Army to occupy parts of Latvia, Lithuania, Ukraine, and Belorussia. But these events brought little cheer to a starving and freezing home front. With the onset of winter and steadily rising fuel prices, the daily bread ration was

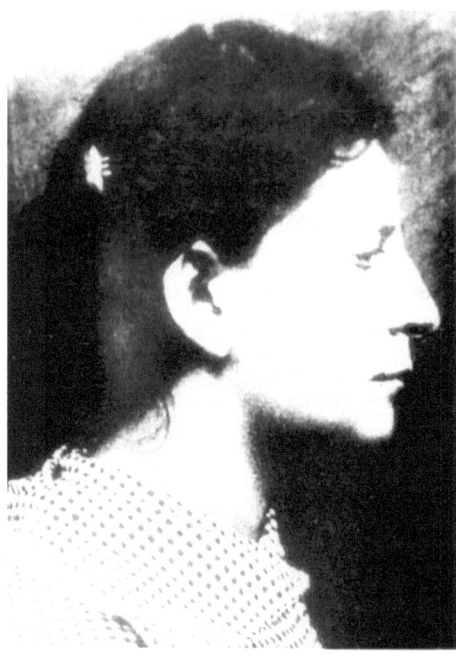

Fanya Kaplan was a Socialist Revolutionary who shot Lenin at close range on August 30, 1918. Lenin was badly wounded but survived. Kaplan, here shown sometime in the 1910s, was executed three days later. Photographer unknown (courtesy Memorial International Photo Archives from David King, *The Commissar Vanishes*).

lowered to fifty grams per person. No less worrisome was the dramatic increase in the crime rate, which put everyone at risk, including Comrade Lenin. On the evening of January 19, his car was stopped by three armed men who forced him, his sister Maria, and a lone bodyguard to alight in order to be searched for valuables. At one point, one of the robbers held a gun to Lenin's head as he checked his pockets. In panic, Maria cried, "What are you doing? This is Comrade Lenin! Who are you? Show us your permits!" To which came the reply, "Criminals don't need permits."[19]

As the fighting continued into 1919, the decisive battles of the Russian civil war had yet to be fought. The Whites had four armies in the field: one in Siberia under Supreme Commander Admiral Alexander Kolchak; one in southern Ukraine under General Anton Denikin; one in Archangelsk under General Evgenii Miller; and one in Estonia under General Nicholai Yudenich. The Bolsheviks had good reason to fear that if the Whites succeeded in coordinating their efforts, the Bolsheviks just might be forced out of power. That this never happened is due less to the prowess of the Red Army than it was to the disunity and incompetence of the Whites. Miller proved to be a disappointment as a military leader. His army failed to link up with Kolchak's and did not achieve anything of note against the Bolsheviks on its own. Kolchak, on the other hand, got off to quite a promising start. In January his army captured Perm and beat back all Soviet attempts to recapture the city. The Supreme Commander then began a march toward the Volga, capturing a number of cities and towns along the way. Among these was Ufa, which cut off the Soviets from Kazakhstan. But Kolchak's army could not sustain its momentum once the Reds began to concentrate their strength on the eastern front. In June they recovered Ufa and, in July, Perm.[20]

Meanwhile, Denikin made the most of the Bolsheviks' preoccupation with Kolchak and led an army of 300,000 into Ukraine in May. Over the next few months he won a string of victories at Odessa, Kiev, Tsaritsyn, Kursk, and Orel. By early fall, his army was within striking distance of Tula and only one hundred miles south of Moscow. At the same time, Yudenich was closing in on Petrograd and was now only 150 miles short of the former capital. It now seemed probable that both cities would fall simultaneously and that the Soviets would be driven from power. But the tide of the civil war was decisively changed when the daring and charismatic leader of the Insurgent Army of Ukraine, Nestor Ivanovich Makhno, savagely struck Denikin's force on September 26 near the village of Peregonovka. The *Makhnovitsy*, as they were called, destroyed three White regiments and completely disrupted Denikin's supply train. This allowed the Red Army to counterattack and drive the Whites into a disorderly retreat.[21]

Makhno, who must surely rank as one of the most remarkable characters in Russian history, was, in many ways, the ideal revolutionary hero. Born into an impoverished Ukrainian peasant family at Gulai Pole in 1888, he had labored on a farm as a small child for a number of years before finding employment in a foundry at age fifteen. He found the latter experience so brutalizing that he soon became an active revolutionary dedicated to the destruction of tsarism. In 1908, he participated in a robbery that took the life of a police officer. Quickly apprehended, tried, and convicted, Makhno barely escaped the death penalty. Instead, he was sentenced to an indefinite term in Moscow's dreaded Butyrki Prison. There, some of his fellow inmates introduced him to the teachings of Piotr Kropotkin, whereby he became a committed anarcho-communist.[22] Released from jail after the February Revolution in 1917, he returned to his family home at Gulai-Pole to agitate for the overthrow of the Provisional Government. He also became active in helping peasants build anarchist communes based on the principle of mutual aid. To this end, he assisted in the breakup of the large estates of the gentry and the redistribution of the land among the poor. In January 1919, he convened the first of four Regional Congresses of Peasants, Workers and Insurgents to discuss the practical problems of building anarchism and to criticize the Soviet regime.[23]

All this unauthorized activity soon caught the attention of the Bolsheviks, who denounced Makhno as an "enemy of the people." This was deemed necessary not merely because of his seditious rhetoric against the regime, but because he urged common people to reject a central tenet of the Bolsheviks' program: the dictatorship of the proletariat.[24] When he defied a Red Army commander's order against convening a third congress of workers, peasants, and insurgents, the Cheka sent two agents to Ukraine to assassinate him. The attempt not only failed (the agents were caught and executed), but actually emboldened the intended victim. Soon Makhno was urging soldiers in the Red Army to send representatives to a fourth congress scheduled for June. Trotsky was furious and ordered a military force to Gulai-Pole to destroy the communes and to arrest Makhno. The soldiers succeeded in the first task, but failed in the second.[25]

Amazingly, the Makhno rebels resumed their cooperation with the regime when Denikin began his march toward Moscow that summer. To be sure, they still distrusted and loathed the Bolsheviks, but they hated the Whites more. They were also committed to protecting the gains of the Revolution. It was this sense of duty and heroic resolve that made possible the victory at Peregonovka and that allowed Makhno and his followers to resume their anarchist agenda. One of their first efforts was to turn two recently liberated Ukrainian towns, Ekaterinoslav and Aleksandrovsk, into model anarchist communities. The townspeople were encouraged to organize their lives as they saw fit and to resist outsiders claiming to have authority over them. Freedom of speech, the press, and assembly were proclaimed as all prisoners were released from jail. The Bolshevik revolutionary committees were disbanded and their agents advised to find jobs and work for a living.[26]

Once again the regime was forced to tangle with a man whose ability to evade and confound them was a major source of embarrassment. This time Trotsky hoped to trick Makhno by ordering his army to proceed to a new location near the Polish border for what seemed like a purely military assignment. The real reason was so that the Soviets could undo the results of Makhno's activism in Ukraine and establish new settlements that were properly Bolshevized. But when the anarchist commander refused to comply, Trotsky again resorted to force. For the next eight months, the rebels employed every trick at their disposal to defend themselves against the Red Army. This included some very effective propaganda. In one of the leaflets disseminated to Bolshevik troops, they were urged to show solidarity to a noble people, who only wanted to be allowed to create a "free soviet order."[27] The fighting that ensued was costly to both sides and made worse by a severe typhus epidemic that initially could not be arrested due to a shortage of doctors and medicine.

But while the regime struggled with the rebels, a whole series of new challenges began to accumulate. In April of 1920, the Poles invaded Ukraine to seize territory that they claimed was part of their ancient heritage. In May, the Siberian Peasants' Union in Omsk staged a revolt against Soviet rule and called for a Siberian Constituent Assembly. In June, a White Army led by General Piotr Wrangel abandoned the Crimea and captured the town of Melitopol near the Sea of Azov. In August, there was an enormous anti–Bolshevik peasant rebellion in Tambov Province led by a former Socialist Revolutionary named Alexander Antonov. Finally, in February 1921, factory workers in Petrograd went on strike demanding food and fuel and calling for radical changes that threatened the very core of the regime.

Somehow, the Bolsheviks were able to answer these challenges and prevail. In June, the Red Army under General Tukhashevsky counterattacked, drove the Poles back into Poland, and nearly captured Warsaw.[28] Another military force suppressed the western Siberian rebels, who were simultaneously appeased by an end to the policy of food requisitioning. Another Red Army force (helped again by Makhnov's rebels) forced Wrangel's army back into the Crimea, where it defeated them for the last time. The remaining Whites were allowed to board ships and sail into exile. Finally, Antonov's rebellion in Tambov province was ended in July 1921 by a mixture of military power, terror, and some conciliatory gestures to win over those who were tired of fighting but who had been afraid to surrender.[29]

The defeat of the workers' opposition in Petrograd, though it occurred several months earlier, proved to be a special case. The fighting took place at a naval base on the island of Kronstadt in the Gulf of Finland just five miles from Petrogad. The sailor stationed on the base were mostly young, illiterate, and aggrieved by the mistreatment of their officers. It involved fighting as intense and savage as any that occurred during the civil war. There was no hope for compromise because the rebels made demands that the Soviet government would not even consider. These included a restoration of the Constituent Assembly, a revival of free soviets and factory committees, free speech, freedom for political prisoners, an end to the Cheka's police state and the elimination of Trotsky's labor battalions.[30] More demands were added by the sailors and workers at the Kronstadt naval base, who upon learning of the revolt supported the strikers. They called for the abolition of Communist-appointed political organizations, the dissolution of Communist fighting detachments in the army, and the removal of Communist guards from the factories.

The Kronstadters had initially been among the most enthusiastic supporters of the Bolsheviks after the October Insurrection. But they could not abide the regime's increasing authoritarianism. By the early days of March 1921, propaganda leaflets were being disseminated on the base that were fiercely anarchist both in content and tone: "Where there is authority, there is no liberty," read one.[31] Other pronouncements called for workers' control, an end to forced labor, and the destruction of the communist bureaucracy. In one of their own revolutionary journals, the Kronstadters described their rebellion as the beginning of the third revolution, "striking the last fetters from the laboring masses and opening a broad new road for socialist creativity."[32] Anarchists elsewhere were much inspired by the sailors' militant stance. Many compared them to the Paris communards of 1871,[33] who had revolted against the French government after the country's loss to Prussia. No doubt they also recalled and worried that the Commune had ultimately been destroyed after much bloodshed.

Meanwhile, at the Tenth Party Congress in Moscow, the delegates were both alarmed and embarrassed by the Kronstadt uprising. Seeking to portray the sailors as counterrevolutionaries who were being manipulated by the Whites, they called for their complete annihilation. Two prominent anarchists, Emma Goldman and Alexander Berkman, pleaded to be allowed to negotiate with the rebels in order to avoid what looked to be a massacre. The request was scorned by Lenin, who declared, "We have had enough opposition."[34] Trotsky put it even more succinctly, calling upon the Kronstadters to surrender unconditionally or "be shot like partridges." But when the rebels did not surrender, the Red Army had a hard time making good on Trotsky's threat. On March 8, 25,000 crack troops under the command of General Tukhachevsky began the five-mile trek across the ice separating Kronstadt from the mainland. The defenders, who numbered about 15,000, fought ferociously and repelled the invasion. However, in a second attack on March 17 with a force augmented to twice its original size, the starving, freezing, and exhausted defenders were overwhelmed. When the fighting ended on the following day, 600 rebels had been killed and 2,500 taken prisoner. Eight thousand defenders had escaped across the ice to Finland. The Red Army had suffered some 10,000 dead, wounded, and missing.[35]

Ironically, many of the economic demands of the workers and sailors were in the process of being addressed at the Tenth Party Congress. Lenin, in his New Economic Plan, called for postponing the construction of socialism in order to rebuild the country's shattered economy. To this end, he proposed a limited return to free enterprise and a market economy. For many, this was a shocking betrayal of the revolution's most fundamental goals. But Lenin staunchly defended the plan, insisting that the Soviet state could not build socialism until the country had recovered economically. Thus, small consumer-oriented businesses (i.e., those with fewer than twenty workers) would be allowed to operate for profit. This was accompanied by an end to the requisitioning in the countryside that had made the regime so many domestic enemies. Henceforth, peasants would be allowed to sell their products on the open market after paying a tax in kind. To encourage increased productivity, farmers would also be permitted to hire laborers and lease land.

Nearly everyone in the party considered the NEP to be a shameful betrayal of the socialist cause. Many feared that any deviation or delay in constructing the new order would jeopardize the entire enterprise. Lenin was not deaf to these concerns, but he tried to remain sanguine. The Bolsheviks still controlled the country's financial institutions, heavy industry, the transportation system, foreign trade, and wholesale commerce. Political activity outside the party was virtually impossible, in large part because all public forums were subject to strict censorship and because the regime had a monopoly on force. Still, even Lenin was troubled by the likelihood that the NEP would have to remain in force at least ten years. Thus, with the upheavals of the recent past fresh in his mind, he took a fateful step that was intended to end all dissident activity. To this end, he urged the delegates to the Tenth Party Congress to outlaw all party groupings independent of the Central Committee.[36]

The importance of this ban on factions, which passed by a two-thirds vote, is almost impossible to exaggerate. Henceforth, the Central Committee would be able to rule the party as absolutely as the party ruled the country. No one would be able to challenge the leadership without risk of being branded an "enemy of the people." To enforce this initiative, and to deal with recalcitrant workers and other agitators, Lenin created the position of General Secretary of the Communist Party. In April 1922, he assigned Josef Stalin to be the first to serve in this post. It was a job no one else wanted, since it involved duties that were mostly bureaucratic and unexciting. Stalin alone seemed to appreciate the possibilities it offered and remained in the position for the rest of his life. It was as General Secretary that he was later able to control the Central Committee and to eliminate anyone who threatened, or might threaten, his policies or hold on power.[37]

But all this was in the future. In the meantime, there were urgent practical problems relating to the country's economic recovery. Seven years of war and revolution had claimed ten million people and ruined the economy. The output of mines and factories had fallen by 80 percent of what it had been in 1914. The amount of land under cultivation had declined by 38 percent and the annual harvest by 63 percent. There was also a crisis of sanitation and health. Cities and towns, with no functioning municipal services, had become littered and befouled by all kinds of debris, trash, garbage, and even raw sewage. Moreover, the dearth of basic consumer goods reduced people to scrounging for items that ordinarily might have been discarded. Thus, the felt of old billiard tables was made into hats, velvet curtains became dresses, and bearskin rugs overcoats.[38]

To be sure, the first few years after the civil war were a period of unrelieved misery for anyone who lacked privileged status. Ordinary people had to struggle to find food and fuel and to adjust to the new order. In theory, they were to be assisted by the new Soviet bureaucracy, whose main concern, ideally, was the welfare of the people and the building of socialism. In fact, Soviet officials proved to be every bit as arrogant and corrupt as those under the tsars and to have even more power. Bureaucrats controlled access to the most basic necessities, such as plumbing and house repairs, clothing vouchers, firewood, meal tickets, train tickets, burial permissions, and coffins. The new system involved red tape, bribes, and long waits in line, all of which tended to discourage people from applying in the first place.

Indeed, people were required to do extra work just to protect their basic rights as citizens. To promote the communist ideal of the *kollektiv* and to get things done on the cheap, people were assigned chores at their apartment houses and workplaces. These included cleaning and sweeping up in areas of common use, shoveling snow, carrying water and firewood, and disposing of trash and garbage. Citizens were also expected to participate in *subbotniki,* or days of "voluntary" labor to the state without pay. The idea had originated with a group of some 200 railway workers, who decided to work all day on Saturday, May 10, 1919, to finish jobs that they had not been able to complete during the week. Lenin and other Bolshevik leaders were surprised and delighted by this display of working-class civic-mindedness. They hailed it as the beginning of true communism in Russia and the key to exporting it elsewhere. Within a year, however, the *subbotniki* had become mandatory. In the future, they achieved less and less and were resented more and more.[39]

The worst was yet to come. A bad harvest followed by a series of extreme frosts and a summer drought created one of the most horrific famines in recorded history. By the end of 1921, one-fourth of the peasantry were suffering from starvation in a vast area that included the Volga, Ural, and Kama basins, parts of Kazakhstan, southern Ukraine, and western Siberia. The few crops that were grown were soon devoured by swarms of locusts and field rats. In the past, the peasants had usually been able to cope with such emergencies because of their practice of keeping large amounts of grain in reserve. But the requisitioning of the civil war had deprived them of this cushion, and by the end of 1921, people were eating almost anything they could find, including grass, tree bark, weeds, leaves, sawdust, clay, horse manure, and acorn flour. As thousands starved, others tried to escape to the towns in a vain attempt to find food. In desperation, many turned to cannibalism.[40]

Unable to deal with the famine on its own, the Soviet government was reluctant even to acknowledge it. When the writer Maxim Gorky led a group of prominent citizens to request permission to set up the All-Russian Public Committee to Aid the Hungry, Lenin only grudgingly gave his assent. He feared it would give rise to the same kind of public outrage against government incompetence that had happened during the famine of 1891.[41] However, when the Committee secured the aid of Herbert Hoover and the American Relief Administration (ARA), Lenin decided the Committee itself was no longer necessary and shut it down. All but two of its seventy-three members were arrested for counterrevolutionary activities. Those found guilty were sent into foreign exile or confined to specific areas within the country.[42]

By the end of 1922, the famine was ended thanks in large part to the efforts of the ARA. Most of the agency's total operating budget of $61 million had been spent feeding the hungry and on providing such necessary items as medicine, clothes, tools, and seed. The official Soviet response to this generosity, however, was stunning in its hostility. Not only had ARA workers been slandered and harassed while performing their labors, but they were subsequently accused of spying and of trying to overthrow the Soviet government. Still, the intended good will was not entirely lost; one man who dared to express his gratitude was Maxim Gorky. In a heartfelt letter of thanks to Hoover, he wrote: "Your help will enter history as a unique, gigantic achievement, worthy of the greatest glory, which will long remain in the memory of millions of Russians whom you have saved from death."[43]

Still, the famine of 1921–1922, which devoured some five million lives, was a catastrophic event by any standard. The full extent of the damage it caused to a society already traumatized by years of war and revolution is difficult to appreciate. In many ways, the very fabric of civic life had come dangerously unraveled as people became inured to death and human suffering. Murder and suicide became commonplace as the near complete lack of health care caused a similar rise in the death rate from natural causes. This somber reality victimized those least able to fend for themselves: the children. By the early 1920s there were seven million orphans at large in the country. Many were reduced to a hobo's existence, wandering about and living from hand to mouth. Homeless, ill clad, and starving, they stole, robbed, and murdered to stay alive. Many joined crime gangs and became alcoholics, drug addicts, and/or prostitutes. Some as young as six were put to work in factories to labor long hours. Others were taken in by the Red Army, where their willingness to kill on command was much appreciated. Those who were least lucky ended up in prison or labor camps.[44]

For Bolsheviks who had triumphed in the civil war and endured so much adversity, this was still a time more of anxiety than relief. Now that the construction of socialism had been postponed indefinitely, it was the task of Party faithful to protect the future by making the most of the present. To this end, many sought to employ the Constitution of the Russian Federated Soviet

Socialist Republic of 1918 as a means of preparing the state for socialism. This document, which identified the workers as the dominant class in Soviet society, also enumerated their obligations and responsibilities. These included military service for men and the obligation of every able-bodied citizen to work in order to receive food and shelter. The constitution also provided for a government based on democratic centralism. The idea was to combine democracy and centralism by allowing debate on important issues before, but not after, a decision had been made. Inevitably, the democratic element suffered, especially when members of the party elite decided to impose their authority.[45]

On December 30, 1922, the long-anticipated Union of Soviet Socialist Republics officially came into being, consisting of Russia, Ukraine, Belorussia, and the Transcaucasian Federation (i.e., Georgia, Armenia, and Azerbaijan) The problems faced by the new government were enormous and would undoubtedly demand years of peace coupled with hard and continued privation for citizenry. Still, there was reason to hope that things would soon get better. For one thing, the Cheka had been abolished the previous February and replaced by the GPU or State Political Administration (*Gosudarstvennoe Politicheskoe upravlenie*). At Lenin's behest, the functions and powers of this new organ were sharply defined, as its work was limited to political problems. Henceforth, it was to operate according to a strict set of guidelines. Suspects could no longer be detained indefinitely without being formally charged; nor could they be denied due process.

For those who had long fretted about the arbitrary arrests and brutality of the Cheka, this was a great victory. Unfortunately, it was not to last. The head of the GPU was to be the same Felix Dzerzhinsky who had created the Cheka. Having been hardened by many years of exhausting activism during the revolution and the civil war, he was more determined than ever that the agency remain vigilant and powerful against those who would threaten the world's first socialist state. In August 1922, the GPU was allowed to bypass normal procedures and exile those suspected of counterrevolutionary activity for as long as three years. In October, it was given permission to try and sentence armed criminals to long years in prison or even death. In short, the more the Soviet security apparatus changed, the more it remained the same. Soon it would be aggressively hunting new "enemies of the people" in order to make the USSR safe for socialism.[46]

Chapter III

Russian Orthodoxy and the Soviet State

IN THE DAYS AND WEEKS FOLLOWING their seizure of power, the Bolsheviks wasted no time attacking one of their most despised enemies: the Russian Orthodox Church. On October 26 (November 8), 1917, one day after the Bolshevik takeover of the Winter Palace, the newly formed Sovnarkom issued a decree that nationalized all land and thus deprived the Church of a major source of its wealth and income. This fundamental policy made life especially difficult for Russia's rural priests, who needed their parish land allotments just to subsist. On January 20 (February 2), separation of Church and state was declared the law of the land. The Church was deprived of its right to open schools or to engage in religious education for anyone under eighteen years of age. Marriage became a civil ceremony, and divorce was legalized. Church holdings, including houses of prayer, schools, seminaries, monasteries, orphanages, old age homes, and candle factories, were expropriated by the regime. Included were some 6,000 churches and monastic buildings deemed to be of historical or architectural value. In theory, freedom of conscience was granted to all, but those who wished to participate in organized worship were now required to lease space from local government authorities. No money was charged for this, although such property was subject to the same taxes that were levied on individuals who engaged in business activity.

Of course, the Russian Orthodox Church had suffered interference and mistreatment under the tsars as well. Ivan the Terrible (r. 1547–1584) convened three Church councils to purify the clergy and to impose other changes he thought necessary. He also had the Metropolitan of Moscow arrested for sorcery and executed. Tsar Alexei (r. 1654–1676), under the influence of the

Patriarch Nikon, sought to introduce changes in liturgy and ritual in the Russian Orthodox Church service in order to bring it into conformity with those of the Greek Orthodox Church. This so outraged a significant portion of the Russian Orthodox community known as the Old Believers that they withdrew into the forests to form religious committees in order to worship in a manner that was pleasing to God. When Tsar Alexei sent troops to hunt them down, the Old Believers locked themselves in their churches and committed mass suicide by setting the churches on fire.

Probably the most offensive of all the tsars to Russian Orthodoxy was Peter the Great (r. 1682–1725). He was reviled by many Orthodox believers as the devil incarnate. Having been introduced as a youth to Western ways during his frequent visits to Moscow's German Suburb, he ignored the Church's warnings against innovation and all things foreign. His unorthodox lifestyle and apparent lack of piety deeply troubled Patriarch Adrian, who frequently admonished the young tsar in a futile attempt to restrain him. In March 1698, Peter became the first tsar to travel to Western Europe in order to learn even more about foreign technology and culture. When he returned to Moscow in August 1698, he was determined to make fundamental changes in Muscovite society. These included the introduction of the Julian Calendar, ordering men to shave their beards, and forcing people to adopt a more European style of dress. Patriarch Adrian was appalled by these initiatives and complained bitterly. When the old prelate died in October 1700, Peter refused to appoint a successor and eventually abolished the patriarchate altogether. This virtually ended the Church's interference in affairs of state. In the meantime, the tsar continued to press his reforms and fight his wars. To satisfy Russia's need for human and material resources, he forced many priests and monks into military service and ordered church bells melted down for cannon. In 1722, he made complete the subordination of the Church to the state by establishing a new body, the Holy Synod,[1] to administer religious affairs.

There was, however, a fundamental difference between the tyranny of the tsars and that of the Bolsheviks: the former strove to use Russian Orthodoxy to enhance and glorify the state; the latter were determined to destroy the Church in order to make way for a socialist society based on secular values. The Bolsheviks were influenced by the secular philosopher Ludwig Feuerbach's book, *The Essence of Christianity*, which portrayed Christianity as the product of fear, deceit, and irrationality. Karl Marx, who had been deeply impressed by Feuerbach's book, later described religion as the "opiate of the people," because it distracted them from the need to agitate for revolution. The Bolsheviks' hostility to religion, however, was far more lethal than Marx's. Their success would surely inspire other countries to do the same, and a new age on earth would begin. The Russian Orthodox Church, rotten and corrupt as it was, could only impede this process and had to be destroyed one and for all.

But in the aftermath of the tsar's abdication in February (March) 1917, Orthodox leaders were actually in the process of reorganizing and reinvigorating the Church. To this end, they convened a Church Council in the fall of 1917 to restore the office of patriarch, which had been vacant since 1700. In November, after much compromise, the Council chose fifty-one-year-old Metropolitan Tikhon to fill this position. The new patriarch, however, did not arouse much enthusiasm. Those who supported him admired his humility and piety and the fact that he was an experienced Church administrator. His detractors deplored his poor education, his inability to inspire as a speaker, and his lack of personal charisma. Few believed that he would prove equal to the crisis at hand. In fact, Tikhon proved to be a surprisingly effective leader, who acted with dignity and courage under the most adverse circumstances.[2]

On January 19, 1918, the patriarch, thoroughly alarmed by the Bolsheviks' radical ideas and disdain for time honored traditions, issued an encyclical, which was read in churches across the land. In it he lashed out at the Bolsheviks for their hostility to everything the Church held sacred and called on all true believers to resist "these monsters of the human race." Tikhon's message seemed to have an immediate effect. That very day, when the People's Commissar of Social Welfare, Alexandra Kollontai, sent a detachment of sailors to occupy the Alexander Nevsky Monastery in Petrograd, a crowd of worshippers rose to defend it. In the violence that ensued, one priest was killed and many more injured. Lenin, who at the time was struggling with other problems, was not eager to open a new front against the Church. Still, he could not tolerate this brazen challenge to Soviet authority and promptly declared all Church property to belong to the state. Soon squads of Bolshevik vandals began looting churches and monasteries for anything valuable they could find.[3]

The Church had no hope of winning this fight, but Tikhon continued to speak his mind forcefully. That summer he condemned the murder of the imperial family and denounced the regime for its lawlessness and savage use of force. In November, on the first anniversary of the Bolshevik coup, he sent a bold letter to Lenin in which he listed the crimes of the Soviet regime and blamed it for most of the county's woes. At the same time, he seemed to leave open the possibility of some kind of accommodation as he called for an end

Metropolitan Tikhon after he was elected patriarch of the Russian Orthodox Church in Moscow in 1917. The post had been vacant since the death of Patriarch Adrian in 1700, when Tsar Peter the Great refused to name a replacement. Photographer unknown (courtesy Russian State Archives of Film and Photo Documents, Krasnogorsk).

to the violence against the Church. But the Soviets merely intensified their campaign against those whom they considered counterrevolutionaries. Over the next two years, twenty-eight bishops were executed and thousands of priests and laypeople were imprisoned or shot.[4]

During the Russian civil war, Tikhon modified his stance somewhat and was careful to maintain the strictest neutrality. He even refused to offer the White armies his blessing, ostensibly because he believed it immoral to encourage fratricidal warfare. At the same time, he urged Church members to obey the new government so long as in doing so they did not violate the dictates of their consciences. Finally, in recognition of the fact that Church and state were now separate according to the new Soviet constitution, he freed Church members from all political obligations. It was a clever move, because it allowed each man or woman to decide individually whether to take sides or remain neutral. Thus when some groups of Orthodox clergy organized armed regiments to fight against the regime, Tikhon could plausibly deny that the Church had any institutional responsibility. This argument infuriated the Bolsheviks, many of whom called for his arrest. But the regime did not want to inflame international opinion at a time when it was trying to win recognition abroad. For the time being, the Bolsheviks had to be content to denounce Tikhon as a "bourgeois parasite" and to deny him a ration card.[5]

The horrific famine of 1921 seemed to offer the Church an opportunity to establish itself as a useful part of the new order. With the Soviet government overwhelmed by the magnitude of the crisis, Tikhon, on his own initiative, appealed to Christian churches abroad to send aid. He also called for the formation of a national ecclesiastical committee to take up collections at every church to feed the hungry. To this end, he gave permission for churches to sell items of value, with the exception of those used to administer the sacraments, in order to buy food. At first, the regime was cooperative and agreed to convey the patriarch's message over the radio and in the newspapers. This arrangement worked for several months, until Lenin began to fear that the Church was gaining in popularity at the expense of the Soviet government. To put a stop to this, he signed a decree on February 26, 1922, which now demanded that *all* items of value, including those thought to be most sacred, be removed from the churches.[6] Tikhon reacted swiftly to this turn of events and appealed directly to the people. He declared unequivocally that the confiscation of such items was sacrilegious and could not be allowed. This is exactly what Lenin had hoped he would do. The regime promptly denounced Tikhon and the

Church as heartless and indifferent to human suffering and declared them "enemies of the people."[7]

Lenin believed that he could use this confrontation to destroy the Church once and for all. To this end, he authorized armed gangs to break into churches and seize anything of value. The most infamous of these raids took place on Sunday, March 12, 1922, in the town of Shuya, some 200 miles northeast of Moscow. There a crowd of angry believers managed to fight off one of these requisitioning gangs, only to be confronted three days later by troops armed with machine guns. The parishioners resisted as best they could but were ultimately subdued after several were gunned down. Back in Moscow, Lenin was absent from the Politburo meeting at which it was decided to suspend further attempts to raid churches. When he learned of the events at Shuya, however, he promptly countermanded these orders and demanded that a war of extermination be waged against the Black Hundred[8] clergy "with such cruelty that they will not forget it for decades to come."[9]

Lenin's fury and determination on this matter can best be measured by the extent to which he personally involved himself in the struggle. On May 4, at his behest, the Politburo passed a decree ordering the death penalty for all priests.[10] He also composed a six-page letter, which he addressed to the Central Committee. In it he talked of the events of Shuya and the need to crush the enemy and to take all the Church's valuables wherever they could be found. Perhaps with Machiavelli in mind, he suggested that when committing cruelties, it is better to do it all at once before people can organize any resistance. Thus, he urged his comrades to be tough: the more clergy and bourgeoisie that could be shot the better. This was especially true of the Shuya rebels, who were falsely accused of having opposed famine relief. Lenin further called for quick trial and the shooting of as many Black Hundredists as possible.

In 1922–1923, the Soviet press reported 1414 violent confrontations in which 7,100 clergy were killed and thousands more were sent to prison. Even so, Lenin was far from satisfied. At the trial for the Shuya rebels, eleven received the death penalty, and many more were sentenced to long terms of incarceration. In an apparent attempt to assuage international opinion, the Politburo granted pleas for clemency to six of the eleven who were originally condemned to death. But there was no let-up in the Bolsheviks' determination to expropriate the Church's wealth and to vandalize its most sacred treasures. When Lenin learned that the relics of St. Barnabas of Vetluga were encased in a silver tomb, he had them removed and the tomb confiscated. A similar fate befell the Monastery of the Caves in Kiev, a sacred Orthodox site that had been occupied by monks since the eleventh century. Most of the wealth that was gathered there was sent directly to Moscow. Perhaps the most demoralizing act of vandalism involved the tomb of St. Sergius of Radonezh,[11] one of the Russian Orthodox Church's greatest heroes. The regime then decided to make a propaganda film of the venerable saint's exhumation to prove relics were not miraculously preserved as the Church fathers claimed, but had decayed like any other corpse. Tikhon strenuously protested this blasphemy, only to be ignored.[12]

On March 20, 1922, just eight days after the Shuya uprising, the Cheka indicted Tikhon for counterrevolutionary activity. He was incarcerated in the Donskoi Monastery until a case could be built against him for trial. Among the first to interrogate the patriarch was Evgenii Tuchkov, who was "curator" of Church affairs. His assignment was twofold: to goad the elderly prelate into making treasonable statements and to devise a plan to split the Church into competing factions. With regard to the latter, Tuchkov seemed to have embraced a new strategy in dealing with the Church. Recognizing the unlikelihood that the regime would be able to eradicate Orthodoxy anytime soon, Tuchkov sought to weaken it by exploiting the natural antagonism that existed between the "white clergy," who were married, and the "black clergy," who were celibate. In a report to the Politburo in October 1922, Tuchkov explained how he intended to use this and other ploys to push the supporters of Tikhon out of both the patriarchate and the parishes.[13]

Included in Tuchkov's strategy was his open support for the "renovationists," a group of left-leaning clergy and laity who believed that the Church could only hope to survive by combining Orthodox Christianity with the social and economic goals of Soviet communism. The renovationists were prepared to swear allegiance and to support the Bolsheviks even if this meant allowing the state to appropriate some of the Church's most valuable and sacred items. In return, they were given leave to establish a rival Church organization and to reform Russian Orthodoxy. That this ultimately did not work well was due in large part because the leaders of the new movement differed widely in their aims and styles. Archpriest Alexander Vvendensky, a Christian socialist and intellectual, who had enthusiastically greeted the Bolshevik takeover in October of 1917, was a highly emotional man who liked to chant the liturgy as if it were poetry. He also declared Marxism to be the Gospel printed in atheist language and yearned for the opportunity to defend Christianity in debate with the Bolsheviks. Another renovationist leader, Bishop

Antonin Granovsky, had an entirely different emphasis. His main goal was to simplify the liturgy and to conduct services in modern Russian to make it more accessible to the common worshipper. Finally, Archpriest Vladimir Krasnitsky, notorious for his extreme right-wing and anti–Semitic views, favored expanding the rights of the "white" or parish clergy, so that they could remarry and also become bishops.[14]

In the meantime, the regime continued to prepare for Tikhon's trial, which had to be postponed again and again because of pressure from the international community. The protesters included Pope Pius XI, a number of German socialists and Swedish pacifists, and the famous Norwegian explorer Fridtjof Nansen. The latter was also head of the League of Nations' High Commission for Refugees. Lenin, who was now in very bad health, found all this enormously frustrating. Even so, he insisted that the interrogations continue until the political climate was right for a trial.[15]

The renovationists, urged on by the GPU secret police, visited Tikhon in prison in May 1922 and persuaded him temporarily to stand down. They convinced him that this was necessary for the good of the Church, since he was not free to perform his duties as patriarch. In fact, this was a ruse to oust him from religious life altogether. Soon the renovationists had set up their own Higher Church Administration headed by Bishop Antonin, who claimed that Tikhon had willingly transferred his powers to him. At a Church council one year later, the renovationists passed a number of resolutions in support of Soviet power. They also voted to defrock Tikhon and to deprive him of his clerical status.[16] In June 1923, the aged prelate was forced to sign a prepared declaration of repentance in which he begged to be forgiven and released from custody. He further pledged that he was no longer an enemy of the regime and promised to disassociate himself from any and all White Guardist counterrevolutionaries. Tikhon never did stand trial, but neither did he ever become entirely free. He remained under surveillance until his death of angina pectoris on April 7, 1925, and was buried in Donskoi Monastery.[17]

Tikhon's demise marks a very low point for the Russian Orthodox Church, especially since the regime would not permit the election of a new patriarch. However, it was by no means the end of organized religion in the Soviet Union. Indeed, a new secular faith was already on the rise, occasioned in large part by the death of Lenin on January 24, 1924, at Gorky, a country estate outside Moscow. Having suffered a massive first stroke in May 1922, his health deteriorated steadily over the next twenty months. The news caught many by surprise, since the seriousness of Lenin's condition had been a closely guarded secret. Now that he was gone, a struggle for power was inevitable. His eventual successor, Josef Stalin, soon came to understand that his legitimacy as ruler in large part depended on his ability to immortalize Lenin's memory and to become its guardian. To this end, he encouraged as much public mourning as possible in order to sanctify the fallen leader's status as a kind of communist saint. Plans were soon underway for a magnificent state funeral. Lenin's body was brought by train into Moscow the next day to lie in state in the House of Soviets. For the next three days, thousands of people stood in line braving temperatures as cold as thirty below zero to file past the bier of possibly the most successful revolutionary of all time.[18]

The Central Executive Committee had assigned Felix Dzerzhinsky to head a special Funeral Commission to make all the necessary arrangements. However, it was Stalin who somehow had the last word on every important decision. As a former seminarian, he had a keen appreciation for the power of religious ritual. Soon Lenin's image began to be displayed publicly in busts, statues, and portraits all over the country. Dramatic biographies emphasizing the great leader's heroic accomplishments were written, and his speeches, essays, and books were reprinted and widely disseminated. These soon came to be looked upon as "holy scripture" as they were introduced into schools and universities. The public clamor surrounding Lenin's death caused ordinary citizens to become surprisingly emotional. Some fainted in public while others sobbed openly in the streets. Funeral wreaths and letters expressing grief came from all over. Theaters and shops closed down, and the Communist Party was flooded with new applicants. Schools, factories, parks, and government institutions were renamed in honor of the great revolutionary. Perhaps the grandest gesture of all came from the Petrograd Soviet, which announced that the former imperial capital was to be renamed Leningrad.[19] The Politburo was so impressed by the intensity of public feeling that it postponed Lenin's funeral by a day so that the body could lie in state that much longer.

No one knows who first proposed the idea of mummifying Lenin's corpse. Possibly it was the public's fascination with the discovery in 1922 of Tutankamen's tomb in Egypt that prompted some to think in these terms. In any case, Stalin was attracted to the idea and applied his influence accordingly. Those who opposed the project were struck not only by its absurdity, but also the irony. Only a few years earlier Lenin himself had sought to discredit the Church by initiating a furious campaign to stamp out the "cult of dead bodies and of dolls." It was he who had personally ordered the public desecration of a number of important Church relics. And now he was being made into one himself! A number of prominent Bolsheviks, including Trotsky, Bukharin, and Kamenev, spoke out against the plan, but Stalin was not to be denied.[20]

The funeral took place in Red Square on January 27 in temperatures that reached thirty-five below zero centigrade. Many thousands of people attended, some with banners that read ambiguously, "Lenin's grave is the cradle of the revolution."[21] Most of the leading Bolsheviks spoke, describing the fallen leader in the most fulsome terms as if trying to outdo one another. Stalin, who was also one of the pallbearers, gave a medium-length address that was notable mainly for its religious tone. After declaring Lenin to be "a genius among geniuses among the leaders of the proletariat," he ended his panegyric with a solemn pledge: "We swear to you, Comrade Lenin, that we will not spare our own lives in strengthening and broadening the union of the laboring people of the whole world—the Communist International."[22]

Over the next few years, the campaign against the Church became less obvious but no less determined. Tikhon had named Piotr Poliansky to carry on unofficially as *locum tenens,* but he was arrested almost immediately because he refused to cooperate with the renovationists. He spent the rest of his life in jail until his execution in 1937. His successor, the Metropolitan Sergei, also refused to have anything to do with the renovationists and actually tried to carry out a secret election for a new patriarch. But the plan was uncovered and denounced as an anti–Soviet plot. Sergei was arrested in December 1926 and spent eight months in jail, where he devised a more conciliatory strategy to deal with his tormentors. On July 19, 1927, he issued a Declaration of Loyalty to the Soviet State, which shocked believers in and out of the Soviet Union. In this pronouncement he declared that there had never been any persecution of religion in the Soviet Union and thanked the Soviet government for considering the spiritual needs of Orthodox believers. He called upon the émigré clergy to submit to Soviet rule and declared every blow against the USSR to be a blow against the Church.[23]

But Sergei's willingness to make concessions was not reciprocated. The regime was determined for ideological reasons to suppress religion as much as possible and to work toward its eventual extermination. In 1923, it had authorized the creation of a new journal, *The Godless,* the purpose of which was to denigrate all forms of spiritualism and to promote atheism. Later it sponsored a youth and workers' movement called The League of the Militant Godless to conduct anti-religious propaganda in schools, trade unions, villages, and the Red Army. The party leader who was most active in this struggle was Emelian Yaroslavsky, a member of the Central Committee and Stalin's official biographer. His *Bible for Believers and Non-Believers* was accepted as a serious scholarly work and was widely read. However, Yaroslavsky was not content to limit his attacks to academic arguments; he also urged his subordinates to mock Church rituals in vulgar parodies and to create cartoons and posters in which priests were depicted as "black crows" and "filth."[24]

The League of the Militant Godless sought to eliminate religious propaganda by any means possible. New laws barred priests from residing in cities and forbade the ringing of church bells. Churches and other kinds of religious structures were closed for the most minor technical infractions, and vandals broke into abandoned churches, smashing icons, covering frescos with lime, and cutting the crosses from the tops of cupolas. Moreover churchgoers were regularly punished by being excluded from work as government officials, teachers, or university professors. In 1929, the regime also introduced the "uninterrupted work week" in order to eliminate Sunday as a day of rest. Henceforth, days off were to be staggered: for some it was Monday, for others Tuesday, and so on.[25] It was also made illegal to organize prayer meetings for young people and women and to open religious libraries and reading rooms.[26] Congregations were even forbidden the right to provide medical care or material aid for their own members.

In 1932, the Soviet government, as part of a grand scheme to remodel and rebuild Moscow, destroyed one of Russian Orthodoxy's most famous churches. The Cathedral of Christ the Savior, which had been built to commemorate the great victory over Napoleon in 1812, had taken forty-four years to build before it was opened on May 20, 1883. As the largest cathedral in Russia, it could accommodate as many as 10,000 worshippers, and its spectacular golden dome was easily visible from as far away as the Lenin Hills. However, on December 5, demolition experts set off a series of explosions causing the church to collapse upon itself "like a house of cards." This wanton and destructive act, wrote *New York Times* reporter Walter Duranty, "was carried out with such nicety that no explosion was heard half a mile across the river, or broke the windows of neighboring houses."[27] Of course, most of the church's valuables, and all of its gold, had been previously removed. Also taken were 177 marble slabs, upon which was chiseled a description of the campaign against Napoleon and the names of the soldiers who perished on the battlefield. In its place, the Soviet government planned to construct an enormous Palace of Soviets large enough to accommodate 21,000 people. It was designed to stand higher than the Empire State Building and to be topped by a statue of Lenin.[28]

In Leningrad, the Cathedral of Kazan was subjected to what many believers probably considered an even worse fate. It, too, had been an important, albeit controversial, monument under the old regime. Having been commissioned by Tsar Paul in 1801, it was modeled after the Basilica of St. Peter's in Rome. Although many devout Orthodox believers found its resemblance to a Catholic church highly offensive since it was here that the commander-in-chief of Russian armies, Mikhail Ilarionovich Kutuzov, had prayed before leading his army to meet the French at Borodino in August of 1812. General Kutuzov's death in 1813 was followed by his interment in the Cathedral, which also became the depository for the keys to seventeen cities and eight fortresses—all taken by the victorious Russian army as trophies of war in Europe. The cathedral was closed in 1917, but reopened in 1932 as the Museum of the History of Religion and Atheism.

Indeed, the 1930s were a bad time for anyone bold enough openly to practice religion in the Soviet Union. The regime was determined to finish what it had begun a decade earlier by treating believers like "enemies of the people." To this end, it intensified its crusade of church closings and converting many surviving religious structures that remained to secular uses such as clubs, movie houses, granaries, and warehouses. Previously, there had been some popular opposition to such vandalism, but now even the most devout believers seemed to have gone into hiding. One man who was not intimidated, however, was a gifted doctor and surgeon named Valentin Felixovich Voino-Yasenetsky. A humble, enlisted medic during the Russo-Japanese War of 1904–05, he later earned a degree in medicine and became chief surgeon at the municipal hospital in Tashkent, Uzbekistan, during World War I. He survived the turmoil of revolution and civil war only to have his beloved wife fall ill and die. The doctor, now in his early forties, was beside himself with grief. He sought solace in Russian Orthodoxy and began to attend church on a regular basis. As his commitment to the Church intensified, he became increasingly offended by the Bolsheviks' campaign of hate and mockery against Orthodoxy and religion in general. In 1920, he made a bold decision: he would study for the priesthood as he continued to practice medicine.

He could hardly have chosen a more dangerous time to receive Holy Orders, since the Soviet government's campaign against religion had reached a fever pitch. But Voino-Yasenetsky was eager to confront the enemies of the true faith. In 1921, he testified in court in defense of a colleague who had been accused of "wrecking." After taking the stand, he was interrogated by the notorious Chekist prosecutor Yakov Peters. At one point, Peters sarcastically

Leningrad's Cathedral of the Annunciation (shown here in 1933) was demolished in part because of the regime's hostility to religion, but also so its bricks could be used at other worksites. Photographer unknown (courtesy Russian State Archives of Film and Photo Documents, Krasnogorsk).

III. Russian Orthodoxy and the Soviet State 61

According to a popular Soviet slogan of the time, "Church bells are for the industrial needs of the USSR!" Thus, this ten-ton bell in Kiev was removed from the Cathedral of St. Vladimir in 1926 so that its metal could be put to constructive use. Photographer unknown (courtesy Russian State Archives of Film and Photo Documents, Krasnogorsk).

wondered aloud how the good doctor could pray at night and carve people up during the day. Yoino-Yasenetsky's answer was bold: unlike the Cheka, he cut people to *save* lives.[29] If such impertinence angered the likes of Peters, it won the admiration of his co-religionists. The following year, when Innokenty, metropolitan of Tashkent and Turkistan, was arrested and incarcerated by the Cheka, a church council chose Dr. Yoino-Yasenetsky to succeed him. Thus, the doctor/priest assumed his new religious name of Luke as he was shorn as a monk.

Luke wasted no time in protesting the anti-religious policies of the Soviet government and was promptly arrested for being a counterrevolutionary and a British spy. To be sure, the Bolsheviks saw him as a dangerous opponent; here was a man of science and learning whose arguments could not be so easily dismissed. Over the next twenty years, he would endure three periods of incarceration totaling twelve years. But with the outbreak of war in 1941, Luke was released from prison and allowed to work as a surgeon in the military hospital in Krasnoyarsk. Despite his advanced age, he worked long hours to save the most gravely wounded soldiers. The very fact that Luke had been allowed to perform such a useful service to the country was due in large part to the boldness of Metropolitan Sergei. In the hours following the initial German attack, he made a dramatic appeal in his Sunday sermon urging the faithful to support the government, fight the enemy, and pray for victory. Over the next few years, he made no less than twenty-three appeals to believers all over Russia to give all they could for the defense of the motherland.[30] The Soviet government soon saw that it was in its interest to end its policy of repression and to allow the Orthodox faithful to participate in the fight against fascism. Thus, it approved the Church's request to open a bank account in order to collect contributions for the war effort.[31]

Another priest who performed heroically under even more difficult circumstances was the metropolitan of Leningrad, Alexei. As a previously declared "enemy of the people," he had served his congregation during the prewar years under constant fear of arrest. But in the summer of 1941, after the Germans laid siege to Leningrad, he patriotically called upon all true believers to obey the Soviet government and to fight the invader. Over the next two and one-half years, conditions in the city completely disintegrated. One million people died from the constant bombardment, cold, disease, and starvation. Alexei, who lived in the cellar of his church on scavenged bits of food, could occasionally be seen walking in procession around the Church of the Transfiguration carrying icons even during aid raids. He became one of the last

In 1929, another huge church bell in Kiev was smashed into smaller parts to make use of its bronze. Photographer unknown (courtesy Russian State Archives of Film and Photo Documents, Krasnogorsk).

surviving priests in the city, as his flock gradually disappeared around him. On one occasion, his choirmaster dropped dead during a service. Soon the aged and exhausted metropolitan, in addition to his priestly chores, was doing all the janitorial work himself. These included making minor repairs around the church, cleaning, and shoveling snow.[32]

Alexei's patriotism and dedication did not go unnoticed. In early September 1943, he, along with two other high-ranking metropolitans, was invited to Moscow to participate in a meeting with Stalin. The occasion was as amicable and productive as it was unexpected. Repression against the Church had already stopped, and the League of Militant Atheists was no longer authorized to abuse the Orthodox faithful. But now, Stalin took a giant step toward normalizing relations with the Church when he gave his permission to elect a new patriarch. This was quickly accomplished when a council of nineteen bishops and several dozen priests and laymen unanimously elected Metropolitan Sergei of Moscow, who was still administering the Church as *locum tenens*. Stalin also approved the resumption of the monthly publication of the *Journal of the*

Moscow Patriarchate and authorized the reopening of eight undergraduate seminaries and two graduate seminaries. All this was accompanied by the release of large numbers of incarcerated bishops and priests from the prisons and camps.[33]

Sergei's death after only eight months as patriarch might have become yet another crisis for the Church, but as the end of the war approached, its status had clearly changed. Perhaps the fact that Orthodox believers had contributed some 150 million rubles to the war effort prompted Stalin to reconsider its role in society. In any case, he permitted the convocation of a national church council to elect a new patriarch. The man chosen to lead the Church in January 1945 was none other than the same humble "enemy of the people," Metropolitan Alexei, who had nearly starved to death during the Leningrad blockade. The changes that the new patriarch had lived to see must surely have seemed miraculous. In 1941, there had been only 380 working Orthodox churches in the USSR and not a single monastery. By 1945, there were 10,547 churches and seventy-five monasteries. Many structures and relics that had been previously confiscated were now returned to the Church. A few outstanding clerics were actually honored for their sacrifices and accomplishments. Among these was the Archbishop Luke, who had been assigned to head the archbishopric of the Crimea in 1945. The following year, he was awarded the Stalin Prize First Class for two scholarly books on medicine.[34]

The regime's qualified toleration of the Church during World War II, however, was soon to be challenged. Doctrinaire communists were increasingly uneasy about the status of an institution that had been identified as counter-revolutionary by Lenin and other important socialist thinkers. Many feared that the Church would eventually become a source of opposition to the regime. As early as 1948, a distinct chill began to develop between Russian Orthodoxy and the government, which prevented the consecration of any new bishops until just days before Stalin's death in March 1953. Stalin's successor as First Secretary of the Communist Party was Nikita Khrushchev, a man who would be remembered for his denunciation of his predecessor's crimes as well as his impulsive behavior and intemperate speech. The new leader moved slowly at first, but toward the end of the decade he began to speak ominously about his intention to take "God by the beard."[35] He also predicted that the Soviet Union would attain true communism by 1980, at which time the country's last Christian would be displayed on television. Khrushchev also made his intentions clear to the Patriarch Alexei, whom he met in 1958. The prelate was deeply troubled by the First Secretary's tone and language and warned of a coming storm.

Alexei's worst suspicions were soon confirmed. The regime began a determined campaign of vicious anti-religious propaganda in the media, which encouraged speculation that the Church would be eliminated from Soviet life as early as 1966. Such talk was accompanied by church closings across the country, which reduced the number from roughly 20,000 to 7,560. Seminary students were no longer deferred from military service, and women under thirty were forbidden to enter the convent. Many priests were arbitrarily deprived of their registration by civil authorities, while others were forced to get special permission from local officials in order to administer sacraments to the ill and the dying. Perhaps the most demoralizing blow came on December 6, 1959, when Soviet citizens were informed by *Pravda* that Alexander A. Osipov, a distinguished professor of Old Testament Theology at the Leningrad Theological Academy, had renounced his religion and become an atheist. Many believers thought the timing of the scandal deliberate since it coincided with a visit by a delegation from the World Council of Churches, a body that many believers had hoped the Church would join.[36]

Patriarch Alexei sought to counter this offensive by publishing a declaration on December 30, 1959, threatening excommunication against all who "publicly reviled the name of God." On February 16, 1960, he gave a speech in the Kremlin at a peace and disarmament congress, in which he lauded the Church for its glorious culture and its historic role as a defender of both Russia and the Soviet Union. He also denounced the communist regime for the insults and abuses it had inflicted on the Church over the years. On February 25, Alexei celebrated his name day by complaining about the "enemies of God" and the harm they had done to the Church. Such impertinence outraged Party officials, who were quick to take revenge. They soon brought about the dismissal of the head of the Council on the Affairs of the Orthodox Church, Georgi Karpov, who was often jokingly referred to as *Narkombog* (the People's Commissar of God), or sometimes *Narkomopium*. The problem was that Karpov had cultivated such a good working relationship with the patriarch and his assistants that many believed that he was unable properly to supervise and control Church affairs.[37] His replacement was Vladimir Kuroedov, an apparatchik known for his hostility to religion and brusque personal style.[38]

Kuroedov embarked on a program of petty harassment, which he hoped would chasten and demoralize those churchmen and women who dared to criticize Soviet power. His first act was to close the main cathedral in Perm, which local authorities lamely alleged was causing traffic problems. He also supported legislation to impede the normal functioning of the Church. One

Anti-religion demonstration of collective farmers in the kolkhoz "Artillerist" of the northern Caucusas, 1931. The front placard reads: "Down with the sermons about the Ascension. Long live the hard fight against the weeds [scum] of society. Let us complete our plan 100 percent!" Photographer unknown (courtesy Russian State Archives of Film and Photo Documents, Krasnogorsk).

such law prohibited Church authorities from giving financial help to poor local parishes struggling to survive. Others stipulated that baptismal fonts could not be located in buildings separate from the main church; that only one church could be open per village; that churches in the larger cities and towns had to be sufficiently far from one another in order to remain open; and that no single priest could serve in more than one church. The cumulative effect of these measures was to bring about many more church closings.[39]

Needless to say, the prelates who administered dioceses were confounded and distraught by these measures, but those who protested paid a serious price. Among the first to be punished was the Metropolitan Nikolai, who had written the patriarch's February speech. In June he was removed from his position as head of the Church's Office of Foreign Religious Affairs and forbidden to celebrate the liturgy or publish any of his writings. In September he was pressured into retiring as metropolitan of Krutitsy and Kostroma. Another target was Archbishop Iov (Job) of Kazan, who, in mid–1960, was accused of swindling and embezzlement and eventually sent to jail. His real crime, according to his parishioners, was his refusal to comply with church closings in his diocese. A similar case occurred the following year when the Archbishop Andrei of Chernigov likewise resisted the church and convent closings demanded by the regime. He was declared guilty of conducting unlawful religious propaganda and of evading taxes. He spent the next eight years in jail.[40]

In his address at the Twenty-Second Party Congress, Khrushchev called for a greater effort to eradicate "religious prejudices and superstitions" and a more vigorous "scientific and atheistic education which would ... prevent the spread of religious views."[41] But Khrushchev, whose domestic policies were under attack by many in the Party, suffered an additional blow in October 1962 from the Soviet Union's perceived defeat during the Cuban Missile Crisis. Two years later he was removed from power; Leonid Brezhnev replaced him as First Secretary, and Alexei Kosygin replaced him as premier. If this change in leadership did little to improve the status of Russian Orthodoxy in the Soviet state, it did signify that the terror of the 1930s was not about to be repeated. Khrushchev, though now reduced to the status of a non-person, was neither imprisoned nor executed. He was allowed to retire and live out his years peacefully at his country dacha outside Moscow.[42] The religious faithful, though still repressed, were no longer denounced as "enemies of the people," as the term itself had become an anachronism.

This is not to say, however, that the regime's fundamental hostility toward religion was much diminished. In the last quarter century of Soviet power, Church and state remained locked in a tense and hostile relationship. It was a strange situation in which things were not what they seemed. On the one hand, there were many among the ruling elite who were still committed to suppressing religion in the Soviet Union. On the other, there were those who urged that the Church at least be allowed to appear to be independent and vibrant in order to prove to the outside world that Soviet citizens enjoyed complete freedom of conscience. To accomplish these seemingly contradictory objectives, the regime infiltrated the Church with dozens of KGB "bishops" to act as informers and to manipulate ecclesiastical appointments. At the same time, it continued to close churches and monasteries in remote areas while it renovated those in the big cities, which were likely to be visited by foreign tourists. The Politburo also bade the patriarch to travel abroad to praise the Soviet Union's foreign and domestic policies.[43]

Throughout the 1970s, the Soviet government continued its attempts to limit the role of the Church in everyday life. Parents were advised to conduct family life in the "spirit of communism" or risk losing custody of their children. Students were enjoined not to attend church, sing in choirs, or participate in religious study circles lest they jeopardize their future educational and professional opportunities. At the same time, the state saw fit to cooperate when it seemed in its interest to do so. One such occasion occurred with the death of ninety-two-year-old Patriarch Sergei in April of 1970. The following month, the regime did not interfere when a national church council chose Metropolitan Pimen as his successor. The new patriarch was much admired for his deep spirituality, ability as a poet, and knowledge of Church music. However, his unwillingness to criticize Soviet power for its attempts to restrict and control the Church led many to suspect that he was under the influence of the KGB.[44]

But if the patriarch was reluctant to confront the regime for its continuing oppression and interference, there were others who could not be prevented from doing so. In the final two decades of Soviet power, a number of defiant priests came forward to demand religious freedom for the Orthodox faithful. Among them were Father Gleb Yakunin and Father Sergei Zheludkov, both of whom spent many years in prison and exile for their willingness to defy the state. The former became the leader of the Christian Committee for the Defense of the Rights of Religious Believers. The latter became known for his seditious sermons and his refusal to submit to official threats even after he had been driven from his parish. That these men survived at all is testimony to the extent times had changed. The regime did not want to make martyrs out of those they wished to silence.[45]

But not all religious dissidents were content to behave as expected. One such maverick was Father Dmitri Dudko, who had long been a thorn in the side of the Soviet government for his relentless fight against atheism. He was first arrested in 1948 while at the Moscow Theological Seminary for the crime of having written religious poems during World War II. Upon his release from jail in 1956, he resumed his studies and four years later was ordained as a priest. His radical views and growing popularity, especially among young intellectuals, resulted in his transfer from Moscow to a remote location in 1974. But this did not prevent him from agitating for religious freedom. In 1980, he was arrested for giving slanderous materials to a reporter from the *New York Times*. Then, after six months in jail, he completely reversed himself by begging forgiveness on Soviet television and by reading the following statement: "I repudiate what I have done and assess my so-called struggle against godlessness as a struggle against Soviet power." After the collapse of the Soviet Union in 1991, Dudko became associated with a nationalist newspaper called *Zavtra* or *Tomorrow,* which praised Stalin for his asceticism and for having created a great empire. "The time has come to rehabilitate Stalin," said Father Dudko, adding, "I even pray for the repose of his soul."[46] This was a turn that no one would have predicted.

In any case, the 1980s brought changes that most people never believed would happen. The Soviet Union's last general secretary, Mikhail Gorbachev, who came to power in March 1985 was, to be sure, a confirmed atheist. He was not, however, inclined to continue the government's war against the Russian Orthodoxy. In fact, he saw in the Church a potential ally to implement *perestroika*—his plan to restructure the USSR's socialist economy. Gorbachev seems to have calculated that the kind of changes he envisioned required a moral commitment on the part of ordinary citizens that communist ideology could not provide. Thus, he appealed to the Church fathers for support early on in his tenure as First Secretary and met with Patriarch Pimen in April 1988, when he declared believers to be Soviet working people who "have every right to express their convictions in a fitting manner."[47] It was a joyous occasion for all concerned. Never had an "enemy of the people" been resurrected so completely. And it was also a good omen for what was to follow: more than 800 new parishes were permitted to open that year, and the millennial anniversary of the Baptism of Kievan Rus' was celebrated all across Russia *with* the support of the government.

The resurrection of the Russian Orthodox Church in the last years of Soviet rule must rank as one of the most startling changes of all that occurred during the tenure of Mikhail Gorbachev. But it was something that had to happen if the new Russia was to be accepted by the international community as a civil society in the making. Today, however, many concerned believers fret about a new problem: secularism. They worry that although a high percentage of Russians identify themselves as Orthodox Christians, most do so only in the cultural sense and feel little for the spiritual. In an increasingly prosperous and materialistic society, this could prove to be far more lethal to the Church than the communists ever were.

Chapter IV

Trotsky and Trotskyism

For most Bolsheviks, the period following Lenin's death was one of concern and apprehension about the future. The new Soviet state had nearly collapsed from the ravages of civil war and one of the most horrendous famines in history. Although the economy had started to improve, a majority of the population was still in wretched conditions. Under such circumstances, there could be no talk of a glorious march to communism. The emphasis now was on recovery and survival, but Lenin's plan to achieve this, the NEP, seemed to betray the highest ideals of the revolution. It had taken virtually all of his powers of persuasion to gain the Party's acquiescence. Now that he was gone, many questioned how long it should be continued and worried that it would revive old bourgeois habits and impede the construction of socialism in the USSR.

The need to unite behind a strong, confident leader was a high priority among the Party faithful. Many thought Lev Davidovich Trotsky, the son of a moderately prosperous Jewish farmer from Ukraine, to be the logical choice to succeed Lenin. That his credentials as a revolutionary leader were impressive, no one could deny. Having become a Marxist at eighteen, he was arrested for trying to incite the workers in the southern town of Nikolaev in 1898. He spent time in a number of prisons while awaiting trial, including one in Moscow, where he married a fellow revolutionary and prisoner, Alexandra Sokolovskaya.[1] Not long after that, they were both exiled to the Lena River in Siberia, where they lived in various towns such as Ust-Kut, Irkutsk, and Verkholensk. Security in these places was somewhat relaxed since the inmates were not actually behind bars, but living in small houses. In 1902, he fled captivity by riding in a cart under a pile of hay, leaving his wife and daughters behind. Trotsky eventually made his way to London, where he met Lenin, whose great work, *The Development of Capitalism in Russia,* he had already read and admired. The two initially liked each other, but their relationship soon soured because of personal and ideological differences.

Trotsky's fame as a revolutionary dates to the Revolution of 1905. He returned to Russia after learning of the Bloody Sunday massacre, which had taken place in January. Russian troops had fired into crowd of workers and their families, who had come to the Winter Palace to present a petition to the tsar. This atrocity aroused indignation worldwide, and in the months that followed, strikes and demonstrations spread across Russia. Trotsky seized the opportunity before him and soon became chairman of the St. Petersburg Soviet of Workers' Deputies. When the members of the Soviet were arrested and charged with planning an armed insurrection, Trotsky's defiant and stirring oratory at the trial won the admiration of even the prosecution. Pronounced guilty by the court and banished to Siberia for life, he escaped his jailors en route by hiring a sleigh to take him across the frozen tundra to freedom. Trotsky eventually made it to Western Europe and finally the United States. He remained abroad for ten years.

In May 1907, Trotsky attended the Fifth Party Congress in London. Thereafter, he resided in many other European cities including Berlin, Vienna, and Paris. He never ceased agitating for revolution—publishing articles, editing newspapers, and working to promote unity among Russian Marxists. In 1914, the outbreak of the First World War found him in France, from which he was expelled two years later for his opposition to the war. In January 1916, Trotsky moved with his second family[2] to the United States and took up residence in the Bronx. He had been there only about ten weeks when he learned of the tsar's abdication. He immediately made plans to return to Russia, but his notoriety as a radical held up his arrival in Petrograd until May 29. That summer Trotsky worked closely with Lenin to undermine the Provisional Government. When the Bolsheviks took power in October, he became Commissar of Foreign Affairs and later Commissar of War. It was in this latter capacity that Trotsky performed his greatest service to the Revolution. Without any previous military experience, he built the Red Army almost from scratch and led it skillfully to defeat the Whites and the forces of counterrevolution.

But for all his many accomplishments, and despite Lenin's support, Trotsky never became the leader of the Party. This was due in large part to his many personal shortcomings and his tendency to antagonize even his admirers. Trotsky was arrogant, vain, ambitious, condescending, and generally dismissive of any point of view that differed from his own. He also had a controversial

Commissar of War Lev Davidovich Trotskey meets with some soldiers of the Red Army in front of the Bolshoi Theater as they prepare to do battle with the enemies of the Revolution. Moscow, 1918. Photographer unknown (courtesy Russian State Archives of Film and Photo Documents, Krasnogorsk).

past: he had originally been a Menshevik and then became an independent Marxist. He was an opponent of Bolshevism for many years and did not formally join the Party until the summer of 1917. Too, Trotsky had often been scathingly critical of Lenin, whose theories he once predicted would result in a one-party dictatorship. All this would come back to haunt him in the struggle for power after Lenin's death. In the end, Trotsky and his supporters were vanquished, and he was declared an "enemy of the people." For this he was removed from all his posts, expelled from the Communist Party, sent into exile, and eventually murdered. Indeed, by the mid–1930s, he had become one of the most vilified persons in Russian history, his very name synonymous with treason.

Stalin was in many ways Trotsky's opposite. Short and pockmarked, he had a slightly withered arm after nearly dying of blood poisoning as a child. He was neither a stirring speaker nor a sophisticated intellectual. Having become a Bolshevik in 1903, he served the Party for many years at the grassroots level, publishing anti-government propaganda and organizing workers for strikes and demonstrations, even traveling abroad to Stockholm, London, Krakow, and Vienna on Party business. Later, in Georgia, he participated in a series of bank robberies to raise money for the Party. Arrested and incarcerated many times, Stalin always managed to escape and resume his work for the Party. Lenin appreciated dedication and considered him the most reliable of men. Others saw a morose and taciturn man, who was easily offended and inclined to hold grudges for the most trivial of reasons.

Stalin seems to have become aware of Trotsky well before Trotsky became aware of Stalin. In 1907, they had both attended the aforementioned three-week-long Fifth Party Congress in London, but the two had very different experiences. Trotsky, who was already recognized as an experienced revolutionary, won the delegates' adulation with his masterful speech to the Congress. Stalin, by contrast, was nearly turned away from the proceedings because the Transcaucasian Social Democrats refused to accept his credentials. Lenin finally got him admitted as a non-voting member, which would have entitled him to address the Congress had he chosen to do so. But there is no record of his uttering single public word, and Trotsky later claimed not to recall having seen him there at all. Thereafter, Stalin and Trotsky went their separate ways and were not formally introduced until 1913, when they were both in Vienna.[3] Stalin had gone there to visit Lenin to discuss the national problem in a future socialist Russia. That conversation resulted in Stalin writing an article for the Bolshevik journal *Prosveshchenye* (*Enlightenment*) entitled *Marxism and the National Colonial Question*. Upon his return to Russia, Stalin was arrested and exiled for the fourth and last time. When the tsar abdicated in March of 1917, he was still in the tiny town of Achinsk in the Arctic Circle, serving out his term.

Stalin was among the first Bolsheviks to return to Petrograd after a general amnesty was proclaimed for all prisoners by the newly formed Provisional Government. By now he was a man of some stature within the Party and was named to the Russian Bureau, the *Pravda* board, and as a Bolshevik delegate to the Executive Committee of the Petrograd Soviet. Interestingly, although he relied on Lenin's patronage, he sometimes took positions that were initially in contradiction to those of his mentor. He often did come around to support Lenin's point of view in the end. Stalin could also act decisively. In July 1917, when many of the Bolsheviks' most important leaders, including Lenin and Trotsky, were either in hiding or jail, Stalin teamed up with Jacob Sverdlov to manage the Party's business until the crisis had passed. Curiously, he did not play a role in the October (November) coup that put the Bolsheviks in power.

Nevertheless, he was Lenin's choice to become Commissar of Nationalities in the new Soviet government.[4]

A major turning point in Trotsky's and Stalin's relationship seems to have occurred just before the first meeting of the Sovnarkom in the last days of October. According to Trotsky, he and Stalin had been waiting in a room when Stalin overheard the new Commissar of the Navy, Pavel Dybenko, chatting with his mistress, Alexandra Kollontai, who was an enthusiastic advocate of free love. Much to Stalin's amusement, the conversation contained intimacies of a sexual nature that were clearly meant to be private. Stalin made a gesture at the partition and, with a wink and a smirk, continued to eavesdrop. But Trotsky "drew himself up" and made clear by the expression on his face his stern disapproval. Stalin immediately realized his mistake and was acutely embarrassed. From that time on, relates Trotsky, Stalin never again attempted to speak to him on matters other than business.[5]

Roughly eight months later, in June 1918, at the beginning of the civil war, Stalin was sent to Tsaritsyn (today Volgograd) on the Volga River to deal with a severe food shortage. The situation had become especially acute because the Germans had occupied the grain-rich Ukraine after the treaty of Brest-Litovsk. Tsaritsyn was therefore a crucial supply point for food produced in the lower Volga region and the North Caucasus. He arrived in an armored train with a bodyguard of 400 men, invested with more power than he had ever had in his life. Stalin initially did his job quite well by fixing food prices, improving rationing, and by finding new sources of meat and fish. But he soon took on other responsibilities, which he seems to have found more compelling. These included reorganizing local Cheka branches and rooting out anti-Soviet plots, real or imagined. Suspects were often executed even when the evidence was weak. Stalin also cast a jaundiced eye on Trotsky's preference for former tsarist officers as military specialists for the Red Army. On July 7, he wrote a letter to Lenin criticizing this practice. He refused to believe that those who had previously served the tsar would defend the revolution.

Stalin soon began to take matters into his own hands. On July 10, and without Trotsky's approval, he appointed Klimenti Voroshilov, an old friend and former Chekist, to active command on the Tsaritsyn front and told him to ignore orders issued by Trotsky. Like Stalin, Voroshilov deplored the use of former tsarist officers in the Red Army. He was also incensed by Trotsky's harsh treatment of loyal Bolsheviks whom Trotsky had suspected of cowardice.[6] Lenin soon found himself in an awkward position. While Stalin was imploring him for the power to dismiss incompetent and unreliable army commanders and commissars, Trotsky was demanding that Stalin be recalled. The Commissar of War also threatened to court-martial Voroshilov for insubordination. Not wanting to antagonize either man, Lenin played for time. Ultimately, he granted Stalin the powers he wanted with the understanding that Voroshilov would submit to the chain of command. But even before this arrangement could be put into effect, Stalin had again begun ordering arrests and summarily shooting former tsarist officers as "enemies of the people." Nor would the "magnificent Georgian," as Lenin once called him, agree to halt the executions pending further investigation. In one instance, he had a group of officers imprisoned on a barge in the Volga River with the hatches nailed shut. When the barge sank, killing all aboard, Stalin claimed it was an accident.[7]

In the end, Voroshilov was transferred to Ukraine and Stalin was ordered back to Moscow. Although the Commissar of Nationalities was officially received as a hero, it was clear that his removal had been intended as a reprimand. Still, none of this did Trotsky any good. Stalin had not been the least bit chastened by his "punishment," and Trotsky had still failed to see him as the threat he would later become. This began to change somewhat one year later, when the Central Committee replaced Trotsky's appointed commander in chief, General Joakim Vatsetis, with General Sergei Kamenev and then reorganized the Revolutionary War Council without his input. Trotsky believed that this was a deliberate affront orchestrated by Stalin, although the initiative had been supported by others in the Central Committee. Trotsky also blamed Stalin for the Red Army's disastrous defeat at the gates of Warsaw in August 1920 because the latter had used his forces to capture Lvov, rather than support the main drive on Warsaw. In retrospect, however, there is little reason to believe that Stalin's diversion could have affected the outcome of the battle.[8]

The ultimate triumph of the Red Army in the civil war should have enhanced Trotsky's position within the Party, but he soon lost whatever prestige he might have earned as the architect of victory. His Bolshevik colleagues were morbidly suspicious that he intended to use his control of the military to take power, as Napoleon had done during the French Revolution. Trotsky made no effort to allay these concerns and soon took on more responsibility by assuming the post of Commissar of Transport in March of 1920. It was a daunting task, since the railroad system was near collapse and Trotsky was already busy enough as Commissar of War. Still, he threw himself wholly into this new job, determined to fix what was wrong. To this end, he created a new agency called Tsektran and employed the harshest dictatorial measures to reinvigorate the transportation system. Though he was largely successful, his arbitrary manner and occasional brutality caused deep resentment.[9]

Similarly, his decision to force ordinary soldiers into labor armies in order to increase the country's productivity (described in Chapter II) was yet another reason to question his motives and his judgment. Not only was the project impractical, it made virtual serfs of soldiers who had served and suffered during the civil war. Amazingly, Trotsky believed that the drudgery of the tasks assigned (peat mining, timber cutting, and railroad repair) could be offset by a campaign of uplifting propaganda. Others had their doubts, and although Lenin and many other high-ranking Bolsheviks originally supported the plan, they were disappointed by the results. These included high costs, low productivity, and endless discipline and morale problems among the soldiers. In the end, the project was recognized as "an empty bureaucratic fantasy" and abandoned. True to form, Trotsky would not admit that he had been at all mistaken.[10]

In 1921, Trotsky took on another losing cause when he became involved in a trade union dispute. The issue had been festering since the fall of 1919, when a group of trade union leaders and industrial administrators had formed the Workers' Opposition to criticize Soviet economic policies. Specifically, they objected to the growing bureaucratization in society, which they alleged was stifling the creative potential of Soviet workers. The group's most prominent member was Alexander Shlyapinkov, who was the chairman of the All-Russian Metalworkers' Union. Not only did he advocate the election of worker assemblies to manage the economy, but he believed that trade unions should also protect the rights of the workers. Trotsky, however, took the view that the main function of the trade union leaders was to find ways to get the workers to increase production. He saw no reason for them to become involved in labor disputes, which could only put them into opposition with Soviet power. To put an end to such talk, Trotsky called for a thorough reorganization of the trade union leadership and, in the process, put himself at the center of a controversy that showed him in a bad light.[11]

Lenin himself was no proponent of trade union democracy and probably sympathized with Trotsky's militancy on this issue. But because of the crisis facing the Soviet economy was so dire, he was inclined to seek a compromise in order to avoid antagonizing the workers and splitting the Party. But Trotsky would not back down. To promote his point of view, he wrote a controversial pamphlet entitled *The Role and Tasks of the Trade Unions*. It was not one of his better efforts, as Lenin himself noted, since it contained numerous "theoretical mistakes and glaring blunders." Still, Trotsky continued to press his argument in speeches and in print. At the Tenth Party Congress, which met in Moscow on March 8, 1921, the issue was finally put to a vote. Lenin's plan to allow the trade unions some autonomy was accepted by a wide margin. Trotsky's position, which was also supported by Nikolai Bukharin, won only 12 percent of the vote. To Trotsky's satisfaction, however, the Workers' Opposition had almost no support and was soon officially banned as an illegal faction.[12]

Lenin no doubt keenly appreciated Trotsky's intellectual brilliance, decisiveness, and energy. And though the two had little personal chemistry, they felt a mutual respect for each other as revolutionaries. Even so, Trotsky often confounded his older colleague by resisting his position even when it was most compelling. In April 1922, shortly after Stalin's title of General Secretary became official, Lenin proposed that Trotsky become deputy premier of the Council of People's Commissars. His intention was to honor the Commissar of War with a position in the Soviet government that was nearly equivalent to Stalin's position in the Communist Party. But Trotsky seems to have considered this a demotion and refused it outright.[13] In the process he offended his most important ally. The following month, when Lenin suffered his first stroke and was forced to convalesce in the countryside outside Moscow, Trotsky did not visit him once the entire summer. In September, Lenin again tried to appoint Trotsky deputy premier of the Council of People's Commissars. This time it was formally approved by the Politburo, although once again Trotsky turned it down.[14]

In contrast to Trotsky, Stalin was careful to cultivate an image as a dutiful servant of the Soviet state and a man without vanity or personal ambition. The General Secretary lived modestly with his second wife,[15] Natalya Alliluyeva, and infant son, Vasily, in a small Kremlin apartment and went about his business without fanfare. His knowledge of the complex Soviet bureaucracy won him the nickname "Comrade Card-Index." Most saw him a loyal colleague, moderate in his political views and a careful listener. But beneath the calm exterior, Stalin was consumed by anger, envy, and a desire for power that few suspected. Determined as he was to outmaneuver his enemies, he always thought far in advance and, unlike Trotsky, was a master of timing and strategy. He also made a practice of assigning his own people to important positions in the bureaucracy. This enabled him to have the phones of his Kremlin colleagues tapped so that he might never be taken by surprise.[16]

One of the few times Stalin *was* taken by surprise concerned the state's monopoly on foreign trade. Lenin was insistent that it be maintained while many others in the Central Committee, including Stalin, wanted to relax it. Three days before Lenin's first stroke, the Politburo accepted his position. However, in the months that followed, while Lenin was convalescing, the Central Committee had voted to weaken it. Upon learning of this, Lenin promptly appealed to Trotsky to support his view and the latter effectively complied. Stalin was surprised by Lenin's fervor on this issue and quickly acquiesced. He actually cared less about the trade issue than he did about the prospect of Lenin and Trotsky conspiring against him. Others were alarmed as well, including Lev Kamenev and Grigori Zinoviev, who saw Trotsky as a schemer bent on exploiting Lenin's incapacity for his own political benefit. With this in mind, Kamenev and Zinoviev approached Stalin during the summer of 1922 with a plan to isolate and outmaneuver Trotsky. To this end, they formed a kind of triumvirate or *troika,* by which they agreed to discuss Party business beforehand and arrive at decisions without Trotsky's input.[17]

Actually, Trotsky had been left out of the loop on important issues even before. In February 1921, the Commissar of War had not been informed that the Politburo had approved a military operation to invade Georgia and overthrow the elected Menshevik government. The campaign, led by Stalin's good friend Sergo Ordzhonikidze, had been easily won, and Soviet troops entered Tbilisi on February 25. But the situation was delicate: the Georgian people had long resented Russia's domination of their homeland, and they preferred the Mensheviks, whom they had elected, to the Bolsheviks, whom they feared. Under the circumstances, Lenin urged moderation and tact. He sought to win them over by granting them the status of a "sovereign republic." This would allow them broad cultural freedoms and the right (at least in theory) to secede from the union.[18]

Naturally enough, the task of drawing up a plan for the new federal union fell to the Commissar of Nationalities. But Stalin's ideas on this question differed significantly from Lenin's. He believed that new republics should enter the federation as autonomous regions, which meant essentially that they would have the same status as they did under the tsars. He sent Ordzhonikidze to Tbilisi in March to pressure the Georgians to join Armenia and Azerbaijan in a Transcaucasion Federation. Ordzhonikidze tried to bully the Georgian Central Committee to accepting Stalin's plan for a federal union. The Georgians were so incensed by this treatment that their Central Committee threatened to resign in protest. Lenin was much angered when he learned of this. Although he had not liked Stalin's plan, he resented the fact that the Georgians should presume to issue an ultimatum. When he expressed this sentiment in a cable on October 21, the Georgian Central Committee made good its threat. Ordzhonikidze countered by appointing a new Central Committee on his own, but this served only to add insult to injury. Amid the anger and recriminations, Ordzhonikidze struck a prominent Bolshevik in the face for insulting him."[19]

For a while, Stalin was able to cover up the nasty details of the Georgian affair. But as the facts gradually became known, Lenin began to worry about Stalin's methods and intentions. The head commissar had hoped to rely on Trotsky to defend his position on the nationalities issue, but the latter showed little inclination to get involved. In retrospect, this was a huge mistake on Trotsky's part. Had he been willing to use Lenin's mandate to aggressively attack Stalin, he might have been able to check the Georgian's growing power and influence. But like so many other prominent Bolsheviks, Trotsky grossly underestimated the General Secretary, whom he judged a plodding mediocrity best suited for dull, bureaucratic tasks. Thus he made no objection on December 18 when the Central Committee made the Georgian responsible for all questions regarding Lenin's medical treatment. Stalin now controlled the health care of the one man who could block him from attaining supreme power.[20]

But Stalin, too, was capable of making serious blunders. Just four days later, he flew into a rage after learning of a congratulatory telegram sent by Lenin to Trotsky over their victory on the trade monopoly question. Seeking to reprimand Lenin's wife, Krupskaya, who had taken dictation, he unleashed a torrent of vulgar abuse that included the term "syphilitic whore."[21] Krupskaya was devastated by Stalin's verbal assault, but out of consideration for Lenin's health, she did not inform him about the incident until much later. This, too, seems to have worked in Stalin's favor. Three days later, Lenin began to write his Testament in order to offer advice to the Party about a successor for his position. He intended that the document be kept secret until after his death.

The Testament was actually composed in two parts. The first, written on December 25, praised Trotsky as "perhaps the most capable man in the Central Committee," but feared that his excessive self-assurance and tendency to become preoccupied with administrative matters would impede his ability to lead. Stalin, on the other hand, had accumulated almost unlimited authority, and Lenin doubted that he would be able to use it wisely. On January 4, after learning more about the Georgian affair, including Ordzhonikidze's violent attack, Lenin wrote a postscript to his Testament in which he expressed his negative appraisal of Stalin. The General Secretary, he now decided, was too "crude" and therefore was unfit to lead the Party. He urged that another man be found for this office, "more loyal, more courteous and more considerate." One can only imagine what Lenin might have written had he known about Stalin's obscene outburst on his wife.[22]

All the while, Lenin continued to rely on Trotsky to help him defeat Stalin on the national question. He was particularly insistent that those who had behaved badly in the Georgian affair be severely punished. But Trotsky let him down again. Using Kamenev as the go-between, Trotsky made what Lenin called a "rotten compromise" with Stalin. He agreed *not* to seek punishment for those who had abused the members of the Georgian Central Committee in return for assurances that such behavior would not repeated. Trotsky also demanded an end to the administrative oppression of the Party, a firmer policy with regard to industrialization and "an honest cooperation in the higher centers." Stalin readily agreed to these conditions. He knew that with Lenin in bad health there was no way he could be forced to keep his word.[23]

Stalin's position was further strengthened on March 7 when Lenin suffered another cerebral stroke, depriving him of his power of speech. This effectively ended his political career. It was an end of sorts for Trotsky as well, since he would no longer be able to count on Lenin's favor. The following month, when he attended the Twelfth Party Congress in Moscow, he was far from his commanding self. Quite uncharacteristically, he seemed content to blend in rather than to stand out. In recollecting this event years later, Trotsky was full of regret that he did not use the Congress to rally his supporters to wrest leadership of the Party from the "epigones of Bolshevism." Instead he scrupulously avoided controversy, and this allowed Stalin to do the same. Trotsky's lone major address during the Congress focused on economic theory. He spoke thoughtfully, but without passion, about the problem of high industrial prices and low agricultural prices.[24] He also called for a gradual elimination of the NEP as the state enlarged the public sector at the expense of the private.

The surface of cooperation and harmony that prevailed during the Congress was short-lived. In September, the *troika,* seeking to diminish Trotsky's hold on the military, nominated a number of new people to serve on the Revolutionary War Council, including Stalin himself. Trotsky was outraged and threatened to resign his positions and go to Germany to promote revolution there. When the appointments were confirmed anyway by the Central Committee, Trotsky left the hall in great agitation. He attempted to dramatize his anger by slamming the door, which had somehow become stuck. He ended up looking very foolish when he was unable to move it. The following month,

Trotsky composed an angry letter to the Central Committee to complain about the many mistakes that had hurt the economy and alienated the workers. He decried the lack of industrial planning, the growing bureaucratization of the Party apparatus, and the stifling of free speech of loyal comrades.

Trotsky's letter was dealt with by the members of the Politburo, most whom were suspicious of his dictatorial tendencies. Their response was to dismiss his concerns and to criticize him for having turned down Lenin's request to become deputy premier of the Sovnarkom—"a position that he obviously considers beneath his dignity."[25] But Trotsky's letter was not in vain. Forty-six oppositionists, all of whom were Party members, sought to support Trotsky by signing a declaration criticizing the Soviet leadership and listing its many failures and shortcomings. Prominent among these was the lack of economic progress and the growing dictatorship within the party. This was the beginning of what became known as the Left Opposition. It could have become a force to contend with in Soviet politics, but Trotsky gave his supporters no encouragement and refused to associate with them.[26]

Such behavior was probably the most bewildering aspect of Trotsky's political activism. During the revolution and civil war, he was nearly always at his best when confronted by crises or disaster. But when faced with challenges and attacks of a personal nature, he invariably fell silent and strove to avoid confrontation. Trotsky's supporters were mystified by his unwillingness to fight back even when the situation most demanded it. Some attributed this apparent faintheartedness to his to his fundamental disdain of party politics and his reluctance to mix it up with those he deemed beneath him. There is, however, a less obvious explanation that is also plausible. The fact that Trotsky nearly always became physically ill whenever he was under personal attack suggests some kind of deep-rooted insecurity. The stress engendered by such situations seemed completely to sap his strength. At such times, he would complain about headaches, dizziness, lower back pain, and fever, although the doctors rarely could find anything wrong.[27]

The forty-six continued to agitate on Trotsky's behalf even after being condemned by the Central Committee. The Politburo finally made what seemed to be a major concession by agreeing to publish a resolution in support of Party democracy. It was hoped that this would satisfy the oppositionists. But just days after it appeared, Trotsky published an open letter in *Pravda* in which he sought to offer an analysis of the Politburo's resolution. Unfortunately, he used some highly offensive language by referring to "apparatus functionaries" and "mummified bureaucrats." Stalin responded to this insult with an article in *Pravda* on December 15 that castigated Trotsky for his Menshevik past. This was followed by much debate and a party conference on January 16, 1924, in which Stalin coldly and without emotion analyzed Trotsky's errors. The following day, Stalin's attack was more personal. He proceeded to denounce "this patriarch of bureaucrats" for his slander of the Central Committee and sternly reprimanded him and his supporters for engaging in factionalism. The General Secretary also denounced Trotsky's alleged campaign to revise Bolshevism as a "petty bourgeois deviation."[28]

Trotsky could not move himself to respond to this new attack. On January 18, he left Moscow with his wife for Tiflis, in Georgia, hoping that the warmer climate would benefit his health. Three days later, he received a telegram informing him of Lenin's death. The news caught him completely by surprise; he had not suspected that his friend and colleague was so close to the end. He immediately put into words a moving tribute to remind those who grieved that Leninism would live on despite their loss. But Trotsky once again confounded his family and supporters by not returning to Moscow for the funeral. He later claimed that Stalin had led him to believe that the ceremony would take place earlier than it actually did. He concluded that he would be unable to return in time. In retrospect, however, it is odd that Trotsky did not return to Moscow at all until May. This suggests that he did not understand the nature of the power struggle that was developing in his absence.[29]

The *troika* exploited Trotsky's extended absence from the political scene by undermining his control of the military establishment. One by one, his trusted lieutenants were removed and replaced by those whose allegiance was to Stalin. At the same time, the General Secretary was touting the success of the "Lenin enrollment," by which some 200,000 recruits had been taken into the party under the supervision of the secretarial apparatus. Trotsky's supporters meanwhile were being forced out of the Party as part of a policy to eliminate careerists and opportunists. All this was done in preparation for the Thirteenth Party Congress, which opened in May 1924. But just when Stalin seemed most in control, Krupskaya sent Kamenev Lenin's Testament calling for Stalin's removal as general secretary. Stalin had known it was coming, but he had been unable to prevent it from being discussed by high-ranking Party members. Suddenly, his political future was in grave jeopardy.[30]

Kamenev read the Testament to an expanded session of the Central Committee and then opened the discussion for comments and questions. Trotsky, who was confident that others would speak up and condemn Stalin, sat and said nothing. This made is easier for Zinoviev to offer what became the defining viewpoint. While acknowledging that Lenin's words were sacred, he also asserted that his concerns about Stalin misusing his power as General Secretary were unfounded. As he put it: "All of you have witnessed our harmonious cooperation over the last months, and all of you, like me, have had the satisfaction of seeing that what Lenin feared has not taken place."[31] Stalin also weighed in by noting that Lenin had not been himself when he wrote those things. Even so, he to offered to resign for the good of the Party, which all the members of the Central Committee (Trotsky included) rejected. The Central Committee also decided that the Testament would not be read to the whole Congress or published. It would, however, be read to closed meetings of delegates from each province, who would then be informed that since Lenin was ill when he wrote his Testament, his assessment of Stalin was wrong.[32]

This was the best chance Trotsky would ever have to defeat Stalin and regain his stature in the Party, and it was now gone. He was now a beaten man, and his subsequent attempts to defend himself did nothing to help. His remarks at the Party Congress were predictable and uninspiring. He continued to warn about the growth of bureaucracy in the party and to urge more planning in the economy. He also tried to justify his role in the opposition movement of the previous January and rejected Zinoviev's demand that he recant. Interestingly, when some rank-and-file party members joined in the criticism and Zinoviev and Kamenev tried to have Trotsky removed from the Politburo, it was Stalin, motivated most likely by tactical considerations, who prevented that from happening.

At the conclusion of the Party Congress, Trotsky once again headed south to rest and write. His first effort was a memoir about Lenin in June in which Trotsky emphasized his status as Lenin's closest comrade. He described rather fancifully how their cooperation brought about victory in the revolution and the civil war. Many in the Party were offended by the self-congratulatory tone of the narrative as well as the author's omission of the many times he and Lenin had disagreed and argued. Still, the fact that no one offered any loud objections emboldened Trotsky to compose another essay, which he entitled "The Lessons of October." Not only did he criticize Zinoviev and Kamenev, but touted himself as Lenin's closest disciple as he described their close and fruitful cooperation. This time Trotsky was attacked from all sides. Bukharin wrote an essay entitled "How Not to Write the Lessons of October"; Kamenev and Stalin each gave speeches. The former called Trotsky an "agent for Menshevism"; the latter criticized Trotsky for exaggerating his role in the October coup and lacking "courage and revolutionary steadfastness" during the negotiations at Brest Litovsk.[33]

Stalin's speech was particularly significant, because for the first time, he defined the term "Trotskyism," as a kind of heresy that had certain basic features: (1) adherence to the theory of permanent revolution[34] and refusal to appreciate the peasantry as a revolutionary force; (2) distrust of the Bolshevik principle, of the monolithic character of the party, of its hostility toward opportunistic elements; and (3) distrust of the leaders of Bolshevism and an attempt to discredit and defame them. But his most devastating charge was that Trotsky, far being the ideal disciple, had viciously maligned Lenin in the past. His proof consisted of a letter from Trotsky to a fellow Menshevik in 1913 in which he described Lenin as "a professional exploiter of every kind of backwardness in the Russian working class movement." He also charged that "the whole edifice of Leninism was built on lying and falsification, which bore within itself the poisoned element of its own disintegration."[35]

The impact of this bombshell, especially on the rank-and-file Party members, was enormous. The same man who was claiming to be the ideal Leninist was now shown to be a fraud and a schemer. Trotsky tried to defend himself by claiming that the letter was a forgery, but he had no credibility. Unable to withstand the storm of anger and condemnation, he took to his pen and wrote a lengthy rebuttal to the Central Committee entitled "The Purpose of this Explanation: Our Differences." He did not recant anything, but he denied that he had ever tried to revise Leninism. He affirmed his loyalty to the Party and declared that he had always been subservient to its will. He also offered to accept any work assigned to him and to resign as Commissar of War and as president of the Revolutionary War Council. The Central Committee, in a meeting with the Control Commission, accepted his resignations, but criticized him for having deviated from Bolshevism and for refusing to acknowledge his mistakes. Trotsky remained a member of the Politburo and the Central Committee only because Stalin, once again, blocked Kamenev and Zinoviev's efforts to have him removed from both.

Trotsky, however, was soon in trouble again. Having left Moscow in late January 1925 to rest and recuperate on the Black Sea, he returned in April to learn that an American friend and admirer, Max Eastman, had written a book, *Since Lenin Died*, which described the power struggle in the Communist Party. It also included excerpts from Lenin's Testament, which, of course, had never been intended to be made public. And since Eastman and Trotsky had known each other during the American's stay in Russia from 1922 to 1924, there seemed little reason to doubt that Trotsky had been the source of most of the sensitive information in Eastman's book. The scandal that followed forced

Trotsky to deny the book's accuracy and to state that Lenin's Testament was only a letter "containing advice of an organizational character." He categorically denied that there had been any great secrecy about the letter or that it had been destroyed.[36]

Trotsky was not overtly punished for this episode. Instead, in May 1925 he was assigned to the Supreme Council of the National Economy, which entailed work that was of such a non-political nature as to preclude him from mounting a comeback. But his new appointment occurred at roughly the same time that Kamenev and Zinoviev began to have doubts about Stalin's increasingly strong hold on the party apparatus. Like so many others in the Party, they had underestimated Stalin in assuming that it was *they* who were using *him*. Only now did they understand the reality. Kamenev made a belated attempt to assert himself on December 21, 1925, when he gave a speech warning of the dangers of one-man-rule and calling for freer discussion in the Party. But by now it was too late. Kamenev was soon expelled from the Sovnarkom, the Politburo, and his position as deputy chairman on the Council of Labor and Defense. Zinoviev suffered a similar fate when he was ousted as party boss of Leningrad and his entire organization was crushed.

It was not until the spring of 1926 when the former enemies Trotsky, Zinoviev, and Kamenev agreed to form what became known as the United Opposition against Stalin. To this end, they gathered several thousand anti-Stalinists, including Lenin's widow, Krupskaya, to try to take back the Party. The plan was to have Zinoviev blame Stalin at a Central Committee plenum in July for the chronic shortage of goods and to call for the creation of a program of intensified industrial production and the collectivization of agriculture. But the plan backfired horribly when the Central Committee, packed with Stalin's supporters, denounced Zinoviev for having violating the party's ban on factions. Not only was he removed from the Politburo, but he was also soon to lose his position as president of the Comintern. Kamenev was also demoted and named director of the Lenin Institute.

Still hoping to be heard, the United Opposition took its case to numerous cell meetings of rank-and-file party workers. But the people they hoped to win over were hostile to their message. At one Moscow factory meeting, Trotsky was forced to leave the stage because of the heckling and jeering. At other meetings, thugs sometimes physically assaulted his supporters. By early October, it was clear that the United Opposition was beaten. An agreement was reached by which they would cease all factional activity, admit to violating party discipline, and repudiate their followers both at home and abroad. But just days after the agreement had been signed, the *New York Times* came out with the *full text* of Lenin's supposedly secret Testament. Stalin was furious and ordered Trotsky, Kamenev, and Zinoviev to confess their errors and to disavow their arguments. At the Politburo meeting that followed, in a moment of high drama, Trotsky lost his temper and declared, "The first secretary poses his candidature to the post of the grave digger of the revolution." Stalin was stunned and infuriated by this rebuke, and many of those present gasped in disbelief. Clearly the former Commissar of War had recklessly insulted a man who was far more powerful than he. As Yuri Pyatakov later warned him, "He will never forgive you for this: neither you, nor your children, nor your grandchildren."[37]

In the lull that followed, the United Opposition received a temporary boost from events in the Far East. Stalin's China policy had been aimed at promoting a bourgeois nationalist revolution in the belief that it would be a blow to the imperialist powers and would ultimately lead the way to a future Communist revolution. To this end, he had sent advisers and equipment to China in order to promote cooperation with the Kuomintang's leader, Chiang Kai-shek. For a while, this policy seemed to work. In the summer of 1926, much of south and central China had been freed from foreign control. Eventually, however, the natural antagonism between the Left and Right factions in the Kuomintang became all too obvious. Chiang, who, of course, supported the latter, sought to resolve this tension on April 12, 1927, when he conducted a bloody purge of the Left in the city of Shanghai in which thousands were butchered.[38]

Trotsky sought to exploit the massacre by blaming Stalin's China policy and by declaring that he had always been opposed to the alliance between the communists and the Kuomintang. In fact, Trotsky's fervor on this issue was far less than he claimed. Although he had been uneasy about Stalin's China Policy, he never actually demanded that the Chinese Communists break with the Kuomintang. Indeed, he seemed rather uncertain about how the USSR should react to Chiang's treachery in Shanghai.

One month later, the Soviet regime was confronted with another crisis. The British government had authorized a raid on a Soviet trade delegation in London to find a missing document and subsequently severed diplomatic relations with the Soviet Union. This allowed Stalin to change the subject. He called for patriotic unity and urged "a united front against British Foreign Minister Austen Chamberlain." It was a clumsy attack, but Trotsky's response was not much better. He tried to link the threat of war with Britain to Stalin's errant Chinese policy and called for a new leadership more in tune with the needs of Soviet workers and the international Communist movement. Trotsky no doubt relished the chance to finally go on the offensive, but it did him no good because the Soviet press refused to print his side of the story.[39]

Not long after the threat of war with Britain had faded, Stalin was again provoked when Trotsky and Zinoviev participated in a demonstration to protest the exile of an important oppositionist to a new post in a region far from Moscow. Stalin turned the matter over to the Central Committee and urged that Trotsky and Zinoviev be removed from that body. The debates that followed began in late July and were drawn out over several sessions. When the vote was finally taken, the Central Committee unanimously voted for expulsion. They were temporarily saved, however, when Sergo Ordzhonikidze[40] intervened on their behalf and persuaded Stalin to relent. This was followed by a truce in which Trotsky and Zinoviev were given a "severe reprimand and warning." Again, Stalin came across as the cautious moderate more interested in uniting the Party than punishing the guilty.

But by September, Trotsky and Zinoviev were at it again. Having composed a lengthy critique of Stalin's policies, they were incensed when the Politburo refused to allow it to be printed. In defiance, they did the job illegally by employing an underground press, which was easily uncovered by the OGPU. The sixteen oppositionists who were involved in the deed were expelled from the party. Trotsky and Zinoviev then appealed to rank-and-file party members by organizing secret meetings, but these failed as miserably as they had before. On October 23, 1927, Trotsky and Zinoviev were put on trial again before an enlarged Central Committee to decide whether or not they should be expelled. Trotsky now spoke for the last time before his former comrades. This time he used Lenin's Testament to mount an attack on Stalin, noting that the "rudeness and disloyalty of which Lenin spoke are no longer mere personal characteristics," that now they had become ingrained in the members of the ruling faction, whose willingness to use violence was extended even to members of its own party. But the audience responded with taunts and jeers. Some threw books at the podium, and one man even threw a water glass. Stalin also spoke in rebuttal. He reminded Trotsky of how he (Trotsky) had denied the existence of the Testament two years earlier; and how he (Stalin) had offered to resign; and how everyone, including Trotsky, urged him to remain at his post. Finally, Stalin admitted that he was indeed rude to those who would split the party, but at least Lenin never complained of his making any serious mistakes. The result was a forgone conclusion. By an overwhelming vote, Trotsky and Zinoviev were again expelled from the Central Committee, and this time there was no one to intercede for them.

Trotsky made one last attempt to reverse his disintegrating fortunes. He planned a demonstration for November 7, the tenth anniversary of the Bolshevik insurrection. He would tour Moscow in an automobile with Kamenev and Nikolai Muralov, while his supporters marched in the streets. Zinoviev would do the same in Leningrad with some of his supporters. This was a desperate gamble and contrary to party regulations, but Trotsky knew well he had little to lose. As might have been predicted, his appearance aroused no interest or support, and those who marched carrying placards and slogans were roughed up by Party thugs. All that remained was to wait for the end. That evening he abandoned his Kremlin apartment and moved in with a friend to keep from being forcibly evicted. One week later he and Zinoviev were formally expelled from the Communist Party.[41]

In the aftermath, many figures in the oppositionist movement, including Kamenev and Zinoviev, pleaded for mercy and were allowed to confess their errors. Trotsky would do neither, and in late December, he learned that he and his wife, Natalya, were to be exiled to an undisclosed location, which later turned out to be Alma Ata in Kazakhstan. Their planned date of departure, January 16, 1928, had to be postponed when a large crowd of well wishers gathered at the station to see him off. The following day a group of OGPU officers showed up unannounced at his temporary residence and had to break the door down to get in. Coincidently, the officer in charge had served on Trotsky's armored train during the civil war and was apologetic about the duty he now had to perform. Trotsky urged him to carry on as ordered and promised to offer only passive resistance. The prisoner was then carried off to a waiting automobile and taken to the Yarolslavl station. The trip to Alma Ata lasted eight days.

Trotsky's first site of exile was remote but not entirely bad. Within a short time the deportees were assigned a house and enjoyed a modicum of comfort. Travel restrictions were imposed, however, at times quite heartlessly. When his youngest daughter, Nina (by his first wife), died of tuberculosis, Trotsky was not allowed to attend her funeral. On the other hand, he was not prevented from taking long hunting trips far from Alma Ata. Nor was there any attempt to prevent him from working. At his request, his library and personal papers were sent to him from Moscow, and he was able to augment his government allowance by working for the Marx-Engel Institute as a translator, editor, and proofreader.

In the meantime, Trotsky closely followed events in Moscow. He was heartened and perhaps perplexed that some of the policies he had favored, such as an intense program for industrialization and a vigorous policy of suppressing the kulaks, were now being adopted.[42] But the political nature of his correspondence with friends and supporters soon began to irritate the General Secretary, and a "postal blockade" was imposed to further isolate and demoralize the deportee. In December, after Trotsky continued to contact his supporters, an OGPU official was sent to Alma Ata to warn him to stop. His defiant attitude led to trumped-up charges that he was trying to promote anti–Soviet activities, including an armed confrontation with the regime. For these reasons, it was decided to expel the Trotskys from the USSR altogether. They had been in Alma Ata just a few days less than a year.[43]

It was not until the Trotskys were well on their way that they learned that their next destination was to be Constantinople (Istanbul) in Turkey. They were accompanied by a team of NKVD officers, who were much impressed by their famous prisoner and treated him with deference. The weather was harsh, especially during the first leg of the trip, when the travelers were headed toward Frunze in Kirghyzstan. Traveling over the Kurday mountains, they encountered huge snowdrifts, which required that they switch to sleighs. Later, after having boarded a special train, they were forced to endure temperatures as low as fifty-three degrees Fahrenheit. At one point, the party was forced to stop for three weeks when there seemed a chance that the Trotskys would be sent to Germany. But this hope was dashed when the Germans refused to grant them visas. The last leg of the journey was made when the train pulled into Odessa, a city Trotsky had known in his youth. There the party was transferred to a steamship, which took them across the Black Sea. They reached Constantinople in late February 1929 and for a time lived in the Soviet consulate. But this arrangement proved awkward for everyone concerned and could not last. Soon a more suitable location was found on one of the Prinkipo Islands in the Sea of Marmara, where the Trotskys moved into a spacious villa.

The four years that Trotsky spent at Prinkipo were extremely productive ones. He began a Russian-language journal entitled *Bulletin of the Opposition*, in which he commented critically on events in the Soviet Union and around the world. He also completed his autobiography, which he had begun while at Alma Ata. Trotsky was no more objective than anyone else in describing his own life. Still, after being translated into German and English, it was very well received by the public, which especially admired the beauty of the narrative. His greatest work was also written during this period, a three-volume *History of the Russian Revolution,* which was important not merely for its stylistic brilliance, but also because it author was such an important part of the events he described. Still, Trotsky was restless. He had no desire to spend the rest of his life on an island in the Sea of Marmora, and when the Danish government invited him to deliver a lecture in Copenhagen in the fall of 1932, he readily accepted. Alas, although the lecture, delivered in German, went well, the Danes did not allow him to extend his visa.[44]

The year 1933 brought more bad news, great sorrow, and also a ray of hope. The rise of Hitler and the collapse of the German Communist Party took him completely by surprise. At about the same time, he learned that his eldest daughter by his first wife, Zinaida Volkhova, who had long suffered from depression, had committed suicide in Berlin. About the only positive news that Trotsky was to receive during this period was that he would be allowed to move to France as long as he agreed to live in the provinces under an assumed name. He was quick to accept these conditions, although things did not go as well as he might have hoped. His first residence was at Royan on the Atlantic coast, but only for a few months. In November, he was allowed to move to Barbizon outside Paris. This might have been ideal, but when his true identity was discovered, he was forced to move to a town near Grenoble in the southeast of France, where he stayed eleven months. This location was in many ways more isolated that any other, but his stay was cut short. In the mid–1930s, as the French were trying to improve their relationship with the USSR, Trotsky's presence in the country became a diplomatic problem.[45]

This difficulty was temporarily resolved when the Norwegian Labor Party came into power in April 1935, and Trotsky was able to move to Norway. Unfortunately, the conditions were much as they had been in France. He was forbidden to live in Oslo, but was invited by a socialist editor named Konrad Knutsen to live in his home well outside the city. Soon, however, he began working on a new book entitled *The Revolution Betrayed,* which was a searing condemnation of Stalin's rule and Soviet society in general. He was especially critical of the 1936 Constitution, which he claimed virtually ended the dictatorship of the proletariat in the world's first socialist country. However, when Trotsky was falsely accused of having participated in an anti–Soviet plot during a show trial in Moscow, the Norwegians became uneasy about their guest. The charge seemed preposterous, but the Norwegians wanted no trouble with the USSR. Thus, Trotsky was again told to find another country.[46]

Fortunately for Trotsky, he still had his admirers. One of them was the famous painter Diego Rivera, who had persuaded Mexican president Lazaro

Cardenas to offer him asylum. The Trotskys soon boarded an oil tanker bound for Mexico. There he received a warm welcome and was invited by Rivera and his wife, Frida Kahlo, who was also a painter of note, to reside at their spacious villa in Coyoacan outside Mexico City. But the Trotskys had hardly settled in when they learned of yet another show trial in Moscow. Seventeen defendants, many of them old friends and political allies, were accused of the most fantastic crimes. Trotsky himself was depicted as an agent for Germany and Japan who was working tirelessly to bring about the overthrow of the Soviet Union.[47]

Trotsky urged his supporters to fight this vicious slander. They obliged him by organizing committees of defense to drum up support in the West among the left-leaning intelligentsia. In March 1938, a Joint Committee of Inquiry of eleven members chaired by the American philosopher John Dewey was set up to study the charges and make a decision.[48] Trotsky, who was desperate to be exonerated, drove those around him mercilessly to organize a defense and prove his innocence before the court of world opinion. The hearings, which began in April and were conducted at Rivera's house, lasted for much of the summer. In the end, the Committee declared that the charges against Trotsky were fraudulent and that the show trials in Moscow were a sham. But the effect of this not guilty verdict on the public was negligible. Few people were listening, and the arrests and executions in the Soviet Union went on as before. Among those singled out for special abuse was Trotsky's younger son by his second wife, Sergei Sedov. He had been arrested in March 1935 and sent to the Vorkuta forced labor complex in the Arctic Circle. In 1937, he was declared a "wrecker" after he had allegedly tried to poison a large group of workers. He was shot in October of that year. Trotsky's remaining followers, also at Vorkuta, were shot in small groups during the spring of 1938.[49]

Because most of the news that came out of the Soviet Union was delayed and secondhand, one could never be sure exactly what to believe. The Trotskys were never officially informed of Sergei's execution, although they probably suspected the worst. In any case, they were soon to grieve again for their eldest son Lev, or Lyova, who in February 1938 fell ill while in Paris with an acute case of appendicitis. He needed an immediate operation and was taken to a private hospital, which was run by a Russian émigré doctor. The man who made all the arrangements was Lyova's closest friend, Mark Zborowski. Only much later was it learned that he was an agent with the NKVD, whose purpose to report to Moscow on Lyova's activities. In any case, the operation was performed and seemed to go well. The patient was recovering when his condition suddenly took a turn for the worse. He died a few days later. An inquest was performed, but the specific cause of death was not determined. There were many unanswered questions, although no proof of foul play was uncovered.[50]

On the heels of Lyova's unexpected death came news of what turned out to be the last of the show trials, with twenty-one defendants. All confessed to having committed treason, and all accused Trotsky of having been the mastermind. One of the defendants, Christian Rakovsky, testified that Trotsky, whom he had known since 1903, had been a traitor to his homeland for fifteen years. Trotsky, still in mourning from Lyova's death, suffered all the more since he could not refute what was being said. He continued to grasp at straws and hoped that by convening the Fourth International, he could establish an organization that would overshadow Comintern in promoting world revolution. But the first meeting of the Fourth International in Paris on September 3, 1938, was not auspicious. Trotsky, who could not attend, sent a message of encouragement to the delegates and predicted that in the coming decade the Fourth International would lead millions "to storm earth and heaven." But the new organization soon split into various hostile groups arguing about such things as how to define Stalinism, how to regard communist movements in the Third World, and what slogans they would campaign under. What they did agree on was that Trotsky was to be admired as a brilliant theorist and activist who had preserved Leninism in its purest form. Stalin was to be despised as a traitor and a fraud, who had grossly distorted the ideals of communism.[51]

In the meantime, Trotsky continued to be afflicted with personal problems. He had a falling-out with Rivera, who had inexplicably decided to support a right-wing general in Mexico's upcoming presidential election. Trotsky was aghast and resolved that he could no longer accept this man's hospitality. After a difficult search, he finally found an appropriate dwelling in an isolated part of Coyoacan, which could offer some security to protect him from those who wished to do him harm. The cost of making this change was, of course, considerable. He was forced to borrow money, and in order to make more, he had to put aside other projects and begin a biography about Stalin. Still, life did hold some pleasures in his new residence. These included motoring trips in the countryside, fishing in the Gulf of Veracruz, walks in the mountains, gardening, and breeding rabbits and chickens. But even these were clouded by the ever-worsening international situation, which was made even more ominous by the German-Soviet Non-Aggression Pact of August 1939.[52]

But now Trotsky's life was in danger as never before. Sometime after the last of the show trials in March 1938, the NKVD was instructed to eliminate the aging revolutionary. The job was assigned to Leonid Eitingon, one of their most trusted agents. Eitingon traveled to Mexico in 1939 to find accomplices to carry out a raid on Trotsky's compound. The Mexican Communist Party, which was known to oppose to Trotskyism, was approached for this purpose. Still, its members wanted none of any assassination plots. In time, however, a group of some twenty men was put together under the leadership of the painter David Alfaro Siqueiros. The plan was to dress the raiding party in police uniforms and arm them with pistols, rifles, submachine guns, incendiary explosives, and two large bombs made of dynamite and attack the Trotsky compound at 4 a.m. on May 24, 1940.

Initially, things went well for the attackers. They easily overcame a lone guard at the outside gate to gain entry and opened fire with the machine guns at Trotsky's bedroom. For several minutes they raked the targeted area with hundreds of rounds. Miraculously, Trotsky and Natalya had taken cover on the floor beside the bed and had not been hit. The attackers had also ignited the incendiary bombs, but these had little effect. One big dynamite bomb was placed next to the house, but had not gone off. Still, the damage to the compound and Trotsky's bedroom was so extensive that the attackers believed that they had succeeded in killing him. Interestingly, when the Mexican authorities arrived, they were so amazed that no one was seriously injured after so much damage was done to the house that they accused Trotsky of having staged the attack to vilify Stalin and to gain attention for himself.[53]

Trotsky fully expected that another attempt would soon be made and took steps to strengthen the compound's defenses. These included higher walls, watchtowers, and steel shutters. But the conspirators, under intense pressure from Moscow, had decided on a change in tactics. They now intended to employ a single agent to infiltrate Trotsky's inner circle. The man selected was a young, handsome Spaniard named Ramon Mercader, who was already known to Eitingon. During the summer of 1938, he had been assigned the task of seducing an American woman, Sylvia Ageloff, who was known to have connections with the Trotsky compound. He introduced himself as a Belgian using the pseudonym Jacques Mornard and succeeded in becoming her lover. Somewhat later he changed his name and nationality to Frank Jacson, Canadian, telling Ageloff that he had been compelled to buy some forged documents in order to avoid military service. By January 1940, Ageloff and Mercader were in Coyoacan and began to visit the Trotskys. At first, Mercader merely drove her to the residence and did not attempt to enter. At some point, however, he began to be invited inside and soon became a familiar face. Trotsky took a liking to this relaxed, personable young man, who seemed so affable and eager to be of help.

In June, Mercader left Coyoacan, allegedly to go to New York to conduct business. Instead, he met with Eitingon and another NKVD officer named Ovakimian, probably somewhere in Mexico, where he was informed that he had been assigned the task of killing Trotsky himself. This came as a shock for the young Spaniard, but he was afraid to refuse to do what he was told had to be done. He returned to the compound in late July in a highly nervous and irritable state. Many people noticed the change in his behavior, but no one suspected what he was about to do. He finally got close enough to Trotsky to commit the murder on August 20. On that day, he arrived at the residence carrying a raincoat that concealed an ice-ax. Trotsky had agreed to proofread an article that Mercader had written and hoped to publish. The two went into the study, and when Trotsky bent over his desk to study the article, Mercader dealt him a powerful blow on the head with the ice-ax. Amazingly, the victim did not die immediately, but actually fought back. But with a wound in his head three inches deep, he could not survive. He died at 7:25 a.m. the next day in a nearby hospital. His body lay in state for five days and was cremated on August 27. The ashes were buried at his residence in Coyoacan and marked by a stone obelisk.

Although Trotsky's assassination made headlines around the world, the reaction in Moscow was strangely muted. To be sure, Stalin was well pleased to be rid of a hated adversary, but he took pains to appear disinterested and did not rejoice publicly. In *Pravda,* a short article appeared under the title "The Death of an International Spy," which condemned Trotsky for having organized the assassinations of Sergei Kirov, Valerian Kuibyshev, and Maxim Gorky and for his campaign of slander against the Soviet government. The article stated that Trotsky had been murdered by one of his own disillusioned supporters. Most in the international community suspected otherwise, although Soviet involvement was difficult to prove. Mercader, who was sentenced to twenty years in prison, managed to conceal his real name for many years. It was not until September 1950 that fingerprint evidence revealed his true identity.[54]

In the years following Khrushchev's 1956 secret speech condemning Stalin, Trotsky was not among the victims who were rehabilitated. Indeed, his vital role in the revolution and civil war was not even acknowledged, much less described. The Soviet regime's silence on this topic was not broken until

January 4, 1989, when an article appeared in *Literaturnaya Gazeta* that partially corrected the record. Prompted in large part by General Secretary Mikhail Gorbachev's policy of *glasnost,* or openness, it was finally admitted that it was Stalin who ordered Trotsky's assassination, thirty-eight years earlier. This was followed by some additional information about Trotsky's role in the October insurrection and his leadership of the Red Army during the civil war. These revelations were not entirely positive, but, as historian Adam Ulam put it, "Trotsky is no longer the evil spirit of Russian history. He's simply a political leader who held rather unacceptable views in many ways."[55]

Trotsky has not been rehabilitated in his homeland, and few Russians today are much interested in his crucial role during the early years of Soviet power. Nevertheless, his memory lives on in the minds of many revolutionary activists around the world as a pure spirit whose dedication and fervor deserve to be admired and imitated. In the years following World War II, a new generation of Trotskyites became active in Europe, Asia, and especially South America. In Venezuela, the socialist Hugo Chavez declared himself a Trotskyite just before his presidential inauguration in January 2002. Trotsky's name and revolutionary example are also invoked by a number of international organizations, including the reunified Fourth International and the Committee for a Workers' International. The latter was founded in 1974 and has chapters in more than thirty-five countries.

CHAPTER V

Wreckers and Kulaks

AT THE BEGINNING OF 1928, the major political and ideological differences within the Communist Party appeared to have been resolved. Trotsky and most of his followers had been disgraced and sent into exile. His two main allies from the United Opposition, Kamenev and Zinoviev, had been made to recant their anti–Lenin heresy and had written a letter to *Pravda* denouncing Trotsky and all who supported his ideas. For several months Kamenev and Zinoviev were banished from Moscow, but they were reinstated in June. For all practical purposes their careers were over, although both dared to hope that if they groveled sufficiently, Stalin would restore them to power and influence. It was not to be. Kamenev and Zinoviev would eventually be imprisoned, tortured, and executed together as "enemies of the people" in the cellar of the Lubyanka.

The Right Communists, whose most prominent members were Nikolai Bukharin, Alexei Rykov,[1] Mikhail Tomsky,[2] and Felix Dzherzhinsky, supposedly had reason to be sanguine about the future. Having helped Stalin defeat the Left and United Opposition groups, they assumed he was on their side. But this changed abruptly in January 1928, when the General Secretary made a trip to the Ural Mountains and western Siberia to find out why grain shipments to the towns had fallen off so dramatically. Of course, as he well knew before he left Moscow, the peasants were withholding the grain because the state offered prices too low for them to buy the industrial goods they needed.[3] But Stalin had no intention of listening to explanations or complaints. Instead he meant to teach them a lesson and to issue a stern warning: Soviet citizens had no right to defy the power of the state no matter what the circumstances. Thus, without consulting anyone in Moscow, he demanded that the peasants in these areas deliver *all* their grain to the state. This presaged a return to the disastrous requisitioning policy that had been in effect during the civil war.[4]

In Stalin's eyes, however, the real villain behind this treason was not the ordinary peasant, but his wealthier neighbor, the kulak, who had achieved a fair level of prosperity during NEP by manipulating the free market. Kulaks were "enemies of the people" in agriculture the way capitalists were in industry because both lived by exploiting the labor of others. But this was a deliberate distortion of the term, which was first applied to village extortioners in the wake of the Emancipation Edict of 1861. The original kulaks were not farmers; they were city folk who had gone into the countryside and grown rich by trade and usury. Stalin meant to apply the term to those peasants who were likely to resist collectivization and to excite class differences between the kulaks and the middle and lower peasants. Ultimately, he hoped to bring about a class war in order to "dekulakizise" the countryside and drive the remaining peasants onto collective farms.[5]

Such a project had been seriously considered at the end of the civil war but had been set aside because of the ravaging famine of 1921–1922. Instead, Lenin proposed his New Economic Policy, by which peasants would be allowed to sell what they grew on the open market in order to restore the country's agricultural productivity. At the same time, he proposed limiting collectivization to a relatively small number of sovkhozes and kolkhozes to assure Party faithful that the ultimate goal of socialized agriculture had not been abandoned.[6] By 1926, the free peasantry had restored agricultural productivity to what it had been in 1913, while the sovkhozes and kolkhozes floundered. Fearful that an aggressive entrepreneurial peasantry would become dominant in the countryside, the government promoted consumer and producer collectives by offering easy credit, tax exemptions, and priority access to scarce manufactured goods. These cooperatives generally did quite well, but the increase in population between 1913 and 1928 caused the grain harvest *per capita* to drop by one-fifth. At the same time, the low grain prices offered by the state led to a severe shortfall in grain procurements in 1928 that threatened to grow only wider as the peasants continued to withhold their grain. This made it increasingly difficult for the regime to export grain to finance industrialization.[7]

Stalin's abrupt about-face on the question of dealing with grain shortages and the pace of industrialization took nearly everyone by surprise. Three who were acutely distressed by this turn of events were Mikhail Tomsky, Alexei Rykov, and Nicholai Bukharin. All were members of the Politburo and all had been steadfast in their opposition to Trotsky. Rykov had succeeded Lenin as Premier of the Sovnarkom and had long been committed to the notion of *smychka* or alliance of the farm workers and the industrial working class. He argued that the NEP should be continued and favored raising the price of grain and lowering the price of certain industrial goods. Bukharin, too, was an enthusiastic supporter of the NEP and saw no reason to make any dramatic changes to accelerate economic growth and development. As recently as 1927 had urged the peasantry to "enrich yourselves" as he helped Stalin drive Trotsky and his supporters out of the Party for suggesting essentially what the General Secretary was now proposing.[8]

Although Bukharin believed that Stalin's proposed Five Year Plan would bring disaster to the country, he chose his words carefully when offering criticism in public. Privately, however, he agonized about his dilemma, comparing Stalin with Genghis Khan and predicting that he would destroy the Party. Deeply pessimistic, he nevertheless tried on a number of occasions to dissuade the boss from the path he had chosen. That July, at a plenum of the Central Committee, he urged that some conciliatory measures be undertaken to reassure the peasants that the government could be trusted to defend their interests. It was agreed to raise grain prices so that farmers would be willing to trade their surpluses of wheat and other cereal crops. This gesture, small as it was, seemed to offer some hope that the food crisis was over and that cooperation between agriculture and industry that had been established under NEP had been restored. But it was not to be. The peasants' cooperation was minimal, as they continued to withhold most of their grain.[9]

That summer, Stalin moved to expand requisitioning throughout the USSR. When Bukharin denounced the policy, the General Secretary went on the attack. In January 1929, at a joint meeting of the Central Committee and the Central Control Commission, Stalin accused Bukharin of factionalism. In April 1929, at another meeting of the Central Committee, the two got into a shouting match about who was the better Marxist. In the months that followed, Bukharin continued to press his argument but lost ground in every encounter. There were, to be sure, those in the Party who agreed with him, but few dared to speak publicly. Stalin, on the other hand, had a multitude of hard-core and aggressive supporters—people whom he had elevated into positions of power and who depended on his patronage. Bukharin found himself increasingly isolated and on the defensive. Over the next sixteen months, Stalin had him removed from all his important positions: as a delegate to the Comintern, as editor of *Pravda*, and as a member of the Politburo. On November

26, 1929, he, Tomsky, and Rykov published a statement in which they admitted their mistakes and begged the Party for forgiveness.[10]

Stalin's victory over his former allies roughly coincided with his fiftieth birthday on December 21, 1929, which the nation celebrated with great pomp. This was the beginning of the General Secretary's "cult of personality," by which he was praised for his genius and humanitarian qualities as the nation's great leader and builder of communism. One week later Stalin announced his intention to liquidate the kulaks as a class and to initiate the immediate collectivization of the grain-producing areas of the USSR. This was formalized in a Politburo resolution of January 30, 1930, "On Measures for the Elimination of Kulak Households in Districts of Comprehensive Collectivization." In demonizing the kulaks as "enemies of the people," Stalin had them divided into three categories: counterrevolutionary kulak-activists to be arrested or summarily executed; rich kulaks who were to be deported to remote areas; and those who were to be expelled from the kolkhoz and resettled locally on semi-marsh or forest land. Soon, even the poorest peasants who resisted collectivization were labeled *podkulachniki* or subkulaks, which exposed them to special abuse by Party activists. Many peasants were so desperate to avoid the kulak label that they sold what they owned in order to seem poorer than they were. Others moved to towns to find work or tried to join a kolkhoz.[11]

In any case, what followed was a social and economic upheaval as brutal as anything in recorded history. The country literally went to war against the peasantry. As Stalin told a conference of agronomists: "Either we go backward to capitalism or forward to communism." No longer would the state be content with merely containing the kulaks' exploitive tendencies. They would now be driven from the village and sent into remote exile in Siberia or in the Arctic north. In fact, even before Stalin issued his dekulakization proclamation, the GPU had begun to arrest the heads of kulak families. Some of those rounded up were veterans of the White Armies who believed they had been pardoned years ago. Nearly all were shot. But since this was clearly a waste of manpower at a time when there was a shortage of labor in critical areas, the regime soon saw the wisdom of establishing slave labor camps (euphemistically called "special settlements") in areas where ordinary Soviet workers would never willingly go. These included vast territories of northern and eastern Siberia along the rivers Yenisei, Lena, and Kolyma, which were rich in forests, precious minerals, and ravenous mosquitoes. In many cases, the *zeks* sent to exploit this wealth lived in dugouts as they built their own prisons. Rations were nearly always dangerously inadequate, although this may have been intentional as part of the punishment. At one taiga camp in the far north, prisoners were expected to survive on a pint of soup and five ounces of bread a day. Some camps were so remote and uninhabitable that everyone died, *including* the guards and their dogs.[12]

Resigned to their fate, many kulaks nevertheless did offer resistance. Some made crude weapons and fought to the death to protect their farms. Others burned their houses, killed and ate their livestock, and sold their possessions. Many ran away or committed suicide. The carnage in both human and material terms was ghastly. It was made worse by young party activists, known as twenty-five thousanders, who were sent to the countryside to organize collectives and to confiscate whatever grain they could find. These young men, who were mostly unfamiliar with rural life, were given two weeks of indoctrination and training to transform Soviet agriculture by proselytizing the peasants.[13] Many, however, were so fanatical about their mission that they terrified the very people they were trying win over. The result was chaos. For a while it looked as if the spring sowing would not be accomplished. Soon, even Stalin saw the need to stop and regroup.

On March 2, 1930, Soviet citizens were surprised to read an article written by Stalin in *Pravda* entitled "Dizzy with Success." The General Secretary lauded the country's progress to collectivization agriculture but, at the same time, cynically expressed disappointment about the excesses that had been committed in the process. He reminded Party workers to avoid the use of force but to rely on persuasion to get peasants to enlist in the kolkhoz. To right the wrongs that had been committed, it was announced that those who had been compelled to join the kolkhoz were free to go if they so desired. More than half did. But the respite did not last long. That November following the harvest, a new push to join kolkhozes was on once again. This time, however, the kolkhozes were to be modeled after the artel, which allowed peasant families to farm their own private plots and keep some livestock. Those who elected to remain on their farms were taxed at rate several times higher than those who joined the kolkhoz.[14]

At the Sixteenth Party Congress four months later, a new slogan was proclaimed: "The Five Year Plan in Four." The pressure to produce more in less time was applied to both industry and agriculture. In order to produce more food for export, a new unit of payment was devised for the members of the kolkhoz called the labor day. The idea was to get peasants to work harder and, presumably, to improve their standard of living by accumulating as many labor days as possible over the course of a year. But not all labor days were considered equal; it depended on the difficulty and complexity of one's job. Thus a tractor driver who worked a given number of hours might be awarded four labor days, while a night watchman working the same amount of time might get only one-half of a labor day. But the main problem with this system was that peasants only got paid if the kolkhoz made a profit. This was made difficult by the Soviet government, which, like the landlords under the tsars, confiscated a large part of what was produced. Many peasants grumbled about a "second serfdom," having supposedly been liberated from the first some seventy years earlier.[15]

In addition to grain shortages, Stalin was concerned about the Soviet Union's lagging economic performance in coal production. This became yet another reason to end the NEP and to make a concerted effort to industrialize the country as quickly as possible. For the General Secretary, this question was inextricably linked to national defense. There were enemies abroad who were determined to resist the establishment of a socialist state in Europe. The USSR could not hope to prevail in a modern war without a mighty industrial base. Stalin's suspicions that this was already happening seemed to have been confirmed in the spring of 1928. In the Donbass city of Shakhty in Ukraine, a local OGPU head, Efiim Evdokhimov, reported uncovering a gang of fifty-three engineers, all of them foreigners, who had been accused of destroying equipment and causing accidents. They were also charged with conspiring with the former owners of the mines, now living abroad, who hoped to someday regain their property. Stalin's intention was to try the culprits publicly in order to dramatize to the Soviet people that wrecking by bourgeois specialists was a serious problem and that, far from abating, class warfare in the country was actually on the increase.[16]

This was the first of the show trials, which were to become such an important element of Soviet justice in the 1930s. It began in Moscow's stately Hall of Columns on May 18 and lasted forty-one days. The newspapers played up the proceedings with headlines demanding "Death to the Wreckers." Stalin, intent on producing a courtroom drama, chose his cast of characters with care. He named an old prerevolutionary prison-mate, Andrei Vyshinsky,[17] to be presiding judge. Vyshinsky was notoriously cynical and self-serving. He operated on the principle that "confession was the queen of evidence" and made sure that defendants were properly worked over before testifying. In this he was assisted by prosecuting attorney Nikolai Krylenko,[18] who was known for his sarcasm, angry oratory, and ability to wring confessions out of stubborn defendants. Krylenko also had the instincts of a showman. At one point, he

Defendants for the Shakhty, or miners' trial, being delivered in a police van for their day in court. Moscow, 1928. Photographer unknown (courtesy Russian State Archives of Film and Photo Documents, Krasnogorsk).

summoned a twelve-year-old boy to testify against his own father. Not only did the son declare his father guilty of wrecking, he called for his execution![19]

The verdict was forty-nine guilty with four acquittals. Of the former, eleven were condemned to death and the rest sent to prison. But if the punishments meted out were less than many feared, the trial proved to be a significant turning point in Stalin's ever-tightening despotism. "Wrecking" was now a serious crime that could incriminate not only those accused of sabotage, but those accused of underachieving as well. Thus an "enemy of the people" need not be a capitalist, merchant, priest, landowner, or ideological opponent. He or she could be an ordinary worker or peasant who had failed to fulfill (or overfulfill) his or her assigned quota. In fact, one could be labeled an enemy merely for being present went something went awry. Accordingly, in the aftermath of the Shakhty affair, forty-six food industry officials in Siberia were executed because of food shortages. Later, a group of bacteriologists were blamed for an outbreak of anthrax and distemper among horses. They, however, were in no danger of being punished since they had already died fighting the epidemic.[20]

The defendants seated in the courtroom to listen to the charges, testify, and await the outcome. Moscow, 1928. Photographer unknown (courtesy Russian State Archives of Film and Photo Documents, Krasnogorsk).

Although Stalin was generally pleased with the results of the Shakhty trial, he was aware that the process had not convinced most in the foreign community. Even the *New York Times* correspondent Walter Duranty,[21] a man who would one day be excoriated for his willingness to apologize for the Soviet regime, had been unimpressed. In an article written a full month before the trial began, he allowed that there probably had been acts of sabotage on the part of some disgruntled technicians, but he doubted that there was reason to believe that there had been any foreign plot. In the end, three of the six German defendants had refused to confess, and most of the foreign press had remained highly skeptical throughout the proceedings.[22] Still, Stalin recognized that the show trial approach to justice had tremendous potential as a tool of manipulating Soviet public opinion. Not only did it enable the dictator to divert attention from his own mistakes and shortcomings, it intimidated potential rivals and kept them on the defensive.

On November 25, 1930, a second Moscow show trial was initiated, involving

Prosecutor and Judge Andrei Vyshinsky (center) reads the verdict to the courtroom. Moscow, 1928. Photographer unknown (courtesy Russian State Archives of Film and Photo Documents, Krasnogorsk).

eight high-ranking engineers and technicians who were falsely accused of counterrevolutionary activity and conspiring with émigré Russians abroad. The latter, it was alleged, had formed the *Prompartiia* (Industrial Party) in 1920, which had financed wrecking activities in the USSR. The accused were said to be the executive committee of that party and to have conspired with British agents, with the French intelligence service, and with the French General Staff. It was also claimed that former French president Raymond Poincare had in 1928 and 1929 authorized the payment of 1.6 million rubles to the Industrial Party. This money, it was alleged, was to be used to promote various kinds of wrecking activities in order to overthrow Bolshevism and reestablish capitalism in the USSR. Sometime in 1930 or 1931 it was said that the French planned to invade the Soviet Union with an army of 800,000.[23]

Once again, Andrei Vyshinsky presided and Nikolai Krylenko acted as chief prosecutor. As in the Shakhty Trial, the government produced what one journalist called "planned hysteria." People marched in the streets carrying banners that read "Death to the Traitors" and "Down with the Jackals of Foreign Imperialists." The trial was broadcast to the nation and aroused much interest in the foreign press. The central defendant was Leonid Ramzin, who was a leading specialist in heat engineering and boiler construction in the USSR and the head of the fictitious Industrial Party. Under questioning by Krylenko, Ramzin laid out a highly improbable scenario. He described how he had traveled to Paris and made contact with prominent White Guardists, who put him into contact with some very important people including former President Poincare and Lawrence of Arabia. He also claimed to have met with officials of the French General Staff, who revealed to him the details of the invasion. These included the direction of the main attacks, debarkation points, and time schedules.[24]

In the end, the defendants confessed to all the charges despite the fact that not a shred of documentary evidence had been introduced. All eight were found guilty. Five were sentenced to death, although these were later commuted to long prison terms. Moreover, the court used the testimonies of those convicted to establish the Industrial Party's relationship with an equally fictitious Toiling Peasant Party.[25] This led to yet another public trial in March 1931 involving the Union Bureau of the Central Committee of the Menshevik Party. The fourteen defendants included V.G. Groman, who was a member of the Presidium of Gosplan. All of the accused had once been Mensheviks and had since found work in Soviet economic and planning agencies. Now they were accused of attempting to reestablish the Mensheviks as a political force in the USSR. They were also said to have aligned with certain former Soviet opposition groups and to have engaged in various kinds of wrecking activity. The star witness was the same Leonid Ramzin who had been sentenced to death at the Industrial Trial. This struck many as odd, since there had been no mention of the Union Bureau at the Industrial Party Trial, and there was no reason to suspect that the two were connected.[26]

It seems probable that Ramzin had been offered clemency to testify that there had been collusion between the Industrial Party and the Union Bureau. In any case, he wasn't very convincing. Not only did he get mixed up about the basic facts of the situation, he undermined his own credibility by contradicting the testimony of a previous witness who claimed to have met with him. No matter. The defendants were all found guilty and sentenced to long prison terms. Ramzin, on the other hand, escaped execution and was eventually returned to a position of power and privilege. Although he was indeed sent to prison, he served only five years and was allowed while in prison to conduct research on his academic specialty. After his release his career flourished. In 1935, he received the Order of Lenin and in 1943 a Stalin Prize for his scientific

Leonid Ramzin (seated, left front corner) and other defendants in the industrial trial of 1930 sit glumly in court as they listen to the charges against them. These included accusations of working for foreign countries in order to devise ways to disrupt the Soviet economy. Moscow, 1930. Photographer unknown (courtesy Russian State Archives of Film and Photo Documents, Krasnogorsk).

work. He went on to become a professor at the Moscow Thermal Institute and scientific director at the All-Union Thermal Engineering Institute. He died in 1948 of natural causes.[27]

There was one more public wrecking trial involving Soviet and foreign citizens that took place in Moscow April 19 and lasted one week. Vasily Ulrickh was the presiding judge and Andrei Vyshinsky was the chief prosecutor. Six British engineers and twelve Soviets, all of whom were employed by the British firm Metro-Vickers, were arrested by the OGPU and accused of causing repeated breakdowns in Moscow power stations. They were alleged to have damaged equipment, gathered secret information about the plants, and offered bribes to employees for military secrets.

The case was heard before a special tribunal of the Supreme Court in Moscow's Hall of Trade Unions. There were about 400 spectators, including many foreign journalists. The British recalled their ambassador and broke off negotiations on a new Anglo-Soviet trade agreement. Later they placed an

V. Wreckers and Kulaks

Having heard the testimonies of the defendants, Vyshinsky (center, turning pages) and other members of the Supreme Court reflect before rendering a verdict at the Industrial Trial. Moscow, 1930. Photographer unknown (courtesy Russian State Archives of Film and Photo Documents, Krasnogorsk).

embargo on most Soviet imports. The trial itself had little drama and produced no surprises. Aside from the oral and written statements of the defendants, no documentary evidence was introduced, and only one independent witness was summoned to testify for the prosecution. The Soviet defendants all admitted their guilt and threw themselves on the mercy of the court. The British, with one exception, denied all wrongdoing. When the verdict was rendered, one Soviet and one Britisher were acquitted. The other Soviets were given prison sentences ranging between eighteen months and ten years. Three British engineers were expelled from the country, and two others were given short prison terms. Diplomatic relations between the two countries were soon reestablished and the negotiations on a new trade agreement resumed.[28]

Although these early show trials were regarded with skepticism by the international community, they were taken more seriously by Soviet citizens, who did not admire the twelve-year-old boy who demanded his father's execution. It was easier for the public to accept that capitalist powers, engulfed in the worst depression of all time, did not wish the Soviets' scientifically planned economy to succeed. Perhaps Marx and Lenin had been right after all, and although this was reason for pride, it also called for vigilance; the capitalist enemies of Soviet power would stop at nothing to bring down the world's only socialist government. Thus, Soviet citizens were urged to distrust foreigners and to avoid any unnecessary contact with them.[29]

But the regime also needed the expertise that only foreigners could provide, especially for the country's most ambitious building projects. Such was especially the case in Magnitogorsk (or magnetic mountain city), which in 1929 had been a village of twenty-five people. It had been so named by Russian travelers in the early years of the eighteenth century whose compass needles behaved erratically because of the enormous lode of iron ore beneath the surface. Thus began an important mining enterprise that by 1913 was producing about 50,000 tons of iron and steel a year. After the First World War, however, Magnitogorsk had virtually been closed down until the regime decided to transform it into an industrial marvel. Much of it was fashioned after what the Americans had built in Gary, Indiana, and Pittsburgh, Pennsylvania. For this the Soviets recruited the best foreign experts money could buy. One of these was a German architect named Ernst May, who was contracted to oversee the construction. Soviet planners also purchased high-quality electrical equipment from General Electric Company and imported rolling mill parts from Deming in Germany.[30]

In the winter of 1931, Jack Scott, an idealistic twenty-year-old American at the University of Wisconsin, learned about the Soviet undertaking and resolved to participate. It took him more than a year to prepare for this momentous step. His parents, both American Communists, encouraged him. With unemployment and misery in the capitalist world at high tide, it was easy to believe that a better future was being built in the USSR. Scott, who wanted to make himself useful, sought to prepare himself by enrolling in a seven-month welding course at the General Electric Plant in Schenectady, New York. From there he made his way to Berlin to apply for permission to enter the Soviet Union. Everything went well until he reached Moscow in October 1932. There his inability to speak Russian contributed to his difficulty in obtaining a resident alien's permit. Still, he persevered and was finally assigned to work as a welder in Magnitogorsk, now a city of some 250,000.[31]

What he saw upon arrival shocked him. Magnitogorsk was as bad an industrial slum as any he had ever seen. The landscape was littered with piles of broken bricks, rusted pipes, and jagged metal sheets. Wooden planks were laid across the unpaved muddy streets amid crude huts and dilapidated, overcrowded barracks. As Scott soon learned, there were shortages of virtually every basic necessity. People subsisted mainly on black bread and many had only one set of clothing. Basic hygiene was nearly impossible: there was no running water, no indoor toilets, no sewers, and no way to treat waste and raw sewage. Black smoke from factories polluted the air and left a residue of filth on everything below. Nearly everyone was undernourished and exhausted from tense living conditions and overwork. Disease and sickness were rife, and there was a shortage of qualified medical personnel.[32]

In time, however, Scott also came to recognize that there was much about Magnitogorsk that was positive. The people working to construct this new industrial colossus believed in the future. Many who had never in their lives seen electric lights, machines, or even a staircase, were determined to build socialism and improve themselves in the process. Most toiled long hours during the day and went to school at night. They froze in the winter and sweltered in the summer. Gradually, however, things got better, and Magnitogorsk became more livable. Schools and libraries appeared, a public transportation system was established, and roads were paved and illuminated. Apartment houses were built, along with schools, libraries, parks, restaurants, cinemas, and clubs. And, most importantly, Magnitogorsk was becoming an industrial success story. Between 1933 and 1937 the quantity of coking coal doubled, iron ore and pig iron tripled, and the output of steel rose sixteen times.[33]

But the pressure from above to accomplish more in less time was unrelenting.

Soviet planners had counted on an annual industrial growth rate of twenty percent for five straight years. This had never before been accomplished before anywhere in the world, but one had to believe. As the slogan proclaimed: "There are no fortresses that Bolsheviks cannot storm." Too, the success of the Five Year Plan was being tied to national security. Stalin warned his managers in 1931: "We are fifty to 100 years behind the advanced countries. We must make good this distance in ten years. Either we do so, or we shall go under."[34] Soon demands were being made to complete the Five Year Plan in four. Workers who exceed their quotas were held up as heroes. One of these, a coal miner named Andrei Stakhanov, had cut 102 tons in a single shift and exceeded his quota by fourteen times. Of course, it was all a fraud, since his comrades had performed all the crucial support work for him. Still, a hero was born and the regime had a reason to raise production norms for other coal miners.[35]

Scott, who would someday write a book about his experiences, remembered what it was like to go to work in the morning on an empty stomach and stand atop rickety scaffolding covered with ice at thirty-five below zero while trying to weld a blast furnace. Under these conditions, men grew tired and accidents happened. Scott recalled the horror of feeling a fellow worker "swish" right past him after he fell from the top of the scaffolding at a work site. The man, a rigger, would have plunged to his death had he not hit a bleeder pipe and landed on a platform that was only fifteen feet farther down. Scott was one of many who rushed to help him, but with blood gushing from his mouth, no one knew what to do. The American, recognizing that the man would soon bleed to death, suggested that he be carried to the infirmary immediately rather than wait for a stretcher. It was a good idea; the man was treated by a doctor and survived.[36]

Many workers Scott knew were peasants right from the farm. They were completely unfamiliar with any kind of technology and were accident-prone in the extreme. But at Magnitogorsk individual workers were easy to replace. It was far more difficult to recover the millions of rubles lost to accidents, collisions, and explosions. These were beginning to occur with increasing frequency. As the cost of these "mishaps" began to add up, Stalin and those around him could not allow that it was mainly the system that was to blame. Surely it was wreckers—"enemies of the people"—who wanted to derail the construction of socialism in the USSR. Since a significant part of the work force had backgrounds that invited suspicion for one reason or another, there was soon a drive to round these people up for questioning. This was often followed by accusations of wrecking and treason. In time, some of the most experienced and dedicated people became suspect. These included foremen, shop stewards, department directors, and plant managers whose workers had been involved in accidents or who had failed to fulfill their quotas.[37]

Of course, real acts of wrecking did occur now and then. They were generally perpetrated by people who had been abused by the regime and wanted revenge. One such man was a foreman in the blowing house of the blast furnace department in Magnitogorsk whom Scott knew personally. The fellow was a heavy drinker who sometimes bragged about how he might take revenge on his tormentors. One day he ruined a gas turbine imported from Germany by throwing a large wrench into one of the turbines. He was quickly arrested, made to confess, and sentenced to eight years.[38] Another incident of which Scott knew personally involved a population of kulaks who had been brought to Magnitogorsk to perform the heavy unskilled labor. The deportees consisted of whole families, most of whom were from the area around Kazan. Scott estimated that they numbered about 30,000 and were thus brought to Magnitogorsk in shifts. The process was brutal. After being deprived of everything they owned, they were packed into boxcars and sent hundreds of miles to their destination. Subsisting on black bread and water, they lived in filth and claustrophobic conditions for as long as twelve days. Upon arrival they were housed in tents and promptly sent to work. In an attempt to strike back, one of them poured ground glass into the main bearings and into some of the minor grease cups of the big turbine that was used in the city's powerhouse. Another smashed a crowbar into a large generator and sneered at the guards who came to arrest him.[39]

Most of the time, however, the regime, in its determination to find wreckers, arrested people who were completely innocent of any crime or evil intention. As production norms were raised, more and more workers failed to meet their quotas. This in turn caused shortages in other industries, which lowered productivity. Such was the case in 1933, when the nation's railroad system nearly collapsed from overuse, lack of spare parts, poor track maintenance, and accidents due to human error.[40] This resulted in oil and coal shortages elsewhere because the trains could not make their deliveries. The regime was particularly concerned about the failure of experienced train engineers to perform as expected. A formal study was made of those involved in these accidents. It was shown that not only did all suffer from malnutrition and exhaustion, but eighty percent of them had tuberculosis![41] Yet the only solution the regime could offer was to accuse more people of wrecking and to make more arrests. Soon inexperienced people were being promoted into jobs of tremendous responsibility but lacked the training and skills to carry out their assignments.

In 1937, Jack Scott traveled to the United States for a brief visit. When he returned to Magnitogorsk, it had been declared a closed city and foreigners were being ordered to leave. Most had already left because the atmosphere for non-citizens had become so hostile. For Scott, however, the situation was complicated by the fact that now he had a Russian wife and child. In 1933, he had married Masha Dikareva, the daughter of a poor peasant who had become a teacher. Thus, when Scott left Russia for good in late 1937, it took three years for his wife and child to be granted permission to join him. By then he was no longer a communist, but when Germany attacked the Soviet Union in 1941, he shuddered at the thought of a Nazi victory and urged his countrymen to help the USSR destroy the Third Reich. It was only with the onset of the Cold War after 1945 that Scott became actively opposed to the Soviet regime, urging policies to contain, if not overthrow, the communist system.[42]

Among Scott's most interesting observations in his book were those that dealt with the use of labor as a means of rehabilitating criminals, drunkards, or other anti-social types. At Magnitogorsk there were five Corrective Labor Colonies[43] populated with inmates, most of whom were at best semi-literate and under thirty years of age. Ironically, the creation of these colonies was in large part prompted by western journalists, who in the late 1920s had begun to write unflattering articles about the use of convict labor in the Soviet Union. At first, the Soviets were accused of resorting to slavery to build socialism. Later the concern became that the slave labor practiced in the USSR was a threat to Western business interests. Soon there was agitation for a boycott of the cheaper Soviet goods. This won support in the United States when Treasury Department in 1930 banned the import of pulpwood and matches from the USSR.[44]

Stalin was deeply antagonized by these actions and feared that more boycotts would impede the flow of hard currency needed for industrialization. This was particularly true in the timber industry, which involved one of the of the country's most lucrative exports. Thus, he authorized that the term "concentration camp" (kontslager) be dropped in favor of "corrective labor colony." He then touted the regime's "enlightened" use of convict labor by announcing a massive building project to connect the White and Baltic Seas that was to be constructed exclusively by convicted criminals. The labor on the Belamor Canal, as it was known, included a large contingent of kulaks whose only crime was that they were kulaks. In any case, the project was plainly dictated by propaganda needs and not by economic necessity. Indeed, many in the Party doubted that the expected number of vessels using the canal would justify such a huge expenditure. But the General Secretary brushed aside all these objections. He was enthralled by the notion of building a monument to the humanitarian nature of Soviet power. Thus, those convicts who performed their tasks in an exemplary manner could hope to be pardoned and released.[45]

Construction of the canal began with much fanfare in November 1931. Stalin decreed that the project, which would require 141 miles of digging, five dams, and nineteen locks, be completed in twenty months. The head of the OGPU, Genrikh Yagoda,[46] was assigned to oversee the work and to hold costs down. Money was to be saved by using wood, sand, and rocks instead of metal and cement. Dynamite was also thought to be a needless extravagance. Massive rock formations were to be broken up by *zeks* pounding "hammers" that were really large chunks of metal screwed onto wooden handles. Rock chippings, excess soil, and other refuse were carted away by "Belamor Fords"—a heavy truck body on four wheels fashioned out of tree stumps. Living conditions, of course, were necessarily primitive due to the lack of careful planning and the rush to get the job done. Still, Yagoda, mindful that starving workers tend to achieve less, made a genuine attempt to increase the quality and amount of food.[47]

In fact, the job did get done, and on time, albeit at the cost of some 25,000 workers' lives during construction. In August 1933, Stalin sailed in triumph through the completed waterway, gazing at a portrait of himself 160 feet high on one of the canal banks. The project was declared a great success despite the fact that it was too shallow to accommodate the larger vessels for which it had been intended. Nevertheless, as a gesture of magnanimity, 12,484 *zeks* out of an estimated 170,000 total workers were deemed sufficiently rehabilitated to be awarded their freedom. And, as journalist-historian Anne Applebaum has noted, this was why the White Sea Canal was the only Gulag project to be openly advertised to the world as a triumph of Soviet social engineering.[48]

But the atmosphere of triumph and celebration that attended the opening of the Belomor canal in 1933 did little to assuage the gloom and despair in Ukraine during the same period. Most of that republic was suffering from the aftermath of a famine that was responsible for the deaths of some five million people. It had been caused in large part by poor harvests and by the government's draconian policy of grain requisitioning. In 1931 Ukraine was ordered to turn over 7.7 million tons of grain out of a harvest of 18 million tons. Ukrainian officials had begged Moscow to lower the quota, but to no avail. In the end, only seven million tons were collected, despite the government's fierce efforts to squeeze the peasants for more. In 1932, the quota was grudgingly lowered to 6.6 million tons out of a harvest of 14.7 tons, but this, too, proved unrealistic.[49] And for good reason. According to historian Louis Siegelbaum, a careful re-analysis of the data of the 1932 harvest indicates that the announced yield was exaggerated by as much as 30 percent.[50] Thus the Soviets fell even farther short of their stated procurement goal than was originally thought.

But such shortfalls seemed to make Stalin even more determined to have his way. On August 7, 1932, the General Secretary drafted a new law in his own hand, "On the safeguarding of state property." This was the infamous "Law of Seven-eighths," since it was promulgated on the seventh day of the eighth month. Simply stated, it decreed that anyone caught stealing or abusing property belonging to a collective farm would be denounced as an "enemy of the people." The punishment was to be death by firing squad or up to ten years' imprisonment in the case of mitigating circumstances. Although the law was sometimes applied selectively and lesser punishments might be meted out, its purpose was never in doubt: to crush the peasantry once and for all. To this end, watchtowers were erected in the fields with armed guards to prevent anyone from stealing even a single ear of corn. Soon the decree would be invoked to punish those who falsified kolkhoz accounts or committed acts of agricultural sabotage. In 1932, 20 percent of all sentences throughout the USSR were carried out on the basis of this law.[51]

As Stalin saw it, the future of the USSR depended on winning the war against the peasantry and tightening Soviet control over Ukraine. He was prepared use force to achieve these objectives, which he knew would excite feelings of Ukrainian nationalism and hatred of Soviet power among the populace. Since it was the intelligentsia who gave shape to and articulated these seditious ideas, he was determined to harass and arrest them in large numbers in order to blunt their influence. Many were tried publicly and made to confess to crimes that guaranteed long prison sentences. At the same time he attacked the kulaks that he believed disseminated the sedition of Ukrainian nationalism. Thus began the great deportation of Ukrainian kulaks. Some were resettled in remote areas, some incarcerated, and others shot. Collectivization continued inexorably. By mid–1932, nearly three-fourths of Ukraine's peasantry had been forced onto collective farms. This was a far higher percentage than had been achieved in Russia.[52]

Of course, by 1932 there were no real kulaks in Ukraine, mainly because no one was wealthy enough to qualify. Even so, Stalin urged Party activists not to become complacent about the apparent triumph of collectivization; kulaks were still working to undermine socialist ideals wherever they could. But while some activists embraced the hate-mongering enthusiastically, there were those who were still capable of humane consideration and common sense. As the situation deteriorated throughout the fall and winter, some individuals actually dared to side with the victims. One collective farm chairman flatly refused to collect the grain as ordered. When the OGPU arrested him and the head of the village soviet, the women of the collective rose in rebellion. They demanded the release of the two men incarcerated and a reduction of the grain quota. Predictably, the regime responded with force: there were sixty-seven arrests and a number of executions. But this did not deter many others from resisting orders they knew to be immoral. Such people were officially denounced as "rightist agents of kulakdom."[53]

Many, perhaps most, of those who witnessed the brutality employed against defenseless peasants were convinced that Comrade Stalin was unaware of what was happening in the countryside. This fiction no doubt suited him quite well. But in the fall of 1932 when his own wife, Nadezhda Alliluyeva, confronted him with the horrific truth, the results were tragic. "Nadya" had been taking courses at the Industrial Academy in Moscow and had become acquainted with a number of students who had returned from Ukraine after helping with grain collection. They told her about the famine, describing in lurid detail the brutality, the forced seizures, and the starving children. Her attempts to persuade her husband to send aid led to a violent argument. Just days after this ugly confrontation, on November 8, the couple went to a party in the Kremlin to celebrate the 15th anniversary of the Bolshevik seizure of power. According to one account, Stalin proposed a toast to the destruction of the enemies of the state and noticed that Nadya hadn't raised her glass. He then said, "Hey, you! Have a drink!" whereupon Nadya retorted, "My name's not 'hey'!" and stormed out of the room. She returned to their apartment and apparently brooded for several hours before shooting herself.[54]

Stalin is said to have been deeply shaken by his wife's suicide, but he was determined to finish what he had started. By the early spring of 1933, the famine in much of Ukraine had reached its peak. People staggered about with swollen faces and bloated bellies, tightly drawn skin, bulging eyes, and vacant stares. Many ate their own cats and dogs. Others scrounged for anything even remotely eatable, including tree bark, acorns, leaves, grass, insects, and earthworms.

Some tried to trap mice, rats, and sparrows. In areas where snails could be found people boiled them, sucked out the juices, diced up the meat, and mixed it with leaves. People also made soup with such items as nettles, beet tops, sorrel, and shoe leather. The ingredients varied according to what was available, but the result was usually a slimy, smelly, gooey mess that people readily consumed in order to live.[55]

At some point, however, the lack of anything eatable became so acute that some people resorted to cannibalism.[56] This might mean eating one's own recently deceased relatives, robbing graves, ambushing children, or murdering strangers. Curiously, such cases when reported were not dealt with by the police, but rather the OGPU. This was probably because the USSR, like most countries, did not have a specific law against cannibalism. Thus the question became did the accused murder their victim(s) before devouring them? If the answer was yes, the culprit was usually executed, although some were sent to labor camps in the far north to live out the rest of their days.[57]

In February 1933, Stalin addressed a congress of carefully selected peasants to brag that the collective farms had saved at least twenty thousand from the rapacity of the kulaks and certain poverty. He also promised that once the kulaks were eliminated each household would have one cow. As he put it: "This is an achievement such as the world has never known before and which no other state in the world has tried to achieve." But by now the survivors were so weak from starvation that they had to be prodded back into the fields for the spring sowing. A "seed subsidy" of 325,000 tons had been allotted to Ukraine in February, but now the concern was to find enough bodies to do the work. Most of those who were still alive were unable to toil for a full day. This put the next year's harvest in serious jeopardy, and the government, in some panic, began to send grain back into Ukraine. Clinics were set up to provide milk and buckwheat porridge to nourish those needed in the fields. The situation was equally dire with regard to horses and other beasts of burden, which were unable to pull and carry heavy loads. Some horses were so weak that they needed to be held up with ropes to be kept from lying down lest they be unable to rise again. Thus did the famine-stricken areas of Ukraine, the North Caucasus, and Kazakhstan begin to recover from their brush with extermination.[58]

The results of Stalin's Five Year Plan to promote industrialization and collectivization were decidedly mixed. The General Secretary was pleased the by growth of heavy industry during this period, which featured a jump in the output of machine tools and the establishment of a number of new industrial

Kulaks were among the most abused enemies in the USSR. Here are three accused of murder awaiting the beginning of their trial in 1929. Photographer unknown (courtesy Russian State Archives of Film and Photo Documents, Krasnogorsk).

areas. These included a hydroelectric scheme on the lower Dnieper and metallurgical combines at Magnitogorsk and Kuznetsk. Also significant were the huge tractor factories at Stalingrad (today Volgograd), Chelyabinsk, and Kharkov that were to serve the needs of mechanized agriculture. Unemployment ceased to exist during this period, as the size of the working class doubled. The production of capital goods is estimated to have grown at twice the rate of consumer goods during this period, and this made daily life for the Soviet worker and his family very difficult indeed. There were chronic shortages of important food items such as meat and dairy products. To buy anything at all, one often needed to stand in long lines. Too, living conditions were so cramped that many were assigned to live in long wooden barracks where there were not enough beds. In such instances one needed to sleep in shifts with a family member or simply bed down on the floor. Another common living arrangement was the communal apartment, which might consist of a single room for as many as five families. Since there was usually one toilet and one shower-tub for bathing and washing clothes, there was little privacy and many conflicts. The lone kitchen, of course, was used by all.[59]

But the situation regarding collectivization was even worse. The peasantry had been so traumatized by Soviet policies in the countryside that they had, like serfs in tsarist Russia, been reduced to a permanent underclass in Soviet society. Having been denied internals passports,[60] they could not move freely about the country. Nor could they hope to participate in new opportunities for upward mobility that had been opened to their counterparts in the industrial sector. The brutalities that had been committed in the name of dekulakization had caused the starvation-related deaths of some five million people. The result was a dramatic drop in agricultural productivity, which, coupled with the government's steady increase in procurement levels, made life in the countryside worse with each passing year.[61] These economic after-effects lingered on for decades, and it was not until the mid–1960s that Soviet agriculture would equal the productivity of tsarist Russia in 1913.

Nevertheless, from Stalin's standpoint, collectivization had been a stunning success. It had reduced the peasantry to a state of submission more complete than anything known under the tsars and strengthened Party control in the countryside. And, as brutal as the process had been, the policy itself had drawn little condemnation from the international community. Most of the journalists, scholars, and others who traveled to the Soviet Union during this period were banned from visiting the afflicted areas. Those who defied the ban and told the truth about what they saw were mostly ignored. Yet one journalist, who was acclaimed for his objectivity, actually saw what was happening and denied that it was so. This was Walter Duranty, who by now had become a confirmed apologist for the Soviet regime. While he allowed that there were some food shortages, he dismissed all talk of famine in Ukraine as "malignant propaganda."[62]

Others who also seem to have been willingly duped were a former Prime Minister of France, Edouard Herriot, and the renowned British playwright George Bernard Shaw. Both had gone to the USSR, albeit at different times, and had been given special tours of areas in the country that were relatively prosperous. Both were able to deny that they had seen any evidence of famine in the Soviet Union. Shaw went even further, claiming that he had not seen "a single undernourished person in Russia young or old." But perhaps the most dispiriting testimony came from two respected scholars, Sidney and Beatrice Webb, who probably should have known better. They, too, had visited the USSR in 1932, but chaperoned as they had been, they saw very little. Even so, they blamed the kulaks for deliberately creating a crisis by hoarding food in an attempt to undermine the socialist order. At the same time, the Webbs lavishly praised Stalin for having the courage to attack and exterminate a ruthless class enemy.[63]

CHAPTER VI

Old Bolsheviks, Ordinary People and the NKVD

THE FIRST TWO MONTHS OF 1934 should have been the best of times for those who attended the Seventeenth Party Congress or the so-called Congress of Victors. Despite the enormous sacrifice and cost, the first Five Year Plan (which the government claimed had been completed in four and a half years) was proclaimed a great success. The country was declared to have made enormous progress in industrialization, and the collectivization of Soviet agriculture had been largely achieved. Amid the self-congratulation and euphoria, the Party seemed more unified than ever. Many of those who had previously opposed Stalin's policies now mounted the podium to admit their mistakes and sing his praises. Among the most abject of these was Bukharin, who lauded the General Secretary for being "the Field Marshall of the proletarian forces, the best of the best."[1] No less fulsome was Kamenev, who solemnly declared that future generations would refer to this glorious time as "the era of Stalin." Indeed, the Georgian mountaineer truly seemed to have done the impossible. With the urban economy almost completely nationalized and agriculture collectivized, the Soviet Union appeared to have achieved the basics of a socialist society.

But in the minds of many delegates, all was not entirely well. Despite the real economic growth that had been achieved, the official production totals had been shamefully exaggerated.[2] Thus, although the regime could justly laud such showplace projects as Magnitogorsk, the Turksib Railway, and the Dnieper hydroelectric dam, in the production of items such as machine tools, turbines, and steel, the totals had fallen far short of what had been predicted. There were also shortages of such basic items as nails and packing materials. Even more worrisome was the situation in agriculture. The subjugation of the peasants had virtually destroyed their incentive to work. Moreover, the huge mechanized and productive kolkhozes that many in the Party had fantasized about turned out to be mostly small, dilapidated, and woefully unproductive.[3] Still, the country had survived a horrible ordeal, and the mistakes and imperfections that remained could, it was believed, be corrected. Many of the delegates must have supposed that at long last the Revolution had been won. Hence the name: "Congress of Victors."

Despite all the adulation and praise accorded Stalin, he, too, was tense and dissatisfied. As he spoke to the delegates at the convention in his keynote address, he lauded the progress that had been made and declared, "There is nothing left to prove, and, it seems nobody to beat."[4] In fact, he sensed resistance in those he had previously defeated: Kamenev, Zinoviev, Bukharin, Rykov, Tomsky and others. Nearly everyone in the Party hoped for some measure of relaxation and normalization. Some, weary of Stalin's increasingly nasty despotism and cult of personality, also hoped that he might be persuaded to give up his job of General Secretary and accept a government position that would be less taxing and equally prestigious. Many believed that Lenin's old position of Chairman of the Sovnarkom would be a perfect fit: it would satisfy Stalin's vast ego and keep him out of the day-to-day running of Party business. The trick was to suggest the transfer in such a way so as to not to arouse the dictator's suspicion. But as the weeks and months passed, this proposal was not acted upon. It was buried forever on December 1, 1934, when a mentally deranged loner named Leonid Nikolaev killed a member of the Politburo, Sergei Mironovich Kirov, with a single shot to the back at the Smolny Institute in Leningrad. The circumstances were strange. On two previous occasions the assassin had been caught trying to get close to the victim with a loaded revolver, and yet, not only was he not arrested, he was allowed to keep his weapon. In any case, Stalin's reaction was swift, and he unleashed a spasm of terror that victimized people across the USSR for the next four years.

Many historians believe that it was Stalin himself who arranged Kirov's murder, acting with the help of the Genrikh Yagoda, head of the NKVD. The reason was Kirov's increasing popularity and independence. A Bolshevik since 1905 and veteran of the civil war, he had become a Stalin protégé during the early years of the NEP. In 1926, he was appointed Party boss of Leningrad, and four years later he was elevated to full membership in the Politburo. Kirov seemed to remain in Stalin's good graces until the fall of 1932, when the two clashed. The issue was Marteman Riutin, a non-voting member of the Central

Committee, who had dared to circulate a manifesto in which he condemned Stalin's economic policies and demanded his removal from power. Riutin and his followers were arrested in September and put on trial. Stalin demanded that the culprits be executed, but Kirov objected and most of the Politburo went along with him. Thus, Riutin and his cohorts were sentenced to a "mere" ten years in prison. In the months following the Seventeenth Party Congress, Kirov angered his patron again by urging a policy of reconciliation for those who had opposed Stalin's policies on industrialization and collectivization. Finally, that summer, Kirov refused his mentor's request to leave his post of Party boss in Leningrad and to come to Moscow. Stalin clearly wanted to keep him close by so that he could be easily watched.

Circumstantial evidence notwithstanding, there is reason to doubt that Stalin had anything to do with Kirov's murder. For one thing, it was unnecessary. There were other ways to deal with an errant subordinate that carried far less risk. Also, the assassination of a major figure in the Party like Kirov might be difficult to pull off. Stalin would have had to rely on Yagoda, whom he suspected had lost his zeal for hunting down the enemies of the Soviet state. Nor was it likely that the General Secretary would have allowed someone as unstable as Nikolaev to be involved in such an important task. Whatever the truth, Stalin was quick to exploit this crisis for his own ends. That evening he, Yagoda, and some other high-ranking Party members and NKVD men boarded a train to Leningrad to conduct the investigation. In anticipation of what he expected to uncover, Stalin had prepared a decree to try and execute all terrorists as quickly as possible without appeal. This was amended four days later to stipulate that all investigations be concluded within ten days and that indictments be presented to the accused only twenty-four hours before the trial. The following day, several dozen people who were being held in Leningrad and Moscow for crimes unrelated to the Kirov murder were executed.[5]

Upon arriving in Leningrad, Stalin displayed his grief and anger by punching a member of the honor guard, Filip Medvedev, in the face. It was he who had been in charge of Kirov's security. Stalin then went directly to the Smolny Institute, where he personally interrogated the accused Nikolaev. It was soon decided that the assassin had help from an alleged Leningrad Terrorist Center, the membership of which was composed mostly of Zinoviev's supporters. Those who could be found were tried and shot in the last days of December, along with Nikolaev himself. Also rounded up and executed were Nikolaev's brother, his ex-wife, and a sister-in-law. In January, Zinoviev and Kamenev were tried for moral complicity in Kirov's murder, to which they confessed their guilt. They were sentenced to ten and five years respectively. Subsequently, 663 former supporters of Zinoviev were arrested and condemned to Siberian exile.⁶

The Kirov murder sent a spasm of alarm around the country. Citizens were urged to be vigilant: "enemies of the people" were at work undermining the Socialist fatherland. Yet, at the same time, for many Soviets citizens, especially those living in he capital or some other large city, life was getting better. The New Year in Moscow was celebrated with more cheer and merriment than had been seen in a long time. People actually dared to decorate their homes with New Year's trees, a practice that had been previously condemned as a vile religious superstition. Rationing for bread and flour, introduced in the 1920s, was ended. The first line of the Moscow Metro was opened, and a mammoth project to reconstruct and modernize the capital was announced. Industrial production was on the rise, and more consumer goods were becoming available for ordinary people. Finally, the regime announced that class restrictions for admission to the more prestigious schools of higher education were to be ended. Thus Stalin could boast with some justification at year's end that "life has become better, comrades. Life has become gayer."

Other signs, however, pointed to the opposite. In a law that was published on April 7, 1935, it was decreed that children as young as twelve could be subject to capital punishment. The reaction in the country and especially abroad was one largely of dismay and amazement. Some western socialists sought to explain it by claiming that people matured so quickly under socialism that even a twelve-year-old had to be considered a fully responsible citizen. Later, Stalin would deny that children would ever be held account for the sins of their parents, but who could be sure? Party members who had children and who had opposed Stalin in the past felt increasingly vulnerable. This is probably exactly what Stalin intended. And all the while the General Secretary was planning to resume the staging of public trials to rationalize the regime's economic failures and to eliminate his political opponents, real or imagined, once and for all. His decision to return to this tactic, however, caught many in the Party by surprise. The previous trials had been more or less successful, but the defendants had mostly been foreigners. This made their guilt much more plausible, at least for Stalin's domestic audience. The coming show trials, however, would involve mostly Old Bolsheviks, many of whom were revolutionary heroes who had worked closely with Lenin. In quite possibly in every case, they would be accused of crimes that they did not commit and that didn't happen. How could ordinary people be made to believe that the same public figures they had been taught to respect and admire were now "enemies of the people?" But the former theology student-turned-revolutionary had by now acquired a shrewd understanding of the power of confession. Thus, in the public trials that were to follow, not only did the accused admit to factious crimes they did not commit, but many of them would beg for mercy as they professed their love and devotion to Comrade Stalin.

At this point, as I prepare to describe and analyze the three show trials that took place in Moscow between 1935 and 1937, I must briefly digress to acknowledge my indebtedness to the late Robert Conquest, whose many works I relied on extensively. It was his groundbreaking scholarship that largely paved the way for students and colleagues alike to better understand one of the most the most puzzling and troubling episodes in Soviet history.[7]

To be sure, the procedures leading up to the show trials were carefully planed. The defendants, all hand-picked by Stalin, would be arrested, incarcerated, and interrogated by a system of torture known as the conveyer. This technique had medieval antecedents. Centuries earlier it had been used to force confessions out of "witches" in Scotland. The Soviets refined the system somewhat by conducting the interrogation in a room either too hot or too cold and by shining bright lights in the prisoner's eyes. The trick was to get the victim to confess to the crimes of which they had been accused without withdrawing the confession in court later on. The interrogations could, if necessary, be carried out over very long periods of time, perhaps four or five months. Sessions would generally begin at night and could be interspersed with periods of more direct physical torture. The defendants might be forced to stand until they collapsed or made to sit in a chair that was too small or in some way made to be uncomfortable. Of course they would be allowed food and water, but only enough to keep them going. There would be occasional breaks during the questioning, which allowed the defendant to rest but not to sleep. Most importantly, the victim would never know for sure when the torment had ended and when he or she would be allowed to sleep and recover. In the end, nearly everyone broke down and confessed. Indeed, so successful was the conveyor technique that Stalin used it routinely to purge and transform the Party. Thus, by 1939, 1,108 of the 1,966 delegates that had attended the Seventeenth Party Congress in 1934 had been either shot or sent to the Gulag.[8]

In the third week of August 1936, Kamenev and Zinoviev were taken from their prison cells and brought to trial on the charge that in their previous court appearance, after Kirov's murder, they had concealed the full extent of their guilt. The General Secretary's need to physically eliminate these two pathetic and thoroughly defeated former comrades puzzled even his most devoted followers. But if Stalin's reasoning was inscrutable to others, it made perfect sense when seen through the prism of his own fears and insecurities. After all, too much familiarity can breed condescension and even contempt. Kamenev had known Stalin since 1904, and later the two had served time together in Siberian exile. Zinoviev's relationship with the Georgian went back nearly as far. In 1922, Kamenev and Zinoviev had suggested to Stalin that they form a triumvirate not long after Lenin's first stroke to keep Trotsky from gaining the upper hand. Clearly they considered him the minor partner in this arrangement. But even more galling was the fact that Kamenev and Zinoviev had intervened to save Stalin's career when Lenin's final letter condemning the General Secretary was read to the Central Committee. Stalin, of course, was incapable of sincere gratitude and was loath to admit that he ever owed anybody anything. He was much more inclined to remember how these same two men in 1925 had opposed him at the Fourteenth Party Congress and later joined Trotsky in the United Opposition.

In any case, one of the purposes of this show trial, and the others to follow, was to prove that even the most trusted Communist could betray the Cause and become an "enemy of the people." Such people had to be rooted out and destroyed. To this end, fourteen others joined Kamenev and Zinoviev in the dock in what was to be the first of three major show trials involving Old Bolsheviks. To gain the complete cooperation of the main defendants, Stalin conveyed to them a promise that they would be spared if they confessed their crimes. Since this was their only hope, they had little choice but to go along. As their court date approached, Kamenev remained the more composed of the two. He said little except to plead that his family be spared. Zinoviev, in contrast, was thoroughly terrified by his predicament. He sent frantic letters to the Politburo trying to explain himself and looking for support. He also wrote to Stalin imploring him to accept that he "was no longer an enemy." Zinoviev was a sick man. In addition to his heart and liver problems, he suffered severely from asthma. His condition was aggravated by his overheated cell, which made it difficult for him to breathe and sleep at night.[9]

The trial began on August 19, 1936, and was held in the October Hall of the Trade Union House, which had once been one of the ballrooms of the old Nobles' Club. It contrasted starkly with the much larger Hall of Columns, which had been used in the earlier show trials. Of the roughly 180 people who attended, most were NKVD personnel. There were also some thirty foreign journalists covering the story, but no relatives of the accused were allowed to be present. None of this mattered, of course, because everything had been carefully prepared. Lazar Kaganovich assured Stalin beforehand that he, Prosecutor Vyshinsky, and Judge Vasily Ulrikh had thoroughly prepared the defendants, who knew exactly what was expected of them. The Soviet press did its part to vilify the accused so that the public was sufficiently worked up about the seriousness of the event.

Judge Ulrikh began the proceedings by reading the indictment, which accused the defendants of having been part of a criminal Trotskyist-Zinovievite Center. All sixteen defendants pleaded guilty. The first witness, Sergei Mrachkovsky, explained how the Center had formed and he had received instructions from Trotsky in planning acts of terror. The next to testify was a former Chekist, Efim Evdokimov, who eight years earlier had been working for the prosecution when he had supervised the torture of the fifty-three defendants in the Shakhty Trial.[10] Then in December 1934, and without any evidence, he was convicted of participating in Kirov's murder. Now he was on trial for concealing important facts at his previous trial twenty months earlier. Evdokhov admitted that that the plan had been originally to kill Stalin at the same time as Kirov. Another defendant, Efim Dreitzer, declared that that he had conspired with Trotsky's son, Lev Sedov, and two other terrorist groups to assassinate *both* Stalin and Voroshilov.[11]

Things became still more bizarre when a prominent Party member named Ivan Bakayev told his story. Like Evdokimov, he too confessed to participating in plot to murder Kirov and Stalin, although he denied knowing anything about the plots attributed to the other defendants. Among the last defendants to address the court that day was Richard Pikel, who admitted that he too had participated in a plot to murder Stalin.[12] Thus ended the first day of testimony. One can only imagine how dismayed and bewildered must have been those Soviet citizens who listened to the proceedings over the radio.

The second day of testimony began with Kamenev, who tried mightily to maintain his composure and present himself in the best light. Although Stalin had promised to spare both him and Zinoviev if they cooperated, each must have wondered whether or he would keep his promise. But as Vyshinsky continued to press him about the details of what he had confessed to earlier under interrogation, he began to unravel. He soon gave up all resistance and agreed to nearly everything the prosecutor suggested.

The most pathetic testimony of all was undoubtedly that of Zinoviev, whose sickly physical appearance and inability to speak audibly must have inspired pity even among those who detested him. Not only did he admit involvement in various terrorist groups, he also implicated a number of other conspirators, including Ivar Smigla, the commander of the Baltic Fleet during the Bolsheviks' seizure of power in 1917. Smigla was something of a war hero who subsequently became a member of the Central Committee.[13]

One of the strangest elements of this first show trial involving Old Bolsheviks was the dearth of outside witnesses to corroborate the prosecution's case. In fact, only one testified during the entire trial. This was the ex-wife of Ivan Smirnov, who flatly contradicted her ex-husband's earlier testimony that he was not the leader of the Trotskyite-Zinovievite Center. Not only was he the leader, said she, but he carried out his responsibilities fully intending to do mortal harm to Soviet power.[14]

Valentin Olberg was yet another man who claimed to have been instructed by Trotsky to murder Stalin. He was prevented from carrying out his assignment because he was arrested before he could act. Then K.B. Berman-Yurin took the stand and claimed that Trotsky had instructed *him* to assassinate Stalin. He planned to carry out the deed at the Thirteenth Comintern plenum, only to be foiled by his inability to obtain a ticket for the event! E.S. Holtzman's testimony proved to be equally disingenuous. In addition to conspiring with Trotsky, he claimed to have met with Trotsky's son, Sergei Sedov, four years earlier in the lounge of Hotel Bristol in Copenhagen. Later, it came to light that this was impossible for two reasons: (1) Sedov was in Berlin at the time taking exams at the University, and (2) the Hotel Bristol no longer existed; it had been torn down in 1917.[15]

More improbable testimony was soon to follow. Nathan Lurye admitted to having stalked Kliment Voroshilov for a year and a half, but never got close enough to fire a shot. Lurye later went to Chelyabinsk to assassinate Andrei Zhdanov while marching with him at the May Day parade. But once again his inability to get close enough prevented him from firing a single shot.[16] Moissei Lurye, a relative of Nathan, admitted to having received his instructions from Trotsky through certain German oppositionists leaders. He also claimed to have assisted his relative, Nathan, in his unsuccessful attempt on Zhdanov's life.

The trial ended with the appearance of Fritz David and the reappearance of E. A. Dreitzer. The former testified that he had been charged by Trotsky and Sedov to kill Stalin, but never got close enough to fire a shot. Dreitzer returned to the dock to accuse fellow defendant Vitovt Putna of being a member of the Trotskyite-Zinoviev Center. Moreover, he charged that Putna had pretended to quit the Center in order to conceal his continuing involvement.

Smirnov returned briefly to the dock to deny that Putna was ever a Trotskyite, although three other defendants confirmed it.

Vyshinsky then made his final statement, in which he alluded to the seven individuals still at large who had been implicated by the accused during their testimonies. These included Mikhail Tomsky, Nikolai Bukharin, Alexei Rykov, N.A. Uglanov, Karl Radek, Yuri Pyatakov, Leonid Serebryakov, and Grigori Sokolnikov. Vyshinsky announced that he intended to order an investigation of these men, which could lead to another trial. One of those accused, Tomsky, decided not to wait for the inevitable. Having listened to the court's proceedings over the radio, he clearly saw the handwriting on the wall. As the trial was ending, he wrote a letter to Stalin proclaiming his innocence and shot himself in the head.[17]

On August 22, the defendants lined up to make their final statements. Most seemed resigned to their fate. Mrachkovsky spoke emotionally of his humble beginnings and rise to prominence as a Bolshevik revolutionary. But as he spoke to the court, he warned that anyone, even a worker with impeccable proletarian roots, could betray the Cause. Thus, as he concluded, he declared that that as a traitor he deserved to be shot. Lev Kamenev's plea was similar in tone and memorable for the personal advice that he addressed to his two sons, who presumably were listening to the radio, and declared that no matter what the sentence he would consider it just. Then he added: "Don't look back. Go forward. Together with the Soviet people, follow Stalin."[18]

Then Zinoviev rose to offer his dreary final words. He explained to the court how his defective Bolshevism became anti–Bolshevism, which led to Trotskyism and then to Fascism. But as he ended, he spoke of the shame he felt for being associated with the other defendants, which was worse than any punishment he might receive. In retrospect, this seems to have been a rather odd thing to say. Since Zinoviev knew that he was innocent of the charges against him, surely he must have realized that the other defendants were also innocent of what they had confessed to. Indeed, Evdokimov, who spoke earlier, probably said it best after he spoke of the shame he felt for having lied about his guilt: "Who will believe a single word of ours?"[19]

The verdict, which was delivered the next day, was entirely predictable. All were pronounced guilty on all counts and all were sentenced to death. The executions were carried out within twenty-four hours. The behavior of Kamenev and Zinoviev in their final hours has long been subject of special interest because of their former prominence as Old Bolsheviks who had worked with Lenin. Clearly, they had hoped for a last-minute reprieve, but it was not to be. According to one account, Kamenev seemed shocked when the guards came to take him away, although he did not resist. Zinoviev, however, became hysterical. He was dragged from his cell screaming out to Stalin to keep his word. It became so bad that he never made it to the cell where executions were usually performed. Instead, the head guard shoved him into a side cell and shot him dead.[20]

The aftermath of the trial brought an even greater travesty of justice, since it involved punishing the innocent friends and relatives of the victims. Many of those who were incriminated during the proceedings were summarily executed. One man, Yuri Gaven, who was too ill to appear at the trial, was taken from his sickbed on October 4, put on a stretcher, taken outside, and shot. Others who would eventually be executed were encouraged for a while to believe that they had been spared. One of these was Kamenev's wife (Trotsky's sister), who had been arrested before the trial in 1935. She was exiled to Siberia, retried in 1938, and executed in 1941. Similarly, Kamenev's elder son, an air force pilot, was tried and convicted in May 1937. He was sentenced to a prison term and shot in 1941. But probably no other defendant's family was victimized more than Zinoviev's. His beloved son, Stefan, was shot in 1937 despite his father's impassioned plea to Stalin in his behalf. A sister, a physician who had previously been sent to the Gulag, was shot in 1939. Three other sisters, two nephews, a niece, a brother-in-law, and a cousin were sent to labor camps.[21]

Beyond the borders of the Soviet Union, the trial had been followed with considerable interest. Many informed observers were skeptical about the contradictions, improbabilities, and complete lack of documentary evidence. But, as they must have wondered, why would so many Old Bolsheviks, who had dedicated their lives to the building of socialism, have confessed to have such hideous crimes? In the final analysis, the fact that they all had confessed could not be denied. Thus, almost no one in the international community denounced the trial as an outright fraud. The one man who was in a position to see through the fog and confusion was Trotsky, then living in Norway. He had been effectively muzzled by his hosts, who feared Soviet economic retaliation.[22]

Two months later, Stalin scored another big propaganda success when he introduced the Constitution of 1936. Interestingly, this document for the first time defines the term "enemy of the people." In Part II, Article 131, such an enemy is described as an individual who takes possession of common property.[23] This explanation had to be disturbing to anyone who cared about truth

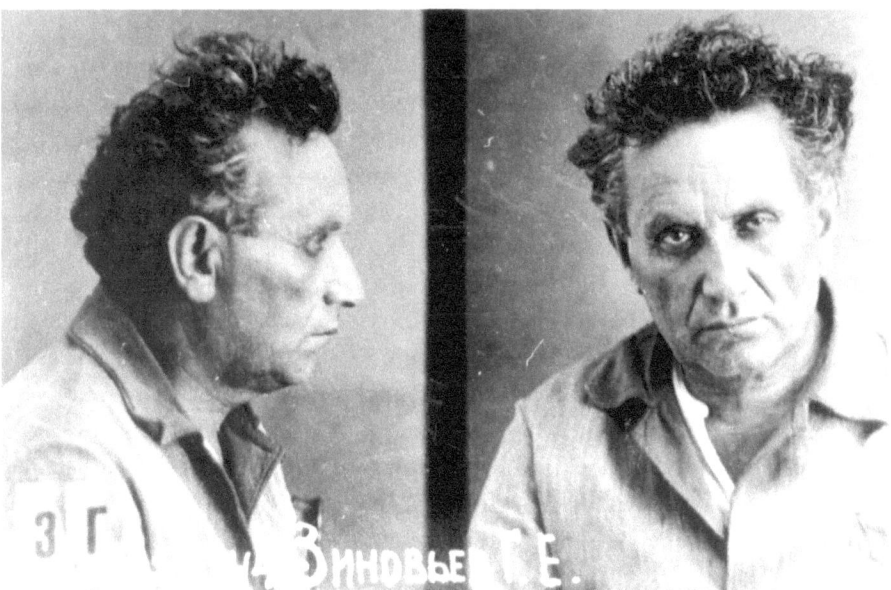

Top: Lev Borisovich Kamenev awaiting execution. Prison mug shot, Moscow, 1936. Photographer unknown, FSB. *Bottom:* Prison mug shot of Grigori Yevseyvich Zinoviev awaiting execution, Moscow, 1936. Photographer unknown, FSB (courtesy Memorial International Photo Archives).

and justice, all the more since the penalties involved were usually lethal. In any case, the announcement was timed to celebrate the completion of the socialist stage of development in the USSR, which now brought the country closer to true communism. In theory, there was much to admire: those who had belonged to the defeated classes, i.e., White Army officers, priests, and kulaks, etc., no longer were considered to be a threat to the state. Thus they would now be granted their full civil rights, including freedom of thought, the press, religion, organization, assembly, and the right to vote. Moreover, as citizens of the world's only socialist country, they were now guaranteed a free education, health care, a subsidized standard of living and, above all, the right to work. The new constitution also benefited the country's eleven soviet republics, which could secede from the Union if their people so desired. At the federal level, the Supreme Soviet was established as the highest legislative organ in the country. Its members were elected by universal suffrage to terms of four years.[24]

It was amid the pomp and self-congratulation that a new face appeared in Stalin's inner circle. Nikolai Ivanovich Yezhov, a man who would one day be remembered as the "Bloody Dwarf," had replaced Genrikh Yagoda as head of the NKVD. Barely five feet tall, Yezhov is described by historian Edgar C. Duin as "a man of limited intelligence and narrow mind who epitomized a breed of sycophant ruthlessly and uncompromisingly used by Stalin, whom he idolized, to achieve his goals."[25] He had become a Bolshevik in March 1917 and participated in the overthrow of the Provisional Government the following November. He joined the Red Army in 1919 and was sent to a radio-telegraphic school at Saratov on the Volga River. Though no weakling (he had once worked in a foundry), he was kept out of combat because of his diminutive size and poor health—he suffered chronically from a hacking cough and frequent bouts of tuberculosis. But Stalin saw potential in Yezhov, whose talent for organization and capacity for hard work were justly admired. He was known to be the kind of subordinate who could be entrusted with any assignment and complete it on time. Yezhov generally got along well with people. Those who knew him thought him a "modest and rather pleasant man," who drank little and was courteous and tactful. But Yezhov's rise up the Party ladder thoroughly corrupted him. In 1929, as deputy commissar for agriculture, he was called upon to assist in the collectivization campaign. Yezhov was as fierce as anyone in intimidating the peasantry and persecuting the kulaks.[26]

In 1934, Yezhov attended the Seventeenth Party Congress and was elected to the Central Committee as a full member. His duties and responsibilities were soon expanded to include membership in the Organizational Bureau, the Party Control Commission, and the Russian Central Executive Committee. In September 1936, Yezhov reached the high point of his career when he was named head of the NKVD. This last promotion marks the beginning of the intensification of the purge[27] and more terror. It is often referred to as *Yezhovshchina* (the terrible time of Yezhov). The victims included high-ranking military officers, heads of the economic sectors, and representatives of the Party apparatus. It was also at this time that many foreign communists were being arrested and executed. Sometimes this took place when they visited Moscow on official business. At other times, such tasks were carried out abroad by an "Administration of Special Tasks," which Yezhov had set up in December as part of the NKVD. This agency consisted of numerous controlled "mobile groups" that could apply deadly force beyond the borders of the USSR.[28]

On January 23, 1937, the second of the public trials involving Old Bolsheviks opened. Once again the site was the October Hall. It became Yezhov's job to produce and direct the event. The thirteen defendants were alleged to be part of the "Anti-Soviet Trotskyite Center." This included such Party notables as Georgii Pyatakov, Grigory Sokolnikov, Leonid Serebryakov, and Karl Radek. Since none of the accused had previously opposed Stalin or his policies in any serious way, it is not entirely clear why Stalin thought this trial necessary. But ever the paranoid, the General Secretary was taking no chances. A mortal enemy could be among the most loyal supporters who might secretly doubt the correctness of the policies that the boss pursued. Such people had to be identified and stopped before it was too late. If that meant rounding up the innocent along with the guilty, so be it. It was a price that had to be paid. Indeed, Stalin had long been nagged by a worst-case scenario that featured the growth of an army of fifth columnists in the Soviet Union. Many of these men and women occupied positions of power and responsibility in society. Their opposition to official policy was carefully hidden for the present as they bided their time to await the war that loomed on the horizon. That is when they would surely rise up and strike against Stalin, the Party, and the country.

The most important of the defendants was Pyatakov, who had been a Bolshevik since 1912. Though he had long been an enthusiastic supporter of Lenin, he had actually sided with Stalin in opposing Lenin's approach to the question of national determination at the Eighth Party Congress. Later, Pyatakov headed the Donbass coal mining industry and became a deputy head of the State Planning Committee (Gosplan), as well as deputy chairman of the National Economy of the USSR. But Pyatakov also had a checkered past.

During the 1920s his views often coincided with those of Trotsky, and for a time, he had been expelled from the Party for this reason. His renunciation of Trotskyism in 1928 led to his reinstatement and to his promotion as Ordzhonikidze's deputy in the People's Commissariat of Heavy Industry. But in 1936, Pyatakov was again expelled from the Party and accused of heading a Ukrainian-Trotskyist Center. Hoping to be spared the death penalty, Pyatakov offered himself to Yezhov as an informer. He also revealed a nest of counterrevolutionary activity (which included his ex-wife) and volunteered to personally shoot them all.[29]

Now that he was on trial as an "enemy of the people," Pyatakov mostly cooperated in the hope of avoiding more torture. He admitted to helping to form terror and sabotage groups and to planning acts of terror and diversion. However, he would not allow himself to be connected to any particular act of violence, nor did he admit to communicating with the plotters. He did, however, describe how he met with Trotsky at his home in Norway in December 1935. The circumstances, however, were highly improbable. Pyatakov had actually been in Berlin at the time attending to government business. However, as he explained to the court, he met one of Trotsky's agents at the Berlin Zoo and arranged for a private flight to Oslo. His plane took off from Templehof Airport on the morning of December 12 and landed at the Kjeillor Airfield in Oslo at 3 p.m. The story was soon exposed as a fraud by a Norwegian newspaper, which had checked the facts and reported that no plane of any kind had landed at Kjeillor between September 1935 and May 1936. Prosecutor Vyshinsky tried to explain this embarrassment by insisting that the Soviet Embassy in Oslo had affirmed that the Kjeillor Airfield received flights all year around, including during the winter.[30]

Karl Radek's testimony on January 24 lent credibility to the prosecution because of details he offered and the confident manner in which he spoke. Radek gave information about Trotsky's followers and their links with Zinoviev's group. He spoke of the fascist and Bonapartist nature of Trotsky's intended regime and his willingness to cede parts of the USSR to foreign aggressors in order to gain and hold power. Radek also implicated Bukharin and mentioned General Mikhail Tukhachevsky, one of the Soviet Union's most distinguished military leaders. However, when he testified again later that evening, he exonerated the general of any wrongdoing.[31] More revelations followed when other defendants gave the prosecution the names of more saboteurs whose activities included sabotaging the railroad system and causing a mine explosion at Kemerovo in Siberia in February 1936. One former NKVD agent, called to testify, described how the Trotskyites sought to make industrial workers angry with the government by creating "impossible conditions" for the workers. Another defendant testified about his plans to blow up the State District Power Station.

The next important wrecker/assassin to take the stand was N.I. Muralov. He had been accused of helping to blow up the Tsentralnaya Mine despite the fact that he had been in jail at the time. Muralov denied this charge but admitted that he conspired with Pyatakov to assassinate two important Party leaders, R.I. Eikhe and Vyacheslav Molotov. The attempt on Eikhe's life never came off, but an attempt on Molotov's life was fabricated after he and his driver, Valentin Arnold, were in a car that went off the road and partially into a ditch. No one was hurt, but the prosecution declared this event to be an attempt on Molotov's life. This required, of course, that Muralov and Arnold memorize a completely fictitious account of what happened. For Arnold this was very difficult, since he had to remember a lot of phony information about his background. In the end, he did not come across as a credible witness.

This time, the more absurd elements of the second show trial were received with some skepticism. Some correspondents even referred to the trials as "frame-ups." Meanwhile, Trotsky, still in Norway, fumed at the way he had been defamed and called upon the Soviet government to demand his extradition so that he could defend himself in person. But the Norwegian government wanted no more involvement in this matter and urged Trotsky to seek asylum elsewhere. This brought him to Mexico, where he continued his agitate for justice. His plea was taken up by the American philosopher John Dewey, who agreed to head a commission to investigate the accusations against the former commissar. After a thorough investigation, it was determined that Trotsky and his son, Lev Sedov, were both innocent of all charges against them. This exoneration, however, gave Trotsky little satisfaction because it changed nothing. The world was occupied by other more compelling concerns, such as the economic recovery after the Great Depression and the rise of fascism in Germany, Japan, and Spain.[32]

Still, the trial went on, and a new defendant, Yakov Lipshitz, was to give a sobering account of the destructiveness of "enemies of the people" in the transportation industry. He, too, was accused of wrecking, planning assassinations, and spying for the Japanese. He confessed to all the charges and named others who assisted him. A junior colleague, I.A. Knyazev, described the carnage caused by the saboteurs in graphic terms. He, too, recited a long list of accomplices, who caused as many as fifteen train wrecks. Among the last to

134 "Enemies of the People" Under the Soviets

Karl Bernardovich Radek (facing, right) in Red Square in 1920 at a memorial service for the American socialist John Reed. Radek was eventually executed as an "enemy of the people" in 1939. Photographer unknown (courtesy Russian State Archives of Film and Photo Documents, Krasnogorsk).

take the stand was an accused chemical wrecker, S.A. Rataichak, whom Vyshinsky denounced as a German or Polish spy and as a "liar, a swindler, and a rascal."[33]

In his closing remarks, delivered late in the afternoon on January 28, Prosecutor Vyshinsky excoriated the defendants as "a gang of criminals and 'Trotskyite Judases.'" He went on to add ominously that "if there is any shortcoming in this present trial, it is not that the accused have said what they have done, but that, after all, the accused have not really told us all that they have done, all the crimes that they have committed against the Soviet State."[34] At the same time, he boasted of the court's strict impartiality and of its refusal to rely on confessions alone to determine "malicious intent without any possibility of doubt." The prosecutor finished his remarks with a crescendo of emotion as he called for the death penalty for all the defendants: "I do not stand here alone! The victims may be in their graves, but I feel that they are standing here beside me, pointing at the dock, at you, accused, with their mutilated arms, which have moldered in the graves to which you sent them."[35]

When the verdicts were pronounced on January 30, thirteen of the seventeen defendants were condemned to death. The sentences were carried out the following day. But even the four who were spared did not have much longer to live. Karl Radek was later retried for having suppressed evidence. He was sent to jail and murdered by a prisoner acting under orders. Also killed in prison at about the same time was Grigori Sokolnikov. He had been personally promised his life by Stalin if he cooperated at the trial. Two others who had initially received long prison terms, Valentin Arnold and M.S. Stroilov, were shot in 1941. But as in the aftermath of the first trial, more retribution was soon to follow. Many of the relatives of those executed themselves became "enemies of the people" and were subsequently set upon, jailed, or shot. Some perished in the camps; others were kept alive for special abuse. Such was the case for the wife of Y.N. Drobnis, who had lost her hearing because of mistreatment during interrogation. She was last seen in 1936 languishing in the isolator at a prison in Krasnoyarsk.[36]

Despite the many omissions, contradictions, and mistakes, the second show trial of Old Bolsheviks mostly achieved what was intended. True, many thought it strange that certain individuals who had been implicated during the trial remained at large and were never brought to justice. Still, there were others who wrote approvingly about the weight of the evidence presented and the fairness of the process. In contrast, the mood of many high-ranking Party members was one of dismay and, in some cases, anger. Such was the case for Stalin's fellow Georgian and long time comrade Sergo Ordzhinikidze, who was Commissar of Heavy Industry. The General Secretary had promised Sergo that his friend Pyatakov would not be executed. When Sergo learned otherwise, he promptly phoned Stalin and threatened to use his position as a member of the Politburo to "raise hell" about the purge. But Stalin seems to have anticipated Ordzhonikidze's reaction well in advance. Some months earlier, he had ordered the arrest of Papuliya Ordzhonikidze, Sergo's older brother. Papiluya was tortured and shot early in February 1937, not long after those condemned at the trial had been executed. At the same time, officers of the NKVD began to collect "evidence" on Sergo's treasonous activities. At one point, the police showed up at Ordzhonikidze's apartment late at night with a search warrant. Although Sergo tried for hours to reach Stalin by phone and demand an explanation, it was only in the morning that he got through and the intruders were ordered to leave.[37]

At 5:30 p.m. on February 18, 1937, Sergo Ordzhonikidze was found dead in his apartment of a gunshot wound. Most historians have concluded that it was a suicide, although the possibility that he was murdered cannot be ruled out. In any case, it is known that Stalin and Ordzhonikidze had met the previous day for several hours. There is no record of what was said, but Stalin is believed to have accused the commissar of siding with the kulaks and of lacking firm proletarian principles. Sergo seems to have tried to get Stalin to recognize that his suspicions were out of control and that the arrests and executions were destroying the Party. The two spoke one more time by phone in the early morning hours of February 18, but the General Secretary was not won over. Later that day, when Sergo's widow, Zinaida, called Stalin to inform him of her husband's death, he came immediately, asked no questions, and feigned surprise. Ignoring the wound and the blood, he said merely: "Heavens, what a tricky illness! The chap lay down to have a rest and the result was a fit and a heart attack."[38] And, indeed, the official cause of death was listed as a heart attack.

Ten days later, Nikolai Bukharin and Alexei Rykov were expelled from the Party and placed under arrest. Next to be taken was Genrikh Yagoda, the former head of the NKVD. Like Bukharin and Rykov, he, too, had seen it coming. Once a member of Stalin's inner circle, he had fallen out of favor with his boss early in 1935 after the Kirov murder. Stalin believed that he had lost his zeal in hunting down those responsible for the crime. In September 1936, he had been replaced by Yezhov as head of the NKVD and demoted to the head of the Commissariat of Communications. Now, exactly one month after Ordzhonikidze's death, Yezhov denounced Yagoda at a meeting of senior NKVD officers at the Lubianka, calling him a spy, a thief, and an embezzler. Yagoda was arrested on April 3, 1937, for "offenses of a criminal nature in connection with his official duties." His dacha was taken over by Molotov, and his wife was sent to the Gulag. Yezhov proceeded to clean up the NKVD with ruthless efficiency, arresting agents thought to be supporters of Yagoda. Most submitted without resistance, almost as if they were obeying the rules of a game. Others committed suicide by shooting themselves or by jumping out of their office windows. Three thousand of Yagoda's men perished in 1937, while Yagoda himself was taken to the Lubyanka. Meanwhile, preparations for a third a third and final show trial involving the Party's Old Bolsheviks were now underway.[39]

Once again, Moscow's October Hall was the venue for the trial, which began on March 2, 1938. This was to be the grandest show trial of all. Eighteen defendants were accused of participating in various crimes including the murders of Sergei Kirov, the writer Maxim Gorky, Gorky's son, Maxim Peshkov, and Party boss Valerian Kuibyshev. (Gorky and Kuibyshev were originally thought to have died naturally.) Also, included in the charges were wrecking, treachery, and espionage. The alleged collective goal of these "enemies of the people" was to provoke a foreign invasion in order to bring about the dismemberment of the USSR, the destruction of the socialist order, and a return to capitalism.[40]

As in the earlier trials, the defendants were rigorously prepared by a combination of torture and threats until they knew exactly what they were supposed to say. All confessed their guilt except Nikolai Krestinsky, a former People's Deputy of Foreign Affairs, who now claimed that he had never been a Trotskyite and had not committed a single crime. The prosecution seemed to take this in stride. A twenty-minute recess followed, and Sergei Bessonov was called to the docket. A former counselor in the Soviet Embassy in Berlin, he claimed to have worked with Krestinsky. When the prosecutor pointed out that Krestinsky had denied this, Bessonov, smiling, not only affirmed it, but claimed that it was Krestinsky who had appointed *him* to be a liaison man for Trotsky! This back and forth went on for some time. Later more defendants came forth to confess to their own crimes and affirm Krestinsky's guilt.

That night, on Stalin's orders, Krestinsky was worked over by the interrogators who specialized in that sort of thing. They dislocated his left shoulder so that he would feel pain without seeming to have been physically abused. The next day, March 3, the prosecution continued the assault. New defendants were called to denounce Krestinsky. One of these was Christian Rakovsky, whom Vyshinsky had called to ask about a letter that Krestinsky claimed he had written to Trotsky, dated November 1927. He had hoped the content of the letter, which had been taken from him as he was being arrested, would exonerate him. But now the prosecution was denying that any such letter existed. Instead, Vyshinsky claimed that a different letter, dated 11 July 1927, was the one taken as he was being arrested. This letter, according to the prosecutor, proved that Krestinsky was still a Trotskyite.

That evening when the court reassembled, Vyshinsky produced the letter of 27 November, which he so recently had claimed didn't exist. At this point, Krestinsky, looking more and more defeated, ended his resistance and admitted to all the charges. On the evening of March 3, he took the stand and confirmed what he had previously denied: that he had met with Trotsky, who instructed him about how to carry out various acts of treason, sabotage, and terror.[41]

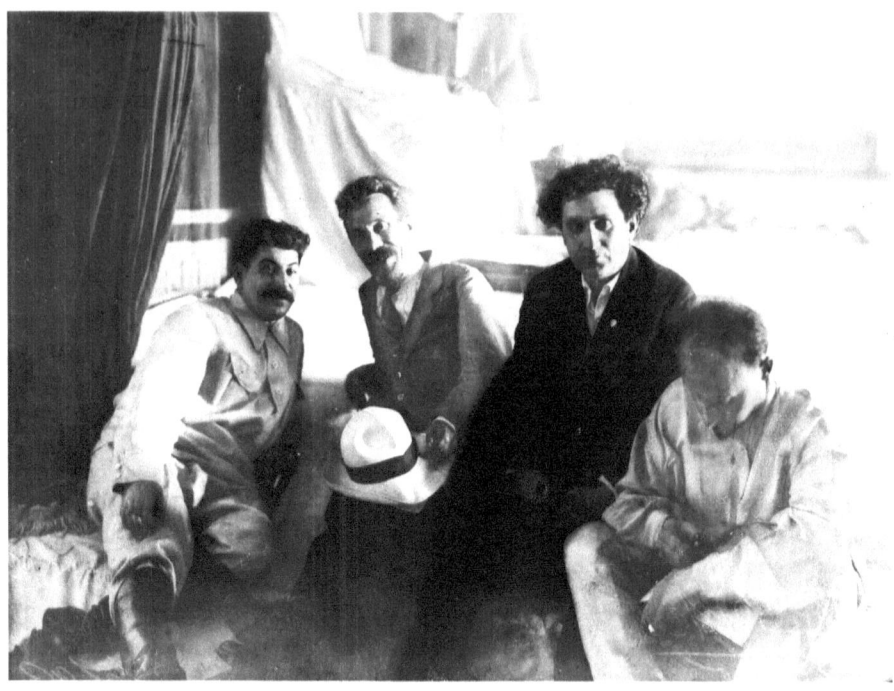

Four friends, sometime before 1927: (from left) Stalin, Rykov, Zinoviev, and Bukharin. Ten years later all but Stalin will have been executed as enemies of the people. Photographer unknown (courtesy Russian State Archives of Film and Photo Documents, Krasnogorsk).

Krestinsky's testimony was interrupted from time to time so that Vyshinsky could question defendants who were accused of various kinds wrecking and economic subversion. This included the People's Commissar of Finance, G.V. Grinko, a Ukrainian, who was accused of financial sabotage—pursuing policies to weaken the ruble. He also urged bank employees to provide bad service to customers, to cause delays in paying wages, mix up accounts, and so on. Another Ukrainian, M.A. Chernov, the People's Commissar of Agriculture, was accused of, among other things, forbidding his subordinates to provide anthrax serum to Eastern Siberia. This resulted in the deaths of 25,000 horses. Chernov was also alleged to have ordered officials to deliberately infect pigs with erysipelas, in various regions all over the USSR. V.I. Ivanov, a former People's Commissar for the Timber Industry, was accused of selling high-quality timber at reduced prices in order to reduce state revenues. Finally, Ivanov implicated Bukharin, who he claimed had instigated such activity as a way of winning support among the bourgeoisie in England.

B.F. Sharangovich, the First Secretary of Belorussia, took the stand and admitted that he had been a spy for Poland for seventeen years. He also confessed that he was part of a national fascist organization and that he helped to form three terrorist groups, two of which had conspired to kill Ordzhonikidze. He also committed acts of agricultural sabotage for which he was denounced as a "bourgeois nationalist" so that Belorussia could achieve economic independence from the USSR. Next to testify was P.T. Zubarov, who seems to have tried to do the opposite. He confessed that he tried to wreak havoc in food production by causing confusion in seed cultivation, bad sifting, and careless storage.[42] Another who assisted in this effort was Isaak Kerensky, a former Secretary of the Central Committee and Secretary of the Moscow Party organization. He testified that he ordered members of his organization to throw glass and nails into butter as it was being produced. Moreover, this was all part of a plot to anger the Soviet people and to discredit the regime.[43]

Such testimony went on and on until it was Bukharin's turn to face Vyshinsky. Thus began what many consider to be the most intense part of this final show trial. The former Right Communist leader was resigned to his fate, but he was determined to insert the truth wherever he could. After his arrest he had resisted his interrogators for three months. He had also written Stalin many times to declare his loyalty to the General Secretary and the Party. Eventually, however, the hopelessness of his situation made him think about saving his wife and infant son. Ten months earlier, in June 1937, he had agreed to confess to all the charges, only to have Stalin make changes to the text of the confession, which he would not accept. This led to a whole new endeavor to craft a confession that would satisfy the dictator and be acceptable to Bukharin. After much wrangling and two postponements, an agreement was finally reached. Thus, the trial went on and Bukharin took the stand the afternoon of March 5.[44]

Bukharin's tactic in dueling with Vyshinsky was similar to some of his co-defendants, although he seems to have succeeded better than anyone else. He accepted general responsibility for the crimes of which he was accused, but denied knowledge of or participation in any specific act of wrecking or terror. For instance, he affirmed that he was a leader of the Right Communist and Trotskyite bloc, which planned assassinations of Party leaders. However, when asked whether Kirov's murder had been among those planned by the bloc, he answered, "I do not know."[45] This infuriated Vyshinsky, but when he posed the same question to Rykov later, he got essentially the same answer. When Yagoda took the stand, he insisted that both Bukharin and Rykov had indeed participated in planning Kirov's murder. He himself admitted to giving instructions to Kirov's bodyguard not to interfere in any attempt to murder Kirov. Another who confirmed Bukharin's and Rykov's guilt was V.F. Sharangovich, who specifically affirmed that both were in contact with the Polish intelligence service and the Polish general staff. He also testified that it was Bukharin who was in charge of his (Sharangovich's) espionage activities. But, try as he might, Vyshinsky could not get Bukharin to say what he wanted. That is, despite having been in contact with Mensheviks and Socialist Revolutionaries abroad, he would not admit that he was guilty of espionage.[46]

The prosecutor's final accusation against Bukharin was that on August 30, 1918, he conspired with the Socialist Revolutionaries to assassinate Lenin. Although the charge itself was patently ludicrous, Bukharin, in fact, had been one of many prominent Party members who had resigned from the Central Committee to protest Lenin's support of the Treaty of Brest Litovsk. Like so many other Bolsheviks, Bukharin believed that, at the time, the treaty was a disastrous mistake. Thus, he acknowledged that there had been a plot to arrest Lenin for twenty-four hours to facilitate the formation of a new government. Vyshinsky, hoping to solidify the assassination charge, produced three former Left Communists and two former Socialist Revolutionaries, but their testimonies were far from compelling. The last of these witnesses, Vladimir Karelin, claimed that it was Bukharin himself who prodded Fanya Kaplan

Andrei Yanuaryevich Vyshinsky (here in 1932) was Stalin's preferred prosecutor during the Moscow show trials. He was notorious for his angry oratory and sarcasm. Photograph SCUSSR (courtesy Russian State Archives of Film and Photo Documents, Krasnogorsk).

to do the deed. Again, this went nowhere. Thus, Vyshinsky ended his examination of Bukharin when the latter refused to agree that the emotional atmosphere in the Party was so intense in late summer 1918 that the assassination of high Bolshevik officials would have been entirely rational.[47]

The conclusion of this final show trial involved a plot by a group of doctors who had been accused of murdering four men, whose deaths had initially been reported as due to natural causes. The alleged victims were V.R. Menzhinsky, a former head of the OGPU; the writer Maxim Gorky and his son Maxim Pleshkov; and Valarian V. Kuibyshev, the former chairman of the Supreme Council of the National Economy. The scheme to charge a group of doctors of murdering their patients was most probably the brainchild of Yezhov, who wanted to impress Stalin and to further disgrace Yagoda, whom he had recently replaced as head of the NKVD.

The first to give testimony was Dr. Vladimir Levin, who claimed to have been recruited by Yagoda, with whom he had planned the murders. Menzhinsky, first to die in May 1934, had been suffering from kidney and heart disease but was poisoned with mercury vapor. Yagoda, a former pharmacist, was accused of having ordered the wallpaper in the victim's apartment to be treated with this deadly substance. This tale holds some plausibility since Yagoda was known to be familiar with various kinds of poisons. He also had a motive: he had wanted Menzhinsky's job and ended up getting it. Pleshkov's death, however, was more complicated. The murderers were said to have plied the young man with alcohol on a cold evening (also in May 1934) and left him in a drunken stupor to sleep on a bench in his own garden. The chill he contracted that night should not have been lethal, but Levin and his two accomplices saw to it that it was. The next to die was Kuibyshev, whose demise was brought about by criminal neglect. He had a bad heart but never received the expert medical attention he so needed. The last to expire was Maxim Gorky, who had long been in bad health. Levin testified that the victim's strange attraction to fire and flames helped to do him in. The doctor admitted that he ordered huge bonfires to be built outside near the writer's residence so that the victim would inhale the harmful smoke. The victim was then taken to visit his grandchildren, who were suffering from colds. Gorky caught cold from them, sickened, and died.[48]

It was an embittered Yagoda who took the stand for the last time on March 8. Over the years he had performed many valuable services for Stalin by taking on the nastiest of jobs. After being arrested the previous April, he had been so affected that he could not eat or sleep. He underwent a long period of interrogation during which he agreed to nearly all the charges, including that of trying to overthrow the state by using the Kremlin guard and the military. He also admitted to participating in the murders of Menzhinsky, Peshkov, Kuibyshev, and Gorky. Now, as Vyshinsky bore down on him, Yagoda, reduced to a mere wisp of his former self, gamely tried to salvage what little remained of his personal dignity by inserting the "truth" wherever possible.

Indeed, Yagoda found the going tough, but was determined to be none too cooperative. When he denied much of what he had confessed to earlier, Vyshinsky pressed him to explain why. "I don't know why," was the answer. Or later, when the prosecutor had asked him why he had made a false deposition, "Permit me not to answer this question." Once when Yagoda was asked to confirm or deny the accusation that he caused the death of Maxim Peshkov he answered, "I admit my part in the illness of Peshkov. I request the court to hear this whole question in camera." In answer to Bulganov's assertion that he had conspired to kill Yezhov, Yagoda admitted that the charge was essentially correct but wrong in certain details. Vyshinsky also tried to get him to confess to espionage; Yagoda denied this charge, but allowed that he had shielded spies in the NKVD. When Vyshinsky suggested that this was tantamount to the same thing, Yagoda objected and responded memorably: "Had I been a spy, I assure you that dozens of states would have been compelled to disband their intelligence services." Yagoda's final public utterances were made under cross-examination by Levin's defense council I.D. Braude, who wanted to know how Yagoda had gotten his client to participate in terrorist acts. To this end, he asked the defendant to confirm what he had confessed to during the pretrial examination. But Yagoda answered dismissively, "It was exaggerated, but that doesn't matter."[49]

Among the very last defendants was a distinguished professor of medicine, Dr. Dmitri Pletnev. At sixty-six, he had a long record of service to the Soviet state as the country's leading heart specialist, and he was one of the doctors who had attended Gorky. The fact that such a valuable scientist could have been singled out for special abuse and ultimately execution was one the most mystifying and, indeed, shameful aspects of the trial. It can only be surmised that Yezhov wanted another big name besides Levin's to rouse the public's indignation against the doctor-defendants. And to make the whole scenario as lurid as possible, it was decided to first involve Pletnev in a tawdry sex scandal before accusing him of assisting in Gorky's murder. To this end, a young female NKVD agent was assigned to visit Pletnev as a patient. She soon made charges that the doctor had molested her and then began going to his home to harass him. He went to the police, but they sided with her. Soon *Pravda* picked up on the story, and on June 8, 1937, it printed an article entitled "Professor—Rapist, Sadist" that describe how Pletnev assaulted the woman and bitten her on the breast. The next month the doctor was tried, convicted, and sentenced to two years in jail.[50]

Pletnev, of course, would never be released from jail and would soon face new charges. Vyshinsky himself conveyed this news when he visited the doctor in the Lubyanka to accuse him of participating in the murders of Kuibyshev and Gorky. Now, beaten down, demoralized, and disgraced, the doctor agreed to confess to the charges in court. He undoubtedly did this to avoid being tortured and to protect his family. Sadly, Pletnev had hoped that his standing as one of the country's most honored doctors would protect him, but it was not to be. The same medical colleagues who had once acclaimed him now lined up to denounce him.[51]

Vyshinsky's summation in this third and final show trial of Old Bolsheviks produced no surprises. The prosecutor spoke self-righteously about the "monstrous crimes" and "foul deeds" that had been committed against "our Socialist Fatherland, the fatherland of working people of the whole world." He also declared that the trial had proven beyond all doubt "that the Rights, Trotskyites, Mensheviks, Socialist Revolutionaries, bourgeois nationalists, and so on and so forth are nothing more than a gang of murderers, diversionists and wreckers without any principles or ideals."[52] He also spoke of the USSR's vast wealth and of the impossibility of shortages existing without the sabotage of traitors and the connivance of foreign powers.

Vyshinsky then commented on the specific crimes of each of the accused. He was especially wrathful in attacking Zelensky for having mixed glass and nails in butter. He called it "a crime so monstrous that all other crimes of the kind pale before it." He referred to Bukharin as "the damnable cross of a fox and a swine" and denounced him for his status a "theoretician" in opposing Soviet policies while staying aloof from the criminal activities that he prodded others to commit. He placed special emphasis on Bukharin and Rykov's refusal to admit their role in Kirov's assassination. Vyshinsky concluded by calling for all but Rakovsky and Bessonov to "be shot like dirty dogs." He also added a note of optimism about the future: "Over the road cleared of the last scum and filth of the past, we, our people, with our beloved leader and teacher, the great Stalin, at our head will march as before onwards and onwards toward Communism!"[53]

The accused were all allowed to make their final pleas. Many accepted their guilt and denounced themselves in the harshest terms, hoping to avoid execution. One defendant, Arkady Rosengolts, after informing the court about his smuggling illegal literature at age ten, actually started to sing a popular patriotic song, which included the line "I don't know any other country where we can breathe so freely."[54] But he soon choked up and sat down, unable to continue. Then Yagoda rose to address the court. He spoke of his long service to the Party, first as a teenager working in the underground, then in helping to organize the security forces of the USSR. He also expressed pride in his contribution to the various forced labor projects he had helped to organize. He concluded his plea by insisting that he had never been a spy.[55]

The two that spoke most ably on their own behalf were Rykov and Bukharin. Rykov began by admitting his general guilt as an oppositionist to certain policies, but stoutly denied that he had anything to do with the Kirov assassination or the four medical murders. He was particularly incensed by the charge that he had help to kill Kirov and claimed that the government's procedure in determining guilt and innocence was deeply flawed. As he pointed out to the court, when an attempt on Lenin's life was made in August 1918, a Soviet court had relied on the testimony of eyewitnesses, or direct evidence, to arrive at a just decision. Twenty years later, a modern Soviet court was content to rely on secondhand information, or indirect evidence, to decide the guilt or innocence of a Party member with a long record of faithful service.[56]

Bukharin was particularly brilliant in admitting what he needed to admit and making the points that he wanted to make. He declared himself guilty of treason and of being an enemy of Socialism. He also admitted to having been a counterrevolutionary conspirator and to having organized kulak uprisings and certain terrorist acts. He declared himself responsible for the defeatist orientation that came to dominate the bloc of Rights and Trotskyites. He also accepted responsibility for the wrecking activities of his followers, but stated that he had no recollection of giving directions of any kind to anyone about carrying out such activities. In fact, he referred to his earlier testimony, in which he recalled telling Radek that he considered "this method of struggle not very expedient." Bukharin also took exception to the accusation that he was part of a special gang of wreckers within the bloc of Rights and Trotskyites. In fact, he was not well acquainted with any of the other members with whom he was supposed to have conspired. Furthermore, the prosecution's charge that the bloc of Rights and Trotskyites, formed in 1928, had been organized under the direction of the fascist intelligence services was ridiculous; the Nazis had only come into power in Germany in 1933.[57]

The verdict was pronounced on March 13 at 4 a.m. after the court deliberated a mere six and one-half hours. The defendants were all declared guilty on all charges, and eighteen of the twenty-one defendants were condemned to death. The three who got jail time were Pletnev (twenty-five years), Rakovsky (twenty years) and Bessonov (fifteen years). But this was only a temporary respite; the three were all shot in prison in 1941. In the meantime, the relatives and, in some cases, friends of the condemned were set upon and abused, some more so than others. Bukharin's third wife, Anna Larina, was arrested within days of her husband's execution and served eighteen years of incarceration and exile, the first six months of which were spent in a small cell that was ankle-deep in cold water. Bukharin's first wife, who was crippled, was arrested in April and deprived of her surgical corset, which left her in much pain. She underwent rigorous interrogation, but refused to confess to crimes she did not commit. She was shot in March 1940. In addition, her brother, brother-in-law, and other relatives were also arrested. Some were shot, others spared. Rykov's wife was already in the Butyrka prison before the trial started. She never learned her husband's fate and died in prison. Their daughter spent twenty years in a camp where she performed hard labor. Yagoda's wife was arrested and initially sentenced to eight years in the camps, only to be shot after one year. Both his sisters and his mother are believed to have to have perished in the camps. Akmal Ikramov's family suffered even more. His wife and four brothers were all shot and his eldest son arrested. His younger son was temporarily spared, probably because he was only ten years old at the time of the trial. He was, however, arrested five years later. Tomsky, who had committed suicide rather than face a show trial, also had his relatives subjected to lethal abuse: his two elder sons were shot while his wife and youngest son were arrested and sent to prison.[58]

Associated with the show trials is the enormous spike in terror that took place roughly from the spring of 1937 to the fall of 1938, during which 750,000 executions took place. During the same period, perhaps twice that number was sent to the Gulag, from which they were not likely to return. That most of these people had done nothing wrong, Stalin well knew. But the General Secretary saw it all in coldly practical terms. After all, how could anyone really be sure who is innocent and who is guilty? A person who is a hero today might become a traitor tomorrow. And since it was his duty to protect the gains of the Revolution, it was imperative to create conditions so that "ordinary people" never got the chance to betray the state. Thus, the purge was a necessary precaution, not unlike an exercise in pest control, with no end in sight. Over the years, he and Molotov signed 383 lists containing 40,000 names. But these were only the prominent people. The fates of the far more numerous ordinary victims rarely came to Stalin's attention. Their numbers tended to increase exponentially because each new prisoner had relatives and friends, who were soon set upon, who also had relatives and friends, and so on.[59] The atmosphere of fear and uncertainty that was created by the purge destroyed normal human relationships. People were urged to be vigilant and to help the government expose "enemies of the people." And all the while, citizens were reminded that even the most beloved members of one's own family should not be immune to critical scrutiny.

To this end, even children were encouraged to inform on their parents, although this had long been the case. The most celebrated of these was fifteen-year-old Pavlik Morozov from the remote village of Gerasimovka in western Siberia. It seems his father, Trofim Morozov, had been accused of selling counterfeit identification papers to "kulaks" exiled to the region. It is not known who informed the OGPU about Trofim's activities, but in November 1931, young Pavlik appeared in court to testify for the prosecution. Trofim was found guilty and sent to a labor camp. He was eventually executed. Pavlik seemed to have felt empowered by his actions and began to snitch on others whom he judged to be anti- Soviet in thought or deed. He was soon hated by nearly everyone in town including his paternal grandfather, who would not allow him in his house. This went on for some time. Then in September 1932 the bodies of Pavlik and his nine-year-old brother Feodor were found in a forest outside of town. The Soviet press picked up the story and had a field day sensationalizing what had happened. In November, five members of Pavlik's family were put on trial for the murder of the two boys. All were found guilty; all but one were executed. But by now, Pavlik had become a national hero. Maxim Gorky actually suggested building a national monument to his memory. Schoolchildren all across the USSR were urged to emulate Pavlik for being courageous enough to put his love of country above that of his own father.[60]

By 1937, life in the workplace had become surreal. Men and women trembled as they saw coworkers disappearing around them. Indeed, the NKVD had informers in virtually every factory, shop, and school across the USSR, who were themselves fearful of not fulfilling their quotas lest they, too, be declared "enemies of the people." Many people kept a small suitcase packed in anticipation of that dreaded knock on the door in the middle of the night, although arrests could also take place during the day and in the most public of places. But by the end of 1938, it was clear that the purge had to be stopped. So many people had been arrested that there was danger that there would not be enough workers to run the economy. Many factories had lost their best engineers and technicians. Stalin now began to slow things down and established a commission to investigate the NKVD. Not surprisingly, the official report that followed exposed incompetence, neglect, and criminality.[61]

The first to be punished was Yezhov, who was removed as head of the NKVD and demoted to People's Commissar of Water Transport. Ominously, this was the same job given Yagoda after his demotion. A Georgian, Lavrenty Pavlovich Beria, became the new head of the NKVD. Yezhov, knowing what was soon to follow, took to the bottle. He also engaged in wild orgies involving lovers of both sexes. In March 1938, he attended a meeting of the Council of Elders to prepare for the upcoming Eighteenth Party Congress and the election a new Central Committee. At some point, Yezhov was nominated to serve another term. Just as some others began to speak in support of his candidacy, Stalin, seated on the side, stood up and walked forward. He accused Yezhov of organizing a conspiracy to kill him. He also declared that the diminutive commissar had arrested the innocent and shielded the guilty. Yezhov was stunned and tried to defend himself by declaring his devotion to the Party and his love for Stalin. But the General Secretary was unmoved, and within a few days Yezhov was under arrest.[62]

Yezhov's fate gives special meaning to the term "hoist on his own petard." His incarceration and interrogation took place in a church within a monastery that he himself had converted into a torture and execution chamber. The former commissar would now face his own torture performed by the very subordinates he had trained. Suffering as he was from tuberculosis and alcoholism, his physical disintegration was swift. At one point, he nearly died from both pneumonia and kidney disease, although he did not escape his day in court. On February 4, 1940, he was tried and found guilty of spying for Germany, Poland, Britain, and Japan, framing innocent people, and plotting to kill Stalin and seize power. "Shoot me peacefully without agonies,"[63] he begged the court. In fact, his execution seems to have been made as terrifying as possible. He was taken to a special cell not far from the Lubyanka that he himself had ordered built. On the night of February 4, 1940, Nikolai Yezhov, screaming for mercy, was shot by Vasily Blokhin, one of the NKVD's most senior executioners. It was a man whose services the diminutive commissar had himself employed many times before.[64]

Unlike Yagoda, who died fully exposed for the scoundrel he was, Yezhov simply vanished. No announcement was made of his execution, although the usual lethal consequences were soon to follow for his friends, relatives, and NKVD colleagues. Over the next few months, some 346 individuals were executed, although his first wife, mother, and sister were left untouched. His adopted daughter, Natalia, was placed in an orphanage and given a new last name. She later became a music teacher and volunteered to practice her specialty in one of the labor camps along the Kolyma River. Natalia spent the rest of her life campaigning for her stepfather's political rehabilitation, claiming that he, like so many others among the Party elite, was corrupted by the man who gave the orders.[65]

Another survivor of the show trials and purge was Stalin's benign image as a great leader, builder of socialism, and defender of the Soviet people. Though his collectivization policies made him very unpopular in the countryside, the urban population saw that life was in many ways improving in the middle and late 1930s. In any case, most did not blame Stalin for the excesses committed during *Yezovshchina*. It was a curious situation, but, as Adam Ulam reminds us in his seminal biography, *Stalin: The Man and His Era*, just as a medieval Christian could not deny the existence of witches, so ordinary Soviets could not doubt the existence of "enemies of the people" in the form of wreckers, spies, and traitors. In addition, the knowledge that the Socialist fatherland was surrounded by hostile powers made people even more inclined

Nikolai Ivanovich Yezhov as head of the NKVD in 1937. He was often referred to as the "Bloody Dwarf" because of his sadistic predispositions and diminutive size. Although he idolized Stalin and served him loyally, he was eventually declared an enemy of the people and shot. Photograph M.S. Nappelbaum (courtesy Russian State Archives of Film and Photo Documents, Krasnogorsk).

to accept Stalin's brutal despotism to defend the country. If mistakes happened, they were the fault of his underlings. At least that's the way film director Vsevolod Meyerhold saw it when he said, "They conceal it from Stalin," and Boris Pasternak when he lamented to Ilya Ehrenburg, "If only someone would tell Stalin about it."[66] The truth, of course, would not be publicly admitted for another two decades.

Perhaps that is the greatest tragedy of all for people who survived the many years of purge and terror. The need to make sense out of what had happened was especially tormenting for those who had endured years in the camps. Many, if not most, returned physically broken and psychologically wounded to a society that was now foreign to them. Historian Orlando Figes wrote of their plight in his book *The Whisperers*. The author's avowed purpose was to learn more about how individual citizens from various walks of life coped with the double lives they were forced to live. Having been inculcated with the highest socialist ideology and worldview, many struggled to make sense of the lies, contradictions, betrayals, and brutality of everyday life. They found themselves groping for answers and trying to believe again in the system that had destroyed their lives.

Chapter VII

The Military, Foreign Communists and Repatriated POWS

THE SHOW TRIALS AND THE PURGE made interesting news in the West, but most people were distracted by other events that seemed more threatening. In the mid–1930s, the world watched in fascination and trepidation as Nazi Germany began to assert its growing power and relative prosperity in Europe. At the same time, Adolf Hitler began to deal seriously with his own "enemies of the people" by promulgating the Nuremburg Laws in 1935. These deprived Jews of their German citizenship and made them targets for various forms of harassment and abuse. In the spring of 1936, he began the systematic dismantling of the Treaty of Versailles by ordering troops into the Rhineland. That summer he invited athletes from around the world to gather in Berlin for the 1936 Olympics as he formed the Axis alliance with two other fascist powers, Italy and Japan. Even more ominously, Germany annexed Austria in March 1938, and the following November Hitler ordered a pogrom (Kristalnacht or Night of the Broken Glass) in which the Nazis attacked Jewish property and businesses across Germany. The damage was severe: ninety-one dead, 101 synagogues and 26,000 businesses destroyed. And because the Jews themselves were blamed for the violence that occurred, 26,000 of them were arrested and sent to concentration camps. And all the while the world watched and worried, but did nothing.

It was a civil war in Spain, however, that seemed to offer the promise of effective international cooperation against the march of fascism. The crisis that led to hostilities began in 1931 when city election results revealed a strong bias for Liberal, Socialist, and Republican candidates around the country, most of whom did not want a monarchy. King Alfonso XIII was distressed enough to leave the country, although he did not formally abdicate. This was followed by parliamentary elections, which gave the Republicans a large majority in the *Cortez* (parliament). After a new liberal constitution was ratified in December, a series of laws was passed that favored the trade unions, workers, and farm laborers at the expense of the privileged classes. The power of the Catholic Church was also severely restricted.

These changes so infuriated conservatives that they formed the Spanish Confederation of Autonomous Rightist Parties and became known as the Nationalists. Amid the increasing political tension, violence broke out in various places around the country. In the spring of 1936, new parliamentary elections were called for. The various Republican groups, having now formed a Popular Front against the Nationalists, won but a slim victory in the *Cortez*. Thus, with the country roughly evenly divided, army units supporting the Nationalists staged revolts all across the country. The Republicans put a mostly volunteer army in the field to defend their regime. Spain was soon embroiled in a full-scale civil war.

Despite the loss of the country's professional army, the Republicans still had some important advantages. They retained control of the navy and they were supported by thousands of idealistic liberal activists, mostly from Europe and America. Many of these men and women came to Spain fully prepared to fight and die for the Republican cause. Too, the Nationalists' most potent military force, the Army of Africa, under the command of General Francisco Franco, was stranded in the Spanish colony of Morocco. But this was quickly resolved when Hitler and Mussolini responded to the Nationalists' request for aid. To this end, they ordered an airlift to fly the Spanish troops to Seville. They also pledged material military support for as long as necessary. This aid by itself was not immediately decisive, but over the next two years it allowed Franco to keep his army unified, well-equipped, and in the field.

Stalin's initial response to the Spanish civil war was one of caution; the USSR had no need to involve itself in a struggle so far from its borders. Things changed when it became clear that the fascist governments of Germany and Italy were aggressively aiding the Nationalists. His primary purpose was to enhance Soviet prestige as the world's first socialist country leading the fight against fascism, although he also hoped the pro–Soviet Spanish Communists would come to dominate republican government. To this end he authorized a covert program of military assistance to defeat Franco and his minions. This consisted of 638 planes, 347 tanks, 1186 cannon, 20,000 machine guns, and nearly 500,000 rifles. Also included were some 3000 soldiers, fliers, tank drivers, and military advisors, of which 158 died between October 1936 and November 1938. Delivering this aid became a rather tricky operation. Stalin did not want to seem too aggressive in supporting the Republicans lest he antagonize public opinion in the West. In a future war against Nazi Germany, Stalin hoped that the British and French would be inclined to side with the USSR. To avoid violating the principal of non-intervention, which was being urged by France and Britain, it arranged that the aid would be paid for in gold by the Spanish National Bank. Since the Republican government in Spain was recognized as legitimate, it was perfectly legal for the USSR to sell it arms. Thus, as was so often the case, Stalin managed to have it both ways. Not only was he able to support the side he wanted, he got reimbursed.[1]

But within the Republican's Popular Front government, there were also problems. The Spanish Communist Party, which was heavily dependent on Soviet aid, was generally inclined to accept Moscow's lead in prosecuting the war. But there were two other leftist groups that sought to impose their own policies. These were the Anarchists and a Trotskyite group called the Partido Obrero de Unificacion Marxista or POUM.[2] These groups accepted the military aid but resisted Moscow's interference on other matters. Stalin's larger concern, however, was that the Anarchists and POUM would unite and promote a Trotskyite agenda in opposition to Moscow's objectives. Seeking to squash this possibility, Stalin sent agents to goad the Anarchists and POUM into trying to overthrow the Republican government in Catalonia, an area known for its radical politics. His plan worked to perfection. The revolt was quickly suppressed, POUM was outlawed, and the Anarchists were ousted from the Popular Front. Thus the position of the more moderate Spanish Communists within the government was enhanced and Soviet influence increased.

But these machinations did little to improve the Republicans' conduct of the war. In fact, by mid-summer 1937, there were unmistakable signs that theirs was a lost cause. The fascist powers were committed to victory, while France and Britain were calling for non-intervention. In any case, Stalin by now was occupied with domestic concerns that were far more compelling: namely the purge of the Soviet Army's high command as "enemies of the people." In June 1937, six of the country's highest-ranking and most decorated generals were put on trial and convicted of treason. They were: Marshall Mikhail Tukhachevsky, Deputy People's Commissar of Defense; I.E. Yakir, Commander of the Kiev Military District; I.P. Uborevich, Commander of the Byelorussian Military District; R. P. Eideman, Head of Osoaviakim (the civil defense organization); Avgust Kork, Head of the Military Academy; Votovt Putna, former Military Attaché in London; Boris Feldman, Head of the Red Army Administration; and Vitaly Primakov, First Deputy Commander of the Leningrad Military District. A seventh traitor/conspirator, Yan Gamarnik, who had been Head of the Political Administration of the Red Army and First Deputy Commissar of Defense, had committed suicide two weeks earlier.

Almost no one had seen this coming. The victims were the very cream of the Red Army's officer corps. Tukhachevsky, in particular, had a reputation as a brilliant and innovative military thinker with an unmatched record of service. He had fought in the imperial army during World War I and was decorated many times for valor. In 1917, he escaped from German captivity to join the Bolsheviks and became a rising star in the Red Army during the civil war. In 1920, he organized the attack on Poland and the following year suppressed the sailors' mutiny at Kronstadt and a peasant rebellion in the Tambov region. But none of this proved to be in Tukhachevsky's favor, in part because of a grudge that Stalin bore him going back to April 1920. The general was at that time leading an attack on Warsaw. He had been expecting reinforcements from Stalin, who was commanding a force to the southeast. The future General Secretary, however, disobeyed orders to support Tukhachevsky and attacked the city of Lvov instead. It occurred to some that the Red Army was repelled at Warsaw because Stalin had selfishly tried to gain an unnecessary victory at Lvov to enhance his own prestige.[3]

Stalin's decision to purge the army in 1937 is mystifying, especially when one considers his well-founded concern about the inevitability of a war with Germany. It makes some sense, however, when seen against the backdrop of the General Secretary's worsening paranoia and his growing awareness that the army's high command had both the power and the motive to destroy him if it so desired. Still, he was in a strong position; he had already eliminated almost everyone in the Party who had ever opposed him or might in the future. These included the relatives, friends, and colleagues of his purge victims, many of whom he had shot on the calculation that they might one day seek revenge. But Stalin could not let it rest. These were the very officers who had emerged victorious in the Russian civil war and who remembered his relative insignificance during that period. Probably they sneered at the cult that he had created for himself and were waiting for an opportunity to strike. Because Tukhachevsky was suspected to be one of these, his fate was sealed. The general was arrested on May 26 after being transferred to Kuibyshev on the Volga to assume a new command. He was taken into custody after giving a short speech to the District Military Command and promptly returned to Moscow. At the Lubyanka, Yezhev himself conducted the interrogation, during which the general was tortured by NKVD thugs. Within days Tukhachevsky had been made to confess that he was a German agent and that he was part of Bukharin's conspiracy. According to Robert Conquest, the general had been beaten so viciously that some of the documents that recorded his testimony were splattered with blood. On June 11, Tukhachevsky and five other generals were executed.[4]

The aftermath of this travesty was sadly predictable. Tukhachevsky's mother, wife, sister, and two brothers were shot. Three of his sisters were sent to concentration camps. His young daughter, who was eleven at the time of her father's arrest, was originally spared but not forgotten. Five years later she was sent to a camp for children for the socially dangerous. Tukhachevsky also had two former wives, both of whom were sent to a labor camp with a special section for wives and mistresses. General Yakir's wife and brother were shot, as were a number of other relatives. General Uborevich's wife was arrested and died in jail in 1941. His daughter was sent to a children's home that was run by the NKVD. The wives of General Kork and Gamarnik were also shot.[5]

Having destroyed many of the country's most gifted and respected military minds and their families, Stalin now turned to Spain. Fearing that the Trotskyite virus might have infected the Soviet advisors working to support the Republicans, Stalin had most of them recalled. Once home they were arrested and in most cases tried, usually for treason and often for other crimes as well. Most were sent to the camps or shot. This included even the Soviet ambassador, Marsel Rozenberg, and the Counsel General in Barcelona, Vladimir Antonov-Ovseenko. The latter was a particularly revered personage in Soviet folklore. This was the same Antonov-Ovseenko who had led a squad of soldiers into the Winter Palace to arrest the ministers of the Provisional Government on October 26, 1917.[6]

But even more inexplicable was Stalin's apparent determination to exterminate younger soldiers, many of whom were not only loyal, but also talented and highly resourceful. One of these was Vladimir Gorev, a military intelligence officer whose heroic exploits helped the Republicans win the Battle of Madrid. Long before he went to Spain, he was an active soldier in the fight for Communism around the world. In the 1920s he served as a military organizer in Germany and later a Soviet military adviser in China. Between 1930 and 1933 he resided illegally in the United States and was among the first to extract

VII. *The Military, Foreign Communists and Repatriated POWs*   155

General Mikhail Tukhachevsky (center of front row, looking left), Marshal of the Soviet Union and Commander in Chief of the Red Army, and other army officers pose in front of Lenin's tomb, 1934. Tukhachevsky was widely thought to be the Soviet Union's most gifted army commander. He was denounced as an enemy of the people in 1937 and executed. Photographer unknown (courtesy Russian State Archives of Film and Photo Documents, Krasnogorsk).

vital information from Whittaker Chambers, who confessed to having been a spy for the USSR. In the fall of 1937, Gorev returned to the Soviet Union to a hero's welcome. He was promoted to the rank of division commander and awarded both the Order of Lenin and the Red Banner Order. But Gorev's days were numbered. Probably it was thought that he had worked too long among Trotskyites in Spain and had been corrupted by their ideological heresy. In any case, he was arrested in January 1938, tried before a military court, found guilty of treason, and shot.

Hero or not, Gorev's execution was not even noted, let alone mourned. He was but one of the many thousands of the best and brightest who perished in the purge. Six months earlier, in the ten days following the Tukhachevsky executions, some 980 officers had been executed. These included corps and division commanders, various specialists, and most of the faculty at the Kremlin Military School and the Frunze Military Academy. One particular instructor, General I.I. Vasetsis, was actually arrested during a class break. When the students returned to their seats someone announced, "Comrades! The lecture will not continue. Lecturer Vatsetis has been arrested as an "enemy of the people." Soon the NKVD began arresting students who had been sent to the academy from units whose commander had been declared an "enemy of the people."[7] Equally absurd was the arrest of a group of Soviet engineers who had been preparing camouflaged guerrilla warfare bases in the event of an enemy attack. They were accused of "lack of faith in the Socialist state" and of training bandits and storing arms for a potential invader. Inexplicably, the NKVD had these bases destroyed only to have to rebuild them in 1941, when the Germans broke through Soviet defenses and penetrated the interior.

As devastating as the initial assault on the army had been in 1937, Stalin made it worse the following year with an even grander display of bloodshed. One of the first to fall was a corps commander named Ivan Belov, who had had acted as one of the judges for the Tukhashevsky trial. Courageously or perhaps foolishly, he had tried to intercede for a fellow corps commander named Serdich. This was considered a criminal offense for which he was eventually shot. Another important officer and battlefield commander to fall was Vasily Bliukher, a hero of the civil war and the first recipient of the Order of the Red Banner in 1918. In 1924, he was sent to China as an adviser first to Dr. Sun Yat-sen and later Chiang Kai-shek. In 1929, he became commander of the Special Far Eastern Army and won great honor for his defense of the Chinese Eastern Railway when it was attacked by Manchurian forces trying to oust Soviet railway and consular officials. Indeed, Bliukher's masterful command of the Soviet Far East seemed to have made him the indispensible man. In 1931, he was awarded the Order of Lenin, and in 1935 he was made a Marshal of the Soviet Union. His final service to his country was to repulse a major Japanese assault on Lake Khasen in the summer of 1938, which involved airpower, tanks, and thousands of troops. In August, Bliukher was recalled to Moscow and harshly reprimanded by Voroshilov. On October 22, he and his entire family were arrested. Three weeks later, Bliukher died in the Lefortovo Prison in Moscow while being interrogated.

Nor did Stalin spare the navy, which, although smaller, suffered proportionately as much as the army. Again, Stalin's reasoning is difficult to divine. With war on the horizon, the General Secretary had wanted to enlarge the fleet and make it competitive with those of Britain and Germany. At the same time, however, he decided that since Soviet warships often put in at foreign ports, it was likely that the crews had been ideologically contaminated. To rid the navy of the same poison that had infected the army and other parts of

VII. The Military, Foreign Communists and Repatriated POWs

society, he turned on R.A. Muklevich, a veteran of the civil war, commander of the Soviet Navy and more recently the Director of Naval Construction. In this capacity he had worked with German naval officers in the late 1920s, when the Weimar Republic and the Soviet Union were cooperating in order to improve their military potential. Muklevich's expertise and competence in this endeavor were highly regarded, but the General Secretary suspected him of being a foreign agent. Thus he was arrested in May 1937 and taken to the Lefortovo Prison, where he died under torture in February of the following year.

More "enemies of the people" were soon to be uncovered among the navy's most accomplished and experienced officers. Vladimir Orlov, like Muklevich, had once served as commander of the Soviet Navy and was then promoted to deputy minister of defense in 1937. He was arrested not long after assuming his position on July 10, 1937, and shot one year later. His successor, Mikhail Viktorov, seemed to be a perfect fit for the job. He had graduated with honors from the Imperial Naval Academy in 1913 and had won the gold medal as first in his class. He served in the Baltic Fleet during World War I and joined the Bolsheviks during the civil war. He subsequently commanded the Baltic Fleet and later became the founding commander of the Soviet Pacific Fleet. Viktorov was appointed commander of the Soviet Navy in August 1937. He lasted only five months before being arrested for unspecified reasons. He was executed in 1939. His successor, Piotr Smirnov, had worked as a smith in a lumber factory before joining the Bolsheviks in 1917. He had fought in the civil war, and had helped to suppress the Kronstadt rebellion in 1921. He had joined the political directorate of the armed forces and had been helping to carry out the purge of the high-ranking military elite. In 1937 he became deputy minister of defense and, finally, commander of the Soviet Navy in December. Six months later he was arrested on unspecified charges and executed in February 1939.

Thus did Stalin's assault on the military continued even as the shadow of war grew ever more menacing on the horizon. In March 1938, German troops marched into Austria, annexing it to the Reich. In September, Hitler met with Britain's Prime Minister Chamberlain and France's President Daladier and bluffed them into allowing him to annex the Sudetenland in Czechoslovakia, which was then inhabited by a German-speaking majority. He promised that this was the "last territorial claim he had to make in Europe," but within six months German troops had occupied the rest of the country. Stalin saw in this a western plot to appease the Führer in order to tempt him to attack the Soviet Union. To counter this threat, the General Secretary began to consider negotiating a deal with Germany. In August 1939, a ten-year nonaggression pact was concluded between the two powers. In a secret clause, Poland and much of Eastern Europe was divided up between them.

The logic of Stalin's decision to come to terms with Hitler becomes even more compelling considering his increasing discontent with Comintern, which the Bolsheviks had created in 1919. Its purpose was to promote anti-capitalist revolutions around the world so that communism could be established without fear from reactionary forces. For a while, the Comintern enjoyed great prestige in socialist circles and was promoted as the "General Staff of the World Revolution." But time passed and not a single revolution occurred. By the mid-1920s, it was clear that the great upheaval that had been so confidently predicted was not going to happen any time soon. Stalin, who had always disliked and mistrusted the cosmopolitan nature of the Comintern, began to talk of Socialism in One Country. He announced that the Soviet Union would not wait for revolutions elsewhere to create communism at home. As this idea gained support, the prestige of the Comintern declined. Increasingly, the organization became an instrument of Soviet foreign policy and was monitored carefully by Stalin's agents.

In the mid-1930s, 133 of 492 Comintern members were purged. These included communists from Western Ukraine, Latvia, Estonia, and Lithuania. Soon, foreigners from any country living in the USSR became suspect. Several hundred Germans, having only recently moved to Russia to escape Hitler, now faced jail or execution. Among the most prominent of these was Heinz Neumann, a former member of the German Communist Party's Politburo, who was living in exile at the Hotel Lux in Moscow. On April 28, 1937, NKVD officers awakened Neumann at one o'clock in the morning to search his apartment for subversive literature. After confiscating about sixty books, they arrested Neumann and delivered him to the Lubyanka for interrogation. In the summer of the following year, he was moved to the Butyrka Prison, where he died. In the meantime, his wife was also arrested and sentenced to five years in prison as a socially dangerous element.[8] Another veteran communist who was arrested at this time was Fritz Platten, a Swiss national who had organized Lenin's return from exile in 1917. This was a feat in itself, since the trip took Lenin through Germany, Sweden, and Finland and then to St. Petersburg. Platten had also been riding with Lenin on January 1, 1918, when assassins fired shots at their car, wounding Platten as he shielded Lenin. None of this spoke in his favor in 1938 when he was arrested and sent to a prison camp near Nyandoma in the far North. He was shot in April 1944.

A foreign communist of much greater renown who also became a victim of the purge was the Hungarian Bela Kun. Born into a middle-class family of modest means, the young Kun embarked on a career of revolutionary activism rife with controversy and scandal. He joined the Hungarian Social Democratic Party at sixteen and later worked as a clerk at Kolozvar Workers' Insurance Bureau, where he was accused of having embezzled money. In the years before 1914, he was a journalist who relished controversy and left-leaning politics. Kun was also impulsive and hot-tempered and was known to fight duels with those who disagreed with him. After the outbreak of the Great War, he was drafted into the Austro-Hungarian army and was taken prisoner in 1916 by the Russians. His conversion to Communism occurred while in a prison camp in the Ural Mountains. It was the major turning point of his life.

Kun remained in Russia even after the Treaty of Brest Litovsk was signed in March of 1918. That same month he founded the Hungarian Group of the Russian Communist Party. He subsequently travelled around Russia, was introduced to Vladimir Lenin, and fought for a time with the Bolsheviks in the Russian civil war. He apparently proved himself a worthy comrade-in-arms. That November he was given a large sum of money to return to Hungary with several hundred of his countrymen to overthrow the government of Mihaly Karolyi and to found the Hungarian Communist Party. Kun was arrested on February 21, 1919, but was able to exercise his leadership even from prison. Exactly one month later, Karolyi's government fell and Kun was freed to unite his communist group with the left-wing socialists to create the Soviet Republic of Hungary. Kun's position in the new government was that of Commissar for Foreign Affairs, but his power and influence were considerable in other matters as well. He called for the nationalization of all private property. Contrary to Lenin's advice, however, he steadfastly refused to redistribute land to the peasants. This alienated Kun's rural supporters probably as much as his dogmatic political style offended others.

The conclusion of the Treaty of Versailles in June 1919 had called for a major adjustment of boundaries in central Europe. Large slices of Hungarian territory were to be distributed to Romania, Yugoslavia, and Czechoslovakia. Kun was committed to defending the country's traditional boundaries, and his small Red Army won some impressive victories early on. But the effort could not be sustained, and the hoped for help from Russian forces never materialized. As the Soviet republic's prospects declined, the Social Democrats attempted but failed to overthrow the government on June 24. Kun responded by calling for a reign of terror in which the secret police executed nearly 600 people, many of whom were scientists and intellectuals. So wanton was the savagery that many of Kun's most devoted supporters were repelled. Then, in late July 1919, Hungary was invaded by Romanian troops. The Hungarian Soviet Republic collapsed, and Kun fled to Austria, where he was captured by anti-communist forces. The following year he was sent to Russia in exchange for some Austrian prisoners of war being held by the Bolsheviks.

Kun's reputation for brutality made him welcome in the new Soviet state. He joined the Communist Party and was assigned to head the regional Revolutionary Committee in the Crimea. Once again Kun gained notoriety when he was alleged to have ordered the murder not only of anti–Bolshevik ethnic minorities, but also many thousands of White Army prisoners. The latter had been promised their lives if they surrendered. Kun was later assigned to the Comintern, where he became an ally of Grigori Zinoviev. One of his first tasks was to go to Berlin to incite German communists to rise in support of miners in central Germany, who were agitating against low pay and poor working conditions. This was the beginning of the Märzaktion or March Action, which ultimately was suppressed with overwhelming force by the Weimar government. Kun's reputation as a revolutionist suffered as a result of this disaster, although he remained in Western Europe until his arrest in Austria while traveling with a forged passport. He returned to Moscow in 1928 and continued to be active in the Comintern, but he was no longer a rising star in the Party.

In May 1937, Kun attended a meeting of the executive committee of the Comintern, where he was accused of having insulted Stalin and of having contacts with the Romanian Secret Police. Kun was shocked, swore his innocence, and begged to be allowed to talk to Comrade Stalin and defend himself. Moments later the NKVD escorted him out of the hall, but he was not yet under arrest. In fact, days later, Stalin called him as if nothing had happened and asked him to meet with a French journalist to prove that he had not been arrested. Kun was happy to comply, but not long after giving the interview, he was arrested and taken to the Lefortovo prison. He was brutally tortured and accused of being an agent for Germany and Great Britain. He was executed on August 29, 1938. As usual, the relatives of the condemned were punished as well. These included his wife, daughter, and son-in-law, all of whom were sent to the Gulag.[9]

If Kun was never formally proclaimed an "enemy of the people," he most surely was treated as one. This was what baffled so many dedicated foreign communists who were ready and eager to promote Soviet policies. Wladislaw

Gomulka once lamented that the NKVD "could extend the category of 'enemy of the people' to everyone who dared to utter a word of criticism." But Kun seems not even to have done that. Indeed, he was like all other foreign communists whose lives depended upon Soviet hospitality and protection. Such people were likely to be very discreet about what they said or did in such a dangerous atmosphere. And yet, Stalin continued to abuse and persecute them, including many of his most ardent supporters. The logic in this resembles that of Stalin's domestic terror: if anyone could be an agent for the opposition, then terror was most effective if those who were arrested were completely innocent. One such individual, a member of the German Politburo named Hermann Schubert, was arrested in July 1937 for allegedly having compared Lenin's 1917 deal with the Germans with Trotsky's fictitious relationship with the Nazis in the 1930s. Another victim was Hugo Eberlein, who had been present at the founding of the Comintern in 1919. Typically, he was arrested for no apparent reason, interrogated, and tortured in the Lefortovo prison. He was sentenced to twenty-five years in the Gulag in the far north. Eventually, he was shot while being moved from one camp to another because he was too ill to travel.

The terror and the purge continued for another year. By the end of 1938, however, the arrests and executions were on the decline. There is no clear explanation of why this happened when it did, but it is likely that Stalin had begun to fret about the country's declining rate of industrial growth, which was surely tied to attrition at the workplace. Then, too, the international situation was becoming increasingly tense. In midsummer 1938, the Japanese encroached on Soviet territory in the Far East near Lake Khasan, which provoked some sharp fighting. The situation was not resolved until August of the following year, when General Zhukov, using tanks, got the better of a large Japanese force. In the meantime, Stalin watched with concern the German annexations of Austria and the Czech Sudetenland in 1938. He was particularly disgusted with the craven behavior of Prime Minister Chamberlain and President Daladier at the Munich Conference in November. When the Germans occupied the remainder of Czechoslovakia in March 1939, the General Secretary became convinced that a major war was inevitable. Since it was clear that the West could not be relied on, Stalin began to consider a deal with Hitler.

On August 23, 1939, the Nazi-Soviet Non-Aggression Pact was signed between two supposedly irreconcilable enemies. The treaty came as a nasty shock to most of the world, even though the published text of the agreement was decidedly less sinister than it was feared. The Soviets would be able to buy German machinery and the Germans would be allowed to buy Soviet coal and oil. The rub, however, was in the secret part of the treaty, which gave the Nazis a free hand to attack Poland and occupy Lithuania. In return, the Soviets were assigned Finland, Estonia, and Latvia as their sphere of influence. Those most immediately concerned were some 570 German communists who had been previously arrested and were now languishing in Soviet prisons. These were the same German communists who had fought the Nazis in the streets in the 1930s and who had escaped to the USSR after the Reichstag fire in March 1933. Most of these were now to be expelled as undesirable aliens and handed over to the Germans. Many were Jews who had gone to the Soviet Union six years earlier to escape Hitler's reach.

When the Germans invaded Poland in September 1939, the Soviets were quick to exploit their part of the agreement by occupying the territory they had lost to the Poles after the Revolution. Soviet troops were accompanied by a large contingent of NKVD personnel, who arrested some 22,000 Polish army officers. All were executed the following spring in the Katyn Forest. On November 30, the Soviets declared war on the Finns, claiming that they had bombarded Soviet territory. In fact, the Finns had merely refused to sign a mutual assistance treaty that would have allowed the Red Army to build military bases on Finnish soil. In any case, the Soviets responded by bombing Helsinki and invading the country, although the ensuing war did not go as expected. The Finns defended themselves furiously, and the Red Army lost some 200,000 men after only three months of combat. But the Finns had limited resources and ultimately had to sue for peace. In March the Soviets gained some territory just north of Leningrad. They were also roundly condemned by the international community for their naked aggression and expelled from the League of Nations. The Finns, on the other hand, preserved their independence and won the admiration of much of the world.

If Stalin was infuriated by the failure of the Red Army to overwhelm Finland, he was ultimately to have his way with Estonia, Latvia, and Lithuania. He imposed his will on these pro–Soviet governments and had them "request" incorporation into the USSR. In July, Stalin seized Bessarabia and northern Bukovina from Romania, which paved the way for the creation of a Moldavian Soviet Socialist Republic. He also renewed his hunt for foreign "enemies of the people" in the new territories by arresting their more prominent citizens as "anti-Soviet elements." Most were shot or sent to the Gulag. In time, the dragnet was expanded to include schoolteachers, independent farmers, and petty traders. Many of these were relocated to "special settlements" in Russia and Kazakhstan. All this was accompanied by a flurry of nationalizations of banks, factories, mines, and estates. A single-party communist dictatorship became the law of the land in all of the affected republics.

Despite the Finnish debacle, by the early months of 1941 Stalin had reason to be sanguine about the overall situation. After the German invasion of Poland, Britain and France promptly declared war, and the General Secretary had imagined that this would lead to a protracted conflict that would occupy the Germans for some time. But the Wehrmacht proved to be far more potent than he expected. In April 1940, the Germans conquered Denmark and Norway, and in May France, Belgium, and Holland. Within six weeks, Hitler could boast of a complete victory over all opponents except for Great Britain. They, having committed their Expeditionary Force to aid the French, were determined to carry on the fight no matter what. Thus the Germans occupied the areas of France of the greatest military importance and established a puppet government at Vichy in the South. Beginning in July, Hitler unleashed the Luftwaffe to destroy British air power and coastal defenses. He had hoped to prepare the way for an amphibious invasion, but the Germans were unable to gain control of the air. This was in large part due to the fact that, unbeknownst to the Nazi high command, the British had radar. Thus the Royal Air Force was able to bring superior force against the invaders and to protect the country's most important military targets.

Fatefully, Hitler now turned his attention to the East and began to plan his most ambitious campaign of all. In this, Stalin himself, who refused to believe the mounting evidence that a Nazi attack was imminent, ably assisted him. Thus did Operation Barbarossa, which began on June 22, 1941, completely overwhelm the unsuspecting Soviet defenses. The invading force, which consisted of 175 divisions and more than three million men, drove deep into the interior across a wide front. So shocked was Stalin by Hitler's treachery that he lapsed into a near-catatonic state for ten days. It was left to Molotov to announce to the nation by radio that the country was at war. Meanwhile the country's defenders, lacking any clear instructions, crumbled. Most of the blame for this disaster fell to a Western Front Commander named General Dmitri Pavlov, who was promptly arrested and shot. Little did it matter that it was Stalin who had completely misjudged the situation from the beginning; that it was he who had insisted that it was a Wehrmacht conspiracy against Hitler and that no counter-measures should be taken. Virtually none were, and the Red Air Force in the early days of the invasion lost 1,000 planes, most of which had been left in forward positions and were destroyed on the ground. When the capital of Belorussia, Minsk, fell on June 29, some 400,000 Soviet troops were taken captive. Smolensk was captured two weeks later. On July 21, German bombers began attacking Moscow. Leningrad was completely blockaded by September 8, and Kiev taken September 19.

The German juggernaut was finally halted some twenty miles outside Moscow early in December. But unlike Napoleon 129 years earlier, Hitler refused to withdraw his army despite the onset of the brutal Russian winter. This enabled him the following spring to resume the offensive, bypassing Moscow and sending the Wehrmacht south to gain control of the oil-rich areas of the North and South Caucasus. At this point, the Germans seemed to be in an exceptionally strong position. They had regained the momentum and occupied Ukraine, Belorussia, and the Baltic States, whose populations were decidedly hostile to Soviet rule. Indeed, some of these peoples had actually received the Germans as liberators and were prepared to cooperate to defeat the Soviet Union. But Hitler spurned the collaboration of those he deemed racially inferior. He promptly ordered them enslaved and their homelands plundered and exploited for the maximum economic benefit of the Reich.

But by the beginning of 1942, Stalin had recovered and was fully restored to his old despotic self. He had long fancied himself a military strategist and was increasingly inclined to meddle in the running of the war. On July 28, he issued Order No. 227, in which he threatened the death penalty for any unauthorized retreat, even for tactical reasons. For professional soldiers who needed to adjust to and improvise with real battlefield conditions, this was not such a welcome thing. Moreover, this order was followed by another order, No. 270, in which Soviet soldiers were required in every instance to fight to the death rather than surrender. To be sure, there was nothing new about such draconian measures for the Red Army. Trotsky had been equally severe with his soldiers during the civil war and had not been shy about resorting to summary justice. But for many members of the high command, it was difficult to forget that just three years earlier the purge had devoured some 40,000 of the country's best military officers. Most had been labeled "enemies of the people" with no supporting evidence. Many in the Red Army had to wonder: Hadn't this helped the Germans? Was there really a need to kill more of our own men? For Stalin, however, such questions were moot. Had he been forced to justify himself, he might have argued that the purge, with some exceptions, had eliminated only those who were predisposed to betray the motherland. In the present situation, with the enemy occupying Soviet territory, he was not punishing any soldiers for what they might do, but only for what they did or failed to do.

Probably the most infamous of these "exceptions" was Andrei Andreevich Vlasov, who was one of Stalin's favorite generals. The youngest of eight children, he was born into a humble peasant family near Nizhnii Novgorod. Like Stalin, he had once studied for the priesthood, but abandoned his studies to join the Bolsheviks. He served with such distinction during the civil war that he was encouraged to make the army his career. Vlasov's service was judged to be stellar by nearly everyone, and he was promoted again and again. In 1930, he joined the Communist Party, even though he had serious reservations. He had long been embittered by the Bolsheviks' murder of his brother in 1919 for his alleged involvement in an anti–Bolshevik plot. Nor could he accept the war against the kulaks, which had victimized his own parents. But Party membership made sense for a man like Vlasic, who was determined to achieve great things in the military. He had particularly impressed his superiors in his capacity as a training officer and was promoted to the position of Chief of Staff of the 72nd Division near Leningrad. Later, he was sent to China to be a military advisor to Chiang Kai-shek. The outbreak of war in 1941 found the highly decorated Brigadier General Vlasov (he had been awarded the Order of Lenin in February) in command of the Fourth Mechanized Corps, Sixth Army, at Lvov. His able defense of the city during the German surprise attack won him still more respect in what was the first major tank battle of World War II. Still, Vlasov's troops could not hold out against such an overwhelming force, although he did manage to rescue much of the Fourth Corps by fighting his way out of the Wehrmacht's many attempts to surround and annihilate them.

Vlasov's next assignment was to command of the 37th Army defending Kiev, which was even more demanding than his previous post. Once again his competence and daring stood out even though the Germans captured the city on September 19. That Vlasov's army was able to survive was due to his leadership and tenacity in breaking through the German lines to the east. It should also be noted that the general helped the defenders gain a measure of revenge when he ordered the NKVD to plant some 10,000 mines around the city. On September 24, after the Germans had settled into their occupation, wireless detonators were used to set off the mines. In the explosions that followed, huge buildings collapsed and fire raged in the city for five days. More than 1,000 German soldiers perished. The Nazis, however, exacted a cruel retribution for this counterpunch. On September 29–30, SS Einsatzgruppen massacred

33,771 Kievan Jews at Babi Yar in what was the largest single massacre of the Holocaust.

The hero of Kiev underwent a brief hospitalization for some minor injuries before being summoned to Moscow. He attended a meeting in the Kremlin along with several other generals to consult with Stalin about the military crisis at hand. When Stalin asked Vlasov to express an opinion about the feasibility of defending the capital, the general bluntly proposed a counterattack as the most likely route to success. This was apparently exactly what Stalin wanted to hear. He promoted Vlasov to the rank of major general and put him in command of the newly forming 20th Army. On December 5, Vlasov's troops broke through the German position to the west and recaptured the town of Solnechnogorsk, which seriously disrupted the enemy's advance. This won time for the arrival of reinforcements from Siberia, which ultimately saved Moscow.

Vlasov, now a lieutenant general, had reached the pinnacle of his success. In March, he was urged by Stalin personally to take over command of the Second Shock Army that had been assigned the task of relieving Leningrad, which was still trapped by the German blockade. But the Soviets were bogged down in the swampy terrain west of the Volkhov River and north of Novgorod and were on the defensive against a superior German force. By the time Vlasov arrived, he could see that the situation was hopeless. He urged Stalin to allow his force to retreat through a mile-wide corridor in order to regroup, but the General Secretary flatly refused and ordered him to fight on. In desperation,

General Andrei Andreevich Vlasov was one of Stalin's favorite generals until he and his men were taken prisoner by the Germans. This fact made them all traitors and subject to execution should they ever return to the USSR. From the book *Moscow, November 1941*. Photographer unknown (courtesy Memorial International Photo Archives).

Vlasov returned to Moscow to present his case to Stalin in person, but to no avail. Thus resigned, the general returned to his men fully prepared to share their suffering and ultimate fate.

The later famous writer and dissident Alexander Isaeevich Solzhenitsyn, who was also serving in the army at this time, took a special interest in the fate of General Vlasov and his men. After his own arrest in February of 1945, for having written critical remarks about Stalin in a private letter, Solzhenitsyn became acquainted with some of the survivors of the Second Shock Army who were being held in the Butyrka Prison. In the first volume of his *Gulag Archipelago*, he described the plight of Vlasov's men, how they "endured starvation and extermination and how they had cut off the hoofs of the dead and rotting horses and boiled the scrapings and eaten them."[10] Only after their situation had become hopeless did Stalin relent and send some reinforcements. In the desperate fighting that took place from June 10–17, the relief force finally did break through and reach Vlasov's men, only to find that it was too late. The escape corridor was nearly closed as German bombers and artillery steadily reduced the ranks of the defenders. Although some men did escape, the general was not among them. Somehow, he eluded the enemy for about three weeks wandering around the swampy and heavily forested area before the Wehrmacht captured him on July 24.

Vlasov was, for the most part, well treated in German captivity, but he was understandably distraught because of his predicament. Having failed to defeat the Germans on the Volkhov front, he had allowed himself to be taken alive by the Germans. He was now an "enemy of the people" and as such could expect to be treated like a criminal were he ever to return to Soviet Union. However, he was not alone. There were about eighty or one hundred other "special" prisoners whom the Germans housed and fed reasonably well. One of them was a Colonel Vladimir Boyarsky, who encouraged Vlasov to co-write a letter with him to the German higher-ups about the possibility of allowing those Soviet officers who were opposed to Stalin and communism to form a Russian National Army to fight the Red Army.

At this time, Vlasov also became acquainted with a number of officers in the Wehrmacht. Among them was a certain Captain Wilfried Strik-Strikfeldt, a Baltic German who spoke fluent Russian. Strik-Strikfeldt had lived and been educated among Russians. He had actually served in the Russian army during World War I. He was apparently quite sincere in his desire that Russians who opposed communism and Stalin should be treated humanely and certainly not as *Untermenschen* (i.e., subhumans). Furthermore, he was convinced that it would be to Germany's advantage to accept them as allies at war with the same enemy. It should be emphasized, however, that Strik-Strikfeld did not have official permission from anyone in authority to promote this idea. Still, he encouraged Vlasov to become the leader in a movement to fight against the Soviet regime. He also urged the general to come up with a program to create a new Russian state after the war. Since Germany seemed likely to win the war, the general agreed to commit himself to these objectives. The Smolensk Declaration of December 1942 was dropped in leaflets both in areas controlled by the Germans and areas controlled by the Soviets. In it the general declared "Bolshevism to be the enemy of the Russian people" and called for the creation of a Russian Liberation Army. Vlasov promised that once Stalin and the Communists were defeated, forced labor and collective farms would be abolished and the land transferred to the peasants.[11]

Vlasov's declaration drew an enthusiastic response, and many began to wear special badges on their uniforms or clothing to indicate their support of the proposed army. During the spring of 1943, Vlasov went on a tour of the occupied areas and published an open letter to further promote his idea. At this point, Hitler ordered him stopped and placed under house arrest. The Führer was not interested in a free and sovereign Russian state after the war and had no intentions of supporting any anti–Stalinist movement among the Soviet people. Nevertheless, the idea did not die. In September 1943, Vlasov met with, of all people, Heinrich Himmler at Dabendorf just outside Berlin. Himmler loathed all things Slavic nearly as much as Hitler. Apparently, however, he was intrigued by the general and saw in him a valuable propaganda tool. He urged him to form the Committee for the Liberation of the Peoples of Russia and the Russian Liberation Army to fight actively against the Soviets. Two months later, a manifesto to this effect was published in Prague, although, to Vlasov's acute frustration, Soviet soldiers who had already joined the Wehrmacht before the general's arrival were not allowed to transfer to the new army.

But things did not develop as Vlasov had hoped, and he soon found that he was the commander of a largely phantom army with no military objective other than the dissemination of propaganda. He lacked the authority to make any decisions or to undertake any initiatives, military or otherwise. Still, he continued to hope that if he cooperated fully with the Germans, they would eventually come to trust him enough to take his men into battle. To this end, he made speeches that were broadcast to Soviet troops at the front encouraging them to desert, although the content of message offended many of his German supporters and especially Himmler. In fact, General Vlasov was a proud and unapologetic Russian patriot, who declared again and again that Russia had never been and would never be a colony of any country, and that "Russia can be defeated only by Russia,"[12] He also reminded his listeners that it was the Russian army that had come to the aid of the German people during the wars against Napoleon. Such candor was well received among ordinary soldiers, and for a time the number of Soviet desertions rose dramatically. But by early 1943, the tide of war had turned. The Red Army's annihilation of the German Sixth Army at Stalingrad was utterly decisive. Soon the soldiers of the Russian Liberation Army began to defect in large numbers to Soviet partisans. Thus in September 1943, Hitler ordered Vlasov's soldiers removed from the Eastern Front.

Ironically, at the same time, and with Nazi troops occupying vast areas of the USSR, Stalin was planning to forcibly remove entire populations far from their ancestral homelands and send them far to the East. In 1941 he had deported Volga Germans because he feared they would support Hitler and the Nazis. Early in 1943, he turned on six other groups: the Kalmyks, the Chechens, the Ingushi, the Karachai, the Balkars, and the Crimean Tatars and sent them to Central Asia and Siberia, where they would inhabit special settlements run by the NKVD. These were small populations that had been traditionally troublesome for both the tsars and the Soviets. In this instance, Stalin believed that they had either supported the Germans or failed to adequately resist their aggression. The number involved in these deportations was about two million. Conquest estimates that one-third died during the trip or not long after arrival.[13] The significance of this operation was not merely that it expanded the "enemy of the people" concept to include ethnicity. Indeed, the victims of this policy were being punished only because they were small nationalities that had no great allegiance to the USSR and no enthusiasm for communism. But the fact that it was conducted during a war in which the USSR was fighting for its life says a lot about the man who thought it was necessary. He couldn't even wait until the final victory. Indeed, the manpower necessary to bring about this upheaval was staggering. Conquest estimates that in addition to the enormous burden to the country's transportation system, it required perhaps 100,000 NKVD men to oversee the operation and guard the prisoners.[14]

In the meantime, General Vlasov's role as Russian collaborator with the Wehrmacht was about to be revived. Heinrich Himmler had become increasingly desperate and fearful as he watched Germany's military situation deteriorate.

Thus he met with the general again to discuss the possibility of reinvigorating the Russian Liberation Army. He also promised to support the creation of a new Committee for the Liberation of the Peoples of Russia or KONR.[15] Vlasov was to be the chairman of the committee, which consisted of thirty-seven members. Thirteen of these were former Red Army officers, nine were Soviet professors or lecturers, seven were émigrés from the period right after the Revolution, and the rest came from other walks of life. Vlasov was also named commander of the new army and supposedly would be allowed some say in deploying his troops as he saw fit. But right from the start there was a major misunderstanding: Vlasov believed that he had permission to form ten divisions and was infuriated to learn that the Germans would allow only two. Only one of these actually became operational.

In any case, the general resolved to do his best to develop and train his Russian force so it could be utilized effectively against the Red Army. The first order of business was to unite as many soldiers as possible under his command. These included those from the Red Army who had been captured or defected early on and were now serving in the Wehrmacht or the SS. Vlasov also sought to unite two Cossack formations, one in Austria and the other in Italy, and two Ukrainian divisions, one in southern Germany and the other in Saxony. Finally, there were the Ostarbeitern or East Workers, most of whom were in their mid-teens. They had come to Germany to work those areas of Eastern Europe under German occupation.[16] In March 1945, a group of some 5,000 escaped Ostarbeitern joined the KONR 1st Division while it was marching to Nuremberg in order to board trains that would take them to Stettin on the Baltic Sea. There they were to await further orders.

As the Red Army moved inexorably closer to Berlin, a sense of anxiety settled over Vlasov's whole enterprise. Most knew the war was already lost and started to think ahead about how they could avoid being forcibly repatriated. Since they were currently fighting on the side of the Nazis, the Vlasovites knew well that Americans and the British would treat them as enemies. But it was also known that there were serious disagreements between the Soviets and their Western allies. It seemed reasonable to hope that the latter would want to help those who opposed Stalin and communism. The trick was to contact the Allies before the end of the war and *before* it was too late. Various plans were suggested for how best to do this. General Zhilenkov headed the department for KONR propaganda but seemed to think it was unnecessary. One of the older émigrés, Yuri Sergeevich Zherebkov, who had been living in France, showed more initiative. He had already contributed to an émigré journal

VII. The Military, Foreign Communists and Repatriated POWs

in Paris to tout Vlasov's patriotic activism. He also thought of engaging neutral counties, including Switzerland, by writing a series of articles about the Russian Liberation Movement. There was even talk of contacting the International Committee of the International Red Cross to protect Russians who served in the Wehrmacht and were now being held by the Allies. But all this came to nothing as the end approached.

The KONR 1st Division under the command of Major General Sergei Kuzmich Bunyachenkov (who had been appointed by Vlasov) fought only one time. That was on April 13, 1945, at Ehrenhof on the west bank of the Oder River. The Germans had ordered Bunyachenkov (without informing Vlasov) to destroy a Soviet bridgehead. The attack failed, and Bunyachenko's men retreated south against German orders, heading toward Prague. On May 2, some Czech army officers met them some fifty kilometers from the city and urged the general to help them in their rebellion against the Germans, which was planned for May 5. The general hesitated but eventually agreed. This was the last Slavic city still under Nazi control, and both Vlasov and Bunyashenko expected that the Americans would liberate the Czech capital. In this way, the 1st Division could prove its loyalty to the Allied cause and its fundamental opposition to Nazism. On May 6, Bunyachenko's 18,000 men changed sides and joined the uprising. They disarmed some 10,000 German soldiers, only to learn that the Red Army would be liberating the city. The Czechs, who had previously been so welcoming, now heaped scorn on the "Vlasov Traitors" for their self-serving conversion.

On May 9, 1945, General Vlasov was taken into custody by the Americans at Schlusselberg, Czechoslovakia. Three days later they set out to drive their prisoner to their regimental headquarters in Pilsen. The convoy had not traveled very far before being stopped at a Red Army checkpoint, which had been on the lookout for Vlasov. A Soviet officer came forward armed with a machine gun and demanded that the turncoat general be handed over to him. The Americans acquiesced, despite the fact that they had superior force at their disposal, including two tanks. Nor did Vlasov resist. Indeed, he is said to have opened his coat and shouted "fire" to his Red Army captor, who would not oblige him. Clearly, the Soviets wanted the general to suffer as much as possible for his treachery. Vlasov was first taken to Dresden and then to Moscow, where he and ten members of his staff would spend the next fourteen months as prisoners waiting for their day in court.

The trial that began on July 30, 1946, bore little resemblance to the show trials of a decade earlier. This one was a strictly private affair. It is true that the defendants probably endured much torture, but now there was no need to fabricate facts or make up stories—the real evidence was overwhelming. Vlasov and his co-defendants really were "enemies of the people" who had committed serious crimes against the state. The general himself, the primary defendant, faced twenty-eight prosecution witnesses and many more accusers who gave sworn depositions. The prosecution had planned its attack with meticulous care, and Vlasov was found guilty of the following charges: that he voluntarily surrendered to the enemy; that he encouraged other POWs and forced laborers to join the German army and to fight against the USSR; that he created the Committee for the Liberation of the Peoples of Russia; and that he "trained agents for espionage and diversionary activity in the rear of the Soviet Army." Later on, Soviet historians and propagandists would claim that he had been a Trotskyite since 1936 and that he had deliberately brought about the destruction of the Second Shock Army in June 1942.[17]

Of course, not all the charges made against Vlasov, either during or after the trial, were entirely true. For instance, he clearly did not set out to surrender to the Germans, but was captured by them after his army had been mostly annihilated. Nor was there evidence that he trained saboteurs or terrorists to work behind Soviet lines or that he was ever a follower of Trotsky. Finally, there is no reason to believe that Vlasov did anything but his best to save the Second Shock Army from destruction. He was impeded in doing so by Stalin's refusal to grant him permission to retreat and maneuver as he thought necessary. The main charge, however, that he fought for the Germans and actively recruited others to serve the enemy, was incontrovertible. Thus on August 2, 1946, Vlasov, was hanged on piano wire with a hook inserted at the base of the skull along with his co-defendants.[18] Though the general was in many ways a high-minded man, the fact remains that he was willing to fight for the Nazis. Thus, it is not hard to appreciate the Soviet point of view that as a traitor he deserved to be executed as an "enemy of the people."

Far more complicated was the fate of the some five and one-half million prisoners that survived their period of captivity scattered all over Europe. Of these, about three million had been captured by the Red Army as it liberated Eastern Europe. Most of those who remained at large were afraid to return to the USSR because they had surrendered and not fought to the death. They knew that they were likely to be accused of treason and executed. In addition, others who had suffered persecution previously due to religious faith, minority status, or undesirable social origins were also reluctant to return. Finally, there

VII. The Military, Foreign Communists and Repatriated POWs

Three generals who somehow were not victims of Stalin's terror: (from left) Semyon Mikhailovich Budyonny, Mikhail Vasilevich Frunze, and Kliment Emremovich Voroshilov. Here they confer as they plan combat with Makhno's bands. Konotop, 1920. Photographer unknown (courtesy Russian State Archives of Film and Photo Documents, Krasnogorsk).

were others who were primarily motivated to avoid repatriation because of the material advantages and political freedoms offered in the West.

But Stalin had his own reasons for wanting all POWs and refugees returned. Perhaps first and foremost, he believed in the necessity of punishing those who had allowed themselves to be taken captive by the enemy. The mere possibility that they could have betrayed the fatherland was reason enough to demand retribution. Too, the Soviet Union needed every able-bodied person for the daunting job of reconstructing the country. Related to this was the firm consensus among Soviet citizens that no other power had contributed more to victory, both in material terms and in terms of human sacrifice, than the USSR. Finally, there was also concern that the West might use aggrieved expatriots to work against the interests of the USSR in the postwar world.[19]

These concerns led Stalin to demand forced repatriation for all Soviet nationals at the Yalta Conference in February 1945. The American and British soldiers understandably approached this issue with some reluctance. It was bound to be unpopular in the West, but Roosevelt and Churchill felt compelled to cooperate if only because they feared for the approximately 50,000 American and British soldiers in areas still controlled by the Red Army. Also, there was concern about the responsibility and cost of feeding and caring for so many soldier-refugees indefinitely. In the end, it was decided to include a clause about forced repatriation in a secret codicil, which was not revealed to the public for more than fifty years.[20]

The repatriation of all POWs and displaced persons was dutifully carried out, albeit not without some cheating. The British were known to have kept certain anti-communist POWs who they thought would prove useful in the postwar period. The Soviets were aware of this and did the same with the British POWs in their custody, albeit in much larger numbers. In the end, some two million former Soviet POWs were rounded up and forcibly repatriated to the USSR, where they were treated as "enemies of the people." Many were summarily executed upon return. Others were sent to filtration camps, where they were interrogated at length and forced to explain the particulars of their capture and time in captivity. This was often the fate of the young Ostarbeitern, many of whom had been traumatized by their long ordeal. These unfortunates were stigmatized as "socially dangerous" and accused of have having aided the enemy in return for an easier life. Most suffered official discrimination, were denied opportunities for higher education, and were sentenced to long terms at hard labor.

The Cossacks felt especially betrayed by the Allies, since some were forced to return who had emigrated after the Revolution and who had never been Soviet citizens. Perhaps the most famous of these was Lieutenant General Piotr Krasnov, a tsarist officer who had fought against the Bolsheviks after their seizure of power in 1917. After the Russian civil war, he immigrated to Germany, where he helped to found the Brotherhood of the Russian Truth, an anti-communist organization dedicated to the overthrow of the Soviet state. Krasnov also worked with the Nazis during World War II and organized a Cossack army unit made up of émigré Russians and Soviet prisoners of war. In May 1945, the general and his men surrendered to the British in Austria after being assured that as White émigrés they would not be forced to return to the USSR. But later that month, Krasnov and some 20,000 of his men were delivered to the Red Army. The old general, now eighty-six years old, was found guilty of treason by the Military Collegium of the Supreme Court of the USSR in January 1947 and hanged.[21]

Eventually, attitudes did change in the USSR, and many citizens and government officials were inclined to feel sympathy for those who had suffered so much in captivity only to return home and be treated as "enemies of the people." In 1955, at First Secretary[22] Khrushchev's initiative, an amnesty for military collaborators was issued. He also authorized the creation of a Committee for the Return to the Homeland that reduced some of the punishment and stigma of POWs or others who spent time in German captivity during the war. This was also reflected in the literature and the cinematography of the period. Such books as Sholokhov's *Fate of a Man* and Solzhenitsyn's *A Day in the Life of Ivan Denisovich* paved the way for a more sympathetic understanding of the kinds of challenges real men and women face during a war. It marked the beginning of a more understanding attitude toward those who had been labeled "enemies of the people.'" It seemed to offer the hope that those who had previously sinned against the State were not necessarily beyond redemption after all.

CHAPTER VIII

The Creative Intelligentsia, Cosmopolitans and Jews

THE END OF WORLD WAR II IN 1945 was a euphoric time for the Soviet Union. The Red Army, which had done more than any other to destroy Nazism,[1] now controlled virtually all of Central and Eastern Europe. The cost had been incalculable in terms of human lives and destruction, but the totality of the victory over a hated enemy had given the country an emotional and spiritual boost that seemed to portend better times. And, indeed, not only did Soviet citizens yearn for an improved standard of living, but they hoped for more personal freedoms as well. They wanted to be allowed to participate in the decisions that affected their lives. They wanted an end to repression, the Gulag, and collective farms.

Stalin, too, savored the great victory, but at the same time he was nagged by serious concerns. One of these was the fact that although the Red Army was arguably the greatest land power in the world, the United States had the atomic bomb. Also, while the Soviet people would spend decades struggling to rebuild the country from the destruction of war, the Americans had suffered virtually no damage at all within the continental United States. Thus, they represented a potential threat to all socialist countries with their powerful economy and ever-improving military technology. Given the increasing hostility between the great powers, this was something Stalin would have to address. But could he lead as he had before? At age sixty-five, the General Secretary had been nearly overcome by the length and intensity of the war. He now suffered from heart problems, fatigue, and memory loss. In the fall of 1945, he spent two months recuperating at his dacha in Sochi on the Black Sea as he thought long and hard about the task of restoring the country and the system of government that he had created as it existed before June 1941.

A similar predicament had existed earlier in Russian history, which Stalin had studied carefully and taken very seriously. Alexander I, who became tsar in 1801, had spoken of the need to introduce reforms including the granting of a constitution and the abolition of serfdom. These plans were put aside during the Napoleonic wars, but once the great victory was won, the tsar's most ardent supporters fully expected him to follow through on his pledges. But by now Alexander was disinclined to do much about either. In 1816, however, he did make one major initiative to alleviate the worst evils of serfdom with the construction of hundreds of military colonies all over Russia. The idea was to improve the lot of the serf by building specially planned communities and by having them combine their agricultural work and military obligations. The tsar believed that this would improve family life for peasants since the men would live at home and be separated from their families far less frequently. Thus the creation of military colonies was not only humane, but practical: families stayed together, military costs were cut, and the country's first line of defense was made more secure. But the military colonies were fatally flawed from very the start and for a number of reasons: the peasants chosen to participate were forced to do so; the conditions under which they lived and worked were often quite brutal; and the man chosen to administer the colonies, General Count A.A. Arakcheev, was a notorious martinet and taskmaster who treated the peasants like inmates, which, in fact, they were.

The Russian officers who had returned from campaigning in the West were aghast at the idea of military colonies. They had seen a better way of life abroad and were dissatisfied with the status quo. When it became clear that nothing was going to change, they formed secret societies and debated among themselves about how to create a better Russia. The one group that finally acted became known as the Decembrists. It consisted mostly of highborn officers who, in December 1825, planned to kill Tsar Alexander I and abolish autocracy and serfdom. Alexander's untimely death on December 14 (by natural causes) coupled with the incompetence of the conspirators doomed the enterprise to failure. The new tsar, Nicholas I, who was the younger brother of Alexander, was quick to take charge. He interrogated many of the guilty himself, had five executed, and sent hundreds more to Siberia. Some years later, he set up a new kind of police force, the Third Section, which was to preserve political security by rooting out subversion in every form. The Third Section also ran state prisons, prosecuted forgers, gathered information on malcontents and foreigners, and imposed censorship of various kinds.[2]

Stalin, an avid student of history, was mindful of all this. In the years following the war, he often brooded about the possibility of a new generation of Decembrists emerging in the Soviet Union and resolved to crush any such movement before it could get started. To this end, he cast a wary eye on his victorious generals, including Marshall Zhukov, whom he seriously thought of arresting as a Western spy. In the end, Stalin had him expelled from the Central Committee and demoted. He was, however, much tougher on a number of other generals and admirals, whom he also suspected of having higher ambitions. This is exactly when the "enemy of the people" label was most useful to the General Secretary—when he wanted to avoid specifying the actual charges. One of his victims at this time was an old friend and comrade, Marshall Kulik, whose bungled operation to break the blockade around Leningrad made him vulnerable to Stalin's anger. Kulik, however, did live to see the end of the war, only to be shot afterward.[3]

Among Stalin's first measures after the war was to repopulate the Gulag by arresting a few hundred thousand army men and accusing them of treason. Included in the roundup were the very officers and men who had met up with the Americans on the Elbe River in 1945. There were also many others who were rearrested after serving their time. The maximum sentence was to be increased from fifteen to twenty-five years and *katorga,* a special regime of hard labor, was reintroduced from the days of the tsars. This meant that inmates were forced to wear chains while working and were denied blankets in the coldest weather. In addition, peoples who had been forced into exile before or during the war were forbidden to return their homelands. Those caught trying faced sentences of up to twenty years. Finally, Stalin gave top priority to the work of the secret-police laboratories to create new poisons and weapons for assassination.[4]

Next, the General Secretary moved to tighten the screws on the cultural front, which he saw as a potential threat to Soviet power. He started by chastising two journals, *Zvezda* and *Leningrad,* for being in "ideological bondage to western ideas and values." For example, *Zvezda* had printed a story by Mikhail Zoshchenko about a monkey that had escaped from the zoo to spend a day wandering around Leningrad. The monkey had all kinds of strange adventures, but was happy to return to his cage at the end of the day. As a satire, of course, the story was not meant to be taken seriously, but Stalin was not amused. The author was accused of "hooligan representations of our reality accompanied by anti–Soviet assaults." He also took exception to the decision of *Zvezda's* editors to publish some poems by Anna Akhmatova. She was denounced as "a decadent drawing room poetess" whose work was "alien to our people." Zoshchenko and Akhmatova were both expelled from the Union of Writers. The former was temporarily deprived of his ration card, while the latter was forced to do janitorial work in order to live.⁵

This kind of hostility to those whose creative talents were thought to be in opposition to Soviet power was not new. In 1917 the Bolsheviks created the Proletarian Cultural and Enlightenment Organizations (*Proletkult*) in order to encourage artists of every kind to promote the goals of the Revolution. This led to all kinds of experimentation in nearly every field, which troubled many Party hardliners. In 1932, Stalin took steps to resolve this chaos with his decree "On the Reconstruction of Literary and Art Organizations." Artist and writers were enjoined to celebrate productive workers as patriotic heroes. To do this, they needed to create works that were concrete rather than abstract and easily understandable to the average worker. Such works needed to be optimistic, uplifting, and based on the highest ideals of Marxist Leninism. The artist was to depict reality as it ought to be rather than as it was. This doctrine came to be known as Socialist Realism, which James Billington described as calling for "two mutually exclusive qualities: revolutionary enthusiasm and objective depiction of reality."⁶

But even before Socialist Realism became the official policy of the regime, innovators and creative artists had to be careful lest they fail to conform to the needs of Soviet propaganda. Among the first of these to feel the pressure of the regime to conform to the new Soviet reality was the great basso and proclaimed People's Artist Feodor Ivanovich Chaliapin. In 1922, he went abroad to raise money for famine victims. Years passed and he did not return. He had been sympathetic to the aims of the Revolution, but he could not tolerate the Bolsheviks' interference in artistic matters. Such was Chaliapin's fame that Stalin himself tried hard to lure him back to the USSR, but he did not succeed until *after* the singer's death.⁷ That is, when Chaliapin died in 1938, his ashes were buried in Paris. In 1984, at the behest of his children, his remains were returned to the Soviet Union.

Two other artists who enjoyed initially enjoyed great favor but who ultimately suffered under Soviet rule were Sergei Esenin and Vladimir Mayakovsky. Both had been early supporters of the Revolution only to be assailed by second thoughts later on. Esenin became disillusioned almost from the beginning and wrote a poem critical of the Bolsheviks entitled *The Stern October Has Deceived Me*. He went on to make a mess of his life by marrying five times and siring four children by three different wives. In time, he became a hopeless alcoholic prone to public fits of rage and violence. In 1925 he suffered a mental breakdown and was hospitalized. Soon after his release, he hanged himself, leaving a farewell poem written in his own blood. He was thirty years old.[8]

Mayakovsky became interested in Marxist literature as a teenager and was imprisoned three times for subversive activities. He went on to join the Moscow Art School, where he became an enthusiastic participant in the Russian Futurist movement. He volunteered for the army in 1914, only to be rejected. He happened by chance to be at the Smolny Institute in October 1917 and witnessed the Bolshevik insurrection. By now he was publishing his poetry and gaining a reputation for his originality and relevance. He defined his work as "Communist futurism" and soon gained great popularity in the new Soviet state. No less interesting were his propaganda posters (Agitprop), which glorified the goals of the Revolution. Mayakovsky was allowed to travel freely around the world and was enthusiastically received everywhere. In time, however, he began to have grave doubts about Stalin's leadership and about the vulgarity and hypocrisy of the regime as a whole. He was also criticized by the Russian Association of Proletarian Writers for being out of step with the needs of ordinary working people. On April 14, 1930, at age 36, he shot himself through the heart, leaving a suicide note that contained his final work, entitled *The Unfinished Poem.*

Chaliapin, Esenin, and Mayakovsky were never actually proclaimed "enemies of the people" despite the fact that they all eventually became profoundly alienated from the Soviet system. Their reluctance to praise the regime without qualification antagonized those in authority. Still, they were never punished or even seriously threatened. The remains of all three were interred with honors in the Novodyevichy Cemetery in Moscow, as their memories were eulogized. In time, however, the tendency of others among the creative elite to antagonize the Party's leadership became dangerous and sometimes fatal. Indeed, this repression of Soviet society's most brilliant and creative people grew to such an extent that Robert Conquest has characterized it as a "holocaust of the things of the spirit."[9]

One of the most tragic victims was the gifted playwright and short story writer Isaac Emileovich Babel, who was born and raised in Odessa on the Black Sea in 1894. His parents had to hire private tutors so he could study at home because of the quota, which limited the number of Jews attending public schools. In any case, the young man's unusual gifts were soon apparent. In addition to the regular academic subjects, he studied the Talmud and music and became fluent in French. In 1915 he moved to St. Petersburg, where he met and was deeply influenced by Maxim Gorky. During the Revolution, Babel worked as a journalist for the Menshevik newspaper *Novaya Zhizyn* (New Life). He also traveled with the First Cavalry Army during the civil war and witnessed and later wrote about the horrors of combat in the story *Red Cavalry*. Babel later became famous for his *Odessa Tales*, which depict the lives of Jewish gangsters in the Moldavanka ghetto of Odessa. The success of this work made him a famous man, but his refusal to conform to the demands of Social Realism also made him powerful enemies. One of these was Field Marshall Semyon Budyonny, who was so infuriated by Babel's graphic depiction of men in battle during the civil war that he demanded the writer be executed. Fortunately for Babel, the Field Marshall's tantrum was not acted upon.[10]

Babel's domestic situation, however, became increasingly turbulent over the years. He married Yevgenia Gronfein in 1919, who bore him a daughter in 1929. But what seemed like an appropriate union ultimately soured because of the writer's many affairs. Yevgenia was devastated by her husband's infidelity and left him and moved to France. Babel later sired two other children by different mistresses before beginning yet another affair with Yevgenia Feigenberg. She, however, was betrothed to the notorious head of the NKVD, Nikolai Yezhov. Foolishly, Babel continued the affair even after Feigenberg and Yezhov were married. The writer was arrested on May 15, 1939, and savagely tortured at the Lubyanka. He confessed that he was an active member of an anti–Soviet Trotskyite organization and a spy for France. At his trial on January 26, 1940, Babel withdrew his confession, but this did him no good. He was convicted and executed by firing squad the next day.[11] Ironically, the "Bloody Dwarf" was by now himself under arrest and awaiting trial. His execution was carried out only one week later.

Stalin's insistence on Socialist Realism in literature and the arts was offensive to some of the country's most gifted writers, including Vsevolod Emilovich Meyerhold. The son of a wine manufacturer of German descent, he was born in Penza just west of the Ural Mountains in 1874. Vsevolod came to love the theater at an early age and worked as both a director and an actor in the imperial theaters for many years. After the Revolution he became a Bolshevik and welcomed the chance to radicalize theater in the world's first socialist country. But to his deep disappointment, the new regime did not welcome his innovations. Still, Meyerhold managed to found his own theater in 1922, which featured a bare stage and stylized gestures. His method of production was called "biomechanics," which seemed to reduce the status of the actor to that of a puppet. He had his actors rehearse certain poses in order to create just the right emotion while performing. Meyerhold worked closely with Mayakovsky,

Vsevolod Yemilyevich Meyerhold in his Moscow study, 1930. Hanging on the wall behind him is a portrait of his wife, the actress Zinaida Raikh. Meyerhold was a much-admired actor and director whose innovations in Soviet theater were frowned upon by the regime. This eventually brought about his tragic demise. Photographer unknown (courtesy Russian State Archives of Film and Photo Documents, Krasnogorsk).

who encouraged his enthusiasm for innovation and the modern. His method was adopted by many of the leading figures of Soviet theater and film. One of these was Sergei Eisenstein, whose films have become cinema classics.

For all its success, however, the Meyerhold Theater was closed in 1938 for being "alien to Soviet art." More than a year later, the director himself was summoned to appear before Andrei Vyshinsky and at a meeting of producers to confess his errors. Meyerhold made the necessary confession, but he also denounced the regime for having made Soviet theater "averagely arithmetical, stupefying, and murderous in its lack of talent." "Is that your aim?" he cried. "If it is—oh!—you have done something monstrous! In hunting down formalism[12] you have eliminated art!"[13]

That Meyerhold would be made to pay for such remarks there could be no doubt. On June 20, 1939, the NKVD came to take him away. Three weeks later his beloved wife, Zinaida Raikh, was found murdered in their apartment. Bandits had broken in and stabbed her seventeen times and made off with her jewels. Her neighbors heard her screaming, but no one came to her aid. Perhaps they feared that her attackers were government thugs acting under orders. Meyerhold's own end was nearly as brutal. He was subjected to many hours of torture during which he was made to lie face-down by his interrogators and beaten with a rubber strap on the soles of his feet and spine. The pain was excruciating and throbbed for many hours. In the end, he confessed to being a spy for the Japanese and British and was shot by firing squad February 1, 1940.[14]

Osip Emilevich Mandelstam was another brilliant poet forced to suffer for his art. He was born in Warsaw in 1891, but grew up in St. Petersburg, a city he came to love. He grew up in relatively comfortable surroundings, was allowed to travel abroad, and received an excellent education. He attended St. Petersburg University, where he studied philosophy and became a member of "Poets Guild." He became acquainted with Anna Akhmatova and Nikolai Gumilov and published a collection of poems in 1913 called *Kamen* (Stone), which was very favorably received by the educated public. Mandelstam survived the triple-trauma of world war, revolution, and civil war and for a while worked for the Education Ministry in Moscow. Later, he became a translator of children's books from English and French into Russian. He also wrote books for children in Russian.

Mandelstam was often critical of the Soviet regime and made powerful enemies. From 1925 to 1930 he ceased writing poetry. Later he traveled to Armenia to become a journalist but soon returned to writing verse. He was arrested in 1934 for writing some offensive lines about Stalin and was exiled to the remote town of Cherdyn in the Ural Mountains. Mandelstam was fortunate to be accompanied by his wife, Nadezhda, who was determined to look after him. But as the poet's mental state deteriorated, he began to brood about suicide. Nadezhda appealed to the Central Committee, and the poet was sent to the more livable city of Voronezh. He was allowed to return to Moscow in 1937 for a time, only to be rearrested in May 1938. At the Butyrka Prison he received his final sentence: five years' forced labor at Kolyma. But Mandelstam never made it to Kolyma. By the time he reached the transit camp near Vladivostok, his dementia had become so extreme that he could travel no farther. He died six weeks later on December 26, probably of starvation.[15]

Another poet of genius who was doomed to a life of tragedy was Marina Ivanovna Tsvetaeva. Born in Moscow in 1892, the daughter of a professor of art history at the University of Moscow, Marina enjoyed a fair amount of privilege as a youth. She attended schools in France and Switzerland and developed a passion for poetry. However, Marina's mother ridiculed her verse and forced her to study music. This created much tension at home, which ended only with her mother's death in 1906. Marina then returned to her poetry and in 1910 published her first collection of poems, entitled *Evening Album*. In 1912, she was married to an army officer, Sergei Efron, with whom she was deeply in love. That same year she gave birth to a girl, Ariadna (Alya), and, in 1917, another girl, Irina. Eight years later a boy, Georgii, was born, whom she loved most of all and spoiled terribly. He never returned her affection and ultimately grew to hate her.

World War I, the Revolution, and the civil war created misery and privation for Tsvetaeva. With Efron away in the army, she became so destitute that Irina died from starvation in 1920. Meanwhile, as the Red Army was triumphing over the White Army in the Russian civil war, Efron fled the country and in 1922 made his way to Berlin, where he summoned his family to join him. That same year the family moved to Prague, where they lived in poverty. Efron came down with tuberculosis and was unable to work. In 1925, the family moved to Paris, where they would live for the next fourteen years. Tsvetaeva found it difficult to get along with the émigré community, who believed that she was pro–Soviet. Actually, it was Efron who was beginning to see things differently. He joined a group called the Eurasians, which advocated the repatriation of Soviet émigrés. He also agreed, unbeknownst to Tsvetaeva, to work for the NKVD. In 1937, he was implicated in the murder of a former Soviet agent. When the Paris Police tried to apprehend, him he fled to the USSR. He had been preceded by his daughter, Alya, who shared his pro–Soviet sympathies and had also wanted to go home. She seems to have been unaware that her fiancé was an NKVD agent ordered to spy on her family. In any case, this left Tsvetaeva alone with Georgii in Paris, without money and without friends. Thus in 1939, she, too, returned to the USSR accompanied by her son, Georgii.[16]

In the Soviet Union, Tsvetaeva found herself stranded in a world she no longer knew. She had no relatives or friends, and most of the established writers wanted nothing to do with her. Pasternak alone helped by occasionally finding her work translating poetry. Things became much worse when the Germans invaded. Mother and son were evacuated to the remote town of Yebuga on Kama River. She and Georgii were assigned a screened-off section of a hut. They were in desperate straits, with no friends and no steady means of support. By the time Tsvetaeva was finally offered a job washing dishes in a canteen, she had already given up. On August 31, Marina Tsvetaeva was found hanged from a hook on the front of her hut. She was interred in the local cemetery, although the exact location is not known. Apparently, no one in the town bothered to attend the ceremony, not even her son.[17]

Boris Pilniak was more compliant than most Soviet artists who suffered persecution. Though he was never a Party member and was generally opposed to urbanism and the mechanization of society, he supported the Party line and had an enthusiastic following among the Soviet elite. However, he brought about his own doom in 1927 when he wrote *Tale of the Unextinguished Moon*, in which he seemed to be accusing Stalin of having caused the death of the great civil war hero General Mikhail Vasilevich Frunze in 1925. The circumstances were highly suspect. The general had been appointed Deputy Commissar for War in the spring of 1924. The following year he fell ill and was ordered by Stalin (through the Central Committee) to undergo an operation. The procedure was performed, but the general died. Many were suspicious at the time that Stalin had had a hand in Frunze's death, since the commissar was known to have opposed Stalin on certain issues. In fact, there is no evidence at all to suggest that the General Secretary was in any way responsible. But Pilniak in his short novel seemed to hint otherwise. In his book, a Red Army commander is ordered to submit to an operation for ulcers only to die from an overdose of chloroform. Later it turns out that the operation had not really been necessary.[18]

Pilniak's situation became even more precarious when he became president of the All Russian Union of Writers in 1929. This was a group that was established to resist the ideological conformity that was being imposed by

RAPP. As if questioning authority in the USSR wasn't dangerous enough, Pilniak decided to have his new book, *Mahogany*, published first in Germany prior to its being released in Russia. In fact, this was done for copyright reasons and was by no means illegal. However, the regime decided to make it an issue by denouncing it as an anti–Soviet and a White Guard provocation. Ironically, it was Maxim Gorky who came to Pilniak's defense and urged that he be allowed to write pro–Soviet literature in peace. But this turned out to be not such a desirable arrangement, since his next novel, *The Volga Flows into the Caspian Sea,* had to be submitted to, of all people, Nikolai Yezhov, to be proofread. The NKVD head identified more than fifty changes that had to be made for the novel to become ideologically acceptable. This was enough to send Pilniak into deep depression. In May 1937, he was publicly attacked for "counter-revolutionary writing," which was roughly equivalent to being declared an "enemy of the people." He was arrested the following October and accused of counterrevolutionary activity, spying for Japan, and terrorism. On April 21, 1938, in a trial that lasted all of fifteen minutes, Pilniak was found guilty and sentenced to death. He was executed the next day.[19]

Novelists and poets were not the only members of the intelligentsia who suffered. In fact, many of the most endangered scholars were historians who supported the theories of Mikhail Nikolayevich Pokrovsky. Pokrovsky was the head of the Institute of Red Professors and, in 1929, became a member of the Soviet Academy of the Sciences. As a confirmed Marxist historian, he had long emphasized the importance of economics in determining the course of history and minimized the role of the individual. In 1920, he wrote *A Brief History of Russia,* which Lenin himself read and highly recommended. But his death in 1924 and the subsequent struggle for power within the Party brought about profound changes in the world of academia. Indeed, Stalin's rise to supreme power and cult of personality caused Pokrovsky's works to be criticized. Historians now found it obligatory to emphasize the great qualities of Lenin and Stalin to explain the victory of Bolshevism in Russia. This led to a huge number of arrests among Pokrovsky's students, many of whom were accused of terrorism. Pokrovsky himself sought frantically to modify and change what he had previously written. His death by natural causes in 1932 undoubtedly prevented him from being arrested. The purge of historians continued into the show trials of 1936 and 1937 as the defendants named a number of historians as active terrorists. The NKVD then began arresting the students of these men because they had been contaminated by a false ideology.[20]

To get a fair idea of how ridiculous things became, one should consider the case of Konstantine Shteppa, a professor of ancient history, who got into big trouble for a series of trivial mistakes he made lecturing to his students in 1937. The first involved some critical remarks about Joan of Arc's role in history. Normally this would not have interested anyone except that in the mid-1930s when the Popular Front came to power in France, the Soviet Union was trying to curry favor with the French. Thus the Party line required Joan of Arc to be treated as a heroine. Shteppa also erred when he referred to the Greek hero Midas in a context that was somehow embarrassing. Later, he repeated a remark made by Trotsky to explain the hold of Christian demonology on the peasants. His final mistake was committed while trying to explain the Donatist movement[21] in North Africa during the days of the Roman Empire. He described it in part as a national as well as a peasant rebellion. This made it a bourgeoisie nationalist movement and contrary to Marxist theory.[22]

The consequences of these mistakes were both strange and serious: Shteppa's friends and colleagues began to be arrested in large numbers, and he himself was taken into custody March 1938. This was followed by seven weeks of brutal interrogation, which led to an accusation that he had tried to assassinate Stanislav Kossior, who had been for a time First Secretary of Ukraine. This, however, was eventually dropped when Kossior himself was arrested and charged with being an "enemy of the people."[23]

Shteppa ended up having to stand trial anyway since he was later accused of being a Japanese spy. The reasoning behind this accusation was even more absurd than the previous charge. Somehow it was decided that because he was the head of the Near East Committee of the Ukrainian Academy of Sciences, he was predisposed to spy for one of those countries even farther east, including Japan. Then it came to light that he had lectured high-ranking Red Army officers about his area of expertise (which didn't include Japan) and that he had met with a least one foreign professor whose specialty was Hittite history. Then an indirect contact was established between Shteppa and a professor in Odessa, who had met the Japanese Consul there. The basis of the prosecution's case was that Professor Shteppa through this contact could have become a spy for the Japanese government. In the end, it didn't matter, because after Yezhov was replaced by Beria as head of the NKVD, the situation became less charged. In the fall of 1939, Shteppa was released, although others continued to be punished by the regime with incarceration and execution.[24]

One of the most militant supporters of Socialist Realism was Andrei

Aleksandrovich Zhdanov. As a longtime supporter of Stalin, Zhdanov had been chosen to replace Sergei Kirov as Party boss of Leningrad after the latter's assassination in 1934. As a prominent member of the Central Committee, no one had been more insistent on the need for vigilance in the hunt for "enemies of the people," especially in academia and the arts. Indeed they seemed to be springing up everywhere. At a plenum in the spring of 1937, he loudly deplored the fact that at the Institute for Red Professors, eighty-five of 183 members had been arrested as "enemies of the people" since 1933.[25] Curiously, he seemed not to have been at all interested in the nature of the evidence against these individuals or whether they were really guilty.

The Kiev Academy of the Sciences was also hotbed of denunciation. At Party meetings, it sometimes happened that when a member was accused of some error or shortcoming, someone else would ask for proof. The latter was nearly always accused of having a counterrevolutionary attitude. He or she would always be silenced and sometimes arrested. The individual most vulnerable to this charge seems to have been whoever was the secretary of the Academy at any particular time. In the years between 1921 and 1938, each and every one of the men who served in this position ended up being arrested for one reason or another. The situation at the Belarusian Academy of Science was similar. A center for the espionage work for "enemies of the people" was discovered that included the school's leading academicians. This same process was also at work at the Kharkov Physics Institute. Of its eight department heads, seven were purged. One of these, Professor Lev Davidovich Landau, was one of the leading theoretical physicists in the country. He was accused of being a German spy and nearly died under the harsh conditions of his incarceration. He was finally released when a brave colleague appealed to Stalin and convinced him of Landau's great value to the country.[26]

Incredibly, Stalin had set into motion a process that was bound to destroy those whose expertise was of the greatest value to the state. A survivor of this bizarre reality was the country's premier aircraft designer, Andrei Nikolaevich Tupolov, who was arrested in October 1937 for wrecking and for selling the blueprints of a plane to the Germans, from which they constructed the Messerschmidt 109. For this he was declared an "enemy of the people" and sentenced to be executed. This prompted a series of appeals, which eventually led to the commutation of his sentence to ten years in a *sharashka*[27] or prisoner research unit. He was released after the German invasion in 1941 and went on to develop a number of planes that were vital in the Soviet victory over fascism. These included the TB-1, a two-engine bomber with a speed of 138 miles per hour and a range of 625 miles. He also developed the TB-3, a four-engine bomber that weighed 43,000 pounds and could carry loads of over two tons.[28]

Perhaps the most reckless injustice caused by Stalin's paranoid policies was the arrest and incarceration of Sergei Pavlovich Korolev, who eventually became the "Chief Designer" of the Soviet space program. Born in Ukraine in 1907, Korolev developed an early interest in flight and glider construction, which ultimately led him into aircraft design. One of his advisers was Andrei Tupolov, who named him chief engineer on the TB-3 heavy bomber project. Later he worked on the development of cruise missiles, a manned rocket-powered glider, and automated gyroscope stabilization systems that allowed stable flight along a programmed trajectory. Korolev's career seemed to know no limits until June 22, 1938, when he was denounced by one of his colleagues for wrecking and arrested by the NKVD. He was taken to the Lubianka, tortured, forced to confess, and sentenced to ten years in a labor camp. Korolev was initially sent to Kolyma, where he spent several months working in a gold mine. Conditions were primitive and the guards brutal. On one occasion, Korolev's jaw was broken by an angry guard and not properly treated. From that time on, Korolev had difficulty opening his mouth wide enough even to eat.

Still, Korolev's value to the Soviet military was such that he could not be allowed to languish in some arctic prison. He was granted a retrial and brought back to Moscow. By now he was a profoundly changed man, although not for the better. He lost most of his teeth from the beatings he received and became almost morbidly introverted. He feared that he would be executed at any time. At his retrial it was decided to reduce his term to eight years and to allow him to work in a *sharashka,* where the living conditions were much better than in an ordinary camp. He was finally discharged from prison on June 27, 1944, and sent to work at the government's aviation industry commission. In 1945 he was awarded the Badge of Honor for his scientific work and commissioned into the Red Army as a colonel. He became chief designer of long-range missiles at the Special Design Bureau. Here Korolev continued to impress his colleagues and superiors with his ability and imagination. In 1952, he was admitted to membership in the Communist Party, although it was not until April 1957 that the Soviet government officially acknowledged that his sentence had been unjust.

By now the Cold War had intensified to include not only the threat of nuclear weapons and ICBMs, but also the race to exploit the cosmos. In many quarters, scientists spoke hopefully of the possibility of sending a satellite into orbit in order to commemorate the International Geophysical Year. The cost of such a venture seemed prohibitive to the U.S. Government, but not to the Soviets. For them it represented an opportunity for a great propaganda victory. On October 4, 1957, thanks mainly to Korolev's inspired leadership at the Special Design Bureau, the first Sputnik was launched into orbit. One month later, a much larger Sputnik 2 was sent into orbit, but this one included a dog named Laika. Soon Korolev began plans to send a man into outer space.

Amazingly, this goal was achieved remarkably sort order. The launch of Yuri Alexeevich Gagarin in April 1961 as the first man in space and to orbit the earth was arguably the most important propaganda victory the Soviets were ever to score. But the scientific knowledge gained by the space program had a value to the regime that was even more rewarding. In October 1964, three cosmonauts orbited the earth sixteen times. The next year, it was a Soviet cosmonaut, Alexei Leonov, who performed the world's first space walk. But the really big challenges loomed in the near future, as Korolev's staff had already begun to design the N1 rocket, which would one day take the first man to the moon. But all this was cut short by the unexpected death of the chief designer on January 14, 1966.

Korolev had been in bad health since suffering his first heart attack in December 1960. At this time, the doctors also identified a kidney disorder that had been caused by the brutal conditions at the labor camp at Kolyma. They urged him to cut back on his work, but Korolev did the opposite. In 1962, the patient was back in the hospital, suffering from intestinal bleeding. In 1964 he was found to have cardiac arrhythmia. Months later, the doctors discovered that he also suffered from an inflammation of his gallbladder. But the condition that brought him down was a bleeding polyp in his large intestine, which the doctors operated on January 5, 1966. During the operation, they discovered a large cancerous tumor in his abdomen, which had to be removed first. To this end, they tried to insert a tube into patient's lungs to assist in his breathing, but were unable to do so. It seems Korolev's mouth could not be opened wide enough due to the untreated broken jaw he had suffered at Kolyma.[29]

In retrospect, it must have rankled those who survived during the terrible years of the terror and purges to know that real "enemies of the people," who had done serious harm to the country, were often celebrated as heroes. Perhaps the most infamous of these was Trofim Lysenko, the son of Ukrainian peasants, who wrote a paper on vernalization in 1928 that promised to revolutionize Soviet agriculture. Due to bitter cold and insufficient winter snow the previous year, many early winter-wheat seedlings had not survived. Lysenko, however, claimed to have developed a chilling process to make the seeds of winter cereals behave like spring cereals. He called this process vernalization and later asserted that the offspring of a vernalized plant would inherit these same traits without undergoing the process themselves. The Soviet news media hyped Lysenko's claims that he had discovered a way to fertilize fields without fertilizer or minerals and that he had proven that peas could be grown in Azerbaijan even during the winter months.

Lysenko's rise to fame and influence was not immediate. He had his supporters, but there were also doubters and critics who demanded to be heard. The turning point seemed to come in February 1935 during a speech that Lysenko gave to the second congress of collective farmers. The "barefoot scientist" compared the kulaks' resistance to collectivization in the countryside to that of the "kulaks of science" in the city, who preferred theoretical work in their laboratories to the great successes of Lysenko's practical approach in the field. Stalin applauded enthusiastically and shouted, "Bravo, Comrade Lysenko. Bravo." Subsequently, Lysenko was named president of the Lenin All-Union Academy of Agricultural Sciences. This gave him all the power and influence he needed to abuse those who failed to accept his theories.[30]

Over the next few years, biologists and agronomists were arrested in large numbers. Among them was the geneticist Nikolai Ivanovich Vavilov, who disagreed with Lysenko about what the best agricultural policy should be for the territory that had been annexed from Finland after the 1939 war. Vavilov was arrested on August 6, 1940, and underwent intensive interrogation for a period of eleven months. He was tried and convicted on July 9, 1941, of participating in a Rightist conspiracy and spying for England. He was initially sentenced to death, but when his fate became known, one of his colleagues actually had the courage to nominate him for a Stalin Prize. Of course, he didn't actually receive the award, but later, when he was elected as a Fellow of the Royal Society in London, the regime commuted his sentence to twenty years. Unfortunately, Vavilov could not endure the harsh conditions of his confinement. Suffering from dystrophy, he eventually died in Saratov Prison.[31]

Meanwhile Lysenko's influence with the General Secretary during and after World War II remained intact. In 1948, he challenged his scholarly detractors to a debate, ostensibly in the interest of determining truth in science. In fact, it was a trick to humiliate and discredit them. Long before the debate, Lysenko had presented his report to the Central Committee and had received its approval. The August session of the Lenin All-Union Academy of Agricultural

Sciences denied the existence of genes and the theory of heredity. Confronted with this, the geneticists assembled had to publicly repent before Lysenko and his supporters. Subsequently all work in genetics was halted and many of the county's most gifted scholars and scientists lost their jobs. In addition, Academician K.M. Bykov and his followers were declared to be the sole defenders of Pavlov's physiological theories. Bykov himself enjoyed high standing in the Party because of his willingness to minimize the importance of Western science and tout the superiority of Soviet science. Thus, as the regime celebrated the 225th anniversary of the founding of Russian Imperial Academy of Sciences, those Soviet scholars who enjoyed recognition and honor in the West were now denounced. Soon inventions and scientific advances previously accepted as Western were now claimed to have been Russian and Soviet achievements. These included inventions in the fields of radio, electric lighting, the electric transformer, diesel-powered ships, the airplane, the parachute, and the stratoplane.[32]

The guiding spirit behind this cultural chauvinism was Andrei Zhdanov. As someone who enjoyed an unusually close relationship with Stalin, Zhdanov had long been a willing participant in some of the General Secretary's worst crimes. He had been a firm supporter of the Terror and co-signer of 176 execution lists. In 1940, he had been sent to Estonia to oversee that country's forced annexation to the USSR as a Soviet Republic. During the war, he had been in charge of the defense of Leningrad, and in 1946, he was named premier of the Soviet of the Union. The following year he organized the Cominform, which was intended to coordinate the activities of the various European communist parties. But Zhdanov's main interest was to create a culture that would serve the USSR's revolutionary goals in the spread of communism. He was especially worried about the infiltration of foreign influences and demanded that Soviet art aid in the struggle against western and bourgeois decadence. In this he had Stalin's complete support. The composer Dmitri Dmitrievich Shostakovich, who had been denounced by Stalin for his dissonant and abstract music, had a number of confrontations with Zhdanov. In his memoir, *Testimony,* he quoted a typical Zhdanov lament: "What would have happened if we had brought up our young people in the spirit of despair and non-belief in our work? What would have happened was that we would not have won the Great Patriotic War."[33]

Such rhetoric, absurd though it may have been, resonated with Stalin as he brooded over the challenges that confronted him in his waning years. During the period between 1946 and 1950, a number of crises emerged that were

The Kresti Prison in Leningrad. Originally built as a wine cellar in the 17th century, it was turned into a prison. By the 1930s its population had grown to about 30,000. Many of these were some of Russia's most brilliant writers and poets. Among these was Nikolai Zabolotstkovo, whose book *The Story of My Incarceration* contains a vivid description of what it meant to be a prisoner in the Kresti. Another victim was one of the Soviet Union's greatest poets, Anna A. Akhmatova. Although she was never incarcerated, she suffered much anguish in being denied information about the fate of her husband and later her son, both of whom were imprisoned in the Kresti albeit at different times (courtesy Russian State Archives of Film and Photo Documents, Krasnogorsk).

highly frustrating for the General Secretary. Many of these were directly related to the ever-intensifying tensions of the Cold War. For instance, the plan to export communism to Greece and Turkey had been opposed by Stalin, but was aggressively promoted by Marshall Tito of Yugoslavia, who wanted to dominate the Balkans. The attempt was foiled when President Truman called for the U.S. Congress to pass an aid package to the two states totaling $659 million in May 1947. The following year, Congress passed the Marshall Plan, which sent $13 billion to help Europe rebuild from the destruction of the world war. This was followed by the Soviet blockade of Berlin, which began in June 1948 to force the Western occupiers (i.e., Britain, France, and the United States) out of Berlin. The relieving airlift succeeded, however, and Stalin eventually lifted the blockade the following May. War was avoided, but tensions were not much reduced. In 1949, the Western powers established the North Atlantic Treaty Organization to counter any future Soviet aggression, and in 1950 the invasion by communist North Korea of the South prompted the United Nations to form a U.S.-led force to support the South Koreans.

Another troubling problem during this period was the creation of the state of Israel in May 1948. Hoping to prevent the new country from aligning itself with the U.S., the Soviet Union became the first country to recognize Israel's nationhood. But the gesture was in vain, since the Israelis immediately sought the support and friendship of the United States. This rejection came at a bad time, when Stalin's paranoid fantasies were dangerously on the rise. He had become particularly suspicious of the Jews, whose inherent cosmopolitanism and prominence in the arts and academia had always been cause for resentment. Stalin was by no means as rabid an anti–Semite as Hitler, but he had certain tribal attitudes that inclined him to be contemptuous of any group with which he could not readily identify. This, however, did not prevent the General Secretary from naming to high positions Jews whom he judged loyal and able. Among the best of these was the highly respected diplomat Maxim Maximovich Litvanov, who was named People's Commissar for Foreign Affairs in 1930. Litvanov served in this position for nine years and gained international respect for his toughness as a negotiator and his passion for disarmament. That same year, however, Stalin also elevated Lasar Moiseevich Kaganovich to the Politburo. Notorious for his brutality and ruthlessness, Kaganovich never hesitated to carry out his master's policies with the utmost severity, especially with regard to collectivization.

Ironically, Stalin had also been among those who favored the creation of a Jewish Autonomous Region in Birobidzhan, an area far to the east and south on the Amur River. Far less desolate than one might imagine, Birobidzhan occupied an area larger than the state of Israel. It was rich in natural resources, including forests, coal, copper, asbestos, and gold. During the 1920s, many in the Soviet government and influential Jews had sought to find a solution for the dire economic problems among the Jewish population in the USSR. Some thought had been given to settling them in Ukraine and later the Crimea, but in both cases, stiff opposition among the local populations made these options less than ideal. In March 1928, however, the Central Executive Committee of the Supreme Soviet began to advertise Birobidzhan as a great opportunity for Jewish people to have their own land, preserve their culture, and prosper economically. Thus, during the next ten years, some 43,000 people moved to this region, although only a little more than half stayed. In any case, the end came sooner than expected. In 1936, as the nation fell into the grip of the Terror and the purges, the government turned Birobidzhan over to the NKVD. Soon the new Jewish Autonomous Region was declared out of bounds for most Soviet citizens. The committees and organizations that had been created to promote Birobidzhan were shut down and their leaders arrested.[34]

Birobidzhan experienced a brief revival after World War II, as Jews once again began to immigrate to the region in large numbers. This, too, was cut short with the creation of the state of Israel and the enthusiasm it inspired among Soviet Jews. This became especially acute when the Ukrainian-born former Milwaukee schoolteacher, now foreign minister, Golda Meir, came to Moscow and was greeted enthusiastically by a small crowd of mostly older people at a synagogue. That the General Secretary could have been aroused and angered by such a minor incident is telling. But with the Cold War intensifying around the world, Stalin resolved to push back against those whose loyalty was misplaced. This gave rise to a surly anti–Jewish campaign across the USSR. The revised Party line linked all Jews with Trotsky, labeling them as rootless cosmopolitans who felt no allegiance to the Soviet Union. They were, in fact, cultural "wreckers" who admired the West and denigrated all that was Russian. It was even suggested that the collectivization campaign had led to famine because Jewish security people had deliberately distorted Stalin's directives in order to sadistically punish the Russian people

Stalin's anger did not always drive him to extreme solutions. He was often content to merely playfully torment those who believed they were in his good graces. Thus, after ordering that Jewish critics be dismissed from Soviet journals and forbidding them to publish, he subsequently admonished the same editors and officials who had carried out his orders for going too far. He toyed with Ilya Ehrenberg, a Jewish journalist who had long been one of his most reliable supporters. Ehrenberg had always been steadfast in his criticism of Israel as "a bourgeois state wholly dependent on American support." However, in February 1949, he was suddenly forbidden to publish and was removed from the critics' reviews. Ehrenberg was mystified by this turn of events and turned to a certain Prospelov, who headed the propaganda department of the Central Committee, to learn why he was being punished. Prospelov promised to look into the matter, but never did get back to Ehrenberg. Two months passed as Ehrenberg waited, anxiously expecting to be arrested at any time. Finally, he could stand it no more and wrote directly to Stalin in an attempt to learn his status. Stalin did not answer the letter directly, but eventually directed Malenkov to call the journalist to inquire about his concerns. Malenkov, feigning bewilderment, explained that the General Secretary had known nothing about Ehrenberg's situation and surmised that it had all been a mistake.³⁵

But, as everyone well knew, Stalin's prejudices and suspicions could have lethal consequences even for those he was inclined to favor. Such was the sad fate of Solomon Mikhoels, a much acclaimed Jewish actor and director whose talents were understood and admired by the General Secretary. Indeed, Mikhoels had been awarded both the coveted title of People's Artist of the USSR and the Lenin prize in 1939. During the war he had been made chairman of the Jewish Anti-Fascist Committee to propagandize for the Soviet Union and to collect funds from Jewish communities abroad, including the United States. But in the intensified anti–Jewish atmosphere, Stalin decided that that Mikhoels was an "enemy of the people" because he staged a play entitled *Tevye the Milkman,* which many deemed pro–Zionist. Thus he ordered Victor Abakumov to devise a plot to murder Mikhoels and to make it look like an accident. The problem was how to accomplish this task in way that would hide the fact that it was actually a murder. To this end, Abakumov assembled a team of assassins and ordered them to do the deed when the intended victim would be at the Belorussian Theater in Minsk to judge plays for the Stalin Prize Committee. It was arranged for Mikhoels to be accompanied by a "friend" (who was also a conspirator) and then lured to a dacha outside of town, where he would meet his end. Thus, on the evening of January 13, 1948,

Solomon Borisovich Mikhoels was a great actor and director in Jewish theater. Here he is in makeup as he prepares to take the stage in 1932. For a while he enjoyed Stalin's favor, but eventually he became an enemy of the state because of his cosmopolitan lifestyle. For this he was brutally murdered on Stalin's personal orders. Photographer unknown (courtesy Russian State Archives of Film and Photo Documents, Krasnogorsk).

the unsuspecting Mikhoels was taken to the dacha, given poison, beaten with a blunt instrument, and shot in the head. The "friend" was also killed at this time for good measure. The corpses were taken back to Minsk by car, where they were laid on the road and run over by a truck so that it would indeed look like an accident. The bodies were then deposited in a field just off the road to be discovered the next day. Mikhoels's corpse was taken to Moscow to be prepared for burial by the renowned biochemist Dr. Boris Zabarsky. This was the same man who was responsible for the care of Lenin's mummy in Red Square. Zabarsky was now ordered to perform a form of ghastly cosmetic surgery to conceal the fact that the victim had been brutally murdered. Days later Mikhoels's corpse lay in state in the Jewish Theater so that his death could be publicly mourned by the people who loved him and his art.[36]

The anti–Jewish campaign was still in its infancy when one of its instigators, Andrei Zhdanov, died of heart failure on August 31, 1948. This gave hope to many who longed for an end to the campaign to purge Russian culture of anti–Soviet influences. Alas, things soon got much worse. The following December, the First Secretary of the Union of Soviet Writers, Alexander Alexandrovich Fadeev, was officially denounced for publishing two once-popular books, *Twelve Stools* and *The Golden Calf*, by Ilf and Petrov,[37] which allegedly defamed Soviet life and government. Fadeev was alarmed, but with the support of Georgii Malenkov, he composed a letter to Stalin claiming that the Soviet art world was infested with enemies and declared his readiness to answer with his life for this charge. This served as a convenient excuse to intensify the campaign against cosmopolitans and Jews.

Not that Stalin ever needed an excuse to annihilate anyone, let alone an "enemy of the people." That November, he disbanded the Jewish Anti-Fascist Committee, which had included Solomon Mikhoels as a leading member. During the war, the group had traveled to a number of western countries to mobilize popular opinion against the fascist aggressors and to raise money to fight the war. In New York City, they had been received rapturously by a crowd of 50,000 and were photographed with such luminaries Mayor Florio LaGuardia, Paul Robeson, and Albert Einstein. But in 1944, the Committee had sent Stalin a letter requesting that an autonomous Jewish republic be created in the Crimea. This proved to be a serious mistake, although it was not immediately apparent. Four years later, however, Stalin used this same letter to prove that the Committee was made up of "enemies of the people," who were devoted Zionists. Their goal was to create a bulwark for American imperialism on Soviet territory.[38]

Stalin's suspicions and doubts were mounting in other areas as well. In 1950, two high-ranking Party officials, Nikolai Voznesensky and Andrei Kuznetsov, had sought to organize a trade fair in Leningrad to stimulate the city's economy and to provide aid to those who had survived the siege of Leningrad and were now destitute. Somehow, this was seen as un–Soviet, and the two were accused of trying to make "the city the capital of a Russia autonomous within the USSR." Victor Abakumov was assigned to make a case against Voznesensky and Kuznetsov and four others. Their trial began on September 30 and lasted one day. The defendants were found guilty and shot. This was followed by a purge of some 2,000 public figures who were removed from their positions. Two hundred more were arrested along with their relatives. Most were exiled or sent to the Gulag. Interestingly, the sentences were not made public, and, according to Donald Rayfield, the campaign to arrest more Jews and other kinds of cosmopolitans did not produce fabrications plausible enough to warrant another show trial.[39]

Even so, the following year Stalin had ordered the Ministry of State Security to eliminate the long-retired former Commissar of Foreign Affairs, Maxim Litvinov, for collaborating with the United States. But Litvinov escaped execution by dying a natural death on December 31, 1951, before he could even be arrested.[40] Not to be discouraged, Stalin ordered the members of the Jewish Anti-Fascist Committee to stand trial for espionage the following May. One of the defendants was the biologist Lina Shtern, whose American brother had helped her get a supply of streptomycin to treat TB patients in the USSR. In the end, about half of those arrested were sent to the camps, and the fifteen thought to be most guilty were held for trial, which took place in May 1952. This included Yitzhak Fefer, whose poem had in lavish praise of Jewish war veterans had irritated Stalin. Fefer and the other defendants, most of them prominent Yiddish writers, were found guilty of anti–Soviet agitation and shot the following August.[41]

Coincidently, it was also in the spring of 1952 that Dr. Vinogradov visited Stalin to perform a routine physical examination on the General Secretary. Vinogradov was alarmed at his patient's weakened state and urged him take a long rest and not to involve himself in politics. Stalin did not accept this advice gracefully. Hadn't Lenin been had been told the same thing some three decades earlier? Sensing a plot, the General Secretary had Vinogradov arrested and began to think about staging another show trial of mostly Jewish doctors, who were allegedly engaged in treasonous activities. This was accompanied in November by a burst of publicity about the sabotage of Jewish wreckers in Ukraine and a vast Zionist conspiracy abroad. Concerning the latter, it was alleged that President Truman and the Israeli president, David Ben Gurion, were actively conspiring to oppose Soviet influence in Eastern Europe and the Middle East. Finally, the Slansky conspirators in Czechoslovakia were accused of using a doctor to try to kill Klement Gottwald, a Czech leader and prominent supporter of the USSR. This may well have been the critical element in Stalin's mind that made him decide in favor of a new show trial.[42]

The first public announcement of the doctors' plot came on January 13, 1953, in *Pravda* under the headline "Murderers in White Gowns." The article described the treachery of nine physicians (six of them Jewish), who were accused of murdering Andrei Zhdanov, Alexander Shcherbakov, and a number of other prominent Party officials. This was followed by a frenzy of anti–Semitic hatred across the Soviet Union. Soon there was talk of an impending pogrom after the guilty doctors were tried, found guilty, and hanged in Red Square. A few leading Jewish Communists were ordered to prepare a letter to *Pravda* calling for "the eradication of Jewish bourgeois nationalists, spies and enemies of the Russian people." They expressed the hope that Comrade Stalin would resettle all Soviet Jews in Siberia, where they would be safe from the wrath of the people.[43]

But the planned trial never took place because the great leader himself died before it could happen. On the evening of February 28, Stalin and four of his cohorts, Beria, Malenkov, Khrushchev, and Bulganin, met at the Kremlin to see a film. They then repaired to Stalin's dacha for some heavy drinking and dinner. The General Secretary was in a good mood despite the fact that he was suffering from a number of ailments, including high blood pressure, rheumatism, dizzy spells, and acid stomach. The party went on until four in the morning when the guests departed. A few hours later, Stalin suffered a deadly stroke and was too weak to summon help. He seemed to have been awake when the lights in his apartment went on at 6:30 p.m. on March 1, but mysteriously he did not appear. It was not until 10:30 p.m. that his bewildered and frightened guards forced open the door so that the deputy commissar of the dacha, Piotr Lozgachev, could check on his master. He found Stalin lying on the carpet in the small dining room conscious but unable to speak. When the other guards came in, they lifted the ailing dictator onto the couch. Someone called the MGB to inform members of the government of the situation, but it was not until 3:00 a.m. (March 2) that two of his guests from the previous evening, Beria and Malenkov, arrived. By the time the first doctors and medical personnel appeared on the scene, it was 9:00 a.m. and too late. Stalin had burst a blood vessel in his brain and was close to death.

Still, he survived in agony for another three days. More people arrived at the dacha. Among these were Khrushchev, Bulganin, Voroshilov, daughter Svetlana, son Vasily, and others. All were grief-stricken and crying except Beria, who behaved in a triumphant manner as he took charge of the situation. At times, he actually seemed to sneer at the dying man. In any case, the doctors continued to treat the patient with medicines and injections and by bleeding him with leeches. They also tried to spoon-feed him tiny amounts of food and liquid. Sometimes he was able to open his eyes and look at his visitors before drifting back into unconsciousness again. At one point he actually raised an arm and pointed to a picture on the wall above him of two children feeding a lamb from a bottle. Khrushchev took this to mean that Stalin now saw himself as helpless as a lamb. As the end grew near, Svetlana described his death as "slow strangulation with his face turning dark, his lips black and his features unrecognizable." He was slowly choking to death. By now the hemorrhaging had spread throughout his brain and his body was shutting down. He died on March 5, 1953, at 9:40 in the evening.[44]

CHAPTER IX

The Secret Speech and Its Aftermath

According to Donald Rayfield, there were three basic reactions to the death of Stalin. Many peasants and ordinary workers were "hysterical with grief" and fearful about the future. The great leader had taken them through some very difficult times. Who could possibly replace him? The opposite reaction was characteristic for those men and women who languished in the Gulag for crimes they didn't commit. Many were joyous even though they may have lost hope of ever being released. Finally, for those in power in the Party and the bureaucracy, this was a time for calculation and sober thinking. They wondered how the transition would happen and whether or not they would survive.[1] Among these, Lavrenty Beria seemed to have the clearest idea of all of what to do and how to do it. One of his first acts after Stalin's death was to merge the Ministry of the Interior (MVD) and the Ministry for State Security (MGB) into one. This put him in the strongest position to control what would happen next.

Stalin's memorial ceremony and funeral took place on March 7. For three days the body lay in state in the Hall of Columns in the House of Soviets. Emotions were high, and on March 9, hundreds of people were crushed to death trying to get a last look at the man who had dominated their lives for nearly a quarter of a century. Stalin's embalmed body was then placed beside Lenin's in the latter's mausoleum. Three days earlier, Georgii Malenkov had become premier of the Soviet Union. He was forced to relinquish that post on March 14 because of the opposition of other members of the Central Committee. Among these was Nikita Sergeevich Khrushchev, who now assumed the role of secretary of the Council of Ministers. But all eyes were on Beria, who was expected to try to make a grab for complete power. At first,

Beria moved cautiously, as if trying to dispel the suspicions of his nervous colleagues. His first big decision was made on April 4 when he called of the off the planned show trial against the doctors Stalin had wanted tried for murder. Three weeks later, in a move that surprised many, Beria ordered the arrest of Vasily Stalin, who was accused of misusing of government property. Thus, Stalin's own son was found guilty and sentenced to eight years in jail.[2]

But Beria was far more vulnerable than he imagined. Working behind the scenes to secure his arrest and removal were a number of Presidium members led by Nikita Khrushchev. On June 26, an unsuspecting Beria arrived at the Kremlin for what he thought was a routine meeting. He was promptly arrested by Generals Zhukov and Moskalenko, who had been lying in wait for him. Beria was taken into military custody and incarcerated. He was tried *en camera* on December 23, found guilty of being a British spy, and shot.[3]

That September, Nikita Khrushchev had been named First Secretary of the Central Committee. This was Stalin's old position, and the new boss was in many ways a welcome change from his inscrutable and vengeful predecessor. For one thing, Khrushchev was genuinely concerned by the privation suffered by ordinary working people and resolved to do something about it. Thus, in order to make it possible for rural and industrial workers to find jobs offering better conditions and more pay, he removed all criminal penalties for absenteeism at work and for quitting. He also allocated funds to build more housing to reduce the severe overcrowding of communal living arrangements. He abolished fees for higher education so that those who were paid least had greater access to higher education. Khrushchev was also determined to increase the food supply by growing grain in the "virgin lands" of northern Kazakhstan, western Siberia, and the southeastern part of European Russia. At the same time he decreed that Ukraine would grow maize to be used as cattle feed. This in turn was expected to make meat and dairy products more available and less expensive. Finally, collective farmers were to be paid higher procurement prices, and taxes were to be reduced on their private plots.[4]

Many of these domestic initiatives were successful and won Khrushchev much popularity among the general population. But his most urgent task was to address the problem of the Gulag, where millions of men and women still languished, some since the 1930s. Many and perhaps most of these inmates or *zeks* had been unjustly sentenced to long prison terms and forced to live under horrific conditions. Although they performed necessary labor for the state, many had special talents that were being wasted as slave laborers. In any case, some attempts had been made in the years following the war to improve

In 1935, A.P. Filatov (left), Genrikh Yagoda (center), and Nikita Khrushchev visit the construction site of one of Stalin's favorite projects: the Moscow-Volga Canal. Twenty-one years later Khrushchev would denounce his former boss before the Central Committee for abuse of power and crimes against the Soviet people. Photographer unknown (courtesy Russian State Archives of Film and Photo Documents, Krasnogorsk).

the lot of Gulag inmates by providing better food, warmer clothing, and even some pay. But all this did little to make a zek's life less miserable.

The problem was further complicated by the fact that the camps were now populated by a new kind of *zek*.[5] These were not the same terrified victims who had been dragged out of their apartments in the middle of the night in the 1930s. These were (mostly) men who had fought in the war and in many cases had seen life outside the Soviet Union. Such men were bolder and more confident and were imbued with a spirit of defiance that their jailors could not stifle. In 1948, the inevitable happened in one of the Arctic camps near Vorkuta. There a group of former Red Army officers, veterans of the war, rose in mutiny. They disarmed and killed their guards and liberated their own camp and one other. They had begun to march toward a third camp but were attacked by dive bombers and paratroopers to end the rebellion.[6]

The Vorkuta rebellion would soon be followed by many more such risings after Stalin's death. The largest of these occurred in Norilsk in May 1953, in Vorkuta in July 1953, and in Kengir (Kazakhstan) in May 1954. By now the inmates had became organized and made a list of specific demands. These included better food, a shorter workday, increased visitation rights for relatives, and removal of numbers from prison uniforms. Moreover, the *zeks* declared their refusal to do any work until a commission was sent from Moscow to hear their grievances. For a time, these tactics seem to promise meaningful results, but as the negotiations dragged on, the authorities in Moscow became impatient and the inmates worn down. This standoff, too, was ultimately ended with overwhelming and deadly force.[7] Indeed, the problem of the camps and the system of Soviet justice that supported them was never resolved, although the number of inmates imprisoned gradually declined in the years following 1970.

Khrushchev also felt anxiety about his potential rivals in the Party, whom he suspected might use force to remove him. To prevent any such eventuality, he created a new agency, the Committee for State Security. Better known as the KGB, it was to be under his exclusive control. This gave the First Secretary a measure of security, which allowed him to travel abroad to establish his own domestic and foreign policies. Indeed, Khrushchev enjoyed his new status and was eager to project his image as the leader of the Soviet state. One of the first trips he made was to China in September and October 1954. As a gesture of goodwill, he returned the navy base at Port Arthur to the People's Republic. In May 1955, Khrushchev also reacted decisively to the admission of West Germany into NATO by creating the Warsaw Pact. The members of this association were Albania, Bulgaria, Hungary, East Germany, Poland, Romania, and Czechoslovakia. Later that month, Khrushchev went to Yugoslavia to normalize relations with Marshal Tito, who, to the First Secretary's disappointment, had elected not to join the Warsaw Pact.[8]

Despite this, the visit to Yugoslavia did yield one very important result: it convinced Khrushchev of the need to admit the truth about the Soviet past and to rehabilitate the millions of "enemies of the people" who had been destroyed by Stalin's policies. During discussions with some high-ranking Yugoslav leaders, the topic of Stalin's terror came up more than once. The visiting Soviets unanimously blamed Beria rather than Stalin as the culprit who sent millions of innocent men and women to the execution chambers or the Gulag. The Yugoslavs scornfully derided the fiction that Stalin had been unaware of the horrors that were being committed in his name, but Khrushchev heatedly insisted that it was so. Years later, however, while dictating his memoirs, he remembered this moment and admitted his mistake: "It's now clear to me that my position was wrong. I didn't fully realize the necessity not only of exposing the crimes but in putting the blame where it belonged so that Stalinist methods would never again be used in our Party."[9] Nine months later, Khrushchev addressed the Twentieth Party Congress in a secret session to denounce Stalin and his methods. Sadly, his courage and candor fell short since he did not entirely put the blame where it belonged.

It is ironic that the same man who had publicly proposed the virtual deification of Stalin just days after his death was now preparing to denounce him. The danger of such a step was great, but Khrushchev was convinced that it had to be done. Twenty-five years of Stalin's cruel dictatorship had left the country almost too traumatized to take on the daunting task of rebuilding the country. Nor could the Soviet people be expected to out-produce the West unless the horrors of the past were confronted. To this end, the Presidium of the Central Committee authorized the director of the Marx, Engels and Lenin Institute, Piotr Nikolaevich Pospelov, to head a commission to investigate the nature and extent of the terror that Stalin had unleashed on the country between 1935 and 1940. Pospelov had always been a devoted Party member and a staunch Stalinist. He seemed genuinely stunned to learn the full extent of the carnage during the terror. On February 9, 1956, when he read his committee's seventy-page report to the Presidium of the Central Committee, his voice was trembling and he could barely speak.[10]

Even so, Khrushchev intended to make full use of the sordid facts contained in the report as he prepared his speech. Not everyone was glad that the truth was finally coming out. Prominent among those who resisted was Vyacheslav Molotov, a former Stalin crony. Fearing that the speech would incriminate him and others, he urged Khrushchev to address the Congress at a night session when fewer members were likely to attend. The First Secretary grudgingly acquiesced, and the speech was postponed to the night of February 24, although the content remained essentially the same.

Khrushchev's main theme was to condemn Stalin for his refusal to tolerate honest dissent and his deviation from Lenin's style of leadership, which had always featured collegiality and cooperation among Party members. Without exception he took vengeance on anyone who opposed him or his policies. Nor did he hesitate to invent charges against the innocent in order to create confusion and uncertainty. Such was the case at the Seventeenth Party Congress in January 1934, when fifty-six percent of the 1,966 delegates were arrested for anti-revolutionary crimes.[11] The percentage was even higher for those who were elected to the Central Committee at the same Congress. That December things became worse still after the murder of Leningrad Party boss, Sergei Kirov. On this occasion, and without the approval of the Politburo, Stalin issued a directive to circumvent normal legal procedures. This led to a huge increase in the number of executions for individuals, all of whom almost certainly had nothing to do with Kirov's assassination.[12]

Khrushchev also blamed Stalin for the crisis in Soviet agriculture, which he claimed was due mainly to the General Secretary's ignorance about the subject itself. The General Secretary refused to heed the advice of the specialists who understood the problems and knew what would and would not work. Nor did he bother to travel to rural areas and meet with kolkhoz workers. In fact, according to Khrushchev, Stalin actually relied on Soviet films for his knowledge about the countryside, which falsely depicted farms that were rich and prosperous. When told that the situation with regard to cattle breeding and meat production was especially bad, he ordered a commission formed to address the problem only to ignore its recommendations. Instead, he demanded that the kolkhozes and the kolkhoz workers across the USSR have their taxes raised by 40 billion rubles! This was a completely unrealistic sum, especially when one considers that during the previous year (1952) the kolkhozes and the kolkhoz workers received only 26,280 million rubles for all the products they sold to the government. As Khrushchev explained to the delegates, "facts and figures did not interest Stalin."[13]

Another important theme in the secret speech was Stalin's abuse of the term "enemy of the people," which Khrushchev wrongly claimed that Stalin invented. In fact, Lenin had used it in November of 1917 to demonize the Constitutional Democrats. But Lenin had not intended it to become an automatic death sentence. With Stalin the term "automatically rendered it unnecessary that the ideological errors of a man or men engaged in controversy be proven." This opened the door for all kinds of outrageous distortions of Soviet justice. Khrushchev underscored this point by describing the recent testimony before the Central Committee of an investigative judge, Boris Rodos, who, during the terror, had interrogated such prominent Communists as Kossier, Chubar, and Kosarev, all of whom were later executed. Rodos plainly admitted to torturing these men until they confessed for the sole reason that they had been branded "enemies of the people." As Rodos explained: "I thought that I was executing the orders of the Party."[14] Under such circumstances, hard evidence was considered unnecessary. Thus, anyone who disagreed with Stalin, or who was suspected of any kind of evil intent could be branded an "enemy of the people." This not only made honest ideological debate within the Party impossible, but people were often too afraid to express their opinions even about routine practical matters. As Khrushchev pointed out, "The formula "enemy of the people" was specifically introduced for the purpose of annihilating people, who, *in Stalin's opinion,* had in some way had opposed the Party line."

Probably no part of Khrushchev's speech was more controversial than his critique of Stalin's conduct just before and during the Great Patriotic War. Between 1937 and 1941, the General Secretary's paranoia had induced him to have thousands of the country's best military officers shot "as enemies of the people." This had a devastating effect on the Red Army's ability to defend the country. In addition, in 1939, Stalin concluded a non-aggression pact with Germany supremely confident that he had outwitted Hitler. Inexplicably, he ignored all evidence to the contrary. In the months before the invasion, all serious observers could see that the Germans were preparing to strike, but Stalin was resolute in his denial. Clearly, as Khrushchev pointed out, the enormous losses suffered by the Red Army in the early months of the war were made much worse by Stalin's delayed reaction. Indeed, the General Secretary remained in a near-catatonic state for ten days until several members of the Politburo came to his dacha and persuaded him to act. But, as Khrushchev explained in his speech, Stalin never really did lead during the war. "He never visited any section of the front or any liberated city except for one short ride on the Mozhaisk highway during a stabilized situation at the front." Actually, this was probably for the better, because often when he did decide to get involved, he actually caused harm by imposing his own ideas about what should be done and how.[15]

Khrushchev's greatest indignation was reserved for Stalin's utter shamelessness in attempting to take all the credit for the Soviet victory in the Great Patriotic War. He was particularly incensed by the film *The Fall of Berlin,* in which Stalin alone is seen as the hero who accomplishes everything by himself. There are no military commanders with whom he consults, nor do any members of the Politburo appear in the film. "Why is everything shown to the nation in a false light?" asked the First Secretary. "To surround Stalin with glory, contrary to the facts and contrary to historical truth."[16]

Nearing the end of his speech, Khrushchev began to talk about what needed to be done in the immediate future. He urged a thorough revision of Soviet history, literature, and the fine arts so that Lenin and the Communist Party could receive their proper due in all that had been achieved since 1917.

He repeated his demand for an end to the cult of the individual and urged the delegates of the Congress to beware of hero worship, which was alien to the spirit of Marxism-Leninism. Too many mistakes and abuses had been committed under its influence. Nor should it be forgotten that the many victories gained during Stalin's rule were not those of one man acting alone. Rather they were the result of workers and peasants acting under wise the leadership of the Communist Party. To regain the momentum for more great achievements, it was imperative to restore "the Leninist principles of Party leadership including that of collective leadership characterized by the observation of the norms of Party life described in the statutes of our Party, and finally, characterized by the main principal of criticism and self criticism."

Khrushchev ended his four-hour address by expressing confidence that the "Party, armed with the historical resolutions of the Twentieth Party Congress, will lead the Soviet people along the Leninist path to new successes, to new victories. Long live the victorious banner of our Party—Leninism!" The delegates in the hall rose to their feet and applauded tumultuously for several minutes.[17]

The Secret Speech did not remain secret for long. Right after the Congress, Khrushchev authorized confidential briefings to be given to Party activists around the country. He also gave transcripts to foreign communist party leaders who had attended the Congress but not the closed session where he delivered the speech. Finally, he ordered the KGB to ensure that the CIA got a copy and sanctioned a brief summary of the speech to appear in the Soviet press. The common reaction nearly everywhere was a mixture of shock, amazement, anger, and possibly even relief. In Tbilisi, Georgia, Khrushchev's revelations caused a riot, and in Poland a workers' revolt. In the latter instance, it led to Wladislaw Gomulka's being released from a Soviet prison so that he could become First Secretary of the Polish United Workers' Party. Far worse, however, for the Soviets was the rebellion that occurred in Hungary in November 1956. There the people made a number of radical demands, including worker management of factories, a role in government for the trade unions and youth, and the withdrawal of all Russian troops. This brought on the Soviet invasion, which consisted of 6,000 tanks and tens of thousands of troops. The rebellion was crushed, but the anger and resentment of the Hungarian people endured.[18]

Khrushchev himself came under fire for the stormy reaction engendered by his speech and the destalinization that followed. These, coupled with the First Secretary's bumptious ruling style and ill-conceived economic reforms, caused his opponents in the Presidium to vote for his resignation. Khrushchev refused on the grounds that since he had been elected by the Central Committee, he would not step down unless the members of that body so demanded. This was followed by days of deliberation, after which Khrushchev received a vote of confidence to remain in office. The First Secretary continued on his way to change the nature of the Soviet regime, particularly with regard to the status of law in society. Khrushchev wanted the law to be more predictable and less arbitrary. He also wanted to change the system so that it was no longer possible to wage campaigns of terror against the innocent. To this end, a new criminal code promulgated the following year that provided for a stricter application of due process of law. The new code also eliminated the terms "enemy of the people" and "counterrevolutionary activity" as a means of gaining a conviction in court. This must have come as good news to Khrushchev's defeated rivals. Although he had demoted all of them to lesser positions, no one was arrested and no one was shot.[19]

But the secret speech and the well-meaning initiatives that followed brought other problems that Khrushchev did not foresee. For one thing, ordinary citizens were plainly confused by the First Secretary's denunciation of Stalin, whom they had previously revered as an infallible genius, builder of socialism, and hero of the Great Patriotic War. Equally troubling were the falsehoods, criminality, and waste of millions of lives that had attended the country's rise to power. People wondered how this could happen in a society that supposedly had been constructed in accordance with the laws of scientific socialism. These revelations gave rise to a new generation of activists who were not afraid to demand the truth and agitate for more freedom and much-needed change. In the decades to follow, however, the regime would be unable to adjust the realities of the modern world or keep up with the pace of economic or technological change. Thus began the slow but inexorable decline of the Soviet Union as a great power.

Epilogue

Sheila Fitzpatrick, in her wonderfully informative and insightful book *The Russian Revolution,* has described the commonalities and traits that revolutionaries in general are likely to share. Among these is a nihilistic obsession with destruction—the need to obliterate the old order in order to create the new, purified of all that is evil and base. They are shrill in their demand for radical change and disdain all that is old or traditional. They are undaunted by obstacles and practical realties and believe in the future the way the ancients believed in a Golden Age. They scorn caution and compromise and are suspicious of those who are anything less than reckless in their commitment. Revolutionaries are essentially Manicheans, who see the world in terms of black and white. They are obsessed with the need for vigilance and relish the prospect of rooting out the enemies of the Revolution.

When the Bolsheviks seized power in 1917, they were inclined to identify with the French Jacobins and, in some ways, copied their brand of activism. Indeed, the two groups were in many ways comparable: Both featured the overthrow of a hated monarchy and a society that was decadent and corrupt. Both sought to impose a social order that was radically new. Both believed in the need for retribution and terror, and both relished the task of exterminating the ubiquitous "enemies of the people." Of course, the Bolsheviks had the advantage of looking backwards. Many of them had studied the French Revolution and lived in fear of a Thermidorian Reaction such as had occurred after the Reign of Terror of 1793–94. They were mindful of the revolutionary malaise that followed the fall of Robespierre and saw how it had made possible the rise of Napoleon, twenty years of warfare, and the eventual restoration of the French monarchy.

The Russians were pleased to believe that they had avoided the worst mistakes of the French revolutionaries. Thus, they and their descendants touted their own revolutionary example for most of the next seventy-four years. They encouraged oppressed peoples the world over to rise up and to destroy the capitalist order. Above all, they urged all those who sought a path to a better future to heed the lessons of Marx and Lenin. Central to this message was the need to eradicate the implacable enemies of the Revolution lest they impede the future. Their message was, of course, not only a warning, but also a call to glorious action. Indeed, the very notion that ordinary workingmen and women could participate in such a vital task was exhilarating. Diabolical "enemies of the people" lurked everywhere but could be defeated with vigilance and determination. This became an essential part of the 20th-century revolutionary tradition all over the globe and especially in China, where many revolutionary activists, and Mao Zedong in particular, at least initially looked to the Bolsheviks as an inspiring revolutionary example.

The Chinese Revolution had some interesting similarities to the Russian experience. As in Russia, China had been the victim of Japanese aggression, although it had occurred a decade earlier, in 1895. The defeat and humiliation that followed led to a period of intense domestic unrest, which prompted the Manchu dynasty to make a serious attempt at reform. Alas, for the imperial rulers in Beijing, it was too little too late. On January 1, 1912, Chinese revolutionary leaders established the Republic of China after forcing the abdication of the Chinese emperor, the eight-year-old boy Pu Yi.

But the new republic had problems almost from the beginning. President Yuan Shikai showed a troubling authoritarian tendency to those who had supported him. In any case, his death in 1916 created a power vacuum, which was exploited by the country's rapacious warlords. These were local military leaders who were determined to rule the country according to their own interests. To counter this aggression, Dr. Sun Yat-sen, a Hawaiian-born physician, created the Kuomintang or Nationalist Party. He also set up an opposition government in Guangzhou, which ultimately led to a protracted civil war that engendered a reawakening of Chinese nationalism and strident demands for political revolution.

To the Bolsheviks, the events in China seemed to justify Marx's prophecy that the success of one communist revolution would ignite others and that creation of a world socialist order was not far off. The Bolsheviks were eager to give history a push in the right direction and to share with others what they had learned. Among the first Russian statesmen to visit China in order to offer encouragement and guidance was the People's Commissar of Foreign Affairs,

G.V. Chicherin. On July 4, 1918, he gave a speech in which he denounced the imperialism of the tsars and repudiated all land claims of Russian citizens in China and Mongolia. He also declared all indemnities remaining from the Boxer Rebellion of 1900 to be officially abolished. Finally and most importantly, he called for the restoration of the sovereign rights of China in the territories along the Chinese Eastern Railway. The Russians had built this stretch of track across Manchuria in 1896 after pressuring the Chinese to allow it after their defeat in the Sino-Japanese War. The new line connected with the Trans-Siberian Railroad and provided the Russians a shortcut to the far eastern city of Vladivostok.

Chicherin's initiative seemed to promise a closer, more mutually respectful relationship between Russia and China, but it never quite became that. Four years later, another commissar, Adolf Abramovich Joffe, came to Beijing with quite a different message. Although he, too, repudiated the imperialism of the tsars, he nevertheless emphasized that Russia had legitimate legal and economic interests in China, especially in the Chinese Eastern Railroad. Joffe now insisted that this section of track was an essential part of Russia's Great Siberian Railroad. The Chinese, to be sure, were not pleased by this reversal of policy. Thus the railroad across Manchuria remained a bone of contention between the two countries for many years to come.

But not only were the Russians unapologetic, they seemed to have presumed that they knew best and that it was their responsibility to guide the Chinese Nationalists through their revolution in order to best promote the cause of world communism. At times, this required the participation of Communist International, which was headquartered in Moscow. The agents of Comintern were not shy about imposing their policies on those they professed to be helping. In July 1921, when a group of some fifty Chinese Communists formed the Konchantang or Chinese Communist Party, one of the founding members was none other than the twenty-eight-year-old Mao Zedong. But the Comintern Bolsheviks thought them of little importance and ordered them to ally with the ideologically more conservative Nationalists under Sun Yat-sen. The Comintern Bolsheviks then assigned one of their own, Mikhail Markovich Borodin, to guide the unification of the two parties. Thus, between 1923 and 1927, it was he who wrote the combined party's new constitution and controlled its political reorganization and military development. Moscow used this occasion to send arms and ammunition as well as hundreds of skilled military and political leaders to help the Nationalists and the Communists in the civil war.

But things did not quite go as planned. Sun Yat-sen's untimely death in 1925 gave rise to General Chiang Kai-shek as the new leader of the Nationalists. Chiang, who had received military training in Moscow, soon demonstrated his skill as an army commander by winning a number of important victories over the warlords. But Chiang was no Marxist and did not trust the Soviet Union. He felt threatened by the large numbers of communist recruits arriving from across the border and soon severed his alliance with the Chinese Communist Party. In March 1927, he went on attack against the Communists in Shanghai, where he ordered the liquidation of tens of thousands of communists and expelled all Soviet advisers. This was a stunning reversal for the Comintern and completely derailed its revolutionary project in China. In the meantime, Chiang's army captured Beijing before moving on to Nanking, which he made his capital. This was the first time in twelve years China had been united under one rule, despite the fact that the new leaders were not yet in full control of the country.

Chiang's assault on the Communists continued into the 1930s, but was put on hold in 1931 when Japan invaded Manchuria. Chiang, however, did not initially fight the Japanese; instead he made an agreement that allowed him to continue his war against the Communists. At one point, Chiang's army was close to annihilating the Red Army, now under the leadership of Mao Zedong. By 1934 the situation seemed hopeless for the CCP until a German-born Russian-trained volunteer, Otto Braun, urged a tactical retreat to Hunan to link up with the Second Army there. Mao embraced the idea, which today is remembered as the Long March and one of the most remarkable military achievements of all time. In 368 days, 87,000 soldiers marched 6,000 miles over some of most difficult terrain in all of China. And although less than 10,000 men survived, they were able to combine with the Second Army and form a force of 80,000, which proved to be every bit the equal of that under Chiang Kai-shek.

The Chinese civil war was interrupted again in July 1937 when the Japanese, now part of the Axis alliance with Germany and Italy, again invaded China. Chiang and his army, having joined the Allies, actually received support from the Russians to hold the Japanese at bay. Meanwhile, Mao's army occupied those territories that had been conquered by the Japanese but had been abandoned. He also took this respite to enlarge his own army and strengthen his Party organization. He confiscated land belonging to the great landlords and redistributed it to the peasants. By the end of the war, the Communists were revitalized and well prepared to continue the fight against Chiang and the Nationalists.

In 1945, General George C. Marshall, on a mission for the State Department, had tried to get the Nationalists and the Communists to agree to a political settlement. Since neither side was willing to budge, the civil war began anew. This time the Chinese Communists were at a distinct advantage: not only had they built up a superior military force, but they had much more support in the countryside. The peasants had been won over by the Communists' program of agrarian reform, which proved be decisive. On October 1, 1949, after a series of impressive military victories, Mao Zedong announced the establishment of the People's Republic of China. He also declared his support for the Soviet Union and the world communist movement. The Nationalists, led by Chiang, escaped to Taiwan, where they sought the support and protection of the United States and other Western countries.

Mao Zedong was a man of his time. Like most twentieth-century revolutionary leaders, he was determined to eradicate all counterrevolutionary elements to force the country to submit to his will. In a speech at the Central Committee of the Seventh Congress of the Chinese Communist Party, he spoke ominously about the future:

> After our armed enemies have been crushed, there will still be our unarmed enemies, who will try to fight us to the death. We must never underestimate their strength. Unless we think of the problem in precisely those terms, we will commit the gravest of errors.[1]

Statements such as this could easily have come from Josef Stalin, especially during the purges and the Great Terror of the 1930s, when most of the Soviet population cowered in fear of being arrested. Mao emulated in Stalin's ruthless revolutionary example and his disregard for human life and may well have surpassed it.

Once in power, the Chinese Communists did much that resembled what the Soviets had done a generation earlier. Land reform was at the top of the agenda, and this meant that the former landowners had to be dealt with decisively. To this end, the Chinese borrowed the "struggle session" that the Bolsheviks had used in the early years of Soviet power. This was a procedure to inflict degradation and humiliation on class enemies. The idea was to make former landlords desire not to be landlords any more. Thus, it was intended to be brutal, but it also made redemption possibly for the landowners who were encouraged to purge themselves of all counterrevolutionary and reactionary thinking. The victims not only had to submit to public criticism, but were expected to criticize themselves as a means of self-improvement. But the struggle sessions could also be lethal depending on the circumstances: if the victim did not appear sufficiently contrite or if the mood of the crowd was unusually vengeful, bad things could happen. In the Soviet Union the struggle sessions had died out in the 1920s, but in China they were not abolished until 1976, the year of Chairman Mao's death.

During his first year in power, Mao's campaign to annihilate counterrevolutionary elements was coupled with the so-called three-anti campaign. This was an effort to cut out waste, corruption, and bureaucracy. The Party targeted former members of the Kuomintang, non–Party bureaucratic officials, businessmen, former employees of foreign companies, and intellectuals. A second such initiative was launched in January 1952, called the five-anti campaign, which targeted bribery, theft of state property, tax evasion, cheating on government contracts, and the stealing of state economic information. These campaigns lasted for several years and took millions of lives. Many disappeared into a system of labor camps similar to the Soviet Gulag, called *laogai*, set up during the 1950s. The term is an abbreviation meaning "reform through labor." Many arrestees were executed according to a quota system set up by Mao himself. Indeed, the terror that gripped China invites comparison with the Soviet Terror of the mid–1930s. It featured a campaign of accusation and denunciation in which workers informed on their coworkers and bosses, spouses informed on each other, and children tattled on their parents.

Borrowing from the Soviet model, Mao also began a five-year plan in China in 1953 to industrialize and to relieve the country's dependence on agriculture in order to become a great power. Helped by considerable Soviet aid, new industrial plants were built that produced so much more wealth than was expected that the Chinese concluded that they no longer needed Soviet support. At the same time, Mao was urging the aggressive collectivization of Chinese agriculture, which also went better than expected. So euphoric was Chairman Mao that in mid–1956 that he proclaimed the triumph of socialism over capitalism in China. He also felt confident that China was stable enough to allow greater tolerance of artistic expression and even urged the country's intellectual class to offer constructive criticism to China's ruling elite. As he put it: "Let a hundred flowers bloom and a hundred schools of thought contend."

The people that Mao was urging to boldly speak up were at first reluctant to do so. The near total silence from those he had hoped to embolden annoyed the Chairman. In February 1957, he gave another speech in which he repeated his demand for constructive criticism for the good of the country. This time people did speak out, albeit cautiously. For the most part, they limited their complaints to the corruption of Party officials. Gradually, however, the tone and content grew sharper as people began to express their misgivings about Marxist-Leninist ideology and the regime's hampering of scientific inquiry through "irrational practices," "inadequate resources" and "unreasonable security restrictions." Some claimed that Party cadres were impeding serious research by dogmatic adherence to ideology. College students were the next to weigh in by hanging wall posters in public places that criticized the Party and called for a reexamination of ideology and doctrine. Some posters went much farther and revealed the raw anger that many people felt. One at Qinghua University cursed Chairman Mao himself for pretending to lead a hard and simple life while living off the fat of the land: "That son of a bitch! A million shames on him!"

Within a few weeks, the Chairman had had enough. He shut down the Hundred Flowers Campaign and began to root out those who had shown themselves to be enemies. To this end, he initiated the Anti-Rightist Movement in which hundreds and thousands of intellectuals, artists, and writers were arrested or executed. Little did it matter that many of those taken into custody had not spoken out at all, but had merely been accused doing so. In any case, the effects of the Anti-Rightist Campaign were soon felt at the universities, which were forced to undergo a thorough reorganization. Party interference in academic policies and administrative matters, which previously had been more of a nuisance, now became overbearing. So many intellectuals were purged as a result of Mao's crackdown that there was a shortage of qualified people to fill all the positions available.

Although chastened, the Great Helmsman was still determined to lead China into the future. In 1958, he initiated a second Five Year Plan, which soon became known as the Great Leap Forward. Mao's thinking on how to build socialism in an economically backward state in some ways resembled Stalin's. The plan was to develop both industry and agriculture by exploiting their interdependent relationship. Thus, in order for industry to expand and prosper, Chinese peasants needed to grow more food. More food would in turn enable Chinese industry to expand and produce the tractors and other items necessary. And since growing more food was critical to the success of the Great Leap Forward, Mao commanded that all of China's small agricultural collectives combine into giant communes, each of which would contain about 5000 families. This policy was carried out with such speed that by year's end, some 700 million people had been relocated into 26,578 communes.

Initially, the Chairman's project aroused enormous enthusiasm, which the regime fueled by nonstop propaganda. Mao promised that the Chinese economy would surpass Great Britain's in fifteen years, and the people wanted to believe. The peasants were especially excited by the prospect of ending the country's food shortages forever. The price of doing this, however, using Mao's Great Leap Forward, proved to be higher than anyone imagined. The peasants' lives were now completely controlled by the commune, which was to provide for all their needs, including food, lodging, health care, and even entertainment. The commune expropriated most of what peasants owned, including their livestock and farm tools. There were day-care services and schools for the children and "houses of happiness" for older people unable to work. Thus, the peasants could devote all their energy and strength to the task of producing food for the country without being encumbered by family concerns. And, much like the Soviet Five Year Plans, people were pressured to surpass their assigned quotas. Finally, Mao's plan also called for the creation of "backyard" production plants, which would enable peasants workers to produce steel and other important items used by the communes. This extra burden proved mostly unworkable.

In the first months, things seemed to go even better than planned. The year 1958 was hailed as a banner year for the Chinese economy. People celebrated in the belief that China had produced the largest harvest in history. This of course justified raising the already high production quotas. Party officials, who knew better, were afraid to object for fear of being labeled "bourgeois reactionaries." But by late 1959, the food shortages became impossible to ignore. China was engulfed in a famine that has been called the worst in world history. Although some of the problem was due to bad weather, which caused flooding in some areas and droughts in others, the human element made things immeasurably worse. The farm machinery that was supposed to help farmers increase productivity was poorly made and quickly fell into disrepair. The backyard furnaces upon which so much depended could not be operated efficiently. They required more coal and manpower than had been expected, which meant that the trains, needing coal for fuel, ran short. Finally, with the harvest rotting in the fields, more workers had to be reassigned from operating the furnaces. and sent back to the fields. Finally, and perhaps worst of all, the steel produced by the backyard furnaces was of such poor quality that it could not be used for the big construction projects for which it had been intended.

It has been estimated that between 1959 and 1962, some thirty million people died of starvation or from famine-related causes. According to Jasper

Becker, not all the deaths were entirely accidental. As food was being rationed throughout China, Chairman Mao manipulated the system so that those whom he considered to be "enemies of the people" received the smallest rations. He also began a vindictive campaign against Party members and others who revealed the truth about the famine. These were labeled "right opportunists" and sent to concentration camps, where many died. Indeed, Mao's reaction to the famine was much like Stalin's to the Soviet famine of 1931–1933. Like his Kremlin mentor, the Chairman was determined to achieve his goals at any cost. But not only did he fail to alleviate the food shortages, he made them worse by increasing the procurement levels. For this he blamed the peasants for concealing grain and sent armed detachments into the countryside to punish the hoarders and to take the grain by force. In the end, even Mao was forced to admit that the Great Leap Forward had been a failure. The program was officially abandoned in 1962. Mao himself was forced to resign his office as president, although he remained Chairman of the Party.

The new leaders of China, who included Liu Shaoqi, Deng Xiaoping, and Zhou Enlai, were far less inclined to take radical measures in order to build socialism faster. Their main concern was to stabilize the economy. Thus, the commune system was restructured so that production brigades and teams had more control over administrative and economic planning. They also meant to discipline the Party in order to make it interact better with the people. To this end, leading Party cadres were urged to adopt a more populist style leadership at all levels. Furthermore, in order to develop and expand industry, the emphasis would now be on realistic and efficient planning rather than ideological fervor and mass movements. Henceforth, factory managers would control production more. Finally, steps were taken to bolster national defense and internal security. Over the next few years, China enjoyed significant recovery under the new, more conservative leadership.

But Chairman Mao took a rather dim view of the new conservative elite and their policies. Moreover, he particularly resented his semi-retired status in the Party and government. The new leadership, he believed, was increasingly alienated from the people they were supposed to serve. Somehow, a way had to be found to reinvigorate the revolutionary spirit in the Chinese people. Thus, in August 1966, he gave a speech at a Plenum of the Communist Party Central Committee in which he called for a cultural revolution to liberate the country from the "Four Olds": old customs, old culture, old habits, and old ideas. To this end, he urged the creation of an army of "Red Guards," made up overwhelmingly of young people, to punish anyone who had grown comfortable with the bourgeois remnants that contradicted the highest ideals of Chinese society.

What followed were two years of chaos and turmoil that nearly destroyed China. In an effort to rid the country of anyone who might impede the building of socialism, the Red Guards engaged in reckless denunciation and persecution against all perceived "enemies of the people." These included people of privilege or those thought a have a superior attitude. More specifically, the list of enemies included bourgeois elements, suspected counterrevolutionaries, engineers, scientists, factory managers, and most of all intellectuals. The Red Guard activists set up special tribunals to deal with these miscreants. Schools and universities were closed as professors and administrators were attacked and beaten. Many young intellectuals who were sent in to the countryside to be "reeducated" by the peasants spent much of their time leaning to sweep courtyards, work on building projects, and clean toilets.

One man who was branded an "enemy of the people" at this time was Deng Xiaoping, a longtime friend and colleague of Mao Zedong. A small man barely five feet tall, he was set upon by Red Guards and forced to endure humiliating "struggle sessions" before being assigned to work in a tractor factory. The Guards also so abused his younger brother that he committed suicide. The same fate befell his eldest son at Beijing University, who jumped out of a window four stories high, hoping to end it all. He broke his back in the fall and for a time was denied treatment. He survived but remained paralyzed for life. Deng himself was finally rehabilitated in 1973, only to be purged again in 1976 as Mao lay dying. This time he was denounced as an "unrepentant capitalist roader," which, ironically enough, is exactly what he later turned out to be. Deng was removed from all his posts and spent most of a year under house arrest. After Mao's death, a comrade from his army days, Marshall Ye Jian-ying, petitioned for Deng to be returned to a position of power and influence.

Soon, however, the chaos and violence became far more destructive than even Mao intended. The Red Guards were determined to banish everything associated with the period before the Revolution. Like the young soviet activists who joined the League of Militant Atheists, seeking to annihilate everything associated with religion, the Red Guards vandalized Buddhist temples, churches, and mosques. They burned sacred texts and continued the struggle sessions, by which political rivals and class enemies were publicly humiliated, physically abused, and forced to admit to crimes that they were alleged to have committed. The struggle sessions were generally conducted before large crowds, sometimes numbering in the thousands. In the beginning, people were required to attend, but in time these spectacles became a form of popular entertainment.

The Cultural Revolution reached a new level of destructiveness when the various Red Guard units began to fight each other because of ideological and tactical differences. They also attacked foreigners and foreign embassies, which resulted in the British Embassy being destroyed by fire. In an attempt to end the violence, Zhou Enlai, who had initially urged Party members to submit to criticism, now feared that the Cultural Revolution would do permanent harm to the country if not brought under control. His plea, however, was not immediately heeded. But by December 1968, Mao himself had come to the same conclusion. Industrial production had fallen by twelve percent in two years. To restore growth, he dispersed the Red Guards around the country so they could cause less harm. To this end, he announced the "Down to the Countryside Movement," whereby urban cadres would be sent to live and work on farms to learn from the peasants. Ostensibly, this was to be understood as a means of leveling society, but in fact, the Chairman sought to end the cultural upheaval he had initiated.

The intra–Party struggles for power, however, were to continue for several years. During this time, the Chairman's second in command, General Lin Biao, had tried to assassinate him, and he, in turn, had tried to assassinate the general. Mao ultimately won this duel when Lin died in a plane crash in 1971 while attempting to flee the country. Meanwhile, a new force had emerged, the so-called "Gang of Four" led by Mao's wife, Jiang Qing, and her three associates. The Gang was opposed to all moderates and used the media to campaign against them. Among those singled out for special abuse was Deng Xiaoping, who had only recently been released from a reeducation camp. But Deng got the upper hand in January 1976 when the popular Zhou Enlai died after a long struggle with cancer. Mourners by the thousands gathered in Tiananmen Square to praise Zhou and denounce the radicals, Mao included. The Chairman blamed Deng for the demonstration and again placed him under house arrest. But the Chairman's death on September 9 brought his handpicked successor Hua Guofeng to power, who promptly had the Gang of Four arrested. This signaled the official end of the Cultural Revolution.

Deng's political comeback was soon to follow. His allies in the military, led by Marshall Ye Jianying, pushed to have him released from house arrest. Hua Guofeng was reluctant to do this, but eventually acquiesced and found himself in a power struggle with Deng, whom he could not defeat. Hua, it seems, had never ceased being a devout Maoist and would not renounce the policies of his mentor. Deng's more pragmatic approach to modernizing the economy had more support. Thus, by December 1978, he was established as China's de facto leader, though he was never head of state or the head of the government. Deng publicly renounced the excesses of the Cultural Revolution, much as Khrushchev had renounced Stalin's atrocities in the great terror. And, like Khrushchev, he sought to expose the sins of his predecessor (Mao) by inviting Chinese citizens to openly criticize the excesses of the Cultural Revolution. He also put China on the road to radical reform by calling for "Four Modernizations" of agriculture, industry, science, and technology.

Deng led China for roughly twelve years and thoroughly transformed the country economically. He opened the country to tourism and improved relations with the West and Japan. He also offered the Chinese people a kind of New Deal when he declared that "socialism does not mean shared poverty." Thus he offered material incentives and bonuses rather than threats and crude propaganda to motivate peasants to produce more. These included the right to sell the produce from their garden plots on the open market. He also changed the country's development strategy to concentrate on light industry and export-led growth. Through it all, Deng was guided more by results rather than ideology. As he used to say: "It doesn't matter whether the cat is black or white as long as he catches the mouse."

But for all his success in promoting prosperity and progress in China, Deng's legacy as a reformer is decidedly clouded. Enormous problems have accompanied the country's new affluence. These have included child labor, sweatshops, the proliferation of fraudulent businesses, criminal gangs, prostitution, and drug trafficking. Moreover, high inflation, panic buying, business bankruptcies, and the threat of unemployment beset a people who were more accustomed to the certainties of socialism. But perhaps most damning was Deng's refusal to cultivate any democratic institutions in the new China that might interfere with his economic reforms. Thus the savage crackdown on the Tiananmen Square protests that followed the visit of General Secretary Mikhail Gorbachev in April 1989 led to soldiers and tanks attacking students in the streets of Beijing, which resulted in more than a thousand deaths. The widespread foreign criticism of this event increased China's wariness about allowing a more open society to complement their more pragmatic approach to economics.

* * * * * *

The year 1933, which was a turning point for so many of the great and powerful countries around the world, was no less so in Cuba. This is when an obscure army sergeant, Fulgencio Batista, played a decisive role in the ousting of the country's unpopular fifth president, Gerardo Machado. This allowed a former university professor, Ramon Grau San Martin, to become president, although his term lasted less than a year. Batista, who had his own ambitions, forced Grau to resign so that he could rule as dictator. The former non-commissioned officer, however, was annoyed by his lack of a title and resolved to become elected president in his own right. To this end, he supported the creation of a new, more liberal constitution before for the presidential election of 1940. The sergeant's victory seemed to portend a long time in power, but the new constitution prevented him from running for a second term in 1944. Batista submitted to the law and moved to Daytona Beach, Florida, to plan a comeback.

In 1952, Batista again ran for president, but this time he took no chances. Lagging in the polls, he turned to his supporters in the military and took the presidency by force. What followed was a nightmare for all but the wealthiest Cubans. Batista began by revoking the 1940 Constitution, which included such basic civil liberties as the right to strike. He actively supported the interests of the most powerful landowners and ignored the widening gap between the rich and the poor. He invited the American mafia and the large multinational corporations to invest and profit in Cuba. He increased censorship, arrested and tortured his detractors, and arranged for public executions for his worst enemies. Interestingly, he seems to have enjoyed the complete support of the U.S. government.

Batista's fraudulent triumph, however, did not go unchallenged. Among those who were determined to defend the democratic process was Fidel Castro, a young lawyer and member of the reformist Cuban People's Party. Castro's first instinct was to take Batista to court by charging him with corruption and tyranny. When this failed, he organized a revolutionary force of 160 men and on July 26, 1953, led an assault on the Moncada military barracks at Santiago de Cuba. He had hoped to precipitate a popular revolt against the dictator, but the result was a complete disaster in which nearly all the insurgents were killed. Castro and his brother Raul were captured and sentenced to fifteen years in prison. In 1955, however, Fidel's former Jesuit teachers intervened and persuaded Batista to free the brothers as part of a general amnesty.

The Castros fled to Mexico to reorganize and meet with other opponents of the regime. It was at this time that Fidel met Ernesto Che Guevara, an

Argentine Marxist who joined the revolutionaries and soon became one of Fidel's most ruthless commandants. This new rebel force became known as "26th of July Movement" in commemoration of the failed attack on the Moncada barracks three years earlier. But the revolutionaries suffered yet another disaster when eighty-two of them traveled by yacht to the Playa Las Coloradas on the western part of the island. They had hoped to establish their main base of operations in the Sierra Maestra Mountains, but they were soon discovered and nearly wiped out by the Cuban army. Amazingly, both Castro brothers and Guevara survived to again rebuild their revolutionary force.

As popular support for the Batista regime plummeted, a new group, the Revolutionary Directorate, which was composed of students and anti-communists, attacked the Presidential Palace on March 17, 1957. The rebels had hoped to decapitate the government by assassinating the president. Although the attempt failed miserably, support for the Revolution grew among ordinary Cubans, who began to believe that the regime could be defeated. The United States gave impetus to this trend the following year when it imposed an arms embargo. The effect on the Cuban army's morale and battle effectiveness was telling. In July 1958, Castro's outnumbered guerrillas defeated a government battalion at the Battle of La Plata and captured 240 of the enemy.

The United States subsequently recalled its ambassador and expanded the embargo. Castro's rebels, outnumbered and undersupplied as always, continued their offensive. On July 28, 1958, during the Battle of La Mercedes, the rebels, who numbered about 3,000, were on the verge of defeat. Castro requested a ceasefire, ostensibly to negotiate a surrender. The ruse worked to perfection. Over the next seven days the talks went on with no result. Meanwhile, the rebels used the delay to sneak back into the mountains to reorganize and to continue the fight.

By now, the momentum had shifted irrevocably to the rebels, who were growing in confidence. On November 7, 1958, the forty-first anniversary of the Bolsheviks' seizure of power in Russia, Che Guevara led his rebel army in a march on Havana. His force grew steadily as other rebel groups joined him along the way. Among the most important of these was the Revolutionary Directorate, whose previous attempt to assassinate Batista had failed so abysmally. This combined rebel force won victories at Yaguajay (December 30) and Santa Clara (December 31). Batista, who was determined not to go down with the ship, fled to the Dominican Republic. He never saw Cuba again. Castro, whose army had recently occupied Santiago de Cuba, now began the long victory march to Havana. He entered the capital in triumph on January 8, 1959, and promptly named himself prime minister of Cuba.

The first order of business for the new revolutionary government was to take vengeance on their former tormentors. As in the Bolshevik victory in 1917, Extraordinary Courts were set up for this purpose. Mass executions were carried out at the La Cabana and Santa Clara prisons. A crowd of 18,000 people gathered in the Palace of Sports to celebrate when some of Castro's more infamous enemies were tried, convicted, and shot. Both Guevara and Raul Castro played important roles in the terror that followed. The former was the supreme prosecutor in La Cabana, while the latter presided over executions of some seventy pro-Batista prisoners after the capture of Santiago.

Throughout the early weeks and months of the Revolution, Castro moved cautiously, mindful of the impression he was making abroad, especially in the United States. He announced repeatedly that he was not a communist and promised to restore the 1940 Constitution. The Eisenhower administration, though wary, was initially prepared to cooperate with the new regime, but this was short-lived. In August 1960, the true nature of Castro's rule became clear when he nationalized all U.S. property in Cuba. Eisenhower responded by freezing all Cuban assets on American soil and by severing diplomatic ties. But Castro, who seems to have anticipated the hostility of the United States, was buoyed by the support his domestic initiatives had engendered at home and abroad. These included a drive to expand education for all children and improvements in medical facilities, health, hygiene, and sanitation. New laws were passed to promote equality for blacks and women, and efforts were undertaken to reduce unemployment and combat corruption.

As so often happens in revolutions, the taste of power and lust for revenge of those who claim to be acting in the name of the people were great. Castro apparently believed that he was immune to such temptations. In 1957, he gave an interview with *New York Times* journalist Herbert Matthew in which he stated flatly: "Power doesn't interest me. After victory I just want to go back to my village and be a lawyer again." But his subsequent actions made a mockery of these words. He, like Batista before him, also refused to honor the Constitution of 1940. He subsequently imposed another that was modeled on that of the Soviet Union. He also postponed elections indefinitely, which he justified in an address to the people of Havana by exclaiming: "Elections? What for?"

In other instances, however, Castro kept his promises even when they were unpopular. Such was the case with land reform. Castro was determined to take decisive action, mainly because seventy-five percent of Cuba's best farmland was owned by foreigners. He ordered that all such lands be expropriated and subdivided into cooperatives. Among those who vehemently disagreed with this policy was Humberto Sori Marin, the very official who had been placed in charge of land reform. Marin fled the country in protest, only to return with weapons and explosives to attempt to overthrow the new regime. He was arrested and promptly executed. When others, however, followed his example, Castro authorized the creation of Committees for the Defense of the Revolution. The purpose of these bodies was to root out all manner of counterrevolutionary activity. To this end, they infiltrated individual neighborhoods and spied on those suspected of disloyalty, keeping records on all aspects of their behavior including contact with foreigners, work and education history, and sexual orientation.

Many of those who had long supported and served Castro were so troubled by these actions that they resigned from the government in protest. These included President Manuel Urrutia, Roberto Agramonte, the minister of foreign affairs, and Rupo Lopez Fresquet, the minister of finance. Castro subsequently eliminated all independent newspapers, including *Avance,* whose fiercely anti–Batista editor was forced into exile. A similar fate befell the editor of *Bohemia,* Miguel Angel Quevedo, who, in 1959, had published the transcript from Castro's 1953 trial, which showed him in a heroic light. All this occurred during a wave of emigration from Cuba of some 50,000 middle-class citizens, many of whom were doctors, teachers, and lawyers. The new regime could ill afford to lose such people, but away they went, never to return.

The enormous number of Cubans who chose to leave the island rather than live under Castro's dictatorship presented the U.S. with what seemed like a golden opportunity. So many of them were resolute anti-communists, who had expressed a willingness to fight in order to oust Castro, that the Eisenhower administration came up with a plan to accomplish that end. It authorized the CIA to train some 1,400 Cuban exiles in Guatemala to attack Cuba and retake the country.

Those who planned the mission were confident that the Cuban people would rise up and support the invaders as liberators. It has been said that President Kennedy, who had replaced Eisenhower in January 1961, had some serious doubts. Still, he allowed the attack to go on April 17, 1961, and the result was an unmitigated disaster. Within three days the operation had been completely routed by the Cuban Army, which captured some 1,200 of the exiles. The U.S. paid $53 million to secure their release. The one truly unintended and fateful consequence of this debacle was that Soviet premier Nikita Khrushchev interpreted Kennedy's refusal to provide sufficient air support as a weakness that could be potentially exploited. He concluded the U.S. would do little to resist Soviet expansion in Latin America or anywhere else.

Meanwhile, Castro savored his victory and further developed his Soviet-style dictatorship. After nationalizing all private commerce and industry, he shut down all religious colleges, including the Bethlehem Jesuit College, which he himself had attended. He also confiscated all property belonging to the Catholic Church, which made it near impossible for the Church to minister to the faithful. Castro seemed to have forgotten how his former Jesuit teachers had petitioned Batista to gain his release from prison. Nevertheless, Castro continued to go hard on the Church as he forced many priests and at least one bishop into exile. As he was later to declare: "Let the Falangist[2] priests start packing their bags." The government was declared to be officially atheist, and although the regime pledged it would allow all Cubans the right to worship as they pleased, it penalized people who did. Thus, religious believers were barred from studying at the university and denied employment in the civil service.

The revolutionary changes that were occurring in Cuba were shaped in no small part by Che Guevara, who was a confidante of Casto. In many ways, Guevara's revolutionary example invites comparison with that of Trotsky. Both men came from relatively well-to-do families; both were intellectuals and cosmopolitan in their attitudes and tastes. Both were intensely devoted to Marxist ideology and eloquent its defense. Both were gifted military leaders who made important contributions to victory in their respective revolutions.

Guevara's success as a military leader, however, did not prepare him for the jobs to which Castro assigned him. As minister of industry and head of the Central Bank, he was clearly a fish out of water and probably did more harm than good. What Guevara could do, however, was to propagate the ideas of Marx and Lenin and extol the Soviet achievement. He wanted Cuba to follow the Soviet Union's road to socialism and to imitate the Soviet cult of the new man. To this end, he adopted the idea of "voluntary work Saturdays," which was copied from the Soviet Subotniki (Saturdays). These were days on which the workers in the USSR gave a free day of labor to the state. He also called for the militarization of youth and praised the "extremely useful hatred that turns men into effective, violent, merciless cold killing machines." Finally and most ominously, he was inspired by the Soviet Union's system of slave labor camps or gulag. According to Regis Debray,[3] it was Guevara and not

Castro who promoted the idea of a corrective work camp, which was in fact much more punitive that the name would suggest.

Eventually, Guevara and Castro had a falling-out. By that time, Che's infatuation with all things Soviet had passed; he became sharply critical of the USSR and now saw China as his revolutionary ideal. He particularly admired the Cultural Revolution in China, with all its destruction and Mao's avowed willingness to wage nuclear war in order to destroy capitalism. Part of this disenchantment was prompted by the Cuban Missile Crisis in October 1962, when American spy planes discovered Soviet nuclear missiles being installed in Cuba. The subsequent American blockade of the island and the real danger of a nuclear armageddon persuaded Soviet premier Nikita Khrushchev to withdraw the missiles. Guevara was one of those who favored a military response and was appalled when Khrushchev backed down in exchange for an American promise not to invade the island.

Guevara left Cuba in 1965 determined to spread the flames of revolution throughout Latin America. He ended up in Bolivia, where he tried to radicalize the peasants, but made few converts. He was eventually hunted down and executed by the Bolivian military on October 8, 1967. Nevertheless, Guevara in death remained a powerful symbol of the Cuban Revolution, of one who was fiercely dedicated to the creation of a communist state in Cuba no matter what it cost in terms of human suffering and deprivation. The evidence for this dire assessment has long been manifest. By April 1980, the misery of daily life in Cuba had become so overwhelming that thousands of poor Cubans mobbed the Peruvian Embassy in Havana, hoping to get exit visas in order to emigrate. The crisis went on for many weeks until Castro finally announced he would allow 125,000 to leave from the port of Mariel. In fact, he used the crisis rid the country of those he didn't want, i.e., the mentally ill and some of Cuba's most hardened criminals. Another such situation arose in 1994, when a large number of people sought to leave the country on rafts called *balsas*. When the police held them up, rioting broke out and dozens of arrests were made. It finally subsided after Castro allowed about 35,000 to leave on this occasion. Since then there have been many more such departures, although Castro has not always been so magnanimous. At times, he has ordered helicopters to drop sandbags on the rafts at sea to prevent people from leaving the island. In the summer of 1994, some 7,000 people lost their lives trying to reach Florida.

Castro has stated that he "would rather die than abandon the revolution." This is probably what will have to happen in order for Cuba to fully face the economic realities of the twenty-first century. Even so, some useful changes have been made in recent years. In 2006, when Fidel became ill, he temporarily turned over control of the government to his brother, Raul. In 2008, Fidel retired and the National Assembly elected Raul to succeed him. The new president soon began introducing economic reforms. These included the lifting of restrictions on consumer access to certain electronic goods, allowing farmers greater control of land use, and the ending the equal pay system, allowing the more productive workers to earn better pay. The United States has responded positively to these moves by easing travel restrictions to the island for Cuban Americans as well as for U.S. academic, cultural, and religious groups. It has also become easier for Americans to send money to relatives in Cuba, and U.S. telecommunication companies are now allowed to operate on the island. All this activity would seem to portend more such positive changes in the near future.

* * * * * *

The revolution that took place in Cambodia in the 1960s and '70s was arguably the most tragic and destructive revolution of the twentieth century. It was largely a side effect of the Vietnam War. A French protectorate since 1863, Cambodia had been a monarchy for more than 1900 years. It was occupied by Japanese and Thai forces during World War II and gained its independence in 1953. Cambodia seemed on the path to political modernization in March 1955 when King Norodum Sihanouk abdicated his throne in favor of his father and involved himself in politics. His great victory in the parliamentary elections the following September enabled him to assume the post of prime minister. In 1960, after the death of his father, Sihanouk was elected head of state, although his official title was that of prince rather than king. These developments, however, were threatened by the ever-intensifying civil war in neighboring Vietnam between the communist north and the noncommunist south. Sihanouk had declared his country's neutrality in the conflict, but his decision to allow North Vietnamese troops to establish sanctuaries in eastern Cambodia in 1965 drew his country into the fighting.

This situation continued for several years until 1969, when President Richard Nixon ordered the bombing of Cambodia in order to clear these areas of North Vietnamese soldiers to prevent them from attacking the South. When this failed to achieve the desired result, the U.S and South Vietnamese invaded with ground troops, but this served only to further destabilize the country. Consequently, in March 1970, General Lon Nol staged a coup and overthrew Sihanouk and declared Cambodia a republic. He then abolished the monarchy, made himself president, and took control of the government. The new regime was soon challenged by the emergence of the Khmer Rouge, a radical communist guerrilla group. Having formed in the 1960s, these rebels operated in the jungles of northeast Cambodia. They identified with the historic city of Angkor, which in the thirteenth century had been possibly the largest preindustrial city in the world. The Khmer Rouge were neither numerous nor well-armed, but for a time the support they received from North Vietnam helped make them a force to be reckoned with. The North Vietnamese broke with the Khmer Rouge in 1973, when they refused to send representatives to Paris to participate in negotiations regarding the withdrawal of American troops from Vietnam. Even so, the Khmer Rouge fought on and declared victory in the civil war after capturing the capital, Phnom Phen, in April 1975.

The all-powerful leader of the Khmer Rouge was Pol Pot, a man who must surely rank as one of the strangest and most mysterious rulers of the twentieth century. He was described by some who knew him in the early days as a sensitive, rather timid man who enjoyed French poetry and was admired by those he taught and advised. As a revolutionary comrade, he was said to be warm and generous and an inspiring leader. But over the years Pol Pot changed and succumbed to what seems to have been some kind of mental illness. Inspired by the glory of Angkar, he became convinced of his infallibility and genius and resolved to create the most perfect agrarian society ever. That August he introduced a Four Year Plan to dramatically raise capital by increasing Kampuchea's agricultural exports. This would finance the industrialization of agriculture, diversify light industry, and eventually promote the construction of heavy industry. Thus Kampuchea would prove its superiority to the world and a new age would have begun. With no hint of the difficulty or the enormous cost of his grand vision, Pol Pot brushed aside all practical considerations: "Because we are the race that built Angkor, we can do anything." He also claimed that the Angkor was really the Communist Party of Kampuchea.

As Pol Pot saw it, the success of his new society depended upon the virtue of those who performed the labor. He was determined to weed out those who were found to be impure and therefore unworthy. To this end, he divided the population into two classes: the country people and the "New People." The former were deemed superior because they worked the land. For this they enjoyed the status of a privileged class. They were allowed to cultivate a small plot of land and were the first to be fed at the canteen. The New People, on the other hand, having come from the cities and towns, had no rights or privileges. They were disparaged for being "the lackeys of foreign imperialism" and treated like "enemies of the people." Their fate was made clear from the very beginning when Khmer spokesmen boasted over the radio that the regime had more than enough people to build the world's most perfect agrarian paradise. Those who were flawed were deemed unnecessary and had little chance of living to see the grand vision realized. Hence the grim Khmer proverb: "To keep you is no benefit, to destroy you is no loss."

Although Pol Pot was the guiding spirit of the whole enterprise, ordinary citizens did not even know his name until much later. He allowed no personality cult to form around him and authorized no official biography. Nor were there any photographs, portraits, or statues of him in public places or writings explaining his thoughts or ideology. These omissions were most likely not due to modesty, but rather his determination to exploit his anonymity as a means of mystifying and intimidating his subjects. Whatever the case, Pol Pot's scary vision of the perfect agrarian society allows no easy explanation. His worst crimes seem to have been engendered by the weird paranoid fantasies that preyed on his mind. Much like Stalin, he came to suspect anyone who showed initiative, leadership, or an independent spirit. His frequent purges of Party personnel were carried out without trials or legal procedures of any kind. In July 1978, the following call for vigilance appeared in the Party's monthly newspaper, *Revolutionary Flags*: "There are enemies everywhere within our ranks, in the center, at headquarters, in the zones, and out in the villages." The carnage that followed was considerable: thirteen of the highest officials in the government and most regional secretaries were executed. Many of those who were eliminated included some of his oldest comrades, who were subjected to the most hideous tortures before execution.

In the new totalitarian order of Democratic Kampuchea, people who were being deported were deprived of all their possessions. They wore black uniforms with long sleeves buttoned up to the top. They behaved according to a strict code, which banned all displays of affection and emotion. Arguments, insults, complaints, and tears of grief or sadness were subject to harsh punishment. Schools were closed and freedom of movement for ordinary people was severely restricted. Medicines were all but impossible to obtain. The practice of religion and the art of writing were driven underground. Perhaps the only thing that wasn't forbidden was the right to work. This, however, became a recipe for death, especially for the New People, who were sent daily into the fields with primitive tools and inadequate food rations. Forced to labor sometimes in excess of twelve hours a day, many died of hunger and exhaustion. Others ended their misery by committing suicide.

Democratic Kampuchea soon gave rise to yet another slogan: "The Angkar kills but never explains." In the new order, almost any behavior that was not specifically allowed was forbidden and usually punishable by death. The most serious crime was stealing food, but those who didn't steal were likely to die from starvation. Thus, people continued to steal, scavenge, and scrounge for anything edible including domestic animals, frogs, snails, lizards, snakes, red ants, spiders, rats, shoots, mushrooms, and forest roots. Too, because the water they drank was befouled with impurities, many suffered from dysentery. Another lethal affliction was edema or dropsy, brought on by an excess of salt in the thin rice soup that everyone ate. Finally, as the hunger crisis intensified, some resorted to cannibalism. This, too, was a capital crime, but it did not deter a former schoolteacher who ate her own sister's corpse. For this she was beaten to death by a crowd in the presence of her daughter. This horrifying act of retribution, however, did not prevent others from cannibalizing the dead. In time, some actually developed a taste for certain human organs such as livers and gallbladders.

In the three years, eight months that the Khmer Rouge ruled Kampuchea, the regime never wavered in its determination to dehumanize and subjugate its subjects. The goal, of course, was to reduce the entire population to a state of helpless subservience to the Angkar. To this end, families were deliberately broken up. Husbands and wives were sent to different work camps and children were raised separately. Those who begged to be reunited with their families were sternly reprimanded by the guards: "You have individualist tendencies.... You must shed these illusions." A soldier who wanted to care for his wounded son was prevented from doing so by a Khmer guard. Later this same soldier was admonished when he tried to help a sick neighbor, who was unable to care for his two children. "You don't have a duty to help these people. On the contrary, that proves that you still have pity and feelings of friendship. You must renounce such sentiments and wipe all such individualism from your mind."

The regime also suppressed Buddhism, a religion that had a sizable following in Kampuchea. The Buddhists were an inviting target because of their otherworldly philosophy and indifference to the practical problems of everyday living. Their belief that one's existence had no meaning in the "great wheel of incarnations" assisted in the regime's determination to snuff out the individuality among its subjects. The Buddhists were appalled when the regime outlawed cremation for the dead and fretted that their loved ones would have to be buried in the cold earth without the necessary rituals to aid in the process of reincarnation. This threatened to condemn an individual's existence to that of a ghost. In the end, however, despite these provocations, the Buddhists could offer no effective resistance to their Khmer tormentors.

Other religious groups suffered even more. The Catholics saw their magnificent cathedral in Phnom Penh completely demolished as nearly half the Catholic population of Kampuchea was either killed or sent into exile. The Catholics were singled out for especially brutal treatment because most came from the cities and were of Vietnamese descent. Another religious minority to suffer was the Cham, most of whom were farmers and fishermen. The Khmer Rouge was especially antagonized that they had adopted an alien faith: Islam. However, because of their reputation as fierce warriors, they were "invited" to join the Khmer Rouge during the civil war. But the Cham were none too enthusiastic about fighting for others' conflicts and much more interested in the profits they earned by selling fish to the people of Kampuchea. For these reasons, Pol Pot ordered the villages of the Cham destroyed, their mosques razed and their Korans burned. In June 1975, thirteen Muslim dignitaries who had agitated for religious rights were executed and the "Cham mentality" was officially denounced and ordered abolished forthwith.

Indeed, minorities of any kind came under lethal attack in Democratic Kampuchea, some of which were almost completely wiped out. These included ethnic Vietnamese, ethnic Chinese, former officers in the republican army, and intellectuals. Of these, it was hatred for Vietnam that was the most intense for having "stolen" Kampuchea Krom two hundred years earlier by integrating it into Cochin China. In 1976, those Vietnamese still living in Kampuchea were suddenly not allowed to leave. In April 1977, a directive was promulgated ordering the arrest and incarceration of anyone who had even a single identifiable Vietnamese ancestor. Those who did were classified as "historical enemies" and subject to all kinds of abuse, including capital punishment.

Despite Pol Pot's boast that Kampuchea would forge its own unique brand of communism, he seems to have been almost mesmerized by Mao Zedong and China's Great Leap Forward. Thus, the communes that were constructed in Democratic Kampuchea had many of the same features of those built in China in during the Great Leap Forward. These included the military control of the workforce, mandatory collective canteens and childcare programs, and the gigantic hydraulic work projects that demanded so much labor at the expense of agricultural productivity. The famine that followed, and the misery it created, peaked in 1977. This calamity was accompanied and made worse by massive purges brought on by political infighting among the Khmer elite. The victims were mostly those who had previously been mostly ignored: schoolteachers, the more prosperous peasants, and the wives of men who had been executed earlier. Sometimes whole families were executed and entire villages wiped out.

Of course, all despotisms apply terror in some form to subjugate those that they rule, but what the Khmer Rouge achieved in Democratic Kampuchea was truly frightening. The entire population was reduced to a level of dazed obedience that rendered them helpless before their tormentors. And for good reason, since virtually any transgression imaginable was punishable by death. Indeed, some people were executed for the sole purpose of making fertilizer. Moreover, the actual executions were designed to make the victims' last moments as horrifying as possible. Thus, the condemned were usually not shot. Most were beaten to death by blows to the head by with iron bars, pickax handles, or agricultural instruments. Others were hanged or had their throats cut. Some were asphyxiated with plastic bags. The worst fate was reserved for disgraced cadres, some of whom were buried up to their necks in the ground and then had their heads doused with gasoline and set on fire.

Perhaps most dispiriting aspect of the Khmer regime was its exploitation and mistreatment of the children of Kampuchea. Children as young as twelve were forced to serve in the army. The regime found that they were they were more malleable than older recruits and obeyed orders without question. Too, such children, when properly indoctrinated, had no scruples even about killing members of their own clan, including babies. Finally, children as young as eight or nine were enlisted to work as spies and apparently performed quite well. Hence they became a valuable asset to the regime. Unfortunately, they, too, were doomed because they were allowed no education, and their training from the Khmer Rouge only encouraged their most savage instincts. Many of these "militia children" wound up in prison despite Pol Pot's claim that in Democratic Kampuchea there were no such institutions. As he put it, "Bad elements in our society are simply given productive tasks to do." The truth, however, was far more sordid. Those who committed transgressions were sent to "reeducation centers," which were housed in abandoned schools or police stations. The conditions were horrific: in some instances as many as thirty prisoners might be crammed into a tiny cell with no toilets and no place to wash. The detainees subsisted on rations that often consisted of nothing more than water with a small can of rice. And there was no need for medical facilities at these "reeducation centers," because all were expected to die in captivity.

The soldiers of the Khmer Rouge soldiers showed no mercy. Children who stole were arrested and executed. Some were shot, some kicked to death, and others thrown into a pond and held down by their feet until drowned. The executioners as a rule sought to inflict as much suffering as possible. One of the worst atrocities was carried out at the central prison, Tuol Sleng, on July 1, 1977. There 114 women, most of which had been identified as wives of prisoners, were all hanged. The next day thirty-one boys and forty-three girls were also executed. All had been the children of prisoners.

As the outside world became aware of the atrocities being committed in Kampuchea, pressure grew to do something to stop the madness. Vietnam had the best reason to take on this nasty chore because of the Khmer Rouge's frequent border attacks on Vietnamese villages, causing death and destruction. In December 1978, Vietnam invaded Democratic Kampuchea. Thirteen months later the Vietnamese captured Phnom Penh and set up a new government to be called the People's Republic of Kampuchea. It was to be run by Hanoi and the Vietnamese military and consisted of a large contingent of Khmer Rouge communists who had agreed to cooperate with the new regime. Meanwhile, Pol Pot and many of his followers had fled westward to an area near Thailand. There they organized an insurgency against the new regime in Phnom Penh. Soon, however, some Cambodian Non-Communists joined in fighting, which reignited the civil war.

In 1982, a coalition was formed between the Non-Communists in Cambodia and the Khmer Rouge insurgents under the titular leadership of Norodom Sihanouk. As the fighting intensified, hundreds of thousands Cambodians fled to refugee camps for safety. Over the next few years, however, the government in Phnom Penh began some cautious economic reforms, which allowed Cambodians to own their own businesses and farms. Vietnam also began to withdraw its troops from the country so that by 1989 the Hanoi-dominated government in Phnom Penh began to negotiate with the various opposition groups to bring an end to the fighting. In 1991, a United Nations-sponsored Peace Treaty was signed, which provided for multiparty elections in May 1993 for a legislative assembly and a transitional government, formed by the parties that won the most seats. This led to a constitution, which provided for a democratically elected government presided over by two prime ministers, Hun Sen and Prince Nordum Ranariddh. The ceremonial office of king was reestablished and filled by Norodom Sihanouk.

The new government didn't work too well in the early years, largely because the two prime ministers didn't get along. After Hun Sen forced Prince

Ranariddh from office in July 1997, the latter challenged the decision, and after years of wrangling, the two reached a power-sharing agreement in 2004, with Hun Sen as prime minister. That same year, King Sihanouk resigned his office for reasons of health and was replaced by his son Norodum. The new king would begin to round up those members of the Khmer Rouge who could be found. King Sihamoni appointed both Cambodian and international judges to a special court that first convened in February 2009 to accomplish this end. Unfortunately, it was too late to try those who were most guilty: Pol Pot died in 1997, and by 1999, the Khmer Rouge had become so reduced in membership that it simply disintegrated. The worst of the killers simply disappeared and never saw the inside of a courtroom.

In retrospect, it is clear that Democratic Kampuchea was deeply influenced by both the Russian and Chinese revolutions. Hence, the regime's boast that "The Khmer revolution has no predecessors" cannot be taken too seriously. Pol Pot was not only an enthusiastic student of the French Revolution, he also took much from Marx, Lenin, and Mao Zedong. His ultimate ideal was the creation of an agrarian utopia within a tightly controlled totalitarian state in which the value of the individual was denied and the collective was all-important. Much like Stalin and Mao, Pol Pot relished the challenge of hunting down and annihilating "enemies of the people" who allegedly lurked everywhere. Virtually anyone could be a target for any reason. The holocaust that devoured the people of Cambodia was frighteningly similar to what occurred in the USSR and China.

* * * * * *

The Iranian Revolution that began in January 1978 was unique among those that had taken place in Russia, China, Cuba, and Cambodia. For one thing, it was a fiercely theocratic and anti-secular movement fundamentally opposed to communist regimes wherever they may be. At the same time, however, as in so many other revolutions, the Iranian people were aggrieved and angry and determined to overthrow the ruling monarch, Mohammad Reza Shah Palavi, whose extravagant lifestyle and hateful domestic and foreign policies had long offended nearly everyone in the country. The Shah was of no great ancient linage; he was the son of an army officer, Reza Shah Palavi, who, in 1925, became the ruler of Iran and founder of the Palavi Dynasty. He had sent his son, the Crown Prince, to Switzerland to be educated in preparation to one day succeed his father. In fact, this happened much sooner than anyone expected when in September 1941, the father was ousted by the British and the Soviets when he refused to allow them to use the Trans-Iranian Railway during the Second World War. Thus, Mohammad Reza Shah, now twenty-two, replaced his father on the Peacock Throne. The young monarch got off to a promising start when he rehabilitated of all those politicians who had suffered disgrace during his father's rule. He also impressed others by his thoughtful and prudent conduct of state affairs, in contrast to his father.

Mohammad Reza's first serious challenge, however, came roughly a decade later when his prime minister, Mohammad Mossadeq, introduced a bill in parliament to nationalize British petroleum interests in Iran. This drew a sharp reaction in the United States and in Britain, whose leaders, President Eisenhower and Prime Minister Churchill, plotted a coup to oust the prime minister. This proved to be not so easy to do. The first attempt failed and the Shah fled the country in panic. Only after the success of the second did he return to Teheran much relieved. He nullified Mossadeq's planned nationalization of the petroleum industry and met with CIA agents from whom he accepted money and promises of help for development and reform.[4] It was an arrangement that proved toxic for him and his dynasty. The Shah had set up his government to resemble a Western democracy, with multiparty elections to the *majlis* or parliament. At the same time, he continued to rule as a despot, denying his subjects the most basic human rights. He also used his Israeli-trained secret police force, Savak, to oppress and abuse all who opposed him.

For the next twenty-five years, the Shah's rule engendered resentment and anger throughout Iran. This was especially true among students and intellectuals, but included even some in his own service. On April 10, 1965, a member of the Imperial Guard entered the Marble Palace with a submachine gun, intent on assassinating Reza Mohammad and possibly others in the royal family. The intruder, who had been trained by a group called the "Devotees of Islam," was intercepted and gunned down by two other Guardsmen who themselves perished in the attack. It was a close call, but Reza Mohammad seemingly did very little in response other than to tighten security and to move his residence north of Tehran to Niavaran, a remote palace intended primarily for state guests. Niavaran was a sumptuous residence and an architectural marvel, built at an altitude of 6,000 feet in a park of old pines and oriental plane trees. There were breathtaking vistas in every direction.

According to historian James Buchan, the Shah's move north exposed a telling irony. This same man who had always insisted that he was loved and admired by his people now felt compelled to travel in and around Tehran by helicopter, mainly for reasons of security. This meant that every house that lay beneath the ruler's flight path had to be vetted by the minister of court. He also began to attend military reviews wearing a bulletproof vest. Otherwise, not much else changed. Mohammad Reza continued to rule as a despot, remaining blissfully ignorant about the needs and concerns of his own people.

In October 1967, the Shah had himself crowned in a glittering ceremony that celebrated his new title: "Shahanshah" meaning "Emperor" or "King of Kings." Mohammad Reza apparently thought himself worthy of such an honor, since the sixties were a time of great prosperity for the country, if not the Iranian people. Much of this had to do with the price of oil, which, of course, had climbed as demand grew worldwide. As Iran's wealth accumulated, Mohammad Reza thought to use it to modernize the country. To this end, he undertook a number of expensive public projects, including two 1,300-megawatt Siemens nuclear reactors for Bushehr on the Persian Gulf and then two more reactors from French industry on the Karun River.

Unfortunately, the Shah never understood the downside of progress and why most Iranians found it so unsettling. For one thing, the country's prosperity had prompted the enormous growth of the country's military establishment, so much so that it seemed to have become an occupying power. Even worse was the fact that much of this had been done at the behest of the United States. During the early summer of 1972, President Nixon and his secretary of state, Henry Kissinger, visited Iran and bestowed on Mohammad Reza the dubious honor of guardian of the Nixon Doctrine, which emphasized America's willingness to help the country with self-defense by offering advice and support, but not with troops on the ground. To this end, the Shah was given to understand that America was prepared to sell him virtually any conventional hardware he wanted. During the next five years, Mohammad Reza bought more than $10 billion of weapons from the Americans, who found doing business with the Shah increasingly lucrative. In the meantime, the U.S. used *its* large military to support Israel during the 1973 Yom Kippur War, further damaging the Shah's image.

Indeed, the 1970s were a frustrating time for Mohammad Reza, who was mystified by the continuing widespread resistance to his most enlightened endeavors. One of his most loyal supporters described his master as a man "who had lavished everything on a beautiful woman for years only to find that she had been unfaithful all along." He was particularly infuriated by the treachery of the radical left, which opposed his every initiative. Thus the Shah commanded Savak to come down hard on these extremists and to show no mercy.

In doing so he committed what may have been his most shameful crime. On 19 April 1975, after capturing nine reputedly dangerous leftist activists, Savak henchmen summarily executed all of them. Afterward, it was claimed that they were shot while trying to escape, but this was contradicted by the testimony of one of the executioners at his trial later that year. He claimed the victims were taken in minivans into the hills above Evin, handcuffed and blindfolded, and gunned down. When the Shah was questioned about this later, he answered dismissively: "There was no choice. They were all saboteurs. They would have escaped and that would have been even worse." In fact, the worst was yet to come.

One year later, in March 1976, Mohammad Reza, in celebration of the 50th jubilee of the House of Palavi, ordered the Islamic solar calendar replaced with a new imperial calendar to commemorate the enthronement of Cyrus the Great in 559 BCE. Devout Muslims were aghast at what seemed like a deliberate affront to their faith. The Islamic calendar, which marked the beginning of the Prophet's ministry in Medina in 622, was sacred to all believers. Among those most angered by the Shah's blasphemy was the Shiite leader Ayatollah Ruhollah Khomeini, who, since 1964, had been living at various places in exile until finally settling in France. The Ayatollah's rage was awesome as he condemned the new calendar by issuing a *fatwa*, which forbade Muslims to recognize or use it in any way. Those who were most resolute in their hatred of the Shah and his regime took notice of this fiery leader and soon began to unite around him. Ruhollah Khomeini was eager to embrace the challenge.

To energize his supporters in Iran, he began to practice his own version of *samizdat* (self-publishing) by recording his angry anti–Shah speeches on cassette. Multiple copies were made of each and passed on to others. In his addresses, the Ayatollah urged his loyal followers not to be discouraged, but to demonstrate, riot, and strike. That they did with a vengeance. By late 1978, the Iranian economy was almost completely shut down. The Shah, now seriously ill with lymphatic cancer, was much demoralized and prepared to leave the country, ostensibly to get some much-needed rest. One of his last acts was to appoint Dr. Shipour Bakhtiar to the office of prime minister. That done, Mohammad Reza, on January 16, 1979, and without officially abdicating, fled the country. He was sustained by the vain hope that his condition could be treated and that he would someday return. The Shah travelled far and wide in search of this treatment. He eventually ended up in Egypt, where he died on 27 July 1980.

Seventeen months earlier, on February 1, 1979, the Ayatollah returned to Iran to a rapturous welcome by some five million people who filled the streets of Tehran. One of his first actions as *faqih,* (i.e., supreme leader) was to dismiss Bakhtiar and appoint the Revolutionary Council to enforce his new laws and edicts. The immediate goal was to purify the country of Western ideas and culture. Thus, alcoholic beverages were forbidden, pro-Western newspapers and magazines were shut down, political parties were banned, and the universities were closed. Revolutionaries also took over the TV and radio stations, most government buildings, and the palaces of the Palavi family. Amid the general celebration and glee, however, many were troubled by the excessive vengeance and lack of judicial procedure that preceded the executions of those who had supported the Shah.

The man chosen to run these proceedings was Sadeq Khalkhali, the humble son of a farmer born in northwest Iran. At seventeen, he entered the seminary at Qum and became acquainted with Mostafa Khomeini, son of Ruhollah Khomeini. Young Sadeq was deeply impressed by the Ayatollah and soon became his devoted follower. Not long after the surrender of the Shah's army, Khomeini appointed him a judge of the revolutionary courts. Khalkhalki did not disappoint his master and soon become infamous for his preference for the death penalty even when there was no evidence to support it. As he later wrote in his memoir: "Lately, I have been thinking how few people I have killed. There were just so many ripe for execution who escaped me." But what offended his detractors was not the number of people he killed, but rather his "slap-dash and indolent way of working." He didn't even pretend to be interested in the truth and was willing to accept vague and unsubstantiated charges such as "war against God" or "corruption on earth" in order to justify the death penalty.

Among the first to suffer from such arbitrary revolutionary justice was a former prime minister, Amir Abbas Hoveyda, who appeared in court on February 12. The accused was in bad health but undaunted by the powers arrayed against him. Unlike the other defendants, he had not tried to escape when the Revolution came. Once in court, he stood up to the prosecutor and answered his questions with poise and confidence. He was also defiant: "I take responsibility for my actions and am not afraid because I believe in God." Indeed, Hoveyda's bravery stood in stark contrast to the lack of it in the other defendants, most of whom were terrified by their predicament. Absent among the accused was General Nassiri of Savak, who was severely beaten and stabbed in the neck and unable to attend the trial. Yet he was declared guilty in absentia of torture, massacre, and corruption on earth. On February 15, all the condemned except Hoveyda were taken to the roof of the Refah School late at night and shot. The former prime minister, however, was temporarily spared so that he could be the sole defendant in a show trial similar to those that were staged in the Soviet Union in the mid–1930s.

On April 7, 1979, Hoveda finally had his day in court. Prosecutor-Judge Khalkhami opened the proceedings by speaking for perhaps three-quarters of an hour about Hoveyda's complicity in the crimes of the Palavi regime over many years. Then Hoveyda, speaking in a calm and dignified voice, explained that he was a "servant of a system" in which much of what a prime minister might normally do was handled by the Shah himself. These included: foreign policy, the armed forces, Savak, the oil company, and certain other departments of state. But Hoveyda did not try to blame Mohammad Reza for all that had gone wrong. He insisted that his former master's vision for the country was right and just and that the Shah had failed only for lack of time. Khalkhami, however, was having none of it. He deliberated just two hours before returning to announce the verdict and the punishment. "You are found to be a corrupter on Earth. You are condemned to death."

This was the beginning of a terror that would continue on and off for the next ten years. The first victims were mostly royalists, cabinet members, senior officials, and members of the Majlis. Also included were numerous generals and Savak agents. The driving force behind this was Khalkhami, who never hesitated to impose the death penalty on the flimsiest of evidence. Over time, however, many Iranians became increasingly troubled by the realization that they had sent one tyrant into exile only to see him replaced by another even more despotic.

In May, the Ayatollah created the Revolutionary Guards to protect the Revolution from what was left of the Shah's army and others groups that were still trying to win control of the Revolution. His intent was to create the ideal Islamic state in which the laws would be strictly in accordance with *Sharia*. But as the Ayatollah constructed his seventh-century theocracy, the world for a while was distracted by other events. Margaret Thatcher became Britain's first female prime minister. Israel and Egypt signed a historic peace treaty that featured the return of the Sinai to Egypt. In June, Pope John Paul II became the first pontiff in history to visit Poland. President Carter and General Secretary Leonid Brezhnev signed Salt II in an attempt to slow down the arms race.

On October 22, however, news from Iran returned to the front page when the Shah was admitted to a New York City hospital seeking treatment for his cancer. This set off an explosion of protest in the streets of Tehran, with demonstrators shouting "Death to the Shah" and "Death to America." That same day, five Iranian students, all members of a group the called the Consolidation of Unity, met in a building near the University of Tehran to plan a response to America's "treachery." At first they talked about the possibility of a sit-in or occupation of the American Embassy for two or three days. As more people became involved, however, the urgency to do something dramatic increased. On November 3, the Ayatollah issued a statement urging students, seminarians, and all devout Muslims to intensify their attacks on the U.S. and Israel in order to force the return of the Shah. That was apparently the go-ahead the students needed.

The next morning at 10:30, some 300 students climbed over the walls of the American Embassy and quickly occupied all the major buildings. The embassy staff had long been prepared for this eventuality and immediately began shredding documents in a sealed room. This was allowed to continue for many hours, since none of the occupiers thought to cut off the electricity. By 2:00 p.m. a crowd of thousands had gathered around the embassy shouting "Death to the Shah"—"Death to America." The attackers, emboldened by their easy success at the American Embassy, later that afternoon broke into the British Embassy. They did relatively little damage and stayed only a few hours. Apparently, one embassy hostage crisis was enough for the time being.

President Carter, who had anticipated the attack on the embassy, was prepared to seek a diplomatic solution. He ordered the freezing of $6 billion in Iranian assets held in American banks. He also solicited the assistance of other Muslim countries to urge moderation on those close to the Ayatollah. In fact, the president got support from a most unlikely source: the Palestine Liberation Organization. The Palestinians, perhaps hoping to win official recognition from the United States, persuaded the release of most of the African American and women hostages on November 17. This reduced the number of hostages being held from sixty-three to fifty-two. At the time, this humane and sensible act seemed to presage an early end to the hostage crisis, but it was not to be.

By the spring of 1980, with negotiations stalled, Carter began to consider a rescue mission code-named Operation Eagle Claw. The final version of this plan proved to be ridiculously complicated. It involved eight helicopters from the aircraft carrier USS *Nimitz* in the Arabian Sea and eight C-130 cargo planes from Oman carrying fuel and ninety U.S. Delta Force commandos that were to rendezvous at an abandoned airfield in southern Iran. The commandos were to be delivered by helicopter and trucks to the American Embassy in Tehran, which they would attack and rescue the hostages. But the mission had to be aborted early on because of technical problems with three of the helicopters. All that remained was to withdraw the aircraft and personnel and return to the USS *Nimitz*. But this, too, proved to be difficult. In the process one of the helicopters collided with one of the cargo plane, causing an explosion that killed eight servicemen. This required President Carter to admit publicly that a rescue mission had been attempted and failed. Thus, the hostages remained in captivity until the inauguration of President Ronald Reagan on January 21, 1981.

In the meantime, the Ayatollah was busy supervising the completion of Iran's new Islamic constitution, adopted on December 3, 1979. Though less than ideal for secular Muslims, it was a near-perfect fit for most fundamentalists who wanted a stern theocracy in which Islamic morality would be aggressively enforced. The Iranian Constitution has been rightly called a mixture of theocratic and democratic elements. All sovereignty is vested in God and all legislation issued by the democratically elected president and Majlis, who reflect the divine nature of God. Of course, all democratic procedures and rights were to be subordinate to the Guardian Council. The Ayatollah was pleased by this document and hoped it would become a model for other Muslim states.

But not everyone in the Islamic world welcomed Iran's new order. Among those who were most hostile to the Ayatollah and his regime was the Sunni president of Iraq, Saddam Hussein. On September 4, 1980, Hussein, sensing weakness in his Shiite neighbor, ordered his army into Iran to win back some disputed territories. These included the oil-rich region of Khüzestan and the Shaat-al-Arab River, which is formed by the confluence of the Tigris and Euphrates rivers. The Iraqis at first made good progress by capturing the city of Khorramshar, but failed to achieve their goal of taking the oil-refining center of Abadan. By 1981, the Iraqis had been forced onto the defensive and had to give up territory. In 1982, they withdrew all their troops from Iran and attempted to make peace. But the Ayatollah refused; he was determined to overthrow his hated foe Saddam Hussein. Thus, the war settled into a long stalemate, which neither side could break through.

This became war at its nastiest. Iran made numerous attacks using untrained and unarmed troops and even young boys taken right from the streets. Hussein used poison gas against the Kurds, whom he believed were aiding Iran. Both sides used aircraft and missiles to attack each other's cities, military bases, and shipping in the Persian Gulf. Iran's attacks on Kuwait's and other Gulf states' oil tankers prompted the U.S. and other countries to send warships to the region to ensure that oil deliveries to the rest of the world not be disrupted.

The loss of oil revenue hit both combatants extremely hard. Both appealed in turn to their allies for help. Iran relied on Syria and Libya for help and aid, while Iraq turned to Saudi Arabia, Kuwait, and other neighboring Arab states. Also favoring Iraq were the U.S. and Soviet Union. Iraq continued to sue for peace even as it used chemical weapons against the Iranians and against the Kurdish population within its own borders. Hussein believed the Kurds to be favoring Iran. But the misery of war for both sides could not be endured forever. By the spring of 1988, Iran's economy had deteriorated to such a point that even the Ayatollah was prepared to accept a UN-mediated ceasefire. It has been estimated that some 500,000 on both sides perished, with Iran suffering the greater losses.

The Ayatollah's death of a heart attack the following year in some ways signaled the end of an era. Ali Khamenei was chosen as the new *faqiq*. He did not come at a good time. In June 1990, an earthquake struck in northwestern Iran and claimed the lives of some 40,000 people. Oil production dropped dramatically, which reduced exports, and this made it nearly impossible for Iran to pay its foreign debts, buy necessary imports, grow the economy, and reduce unemployment.

Khamenei was not to know much tranquility during his one term in office. The Clinton administration accused him of sponsoring international terrorism and of trying to acquire nuclear weapons. In 1995, President Clinton ordered a ban on all trade with Iran. At home, Iranians suffered by the embargo and faulted the government for mismanagement and corruption. By 1997, Iranians had elected a new president, Mohammad Khatami, who promised political reform and a relaxation of some of the harsher policies that had been instituted during the Ayatollah's decade in power. In the parliamentary elections of 2000, various reform groups won a majority in the Majlis. These reformist-minded legislators pushed through a number of enlightened measures, including freedom of the press and less government interference in the personal affairs of ordinary citizens. Khatami's reelection in 2001 seemed to portend a more liberal and democratic Iran. But these hopes were dashed when the Council of Guardians vetoed many of these bills.

In 2005, the former mayor of Tehran, Mahmoud Ahmadinejad, was elected president of Iran. The process was deeply flawed, since the Council of Guardians had disqualified many reformist candidates in advance. Ahmadinejad proved to be a hardliner in every sense of the word. Not only did he strictly enforce Islamic dress codes and harass minorities, but he embraced an anti-gay agenda that authorized the hanging of homosexuals. He also defied the United Nations by continuing to enrich uranium, which many feared would be used to produce nuclear weapons. Finally, as a confirmed anti-Semite, he denied that the Holocaust ever happened and pledged to work for a new world order without Israel and America. Amadinejad was reelected in 2009 by such a wide margin that many suspected fraud. The supporters of his opponent, Mir Hossein Moussavi, turned out by the thousands to protest the results in the streets of Tehran. The government reacted vengefully to this challenge, killing at least twenty demonstrators and possibly many more.

Iran still struggles to recover from its revolution of so long ago. It brazenly defies the court of world opinion as continues to enrich uranium in order to build nuclear weapons. The Obama administration has attempted to engage Iran on issues of common concern, but has achieved little of substance so far. It may well take another violent revolution to put Iran firmly on the road to modernity.

Chapter Notes

Introduction

1. Richard Pipes, *The Russian Revolution* (New York: Vintage Books, 1991), 545.
2. It is well to remember that the notion of guilt due to the identity rather than the actions of the defendant was not unique to France or Soviet Russia. In the years following the American Civil War, General Philip Sheridan declared, "the only good Indian is a dead Indian" as the army endeavored to round up all of the country's Indians and put them on reservations. More recently, in Nazi Germany, the authorities went to great lengths to determine how much Jewish blood a person had to have in order to be declared legally Jewish.
3. Orlando Figes, *A People's Tragedy* (New York: Viking Press, 1997), 510–511.
4. Figes, *A People's Tragedy*, 631.
5. Figes, *A People's Tragedy*, 630.
6. Anne Appelbaum, *GULAG: A History* (New York: Doubleday, 2003), 102.

Chapter 1

1. The earliest socialists, such as Charles Fourier (1772–1837), Henri Saint-Simon (1760–1825), and Louis Blanc (1811–1882) reacted to the evils of industrial capitalism by urging the creation of cooperative communities in order to promote social harmony and economic equality. These "utopian" socialists were opposed to the accumulation of private property as contrary to the best interests of society. Marx and his collaborator, Friedrich Engels (1820–1895) were influenced by these early thinkers, but also criticized their failure to appreciate the need to mount a revolutionary struggle to destroy the capitalist system.

2. Lenin headed the majority, or Bolshevik faction, which called for a tightly knit party of dedicated revolutionaries, which would not hesitate to use subversion and violence to overthrow the state. The minority, or Menshevik faction, was led by Georgi Plekhanov and, later, Nikolai Bukharin. They urged the creation of a mass labor party in order to achieve economic gains for the workers by legal means.
3. Orlando Figes, *A People's Tragedy*, 525.
4. Geoffrey Hosking, *The First Socialist Society* (Cambridge, MA: Harvard University Press, 1993), 58–59.
5. Trotskii, *Sochinenia*, 17, I: 290-I, quoted in Figes, *A People's Tragedy*, 529.
6. Figes, *Peasant Russia Civil War: The Volga Countryside in Revolution, 1917–1921*, 101ff, 132–135; Channon, "Tsarist Landowners," 584; Rudnev Privechernykh, 112–129.
7. Dekrety, I, 469 and IV, 101, quoted in Pipes, *The Russian Revolution*, 798.
8. Ia. Berman in PRiP, No. 1/11 1919, 70, quoted in Pipes, 798–800.
9. Andrei Synyavsky, *Soviet Civilization* (New York: Arcade Publishing, 1988), 88–89.
10. V.I. Lenin, Polnoe sobranie sochinenie, 35, 204, quoted in Figes, *A People's Tragedy*, 524.
11. *Novaia Zhizn'*, 17 January 1918; Steinberg, *In the Workshop*, 145, quoted in Figes, *A People's Tragedy*, 536.
12. Pipes, *The Russian Revolution*,. New York: Vintage Books, 1991, 728.
13. GARF, f. 393, op 2, d. 59, 1. 35–8, quoted in Figes, *A People's Tragedy*, 527.
14. E. H. Carr, *The Bolshevik Revolution* (New York: W.W. Norton, 1980), vol. 2, 88–89.
15. Members of 17th Century sect, who rebelled against the reforms introduced by

Patriarch Nikon in the Russian Orthodox Church. These changes were intended to correct errors in religious texts and rituals that had accumulated over many years since the translation from the original Greek. The Old Believers offered fanatical resistance and eventually formed a separate sect. For their defiance they were severely persecuted by the tsars.

16. James L. West and Yurii A. Petrov, eds., *Merchant Moscow* (Princeton, NJ: Princeton University Press, 1998), 164–165.

17. West and Petrov, eds., 168–169.

18. West and Petrov, eds., 169.

19. West and Petrov, eds., 176.

20. West and Petrov, eds., 176–167.

21. West and Petrov, eds., 177.

22. Robert Service, *A History of Twentieth Century Russia* (Cambridge, MA: Harvard University Press, 1997).

23. Lenin, PSS, 44: 167, quoted in Alan M. Ball, *Russia's Last Capitalists* (Berkeley: University of California Press, 1987), 19.

24. Resheniia partii i pravitel'stva po khozaistvennym voprosam, 1:233–234; SU, 1921, No. 57, art. 356, quoted in Ball, *Russia's Last Capitalists*, 21–22.

25. Ball, *Russia's Last Capitalists*, 22.

26. *Zakony o chastnum kapitale*, pp. 6–7, 19–20, quoted in Ball, 23.

27. Victor Serge, *Memoirs of a Revolutionary 1901–1941* (London, 1967; reprint, 1975), 198–199, quoted in Ball, 42.

28. Ball, 30.

29. Ball, 39.

30. Ball, 40–41.

31. Ball, 47–48.

32. Ball, 53.

33. Ball, 59–60.

34. Ball, 56.

35. Ball, 162–63.

36. Bruce Lincoln, *The Romanovs* (New York: Doubleday, 1981), 577–578.

37. Bruce Lincoln, *Red Victory* (New York: Da Capo Press, 1999), 446.

38. Grand Duke Sergei Alexandrovich was the cousin and brother-in-law of Tsar Nicholas II. He was married to Elizabeth of Hesse, known as Elle, who was the elder sister of the Empress Alexandra. Elle entered a monastery after the assassination of her husband and earned widespread respect and admiration for her piety and good works. However, on the evening of July 17, 1918, she and a number of other high-born prisoners were thrown into a mineshaft near the town of Alapayevsk in western Siberia after being clubbed to death.

39. The home belonged to a retired engineer, Nikolai Ipatiev.

40. Greg King and Penny Wilson, *The Fate of the Romanovs* (Hoboken, NJ: John Wiley & Sons, 2003), 214.

41. In 1912, Grand Duke Michael had married a twice-divorced woman of common birth named Nathalia Sheremetevskaya Wulfert. The wedding was technically illegal because members of the royal family were not permitted to marry without the tsar's explicit consent. In fact, Nicholas had specifically warned his brother not to marry Mrs. Wulfert, whose social ambitions were well known. Eventually, he did allow her to assume the title of Countess Brassova, although he never received her at court.

42. This was a military force comprising Czechs and Slovaks who had initially been part of the Austro-Hungarian Army. After being captured by the Russians, they were granted permission by Tsar Nicholas II in 1915 to serve in the Russian Army as a special unit and at one point numbered as many as 65,000 men. After the tsar's abdication in March 1917, the Legion fought for the Provisional Government. Eventually, it became involved in the Russian civil war and posed a serious threat to the Bolshevik regime.

43. King and Wilson, 206–207.

44. This account of the murder of the imperial family and their retainers closely follows that of King and Wilson in their book, *The Fate of the Romanovs,* 301–311.

45. Telegram from Ural Regional Soviet to Lenin and Sverdlov in GARF, f. 601, op. 2, 27, quoted in King and Wilson, 334.

46. Nicholas Sokolov, *Enquette judiciare sur l'Assassinat de la Famille Imperiale Russe,* Payot: 1925, quoted in King and Wilson, 336.

47. The mineshaft where Yurovsky had originally intended to bury the victims proved to be too shallow. This necessitated a time-consuming search for a new site. Secrecy became impossible because nosy outsiders kept appearing and reappearing. The truck carrying the corpses got stuck three times due to the muddy roads, and Yurovsky fractured his leg when the horse he was riding slipped and fell.

48. As late as the 1980s, guides for the Soviet travel agency *Intourist* routinely misinformed foreign visitors to the USSR that only Nicholas was executed in the Ipatiev House. It was claimed that the other family members and servants were spared and allowed to live elsewhere.

49. The Soviet government also chose to celebrate perhaps the most loathsome of all the murderers, Piotr Ermakov (1884–1952), who as a youth had raised money for the Party by stealing horses and robbing trains and banks. He first attained notoriety when he killed and then beheaded a night watchman during one of his robberies. For the rest of his life after the Ipatiev House massacre, Ermakov enjoyed the status of a privileged member of the Communist Party. The authorities even named a street after him in Yekaterinburg. He was often invited to address groups of students and workers to boast of his role in the murders and to show off the pistol with which he claimed to have killed Nicholas II. Ermakov died of alcoholism at the age of sixty-eight and was buried with honors in the War Memorial in Moscow.

50. King and Wilson, 521.

Chapter 2

1. The zemstvos were institutions of local self-government established in 1864 during the reign of Tsar Alexander II (r. 1856–1879). The municipal dumas were city parliaments with limited power to legislate on matters of local interest.

2. G. Lelevich [L. Mogilevskii], V dni samarskoi uchreditilki (Moscow, 1921) 9–10 passim: also Lenin Sochineniia XXIII 644; George Stewart, *The White Armies of Russia* (New York, 1933) 145, quoted in Pipes, p. 130.

3. Figes, *A People's Tragedy*, 624.

4. Figes, *A People's Tragedy*, 626–627.

5. The declaration of grain as a state monopoly was the first major element of what soon became known as war communism. It was based on the mistaken belief that the abolition of the free market would enable the regime to supply food to the cities and towns. However, the Bolsheviks also saw this as a means of waging the civil war. They intended to extend their power base to the countryside to punish those peasants who were hoarding grain. See Figes, *A People's Tragedy*, 612–615.

6. Antonov-Saratovskii, Sovety I. 54–56, quoted in Pipes, 738.

7. Orlando Figes, *Peasant Russia Civil War: The Volga Countryside in Revolution, 1917–1921*, 249–261, 622.

8. Founded by Victor Chernov in 1900, the Socialist Revolutionaries espoused a left-wing agrarian agenda that advocated terrorism and called for the overthrow of the tsar, equitable land distribution, and the creation of a classless society.

9. Riezler and Erdmann, *Riezler*, 713–714, and Lenin Khronika, V, 606, quoted in Pipes, *The Russian Revolution*, 639.

10. Riezler and Erdmann, *Riezler*, 715, and Baumgart, *Ostpolitik*, 228, note 71, quoted in Pipes, 640.

11. Pipes, 640–641.

12. This was not the first time that Lenin survived an attempt on his life. On January 14, 1918, he was fired at while being driven through the streets of Petrograd. He was pushed to the floor by a fellow passenger, the Swiss socialist Fritz Platten, who was wounded in the right hand by a bullet.

13. N.K. Krupskaya VoVil, vol. 2, p. 312, quoted in Robert Service, *Lenin: A Biography* (Cambridge, MA: Harvard University Press, 2000), 361–362.

14. Maria Spiridonova (1884–1941) was the daughter of well-to-do parents in Tambov province who joined the Socialist Revolutionaries in 1905 and assassinated a government official the following year. She was sentenced to penal servitude for life in Siberia, but she was released after the February Revolution of 1917. She subsequently served a short term as mayor of Chita, where she gained both fame and notoriety by ordering the town's jails to be blown up. Later, after her return to St. Petersburg, her fearlessness and inspiring oratory established her as a leading member of the Left Socialist Revolutionaries.

15. PSS, vol. 37, I. 4; quoted in Dmitri Volkogonov, *Lenin: A New Biography* (New York: Free Press, 1994), 220.

16. In fact, no one actually saw Kaplan fire the shots. Lenin's driver, Stepan Gil, testified to seeing an unidentified woman's hand stretched out from behind a number of other people. In any case, many doubt Kaplan could have committed the deed since she had notoriously bad eyesight.

17. Mal'kov, p. 162, Zapiski Kommandanta Moskovskogo Kremlya, 2nd rev. ed. Moscow, 1961, quoted in Bruce Lincoln, *Red Victory* (New York: Da Capo Press, 1999), 158.

18. Ulyanova, *O Lenine I semie Ulyanovykh*, *Pravda*, 14 January 1925, quoted in Volkogonov, 234.

19. GARF f. 130, op. 2, d. 2, ll. 241–2, quoted in Volkogonov, *Lenin*, 229.

20. Figes, *A People's Tragedy*, 661–662.

21. Paul Avrich, "Nestor Ivanovich Makhno," *Modern Encyclopedia of Russian and Soviet*

History, ed. Joseph L. Wieczinsky, 54 vols. With suppl. (Gulf Breeze, FL: 1976–1990, Academic International Press), vol. 21, 19.

22. Anarcho-communists called for a free federation of agricultural communes and handicraft cooperatives in lieu of large-scale industry and labor organizations. Many anarcho-communist groups such as *Chernoe Znamia* (Black Flag) and *Beznachalie* (Without Authority) advocated terrorism, although the followers of Piotr Kropokin's *Khleb i volia* (Bread and Freedom) group favored tactics that were decidedly more moderate.

23. Avrich, "Makhno," 16–17.

24. Marx had originally used this term when he referred to the political transformation that would take place between capitalism and communism. Lenin developed the concept much more fully in his book *State and Revolution,* written during the summer of 1917. The dictatorship of the proletariat would enable the workers to consolidate political power, suppress all opposition, gain control of the means of production, and reeducate society according to socialist norms. The former upper and middle classes would lose their civic rights as the party put an end to "bourgeois democratic parliamentarianism." Both Lenin and Stalin used this concept to justify the Communist Party's monopoly on power by claiming that it alone represented the true interests of the proletariat.

25. Avrich, "Makhno," 19.

26. Avrich, "Makhno," 19.

27. "Tovarishchi krest'iane!" (leaflet, 3 February 1920), Fedeli Archive, quoted in Paul Avrich, *The Russian Anarchists* (Edinburgh: AK Press, 2005), 220.

28. The Poles were saved when aid from France and other Western powers enabled them to regroup and win a stunning victory to end the war. By the Treaty of Riga in March of 1921, the Poles moved their eastern boundary deep into Belorussia and Ukraine, although they did not acquire all that they had originally sought.

29. Lincoln, *Red Victory,* 470–471.

30. In January 1920, Trotsky became Commissar for Transport and formed the First Labor Army from remnants of the Third Red Army. This was the first of many such initiatives to use military discipline to achieve economic goals. Trotsky eventually created four more labor armies to perform such tasks as constructing railroads, mining coal, and digging peat. The soldiers dragooned to perform this work thoroughly hated it. The labor armies were abandoned when it was seen that little was being accomplished.

31. N.A. Kornatovskii, ed., *Kronshtadskii miatezh;* sbornik statei, vospominanii i dokumentov (Leningrad, 1931), 164–166, quoted in Avrich, *Russian Anarchists,* 229.

32. *Pravda o Kronshtadte,* 83–84; Berkman, *The Kronstadt Rebellion,* 28, quoted in Avrich, *Russian Anarchists,* 230.

33. In 1891 Friedrich Engels wrote a postscript to Marx's *The Civil War in France* to answer critics of this concept. "Well and good, gentlemen, do you want to know what a dictatorship of the proletariat looks like? Look at the Paris Commune. That was the "Dictatorship of the Proletariat." See Ray Taras's article "Dictatorship of the Proletariat" in *Encyclopedia of Russian History,* Vol. I, 394–395.

34. Leonard Shapiro, *The Origin of the Communist Autocracy,* 316, quoted in Avrich, *The Russian Anarchists,* 230.

35. For an excellent account of the Kronstadt Rebellion, see Bruce Lincoln's in *Red Victory,* 489–511.

36. This body served as a kind of parliament to the Communist Party. It consisted of some 300 members who were elected at Party Congresses, which usually occurred every five years. One of the main responsibilities of the Central Committee was to elect all Party, leaders including members of the Politburo. The Committee also met every six months to ratify decisions by the top levels of the party. See Johanna Granville's article in the *Encyclopedia of Russian History,* Vol. I, 221–222.

37. Figes, *A Peoples Tragedy,* 765.

38. Mikhail Keller and Alexander M. Nekrich, *Utopia in Power* (New York: Summit Books, 1986).

39. Yu. A. Poliakov, "Communist Saturdays," *Modern Encyclopedia of Russian and Soviet History,* ed. Joseph L. Wieczinsky, 54 vols. With suppl. (Gulf Breeze, FL: 1976–1990, Academic International Press) Vol. ?, 226–227.

40. In the Bashkir region and the steppes around Pugachev and Buzuluk, the thousands of cases that were reported represent less than half of all that occurred. It was not unusual for parents to use their deceased children to feed themselves and their other children still alive. People hoarded corpses and robbed from cemeteries to get food. They justified their actions by pointing out that the bodies of those interred would have been eaten by worms anyway.

41. In the fall of 1890, the Volga region was

beset by early frosts and a cold winter with very little snow. High winds that spring blew away the topsoil, which was followed by three months with no rain.

42. Volkogonov, 345–346.

43. ARA Bulletin, ser. 2, 28: 6, quoted in Figes, *A People's Tragedy*, 780.

44. Alan Ball, "Survival in the Street World of Soviet Russia's *Bezprizornye*'" *Jahrbucher fur Geschichte Ost Europa*, I, 1991 34, 36–7, 41–2, 47; and Ball, *And Now My Soul Is Hardened: Abandoned Children in Soviet Russia, 1918–1930* (Berkeley: University of California Press, 1994), quoted in Figes, *A Peoples Tragedy*, 780–782.

45. D.L. Zlatopol'skii, "Constitutions of the Soviet Union," *Modern Encyclopedia of Russian and Soviet History*, ed. Joseph L. Wieczinsky, 54 vols. With suppl. (Gulf Breeze, FL: Academic International Press, 1976–1990), Vol. 8, 47–48.

46. Robert D. Warth, "GPU, " *Modern Encyclopedia of Russian and Soviet History*, ed. Joseph L. Wieczinsky, 54 vols. With suppl. (Gulf Breeze, FL: Academic International Press, 1976–1990), Vol. 13, 87–89.

Chapter 3

1. Founded on the Lutheran model, it consisted of ten (later twelve) clerics headed by a layperson appointed by the tsar.

2. Figes, *A People's Tragedy*, 528.

3. Figes, *A People's Tragedy*, 528.

4. Pipes, *Russia Under the Bolshevik Regime, 1919–1924* (London: 1990), 347–349; Vasil'eva, "Russkaia," 43.

5. Dmitri Pospielovsky, "Church-State Relations in the USSR," *Modern Encyclopedia of Russian and Soviet History*, ed. Joseph L. Wieczinsky, 54 vols. With Suppl. (Gulf Breeze, FL: 1976–1990, Academic International Press) Vol. 7, 109.

6. Figes, *A People's Tragedy*, 748.

7. Interestingly, not all people of faith were declared to be "enemies of the people," although Roman Catholics were persecuted nearly as severely as were the Orthodox. However, of the several Protestant groups that resided in Russia in 1917, the Baptists seem to have been accorded the most toleration. Indeed, the regime seems to have so admired their hard work, strict morality, and self-discipline that it allowed them to operate religious collective farms. Nor were the Soviets inclined to try to suppress the Muslims, whose religion was tightly interwoven with their basic culture and daily living practices. Finally, the Jews, who had been so persecuted under the tsars, actually benefited by the establishment of Soviet power, especially when the regime legally abolished discrimination against them. This did not, however, eliminate the very substantial anti-Semitic sentiments that had long been widespread among the Russian people.

8. Members of a fiercely anti–Semitic group, who won praise from Nicholas II for organizing pogroms against Jews and their support of autocracy. The Black Hundreds were also remarkable for their hatred of university students and all professional people. Their slogan was "Beat the Yids and the Intelligents; Save Russia."

9. RTsKhIDNI, f. 2, op. I, d. 22947, quoted in Dmitri Volkoganov, *Lenin: A New Biography*, 379.

10. Dmitri Volkogonov, *Lenin: A New Biography* (New York: Free Press, 1994) 377.

11. Sergei of Radonezh (1314–92): patron saint of Moscow and founder of the Trinity-Sergius Monastery who gave his blessing to Grand Prince Dmitri Donskoy, whose army won a victory over the Mongols at Kulikovo Field in 1380.

12. Volkogonov, *Lenin*, 381–382.

13. Volkogonov, *Lenin*, 382–383.

14. Geoffrey Hosking, *The First Socialist Society* (Cambridge, MA: Harvard University Press, 1993), 231–232, and Pospielovsky, "Church State Relations" vol. 7, 110–112.

15. Volkogonov, *Lenin*, 382.

16. Hosking, 232.

17. Hosking, 233.

18. Volkogonov, *Lenin*, 435–440.

19. Service, *A History of Twentieth Century Russia*, 154.

20. Robert Service, *Lenin: A Biography* (Cambridge, MA: Harvard University Press, 2000), 154.

21. Volkogonov, *Lenin*, 437–438.

22. Service, *Lenin*, 153.

23. Nathaniel Davis, *A Long Walk to Church* (Boulder, CO: Westwood, 1995).

24. Davis, 4.

25. Clive Foss, *History Today*, Volume 54, Issue 9.

26. Foss, Volume 54, Issue 9, 46–47.

27. Walter Duranty, "Christmas Slips By Unnoticed in Russia," *New York Times*, December 26, 1931, 1.

28. Since the ground was too marshy to support such a structure, the palace was never built.

In the late 1950s the Soviet government used the site to build an enormous outdoor circular swimming pool that was heated so it could be used in winter. But with the fall of communism in 1991, the pool was closed and a new Cathedral of Christ the Savior was built to the same specifications as the original.

29. Davis, 37.
30. Pospielovsky, "Church-State Relations in the USSR," 114–115.
31. "Luke Voino Yasenetskii" *Drevo otkritaya pravoslavnaya entsyklopedaya,* http://drevo-info.ru/articles/4137.html.
32. V. Kononenko, Pamyat blokady, *Nauka i Religiya,* No. 5 (May), 1988, 10–11, quoted in Davis, 18.
33. Sergei Gordon, "Russkaya Pravoslavnaya Tserkov v period s 1943 no 1970 god, Zhurnal Moskovskoi Patriarkhii. No. 1 (January). 1993; No. 2 (February), 1993, quoted in Davis, 18–19.
34. "Luke Voino Yasenetskii" *Drevo otkritaya pravoslavnaya entsyklopedaya,* http://drevo-info.ru/articles/4137.html and Eastern American Diocese http://www.edio.org/News/2013/apr/stluke.en.htp.
35. Tserkov v S.S.S.R. posle Khrushcheva, January 15, 1965, p. 2, quoted in Nathanial Davis, *A Long Walk to Church,* 34.
36. Davis, 37.
37. Hosking, 237.
38. Davis, 37–38.
39. *Ibid.*
40. Bourdeaux, *Opiate of the People,* 213–214, quoted in Davis, 40.
41. Michael Bourdeaux, *Patriots and Prophets,* 38, quoted in Davis, 41.
42. Brian Moynahan, *The Russian Century* (New York: Random House, 1994), 209–210.
43. Service, *A History of Twentieth Century Russia,* 369.
44. Davis, 79–80.
45. Davis, 50–51.
46. Sophia Kishovsky, *New York Times,* July 1, 2004.
47. Hosking, 461.

Chapter 4

1. Trotsky married Anna Sokolovskaya in 1899 in Moscow. Anna gave birth to two girls, Zinaida, born in 1900, and Nina, born in 1902. The marriage effectively ended when Trotsky escaped his Siberian captivity in 1902, although the two never formally divorced.
2. In 1903, Trotsky met a student, Natalya Sedova, in Paris. The two entered into a common-law marriage, probably in 1905. Natalya gave birth to two boys, Lev in 1906 and Sergei in 1908.
3. Dmitri Volkogonov, *Trotsky: The Eternal Revolutionary* (New York: Free Press, 1996), 47.
4. Robert Conquest, *Stalin* (New York: Viking, 1991), 66.
5. Conquest, *Stalin,* 70.
6. Trotsky showed no mercy to anyone who retreated without orders. On one occasion, he ordered the political commissar, the commander, and every tenth soldier of a unit shot for cowardice in battle.
7. Conquest, *Stalin,* 79.
8. Robert Warth, *Leon Trotsky* (Boston: Twayne Publishers, 1977), 109.
9. Warth, 109–110.
10. Warth, 106.
11. Figes, *A Peoples Tragedy,* 732.
12. Warth, 110–111.
13. Warth, 115.
14. Warth, 123.
15. Stalin had married Yakaterina Svanidze in 1905, who died not long after giving birth to a son, Jacob, in 1907. When Stalin left home to pursue his revolutionary activities, Jacob remained in Georgia to be brought up by an uncle and an aunt. He did not live with his father until 1926 after moving to Moscow to study. That same year Natalya gave birth to a girl named Svetlana, who left the USSR in the 1950s to live in England and later the United States.
16. Brian Moynahan, *The Russian Century,* 102.
17. Volkogonov, *Trotsky,* 258–259.
18. Volkogonov, *Lenin,* 421.
19. Volkogonov, *Lenin,* 421–422, and Conquest, *Stalin,* 99.
20. Conquest, *Stalin,* 99.
21. Conquest, *Stalin,* 100.
22. Lenin was finally told about the incident on March 4, 1923, and was outraged. He sent a terse letter to Stalin demanding that he apologize to Lenin's wife. But the Georgian offered only a few words of explanation that were delivered orally by a secretary. See Conquest, *Stalin,* 101–103.
23. Isaac Deutscher, *The Prophet Unarmed: Trotsky 1921–1929* (Oxford: Oxford University Press, 1980).
24. This was the so-called scissors crisis, which concerned many in the Party since it caused a significant decline in the peasants' standard of living. This prompted an attempt

by Soviet leaders to keep industrial prices artificially low.
25. Warth, 130–131.
26. Conquest, *Stalin*, 108.
27. Warth, 143,147–148, 154, 179.
28. Warth, 133.
29. TsPa IML, f.2, op. I, d, 27 088, Ii, quoted in Volkgogonov, 266.
30. Volkogonov, *Lenin*, 441.
31. Conquest, *Stalin*, 138.
32. Deutscher, 137–138.
33. Volkogonov, *Trotsky*, 199–200.
34. Permanent revolution rested on the premise that Russia was not yet ready for true socialism and needed socialist revolutions in more developed European countries to prepare the way. But Stalin had developed a different idea and by late 1924 had begun to call for "socialism in one country." Stalin contended that Russia could not afford to wait for socialist revolutions to occur in Europe in order to begin a program of massive industrialization in the USSR. Many Bolsheviks, Trotsky included, balked at this idea as contrary to the theories of Marx and Lenin. Stalin countered by suggesting that those who opposed his initiative clearly lacked faith in the power of the Soviet people to achieve socialism on their own. In time, such people would be branded as "cosmopolitans" and even "enemies of the people" because they held the European revolutionary tradition in higher regard than they did that of their own country.
35. *Byulletin oppozitsii*, No. 33 (1933), quoted in Warth, 141.
36. Warth, 144.
37. *Trotsky's Diary in Exile*, 69, quoted in Warth, 150.
38. Donald Rayfield, *Stalin and His Hangmen* (New York: Random House, 2004), 176.
39. Warth, 152.
40. Ordzhonikidze was very supportive of Stalin on most issues, but apparently he felt a genuine sympathy for the oppositionists because of their long record of hard work and service to the Party. See Warth, 152.
41. Warth, 154.
42. Warth, 157.
43. Warth, 159.
44. Warth, 164.
45. Warth, 68–69.
46. Warth, 171.
47. Warth, 172.
48. Volkogonov, Trotsky, 387.
49. Warth, 175.
50. Warth, 175.
51. Warth, 176–177.
52. On August 23, 1939, Soviet deputy chairman of the state defense committee Vyacheslav Molotov and German foreign minister Joachim von Ribbentrop signed a ten-year treaty that enabled Germany to attack Poland and later France and Great Britain without fear of Russian intervention. It was also secretly agreed that the Baltic States and one-half of Poland would be annexed by the Soviet Union.
53. Warth, 179–180.
54. Mercador was released from jail in Mexico City on May 6, 1960, and went immediately to Cuba, where he was welcomed as a hero. He moved to the USSR in 1961 and was awarded the Hero of the Soviet Union medal, which was presented to him by the then-head of the KGB Alexander Shelepin. Mercador died in Havana in 1978.
55. Craig R. Whitney, "The New Trotsky: No Longer a Devil," *New York Times*, January 16, 1989, p. A.3.

Chapter 5

1. Alexei Ivanovich Rykov (1881–1938) became a Bolshevik in 1905 and was arrested many times over the years agitating for the Cause. After the Revolution of 1917, he became People's Commissar of Internal Affairs and developed a close working relationship with Lenin. Rykov was one of the Party's most attractive personalities. He had a keen sense of humor and loved to poke fun at himself. He is said to have been so fond of vodka that his friends referred to the drink as "Rykovka."
2. Mikhail Pavlovich Tomsky (1880–1936), a factory worker turned revolutionary, joined the Social Democratic Party in 1905 and rose high in the ranks of the Bolshevik Party. He served a pallbearer at Lenin's funeral and seemed destined for further advancement. However, he ran afoul of Stalin for his attempts to gain some measure of autonomy for trade unions.
3. This problem started with the so-called Scissors Crisis of 1923–1924, which was characterized by low prices for agricultural goods and high prices for industrial goods. This caused a worrisome decline in the peasants' standard of living that the government failed to resolve.
4. Robert Conquest, *Stalin*, 147–148.
5. Robert Conquest, *Stalin*, 146–147.
6. The Sovkhoz was a state farm in which peasants were paid a wage for their labor.

Sovkhozy played a part in the cultivation of virgin lands and were also useful in areas of agricultural experimentation. Still, they were notoriously inefficient, and many were changed into collective farms. A kolkhoz was a collective farm in which, ideally, peasants pooled their land and equipment and were paid according to what was actually produced. But because the state always paid low prices, most collective farms made very little money no matter how hard the individual members worked.

    7. Donald Rayfield, *Stalin and His Hangmen* (New York: Random House, 2004), 156, and NA. Shefov, Tysicheletiye Rysskou Istorii, (Moskva: Vech, 2001), 453.

    8. Conquest, *Stalin*, 144.

    9. Sheila Fitzpatrick, *The Russian Revolution* (Oxford: Oxford University Press, 1994), 135.

    10. Shefov, 451, and Conquest, *Stalin*, 150–151.

    11. Geoffrey Hosking, *The First Socialist Society* (Cambridge, MA: Harvard University Press, 1991), 159–163.

    12. Bruce Lincoln, *The Conquest of a Continent* (New York: Random House, 1994), 332–349.

    13. Hosking, 177.

    14. Conquest, *Stalin*, 160, and Hosking, 165.

    15. Hosking, 169.

    16. Conquest, *Stalin*, 152–155, and Hosking, 173–174.

    17. Andrei Yanuarevich Vyshinsky (1883-1954) was a native of Odessa in Ukraine. He joined the Social Democratic Party in 1902 and one year later sided with the Mensheviks and remained with that faction for the next eighteen years. Vyshinsky was both a ruthless revolutionary activist and a serious academician. In Baku, he specialized in murdering provocateurs and police agents not long before he began studying for a law degree at the University of Kiev. When the Revolution came in 1917, Vyshinsky found employment as a prosecutor with the Provisional Government. He made a near-fatal mistake when he issued a warrant for Lenin's arrest. After the Bolsheviks came to power, Stalin protected him and got him a job organizing food supplies.

    18. Nikolai Vasil'evich Krylenko (1885-1938) was the son of an exiled official in Smolensk Oblast. He became a revolutionary in 1904 when he joined the Social Democratic Party. He received a degree from the University of St. Petersburg in History and Philology in 1909 and a law degree from the University of Kharkov in 1914. All the while he was active in the revolutionary movement and was arrested and imprisoned on several occasions. He was twice sent into exile, first to Lublin and later to Kharkov. By 1915, he was living in Switzerland and working for the Bolsheviks, who sent him to Moscow as an undercover agent. In April of the following year, he was drafted into the Russian Army and sent to the front. When the Revolution came one year later, Krylenko was assigned to a number of military and political posts in the new Soviet government. In 1918, he took a position in the Soviet judicial system, where he worked for many years as a prosecutor in the major political trials.

    19. Rayfield, 163.

    20. Hosking, 173–174.

    21. Walter Duranty (1883–1957) was the *New York Times* correspondent in Moscow for fourteen years. He was born in Scotland and came to the USSR for the first time in 1922. His objectivity seems to have suffered somewhat over time. Somehow, he gained a favored status among western journalists, and in 1929 he was granted a private interview with Stalin. Thereafter he seems to have followed a mostly pro–Soviet line that mystified many of his professional colleagues. Malcolm Muggeridge declared him to be "the greatest liar of any journalist I have ever met."

    22. Rayfield, 163.

    23. Roy Medvedev, *Let History Judge* (New York: Alfred A. Knopf, 1972), 114–115.

    24. Samuel A. Oppenheim, *Modern Encyclopedia of Russian and Soviet History*, vol. 52, 6.

    25. It was alleged that the Toiling Peasant Party was a counterrevolutionary group whose members supported the kulaks and who were determined to sabotage collectivization.

    26. Samuel A. Oppenheim, "Prompartiia Trial," *Modern Encyclopedia of Russian and Soviet History*, vol. 52 (Supplement), 5–8.

    27. Ibid.

    28. Mikhail Heller and Aleksandr M. Nekrich, *Utopia in Power* (New York: Summit Books, 1986), 231-232, and Robert D. Warth, "Metro Vickers Case," Modern *Encyclopedia of Russian and Soviet History*, vol. 5, 5–8.

    29. Rayfield, 163.

    30. Bruce Lincoln, *The Conquest of a Continent*, New York: Random House, 1994, 325.

    31. Jack Scott, *Behind the Urals* (Bloomington: Indiana University Press, 1989), x–xiii.

    32. Scott, xiv.

33. Scott, xix.
34. Brian Moynahan, *The Russian Century* (New York: Random House, 1994), 124.
35. Alexei Grigor'evich Stakhanov (1905–1977) was born in a small village in Orel province to poor peasants. At age seventeen he began working in a flour mill owned by a kulak. After five years, he traveled to the Donets Basin to find work as a coal miner. He had hoped to earn enough money to buy a horse so that he could return to his native village. He started as a brakeman of horse-drawn trains, which was the lowest-paying job. Soon he was promoted to driver and then to pick man. In 1933, he was assigned to use a mechanical hammer as part of a program to mechanize the mines. Stakhanov set his record on August 31, 1935, as part of a competition arranged by G.K. Petrov to see who could mine the most coal in one shift.
36. Scott, 19–21.
37. Scott, 180–186.
38. Scott, 186–187.
39. Scott, 291.
40. Moynahan, 130.
41. Moynahan, 126.
42. Lincoln, *The Conquest of a Continent, 324–31* (New York: Random House, 1994), 324–331.
43. Scott, 284 -286. The Collective Labor Colony (Ispravitalno Trudovaya Koloniya) or ITK was administered by the People's Commissariat for Internal Affairs and received non-political prisoners from all over the country to work on heavy construction.
44. Anne Applebaum, *GULAG: A History*, 58–60.
45. Applebaum, 66–70.
46. Genrikh Gregori'evich Yagoda (1891–1938) was of Latvian parentage and before the Revolution had worked as a statistician and in a pharmacist's shop in Nizhnii-Novgorod. He joined the Bolsheviks in 1907 and was twice deported for revolutionary activity. After the Revolution he worked for the Cheka and later the OGPU. He participated in the Shakhty Trial, but his reputation was tainted when he failed to gain confessions from some of the defendants. Later he worked on developing a systematic way to exploit slave labor and in 1930 was assigned to head the Main Administration of Corrective Labor Camps. After the completion of the White Sea Canal, Yagoda participated in a number of other mammoth building projects, including the Moscow-Volga Canal and the Amur-Baikal Canal.
47. Applebaum, 64–65.
48. Applebaum, 66–67.
49. Moynahan, 116–117.
50. Gregory Freeze, ed. *Russia: A History* (New York: Doubleday, 2003), 303. Siegelbaum's larger point was to question the extent to which the famine in Ukraine was "deliberate and genocidal." He concludes that although the regime's decision to feed the urban population at the expense of the countryside was indeed intentional, the shortfall in grain made major food shortages inevitable.
51. Robert Conquest, *The Harvest of Sorrow* (Oxford: Oxford University Press, 1986), 184, and Moynahan, 117.
52. Moynahan, 116.
53. Conquest, *Harvest of Sorrow*, 228.
54. Conquest, *Stalin*, 169.
55. Moynahan, 118.
56. Moynahan, 118–121.
57. Conquest, *Harvest of Sorrow*, 257–58.
58. Hosking, 160–63.
59. Hosking, 150–170.
60. Internal passports for the urban population had been introduced in December 1932 in part to prevent those starving in the countryside from fleeing to the cities. However, the measure was also aimed at controlling the industrial proletariat. At about the same time, a decree was promulgated denying ration cards to those who were absent from or habitually late for work.
61. In 1928, the state took 14 percent of the crop; by 1934, it was taking 38 percent.
62. Brian Moynahan, *The Russian Century*, 122.
63. Moynahan, 121.

Chapter 6

1. The Seventeenth Congress of the All Union Communist Party, quoted in Adam Ulam, *Stalin: The Man and His Era* (New York: Penguin Books, 1992), 373.
2. Sheila Fitzpatrick, *The Russian Revolution* (New York: Oxford University Press, 1994), 151–152.
3. Fitzpatrick, 153.
4. Stalin, Report to the XVII Party Congress, quoted in Robert Conquest, *The Great Terror* (Oxford: Oxford University Press, 1967), 131.
5. Conquest, *The Great Terror* (Oxford: Oxford University Press, 1967), 37–52.
6. Donald Rayfield, *Stalin and his Hangmen*, 256.
7. Robert Conquest (1917–2008) was ed-

ucated at Winchester College, the University of Grenoble, and Magdalen College, Oxford. After earning his doctorate in 1937, he joined the Communist Party of Great Britain. During World War II, he served in the Oxfordshire and Buckinghamshire Light Infantry. In 1944, Conquest went to Bulgaria as a liaison officer to Bulgarian troops fighting under Soviet command. It was during this period that he became disillusioned with Communist ideology and severed his affiliation with the communist movement. In 1950, he served briefly as First Secretary in the British Delegation to the United Nations. In 1962–63, Conquest was literary editor of *The Spectator*, but resigned to better concentrate on his research on the Soviet Union. In 2005, he received the Presidential Medal of Freedom for his outstanding scholarship in Russian studies.

8. Nikita Khrushchev, Secret Speech, quoted in Conquest, *Terror*, 31.

9. Conquest, *Terror*, 104.

10. Conquest, *Terror*, 94–95, quoted in Petrov and Petrov, *Empire of Fear* (New York: Praeger, 1956), 51.

11. Petrov and Petrov, *Empire of Fear*, 51, quoted in Conquest, *Terror*, 94–95.

12. Conquest, *Terror*, 95.

13. Zinoviev Trial, 72, quoted in Conquest, *Terror*, 96.

14. Conquest, *Terror*, 97.

15. Socialdemocraton, 1 September 1936, quoted in Conquest, *Terror*, 99.

16. Report of the Court Proceedings: The Case of the Trotskyite-Zinovievite Terrorist Centre, English ed. (Moscow, 1936), 103, (henceforth referred to as Zinoviev Trial), quoted in Conquest, *Terror*, 126.

17. *Tsugzvang Mikhaila Tomskogo*, 233–234, quoted in Rayfield, 227–228.

18. Orlov, *Secret History of Stalin's Crimes*, 175–76, quoted in Conquest, *Terror*, 103.

19. Zinoviev Trial, 166, quoted in Conquest, *Terror*, 103.

20. Serge, *From Lenin to Stalin*, 145, quoted in Conquest, *Terror*, 104 and Emmanuel d'Astier de la Vigerie, *Staline* (New York, 1951).

21. Conquest, *Terror*, 105.

22. Rayfield, 280.

23. http://ru.*Wikipedia.org/vrag*_naroda.

24. Zoatopolskii, D.L. "Constitutions of the Soviet Union," *Modern Encyclopedia of Russian and Soviet History*, 47–53.

25. Edgar C. Duins, "Ezhov, Nikolai Ivanovich," *Modern Encyclopedia of Russian and Soviet History*, 34–39.

26. Rayfield, 295–297.

27. In fact, there had been a number of purges during the early years of Soviet rule. The first had been ordered by the Central Committee in 1921–1922 to rid the Party of those who were careerists rather than serious communists, or opposed in some way to certain basic communist principles. One could also be excluded from the Party for certain character flaws such being a drunkard, being religious, or being corrupt. There was another purge in 1929–1930 that was carried out for the same reasons, but that also included those who had been part of the Right Opposition. It was about this time that the labor camp population began to swell with those who had been excluded from the Party. By 1933–1934, the purge had become a regular feature of Soviet life.

28. Duins, 36.

29. Rayfield, 271.

30. Conquest, *Terror*, 152.

31. Conquest, *Terror*, 152–153.

32. Conquest, 465–466.

33. Report of the Court Proceedings in the Case of the Anti-Soviet Trotskyite Centre, English ed. (Moscow, 1937), 474 (henceforward referred to as Pyatakov Trial), quoted in Conquest, *Terror*, 161.

34. N.M. Shvernik, speech to XXII Party Congress (*Pravda*, 26 October 1961), 514, quoted in Conquest, *Terror*, 162.

35. Pyatakov Trial, 516, quoted in Conquest, *Terror*, 163.

36. Elizabeth Lermolo, *Face of a Victim* (New York: Harper, 1955), 134–35, quoted in Conquest, *Terror*, 165.

37. Izvestiya, 22 November 1963; I.M. Dubinsky-Mukhadze Ordzhonikidze, 6, quoted in Conquest, *Terror*, 168.

38. Izvestiya, 22 Nov. 1963; Dubinsky-Muhadze Ordzhonikidze, 6, quoted in Conquest, *Terror*, 169.

39. Conquest, *Terror*, 180.

40. Conquest, *Terror*, 341–343.

41. Bukharin Trial, 157–158, quoted in Conquest, *Terror*, 351–352.

42. *Izvestia*, TsK KPSS, no. 9 (1989), quoted in Conquest, *Terror*, 355.

43. Conquest, *Terror*, 361–364.

44. Conquest, *Terror*, 364–365.

45. Bukharin Trial, 374, quoted in Conquest, *Terror*, 365.

46. Bukharin Trial, 424, quoted in Conquest, *Terror*, 365–372.

47. Bukharin Trial, 508–509, quoted in Conquest, *Terror*, 372–374.

48. Bukharin Trial, 537, quoted in Conquest, *Terror*, 375–376.
49. Bukharin Trial, 577–578, quoted in Conquest, *Terror*, 383.
50. Orlov, *Secret History of Stalin's Crimes*, 268, quoted in Conquest, *Terror*, 383–384.
51. Orlov, *Secret History of Stalin's Crimes*, 268, Quoted in Conquest, *Terror*, 384.
52. Bukharin Trial, 676, quoted in Conquest, *Terror*, 390–91.
53. Bukharin Trial, 697, quoted in Conquest, *Terror*, 390–91.
54. This song was from the musical *Circus*, directed by Grigori Alexandrov. It features a woman circus performer, who brings disgrace upon herself by giving birth to a black child. She eventually leaves the country and goes to the Soviet Union, where she is hired by the circus in Moscow. She soon falls in love with its director, who sings the song to her. *Circus* was one of Stalin's favorite musicals.
55. Bukharin Trial, 786, quoted in Conquest, *Terror*, 392–393.
56. Bukharin Trial, 738, quoted in Conquest, *Terror*, 392.
57. Conquest, *Terror*, 393–395.
58. Conquest, *Terror*, 395–396.
59. Lewis Siegelbaum has questioned the accuracy of traditional estimates on the number of how many were imprisoned in the Gulag during the late 1930s. Robert Conquest's estimate is seven million by 1938. Siegelbaum, however, cites the work of researcher Viktor Zemskov, whose access to recently opened archives suggests the camp population was actually less than two million at roughly the same time. See Gregory Freeze, ed. *Russia, A History* (Oxford: Oxford University Press, 1997), 314–315.
60. Conquest, *Terror*, 465–66.
61. Conquest, *Terror*, 431.
62. Ogonek, no. 7 (1988), quoted in Conquest, *Terror*, 432.
63. Aleksei Polianskii, *Ezhov* (Moscow, 2001), 304–305, quoted in Rayfield, 339.
64. Rayfield, 338–339.
65. Rayfield, 339.
66. Conquest, *Stalin*, 207.

Chapter 7

1. John W. Long, "Spanish Civil War, Soviet Intervention In," *Modern Encyclopedia of Russian and Soviet History*, ed. Joseph L. Wieczinsky, 54 vols. With suppl. (Gulf Breeze, FL: 1976–1990, Academic International Press) vol. 21, 19.
2. The Workers' Party of Marxist Unification.
3. Robert Service, *Stalin* (Cambridge, MA: Belknap Press of Harvard University Press, 1997), 181–82.
4. Rayfield, 324.
5. Robert Conquest, *Terror*, 204–205.
6. Having been summoned to Moscow, he was kept waiting a month before being received by Stalin. The General Secretary discussed with him the situation in Spain and then named him Commissar of Justice. Weeks later he was arrested and incarcerated in the Butyrka Prison, where he was shot sometime in 1938.
7. A.T. Stuchenko, *Zavidnaya nasha sudba*, quoted in Conquest, *Terror*, 205.
8. Conquest, *Terror*, 400–401.
9. Conquest, *Terror*, 402–403.
10. Alexander Solzhenitsyn, *The Gulag Archipelago*, 252n.
11. Catherine Andreyev, *Russia and the Russian Liberation Movement* (Cambridge: Cambridge University Press, 1987), 206–207.
12. Mikhail Keller and Aleksandr M. Hekrich, *Utopia in Power*, 433. The phrase "Russia can only be beaten by Russia" was borrowed from Schiller's *Demetrius*.
13. Conquest, *Stalin*, 258–259.
14. Conquest, *Stalin*, 258–259.
15. KONR in Russian is *Komitet Osvobozhdeniya Narodov Rossii* or the *Committee to Liberate the Peoples of Russia*.
16. Beginning early in 1942, these unfortunates had been lured to work in Germany by promises of sufficient food and reasonable working conditions. What they got was starvation rations and slave labor. Once the word got out about the ruse, new workers had to be captured and taken by force.
17. Mark Elliott, "Vlasov, Andrei Andreevich," *Modern Encyclopedia of Russian and Soviet History*, ed. Joseph L. Wieczinsky, 54 vols. With suppl. (Gulf Breeze, FL: 1976–1990, Academic International Press), 188–195.
18. Catherine Andreyev, *Vlasov and the Russian Liberation Movement*, 79.
19. Mark Elliot, "Repatriation of Soviet Refugees of World War II," *Modern Encyclopedia of Russian and Soviet History*, ed. Joseph L. Wieczinsky, 54 vols. With suppl. (Gulf Breeze, FL: 1976–1990, Academic International Press) vol. 31, 16–19.
20. Elliott, "Repatriation of Soviet Refugees of World War II," 16–19.
21. Anne Applebaum, *Gulag*, 437. The British tricked the Cossack officers by summoning

them to a "conference" and then turning them over to Soviet troops.
22. Khrushchev's title of First Secretary had been changed from that of General Secretary to reflect the change in leadership that the new leader intended to offer. When Khrushchev was deposed in 1964, his successor, Leonid Brezhnev, assumed the title General Secretary.

Chapter 8

1. Robert G. Kaiser, *Russia: The People & the Power* (New York: Atheneum, 1976).
2. Of course, Stalin's secret police (i.e., the NKVD and later the NKGB, the MGB, and the MVD) had done all this and more.
3. Robert Conquest, *Terror*, 455.
4. Robert Conquest, *Stalin*, 270.
5. Donald Rayfield, *Stalin and his Hangmen*, 431–432.
6. James Billington, *The Icon and the Axe* (New York: Vintage Books, 1970), 535.
7. Victor Borovsky, *Chaliapin: A Critical Biography* (New York: Knopf, 1988), 531.
8. Biografia Sergeia Aleksandrovicha Esenina. http://www.sa-esenin.org.
9. Conquest, *Terror*, 307.
10. Donald Rayfield, *Stalin and His Hangmen*, 217.
11. Conquest, *Terror*, 298.
12. A typical Soviet definition describes formalism in art as the expression that is of bourgeois ideology that is hostile to the Soviet people. See Solomon Volkov's *Testimony: The Memoirs of Dmitri Shostakovich*, 83n.
13. Conquest, *Terror*, 306.
14. Rayfield, 364–365.
15. Conquest, *Terror*, 304–305 and Rayfield, 328.
16. Ronald Hingley, *Nightingale Fever: Russian Poets in Revolution* (New York: Alfred A. Knopf, 1981), 231.
17. Hingley, 234–235.
18. Conquest, *Terror*, 299.
19. Conquest, *Terror*, 300, and Aleksandrov Belousendrob, Elektronnaya Biblioteka , *Boris Andreevich Pilniak*.
20. Conquest, *Terror*, 291–292.
21. A schismatic group that arose early in the fourth century C.E., whose members believed that only those living a blameless life belonged in the Church.
22. Conquest, *Terror*, 292.
23. Conquest, *Terror*, 292.
24. Conquest, *Terror*, 192–193.
25. Conquest, *Terror*, 293.

26. Conquest, *Terror*, 294n.
27. A special kind of prison invented by Lavrenty Beria in 1938 in which the inmates were all scientists and technicians assigned to work on special projects.
28. Conquest, *Terror*, 295.
29. Yu.B. Biryukob, Entsiklopedia Kirill i Mefodii, Sergei Pavlovich Korolev. http://to-name.ru/biography/sergej-korolev.htm.
30. Heller and Nekrich, 484.
31. Geoffrey Hosking, 310–311.
32. Rayfield, 368–369, and Conquest, *Terror*, 296.
33. Solomon Volkov, *Testimony: The Memoirs of Dmitri Shostakovich*, 270.
34. Arthur Rosen, "Birobidzhan—The Almost Soviet Jewish Region," http://www.Jewishmagwww/75mag/birobidzhan/birobidzhan.htm.
35. Russiapedia Prominent Russians: Ilya Ehrenburg http://russiapedia.rt.com/prominent-russians/literature/ilya-ehrenburg.
36. Rayfield, 440–41.
37. Pseudonym for Ilya Arnoldovich Fainzelberg (1897–1937) and Evgenii Petrovich Katayev (1903–1942), who, in the 1920s, formed a literary partnership in writing such works as *The Twelve Chairs* and *The Golden Calf* that satirized aspects of Soviet society.
38. Anti-Fascist Committee, Jewish. http://www.jewishvirtuallibrary.org/source/judica/ejud_0002_0002_0_01147html.
39. Rayfield, 444.
40. Heller and Nekrich, *Utopia in Power*, 502.
41. Rayfield, 450.
42. Conquest, *Stalin*, 308–309.
43. Rayfield, 450.
44. Simon Sebag Montefiore, *Stalin: The Court of the Red Tsar* (New York: Alfred Knopf, 2004), 637–38.

Chapter 9

1. Rayfield, 455.
2. N.A. Shefov, *Tysyachiletiye Russkoi Istorii* (Moskva: Veche, 2001), 501–502.
3. Heller and Nekrich, 523.
4. William Taubman, *Khrushchev: The Man and His Era* (New York: W.W. Norton, 2003), 261–263.
5. Russian abbreviation for *zaklyuchennyi*, or prisoner.
6. Hosking, 329.
7. Applebaum, 491–2.
8. Shefov, 502.

9. Nikita Khrushchev, *Khrushchev Remembers*, Translated and Edited by Strobe Talbert (Boston: Little, Brown, 1970), 344.
10. Hosking, 334.
11. Moynahan, 138.
12. *Khrushchev Remembers*, 574.
13. *Khrushchev Remembers*, 610–611.
14. *Khrushchev Remembers*, 586–587.
15. *Khrushchev Remembers*, 587–593.
16. *Khrushchev Remembers*, 594–595.
17. *Khrushchev Remembers*, 618.
18. Moynahan, 197–199, and Service, *Lenin*, 341–343.
19. Hosking, 347–351.

Epilogue

1. The Black Book of Communism, 463.
2. Falangism is an authoritarian, conservative ideology widely associated with fascism. It is anti-communist, anti-democratic, and anti-liberal.
3. Born in 1940, Debray is a French philosopher, academician, journalist, and former French official who became associated with Che Guevara in Bolivia.
4. This was the Shah's so-called "White Revolution." It included an extensive land reform that featured the redistribution of the estates of the rich landlords to the peasants who worked the land. He also sought to promote education, improve social services, and give women the right to vote. Finally, he used the profits from Iran's oil industry to develop new projects, which greatly enhanced the country's economic growth.

Bibliography

Alliuyeva, Svetlana. *Twenty Letters to a Friend*. Translated by Priscilla Johnson McMillan. New York: Harper & Row, 1967.
Andreev, Ivan Mikhailovich. "The Trial of Patriarch Tikhon." http://wwwlrussianorthodoxchurch.ws/english/pages/articles/pattikhon.
Andreyev, Catherine. *Vlasov and the Russian Liberation Movement*. Cambridge: Cambridge University Press, 1987.
Applebaum, Anne. *GULAG: A History*. New York: Doubleday, 2003.
Avrich, Paul. *The Russian Anarchists*. Edinburgh: AK Press, 2005.
Ball, Alan M. *Russia's Last Capitalists*. Berkeley: University of California Press, 1987.
Belousenka, Alexandra. "Boris Andreevich Pilniak." http://www.belousenka.com/wr-pilnyak.htm
_____. "Ilya Ehrenburg." http://www.belosenko.com/wr_ehenburghtm
Biographiya Sergeia Aleksandrovna Yesenina. http://www.sa-esenin.org
Borovsky, Victor. *Chaliapin: A Critical Biography*. New York: Alfred A. Knopf, 1988.
Boryukov, Yu.V. *Entsiklopedia Kirill i Mefodii*. Sergei Pavlovich Korolev. http://to-name.ru/biography/sergej-kopolev.htm
Cohen, Stephen F. *Bukharin and the Bolshevik Revolution*. Oxford: Oxford University Press, 1980.
Conquest, Robert. *The Great Terror: A Reassessment*. Oxford: Oxford University Press, 1967.
_____. *Stalin: Breaker of Nations*. New York: Penguin Books, 1992.
Davis, Nathanial. *A Long Walk to Church*. Boulder, CO: Westwood, 1995.
Deutscher, Isaac. *The Prophet Unarmed: Trotsky 1921–1929*. Oxford: Oxford University Press, 1980.
Dorman, Oleg. *Podstrochnik*. Moskva: Izdatel'stvo CORPUS, 2010.
Elliott, Mark. "Repatriation of Soviet Refugees of World War II." *Modern Encyclopedia of Modern Russian and Soviet History,* ed. Josef L. Wieczinsky, 54 vol. with Suppl. Gulf Breeze, FL: Academic International Press, 1976–1990.
_____. "Vlasov, Andrei Andreevich." *Modern Encyclopedia of Modern Russian and Soviet History,* ed. Josef L. Wieczinsky, 54 vol. with Suppl. Gulf Breeze, FL: Academic International Press, 1976–1990.
Figes, Orlando. *Peasant Russia Civil War: The Volga Countryside in Revolution, 1917–1921*. Oxford: Clarendon Press, 1989.
_____. *A People's Tragedy*. New York: Viking Press, 1997.
_____. *The Whisperers*. New York: Henry Holt, 2007.
Fitzpatrick, Sheila. *The Russian Revolution*. Oxford: Oxford University Press, 1994.
Freeze, Geoffrey, ed. *Russia: A History*. Oxford: Oxford University Press, 1996.

Getty, J. Arch. *The Origins of the Great Purges: The Soviet Communist Party, 1933–1938.* Cambridge: Cambridge University Press, 1987.
Hartford, James. *Korolev.* New York: John Wiley & Sons, 1997.
Heller, Mikhail, and Aleksandr M. Nekrich. *Utopia in Power.* New York: Summit Books, 1986.
Hingley, Ronald. *Nightingale Fever: Russian Poets in Revolution.* New York: Alfred A. Knopf, 1981.
Hosking, Geoffrey. *The First Socialist Society.* Cambridge, MA: Harvard University Press, 1991.
Kaiser, Robert G. *Russia: The People & the Power.* New York: Atheneum, 1976.
King, Greg, and Penny Wilson. *The Fate of the Romanovs.* Hoboken, NJ: John Wiley & Sons, 2003.
Khrushchev, Nikita S. *Khrushchev Remembers.* Translated and edited by Strobe Talbott. Boston: Little, Brown, 1970.
Konstantin Feodorovich Shteppa. http://www.tez- rus.net/ViewGood41826.html
Khrushchev, Sergei N. *Nikita Khrushchev.* University Park, PA: Penn State Press, 2000.
Lewin, Moshe. *The Soviet Century.* London: Verso, 2005.
Lincoln, W. Bruce. *The Conquest of a Continent.* New York: Random House, 1994.
_____. *Red Victory.* New York: Da Capo Press, 1999.
Long, John W. "Spanish Civil War, Soviet Intervention In." *Modern Encyclopedia of Modern Russian and Soviet History,* ed. Josef L. Wieczynsky, 54 vol. with Suppl. Gulf Breeze, FL: Academic International Press, 1976–1990.
Lure, John. *The Cossacks: An Illustrated History.* New York: Overlook Press, 2002.
Marrin, Albert. *Stalin: Man of Steel.* New York: Viking, 1988.
Massie, Robert. *The End of the Romanovs.* New York: Randon House, 1995.
_____. *Nicholas and Alexandra.* New York: Atheneum, 1967.
Medvedev, Roy. *Let History Judge.* New York: Alfred A. Knopf, 1972.
Miller, James R., ed. *Encyclopedia of Russian History.* New York: Thompson Gale, 2004.
Montefiore, Simon Sebag. *Stalin: The Court of the Red Tsar.* New York: Alfred A. Knopf, 2004.
Moynahan, Brian. *The Russian Century.* New York: Random House, 1994.
Ozginga, James R. *Communism: The Story of the Idea and Its Implementation.* Englewood Cliffs, New Jersey: Prentice Hall, 1991.
Petrov, Vladimir, and Evdokia Petrov. *Empire of Fear.* New York: Praeger, 1956.
Pipes, Richard. *Russia Under the Bolshevik Regime, 1919–1924.* London: Harvill, 1994.
_____. *The Russian Revolution.* New York: Vintage Books, 1991.
Polonski, Vadim. Entsiklopedia Krogosvet. http://www.c-café.ru/days/bio/10/097.php
Radzinsky, Edvard. *Stalin.* Translated by H.T. Willets. New York: Doubleday, 1996.
Rayfield, Donald. *Stalin and his Hangmen.* New York: Random House, 2004.
Scott, John. *Behind the Urals.* Bloomington: Indiana University Press, 1989.
Service, Robert. *A History of Twentieth Century Russia.* Cambridge, MA: Harvard University Press, 1997.
_____. *Lenin: A Biography.* Cambridge, MA: Harvard University Press, 2000.
_____. *Stalin: A Biography.* Cambridge, MA: Belknap Press of Harvard University Press, 1997.
Shefov, N.A. *Tysicheletiye Russkoi Istorii.* Moskva: Veche, 2001.
Sinyavsky, Andrei. *Soviet Civilization: A Cultural History.* New York: Arcade Publishing, 1988.
Smith, Hedrik. *The Russians.* New York: Ballantine Books, 1976.
Solzhenitsyn, Alexander. *The Gulag Archipelago.* New York: Harper and Row, 1973.
Taubman, William. *Khrushchev: The Man and His Era.* New York: W.W. Norton, 2003.
Volkogonov, Dmitri. *Lenin: A New Biography.* New York: Free Press, 1994.
_____. *Trotsky: The Eternal Revolutionary.* New York: Free Press, 1996.
Warth, Robert D. *Leon Trotsky.* Boston: Twayne Publishers, 1977.

West, James L. and Iurii A. Petrov, ed. *Merchant Moscow*. Princeton: Princeton University Press, 1998.
Ulam, Adam. *Stalin: The Man and His Era*. New York: Viking, 1973.
Volkogonov, Dmitri. Lenin: *A New Biography*. New York: Free Press, 1994.
Yevreiskoe Slova, 19 Marta 2002 goda. *Lina Stern* http://www.Languages-study.com?yiddish/linastern.html

Index

Page numbers in **_bold italics_** indicate pages with illustrations.

Abakumov, Victor 198
Ageloff, Sylvia 93
agricultural planning: collectivization 97; grain requisitioning plan 97–98; under Lenin regime 34, 97
Ahmadinejad, Mahmoud (successor to Mohammad Khatami) 243–244
Akhmatova, Anna (poet) 178–179, 193
Albania (member of Warsaw Pact) 204
Alexander I (Tsar): construction of military colonies 177
Alexander II (Tsar): assassination by the People's Will (1881) 26; Emancipation Edict of 1861 25–26, 97; reform movement 26
Alexander III (Tsar) 7, 26; assassination attempt by Alexander Ilich Ulianov 25
Alexandra Feodorovna (Empress) 27, **_28_**; murder by the Ural Regional Soviet 30–31
Alexei (Metropolitan): election as Patriarch 64
Alexei (Metropolitan of Leningrad) 62–64
Alexei (Patriarch) 64, 65
Alexei (Tsar): interference with Russian Orthodox Church 48–49
Alexei Nicholaevich (Tsarevich) 27, **_28_**; murder by the Ural Regional Soviet 30–31
Alfonso XIII (King of Spain) 151
Alliluyeva, Nadezhda Sergeevna 77; suicide of 115
Alliluyeva, Svetlana 200
All-Russian Central Executive Committee: call for terror against bourgeoisie 38
All-Russian Council for the Economy 34
All-Russian Extraordinary Commission for Combating Counter-revolution and Sabotage see Cheka
All-Russian Metalworkers' Union 76
All-Russian Public Committee to Aid the Hungry 45–46
American Relief Administration (ARA): aid to Russia during 1921–1922 famine 46

Anastasia Nicholaevna (Grand Duchess) 27, **_28_**; murder by the Ural Regional Soviet 30–31
Andreev, Nikolai: assassination of German ambassador 35
Andrei (Archbishop): imprisonment of 67
Andropov, Yuri (head of KGB) 32
Anti-Soviet Trotskyite Center 131
Antonov, Alexander 41
Antonov-Ovseenko, Vladimir (Counsel General in Barcelona) 154
Arakcheev, A. A. (General Count, administrator of military colonies) 177
Armenia (member of Transcaucasian Federation) 47
Arnold, Valentin 133, 135
Avdonin, Alexander (discoverer of Romanov family remains) 32
Azerbaijan (member of Transcaucasian Federation) 47

Babel, Isaac Emileovich 180–181; arrest and execution 181; *Odessa Tales* 181; *Red Cavalry* 181
Babi Yar (site of massacre of Kievan Jews by German SS) 165–166
Bakayev, Ivan 125
Bakhtiar, Shipour (Dr.) 238
Balkar people: deportation ordered by Stalin 169
Baltic States 164; occupation by Germany 164
Batista, Fulgencio 222
Belamor Canal construction project 112–113
Belgium: invasion by Germany 163
Beloborov, Alexander 31
Belorussia (member of Union of Soviet Socialist Republics) 47; occupation by Germany 164
Belov, Ivan (Commander) 156
Ben Gurion, David (Israeli president) 199
Beria, Lavrenty Pavlovich 9, 199, 200; arrest and execution 202; head of NKVD 147, 187;

261

Ministry of the Interior and Ministry for State Security merger 201
Berkman, Alexander 43
Berlin, Germany: Soviet blockade of 193
Berman-Yurin, K. B. 126
Bessonov, Sergei 137, 143, 145
Biao, Lin (General): attempted assassination of Mao Zedong 220; death of 220
Bible for Believers and Non-Believers (Yaroslavsky) 58
Billington, James 179
Black Hundredists: extermination of 53
Bliukher, Vasily (Commander) 156
Bliumkin, Jakob: assassination of German ambassador 35
Blokhin, Vasily 147
Bolshevik party 3
Bolshevik regime: atheism, promotion of 57–58; ideological economic disputes 23; Provisional Government, overthrow of 3, 4, 8, 27, 33, 35, 71, 73, 180; republic of equals, creation of 14; and Russian Orthodox Church 48–69; threats to 6–7, 17, 33–46
Bolshevik Revolution 8; *see also* October Coup
Bolsheviks: China, example for 211; compared to the French Jacobins 210; Lenin as leader 3; Republic of China, intervention in 211–212; scientific socialist beliefs 5, 11
Bonaparte, Napoleon 210; crowned as Emperor of France 5
Borodin, Mikhail Markovich: unification of Chinese Communist Party and Nationalist Party 212
Botkin, Evgenii: murder by Ural Regional Soviet 31; Romanov physician 27
bourgeoisie 11, 24; Decree on Land, effects of 14; as "enemies of the people" 16–17, 38; system of organized violence against 13–17, 19, 38
Boyarsky, Vladimir (Colonel) 167
boycotts of Soviet goods 112
Brassov, Michael *see* Michael (Grand Duke)
Braude, I. D. 142
Brezhnev, Leonid (General Secretary) 240; successor to Khrushchev 67
Brezhnev era 32
A Brief History of Russia (Pokrovsky) 186
Buchan, James 236
Budyonny, Semyon (Field Marshall) 181
Bukharin, Nikolai Ivanovich 23, 24, 77, 96, 119, 120, 127, 132, 138, *138,* 154; arrest of 136; "How Not to Write the Lessons of October" 83; opposition to Stalin's Five Year Plan 97–98; trial of 139–141, 143, 144
Bulganin [Nikolai] 199, 200
Bulgaria (member of Warsaw Pact) 204
Bulletin of the Opposition (journal) 89
Bunyachenkov, Sergei Kuzmich (Major General) 171
burzhui ("enemies of the people") 17
Butyrki Prison, Moscow 40, 145, 167, 184

Bykov, K. M. 192
byvshchie liudi (former people) 13

Cambodia 229–235; bombing by U.S. 228; Democratic Kampuchea, name change to 229; General Lon Nol, overthrow of government by 228–229; Japanese and Thai forces, occupation by 228; Khmer Rouge 229–235; People's Republic of Kampuchea, name change to 234; Pol Pot 229, 230, 235
Cambodian Non-Communists: participation in civil war 234
Carter, Jimmy (President) 240; Operation Eagle Claw 241–242
Castro, Fidel 222–223; attempted revolution 222; Guevara, falling out with 227; overthrow of Batista government 223; religious property, confiscation of 226
Castro, Raul 222
Cathedral of Christ the Savior, Moscow: destruction of 58
Cathedral of Kazan, Leningrad: conversion to Museum of the History of Religion and Atheism 59
Cathedral of St. Vladimir: removal of bells *61*
Cathedral of the Announciation, Leningrad: destruction of *60*
Catholic Church: power curtailed in Spain 151
Central Committee of the Communist Party 9, 44
Chaliapin, Feodor Ivanovich 179
Chamberlain, Neville (British Prime Minister) 157, 161
Chambers, Wittaker 155
Chavez, Hugo 95
Chechen people: deportation ordered by Stalin 169
Cheka 31, 35; attempts to curb excesses of 16; Grand Duke Michael, murder of 29–30; move to Moscow's Lubyanka Square 6; Nicholas Johnson, murder of 29–30; Patriarch Tikhon, arrest of 54; Revolutionary state security agency, creation of 5; terror activities 5–8, 9, 17
Chenier, Andrea (poet): execution during French Revolution 4
Chernov, M. A. 138
Chicherin, G. V. (People's Commissar of Foreign Affairs) 211
China: civil war (1927–1950) 213–214; Mae Zedong 211; Stalin's policy 86
China, People's Republic of 214–220; alliance with Soviet Union 214; Cultural Revolution 218–220; Deng Xiaoping 218; establishment of 214; Gang of Four 220; intra-party power struggles 220; Liu Shaoqi 218; Mao Zedong as leader 214; Red Guards 218–220; Tiananmen Square protests 221; Zhou Enlai 218
China, Republic of: civil war (1927–1950) 211, 213–214; Dr. Sun Yat-sen as leader 211, 213; General Chiang Kai-shek as leader 213

Chinese Communist Party 86, 212; Central Committee of the Seventh Congress 214; Nationalist Party, break with 213; purge of perceived enemies 214–215, 216
Chinese Eastern Railway 212
Chinese Nationalist Party 212; Chinese Communist Party, break with 213; Dr. Sun Yet-sen as leader 211, 213; escape to Taiwan 214
Chinese Revolution: similarities to Russian experience 211
Chubar, Vlas Yakovlevich: execution of 206
civil war (1917–1922) 8, 28, 33, 35–46; economic recovery, problems relating to 44–46; Kronstadt uprising 42–43
class warfare 5
Cold War: Berlin, Soviet blockade of 193; Israel, creation of 194; Korean War 194; Marshall Plan 193; North Atlantic Treaty Organization 194; space race 189–190; Stalin's differences with Tito 193; Truman's aid package to Greece and Turkey 193
collectivation agriculture 100
collectivization 97, 118
Comintern 158, 212; purge of members 158
Committee for a Workers' International 95
Committee for State Security *see* KGB
Committee for the Liberation of the Peoples of Russia 168, 170
Committee of Members of the Constituent Assembly 33
Committees of the Poor *see* Kombedy
Communist International 57, 212; *see also* Comintern
Communist Party: power struggle following Lenin's death 74–88
Communist Party congresses: Eighteenth Party Congress 147; Eighth Party Congress 131; Fifteenth Party Congress 24; Fifth Party Congress, London 71, 73; Fourteenth Party Congress 24, 124; Second Soviet Congress 7; Seventeenth Party Congress 119–120; Sixteenth Party Congress 100; Tenth Party Congress 8, 42–43; Thirteenth Party Congress 82–83; Twelfth Party Congress, Moscow 80; Twentieth Party Congress 9, 205–208; Twenty-Second Congress 67
Communist Party, Spain: Anarchists 152; Partido Obrero de Unificacion Marxista (POUM) 152; rifts within 152; Soviet influence, increase in 152; during Spanish civil war 152
Congress of Victors 119, 120; *see also* Seventeenth Party Congress
Conquest, Robert 123, 154, 169, 180
Constituent Assembly 33, 34, 42; election for 3
Constitution of 1936 128, 130
Constitution of the Russian Federated Soviet Socialist Republic (1918) 46–47
Constitutional Assembly (1917): opening, postponement of by Lenin 4
Constitutional Democratic Party 3; *see also* Kadets

the conveyer: system of torture used by Stalin 123
corrective labor colonies 112–113
cosmopolitans, persecution of: Andrei Kuznetsov 198; Maxim Litvinov 198; Nikolai Voznesensky 198
Council of People's Commissars 3, 16; *see also* Sovnarkom
Council on the Affairs of the Orthodox Church 65
Crimean Tatars: deportation ordered by Stalin 169
Cuba 222–227; Committees for the Defense of the Revolution 225; Cuban Missile Crisis 227; emigration of anti-communists to U.S. 225, 227; Fulgencio Batista 222; Gerardo Machado 222; independent newspapers, elimination of 225; overthrow of the Batista government 223; President Manuel Urrutia 225; Ramon Grau San Martin 222; religion, suppression of 226; revolution attempts 222, 223–224; Revolutionary Directorate 223; Roberto Agramonte, minister of foreign affairs 225; Rupo Lopez Fresquet, minister of finance 225; Soviet Union, alliance with 227; 26th of July Movement 223
Czech Legion 28, 33
Czechoslovakia (member of Warsaw Pact) 204

Daladier, Éduard (French President) 157, 161
David, Fritz 126
A Day in the Life of Ivan Denisovich (Solzhenitsyn) 175
Debray, Regis 226
Decembrists 177
Decree of Nationalization 34
Decree on Land 14
Decree on the Red Terror: results of 7
dekulakization program: proclamation of 99; resistance to 100; slave labor camps 99–100; twenty-five thousanders 100
Demidova, Anna (imperial family maid) 27; murder by Ural Regional Soviet 31
Democratic Kampuchea 229; Cambodia, name change from 229; children, exploitation and mistreatment of 233–234; city dwellers, deportation of to the countryside 230–231; Communist China, influence of 232–233; Communist Party of 229; invasion by Vietnam 234; minorities, persecution of 232; "New People" as "enemies of the people" 229–230; People's Republic of Kampuchea, name change to 234; purges 233; religion, suppression of 231–232
Denmark: invasion by Germany 163
deportations: Balkar people 169; Chechens 169; Crimean Tatars 169; dekulakization program 99–100; Ingushi 169; Kalmyk people 169; Karachai people 169; Ukranian kulaks 114; Volga Germans 169

The Development of Capitalism in Russia (Lenin) 71
Dewey, John 133; Joint Committee of Inquiry, chairman of 91
"dictatorship of the proletariat": organized violence against the bourgeoisie 13
Dikareva, Masha 112
Dnieper hydroelectric dam 119
Dreitzer, E. A. 126
Dreitzer, Efim 125
Drobnis, Y. N. 135
Dudko, Dmitri (Father) 68–69
Duin, Edgar C. 130
Duranty, Walter (*New York Times* correspondent) 103, 118
Dybenko, Pavel (Commissar of the Navy) 74
Dzerzhinsky, Felix 96, 97; arrest by Left Socialist Revolutionaries 28, 36; Cheka, leadership of 5–6; head of GPU 47; Lenin Funeral Commission, head of 56

East Germany (member of Warsaw Pact) 204
Eastman, Max: *Since Lenin Died* 84
Eberlein, Hugo (Comintern member) 161
Efron, Ariadna (Alya) 184
Efron, Georgii 184, 185
Efron, Irina 184
Efron, Sergei 184
Ehrenburg, Ilya Grigoryevich 149, 195–196
Eighteenth Party Congress 147
Eighth Party Congress 131
Eikhe, R. I. 133
Einstein, Albert 197
Eisenhower, Dwight D. (President): Cuban exiles, CIA training of 225
Eitingon, Leonid: role in assassination of Trotsky 93–94
Emancipation Edict of 1861 25–26, 97
"enemies of the people" 8, 10, 32, 75, 132, 133, 135, 137, 146, 148, 210, 211; applied to ethnic peoples by Stalin 169; bourgeoise, concept applied to 17; Cambodia, use of concept by Pol Pot regime 10; China, use of concept by Mao Zedong 10; concept used in Stalin's regime 206–207; Constitution of 1936, Part II, Article 131, defined by 128; Cuba, use of concept by Fidel Castro 10; defined by Lenin 4–5; hunt for in academia and the arts 188; Iran, use of concept 10; Iraq, use of concept by Baathists 10; Lev Davidovich Trotsky 72; Old Bolsheviks 124; Peru, use of concept by Shining Path terrorists 10; rehabilitation of by Khruschev 204; Soviet Army high command 152; Soviet military officer corps 155–157; use of concept during French Revolution 4, 5; widespread use of concept during Bolshevik era 7, 10, 38
Enlai, Zhou: death of 220; leader of People's Republic of China 218
entrepreneurs 18–19

Ermakov, Piotr: assassination of imperial family 31
Esenin, Sergei 179
The Essence of Christianity (Feuerbach) 49
Estonia (as part of USSR) 162
Evdokhimov, Efim 101, 125, 127
Evening Album (Tsvetaeva) 184
Executive Committee of the Petrograd Soviet 73
Extraordinary Assemblies of Factory and Plant Representatives 34

Fadeev, Alexander Alexandrovich: denunciation of 197; First Secretary of the Union of Soviet Writers 197; *The Golden Calf* 197; *Twelve Stools* 197
The Fall of Berlin (film) 207
famine, 1932–1933: Kazakhstan 116; North Caucasus 116; Ukraine 115–116
famine of 1921–1922 46
fascism 127; Germany, rise in 133; Japan, rise in 133; Spain, rise in 133
Fate of a Man (Sholokhov) 175
Fefer, Yitzhak 198
Feigenberg, Yevgenia 181
Feldman, Boris (Head of the Red Army Administration) 153
Fifteenth Party Congress 24
Fifth Party Congress, London 71, 73
Figes, Orlando: *The Whisperers* 149
Filatov, A. P. **203**
Finland: invasion by Red Army 162
Fitzpatrick, Sheila: *The Russian Revolution* 210
Five Year Plan 119; failures 119–120; food shortages 117; growth of heavy industry 116–117; successes 119
foreign trade 77–78
"former people" (*byvshchie liudi*) *see* bourgeoisie
Fourteenth Party congress 24, 124
Fourth International 92, 95
France: Directory 5; Germany, invasion of 163; Reign of Terror of 1793–1794 210; Spanish civil war non-intervention policy 152; Thermidorian Reaction 210; Vichy puppet government 163
Franco, Francisco (General): Army of Africa 151
Franz Ferdinand (Archduke of Austria): assassination 19
French Revolution: Committee of Public Safety 4; "enemies of the people" concept, use of 4; Executive Council of the National Convention 4; Jacobins 4; Revolutionary Tribunal, activities of 4
Frunze, Mikhail Vasilevich (General) 185
Fuerbach, Ludwig: *The Essence of Christianity* 49

Gagarin, Yuri Alexeevich (Soviet cosmonaut) 190

Gamarnik, Yan (General): Head of the Political Administration of the Red Army & First Deputy Commissar of Defense 153; suicide of 153
Gaven, Yuri 128
genetics: halt in work by Soviet scientists 192
George V (King of England) 27
Georgia (nation): Central Committee 78–79, 80; government overthrow by the Bolsheviks 78–79; Transcaucasian Federation, member of 47
Germany: ambassador to Russia, assassination by Left SRs 28, 36; Austria and the Sudetenland 157, 161; Belgium, invasion of 163; Berlin, Soviet blockade of 193–194; Communist Party, collapse of 90; Denmark, invasion of 163; France, invasion of 163; Great Britain, attacks on 163; Holland, invasion of 163; non-aggression pact with the Soviet Union (1939) 92, 157–158, 161; Norway, invasion of 163; Operation Barbarossa 163; Poland, invasion of 162, 163; rise of Nazi Party 150; Soviet Union, invasion of 163–169; Spanish Nationalists, support for 151; Treaty of Brest Litovsk 16, 28, 33, 34, 36, 38
glasnost 95
The Godless (journal) 57
The Golden Calf (Fadeev) 197
Goldman, Emma 43
Goloshchekin, Filip (Ural Regional Soviet) 28
Gomulka, Wladislaw 160–161, 208
Gorbachev, Mikhail: domestic reforms 10, 32, 95; relationship with Russian Orthodox Church 69; visit to People's Republic of China 221
Gorev, Vladimir 154–155
Gorky, Maxim 94, 137, 141, 142, 146, 180, 186; All-Russian Public Committee to Aid the Hungry 45–46
Gottwald, Kelment 199
GPU (State Political Administration) 9; dekulakization program 99; state security agency 47
Granovsky, Antonin (Bishop) 54–55
Great Britain: diplomatic relations with USSR 86–87; military intervention 33; Spanish civil war non-intervention policy 152
Great Depression 133
Great Terror 9, 214; *see also* cosmopolitans, persecution of; intelligentsia, persecution of; Jews, persecution of; Old Bolsheviks; purges, Soviet; wrecking trials, public
Great War 26; *see also* World War I (1914–1918)
Greek Orthodox Church 49
Grinko, G. V. 138
Gronfein, Yevgenia 181
Guevara, Ernesto Che 222–223; arrest and execution in Bolivia 227; Castro, falling out with 227; Cuba, leadership role in 226; overthrow of Batista government 223
Gulag 123, 198; repopulation of 178; uprisings 203–204; White Sea Canal project 113

Guofeng, Hua (successor to Mao Zedong) 220
Himmler, Heinrich 168, 169
history, "scientific" interpretation of 11, 15–16
History of the Russian Revolution (Trotsky) 89–90
Hitler, Adolf 150
Holland: invasion by Germany, 163
Holtzman, E. S. 126
Holy Synod 49
Hoover, Herbert (President) 46
House of the People's Revenge: destruction of by order of Yuri Andropov 32
Hoveyda, Amir Abbas 239
"How Not to Write the Lessons of October" (Bukharin) 83
Hungarian Communist Party 159
Hungarian Group of the Russian Communist Party 159
Hungarian Social Democratic Party 159
Hungary: rebellion (1956) 208; Warsaw Pact, member of 204
Hussein, Saddam (President of Iraq) 242

Ikramov, Akmal 145
industrial capitalism 12
industrial capitalism, Russian: destruction of 12
industrial powers, 19th century: acquisition of colonial empires 12
Industrial Revolution: industrial capitalism, impact of 11–12
Ingushi people: deportation ordered by Stalin 169
Institute for Red Professors 188
Insurgent Army of Ukraine (*Makhnovitsy*) 39
intelligentsia, persecution of: Andrei Nikolaevich Tupolov 188–189; Belarusian Academy of Science 188; Boris Pilniak 185–186; Dmitri Dmitrievich Shostakovich 192; Feodor Ivanovich Chaliapin 179; Institute for Red Professors 188; Isaac Emileovich Babel 180–181; Kharkov Physics Institute 188; Kiev Academy of the Sciences 188; Konstantine Streppa 187; Marina Ivanovna Tsvetaeva 184–185; Mikhail Nikolayevich Pokrovsky 186; Nikolai Ivanovich Vavilov 191; Professor Lev Davidovich Landau 188; Sergei Esenin 179; Sergei Pavlovich Korolev 189; Vladimir Mayakovsky 179–180; Vsevolod Yemilyevich Meyerhold 183, 185; Zinaida Raikh 183
Iov (Job) (Archbishop of Kazan): arrest of 67
Ipatiev House, Yekaterinburg (imperial family murder site) 30–31; *see also* House of the People's Revenge
Iran 235–244; Ali Khamenei, successor to Ayatollah Khomenei 243; American Embassy attack 241; Amir Abbas Hoveyda 239, 240; Ayatollah Ruhollah Khomeini 238–240, 242; Constitution 242; "enemies of the people," use of concept 10; General Nematollah

Nassiri 239–240; Mahmoud Ahmadinejad 243–244; Mir Hossein Moussavi 244; Mohammad Khatami 243; reign of terror 240; revolution 239–243; Revolutionary Council 239; revolutionary courts 239; Revolutionary Guards 240; Sadeq Khalkhali 239; Trans-Iranian Railway 236
Iranian Revolution 239–243
Iran-Iraq War 242–243
Iraq: "enemies of the people," use of concept 10
Israeli-Egypt peace treaty 240
Italy: support for Spanish Nationalists 151
Ivan the Terrible (Tsar): interference with Russian Orthodox Church 48
Ivanov, V. I. 138

Jacobins: compared to Russian Bolsheviks 210
Jacson, Frank *see* Mercader, Ramon
Japan: Cambodia, occupation of 228; China, invasion of 213; encroachment on Soviet territory 161; Manchuria, invasion of 213; military intervention 33; Russo-Japanese War (1904–1905) 26
Jewish Anti-Fascist Committee: disbanding of 197
Jewish Autonomous Region, Birobidzhan 194–195
Jews: anti-Semitic campaign 195
Jews, persecution of: Alexander Alexandrovich Fadeev 197; doctors' show trial 198–199; firing of critics from Soviet journals 195; Ilya Grigoryevich Ehrenburg 195–196; Jewish Anti-Fascist Committee 198; Lina Shtern 198; Solomon Borisovich Mikhoels *196*, 196–197; Yitzhak Fefer 198
Jianying, Ye (Marshall) 219, 220
Joffe, Adolf Abramovich 212
John Paul II (Pope) 240
Johnson, Nicholas: Grand Duke Michael, secretary to 29; murder by Cheka 29–30
Joint Committee of Inquiry 91
Joint State Political Directorate *see* OGPU
Journal of the Moscow Patriarchate 64

Kadets: "enemies of the people" 4
Kaganovich, Lazar Moiseevich 125, 194
Kahlo, Frida 91
Kai-shek, Chiang 86, 156
Kai-shek, Chiang (General): Nationalist Party, leader of 213
Kalmyk people: deportation ordered by Stalin 169
Kamenev, Lev Borisovich 23, 78, 80, 82–83, 86, 88, 119, 120, *129*; execution as "enemy of the people" 96, 127, 128; imprisonment 121–122; Party posts, expulsion from 85; show trial of 124–127
Kamenev, Sergei (General) 75
Kampuchea, People's Republic of: Democratic Kampuchea, name change from 234

Kaplan, Fanya: Lenin assassination attempt 37, *38*, 140
Karachai people: deportation ordered by Stalin 169
Karelin, Vladimir 140
Karolyi, Mihaly 159
Karpov, Georgi: Council on the Affairs of the Orthodox Church 65
katorga 178
Katyn Forest, Poland: Polish army officers, execution of 162
Kazakhstan: famine 116
Kennedy, John F. (President): Bay of Pigs invasion 225–226; Cuban Missile Crisis 227
Kerensky, Alexander (Prime Minister of the Provisional Government) 27; protection of imperial family 27
Kerensky, Isaak 139
KGB: creation of 204; influence with bishops 68
Khalkhali, Sadeq (judge of revolutionary court) 239, 240
Khamenei, Ali (successor to Ayatollah Khomeini) 243
Kharitonov, Ivan (imperial family chef) 27; murder by Ural Regional Soviet 31
Khatami, Mohammad 243
Khmer Rouge 229
Khomeini, Mostafa 239
Khomeini, Ruhollah (Ayatollah): anti-Shah speeches 238; death of 243; *fatwa* against Shah's imperial calendar 238; Iran, return to 238–239; Mostafa Khomeini 239; Revolutionary Guards 240
Khrushchev, Nikita 199, 200, *203*; actions following Stalin's death 202–209; Cuban Missile Crisis 67, 227; domestic initiatives 202; First Secretary of the Central Committee 202; Stalin, condemnation of 9, 94, 205–208, 209; successor to Stalin as First Secretary of the Communist Party 64
Kiev Academy of the Sciences 188
Kirov, Sergei Mironovich 94, 137; murder by Leonid Nikolaev 120, 206; Stalin, clash with 120–121
Kissinger, Henry: Nixon Doctrine 237
Knyazev, I. A. 133
kolkhoz 97, 99, 100; artel, modeled after 100
kollektiv 45
Kombedy 34–35
Komuch *see* Committee of Members of the Constituent Assembly
KONR *see* Committee for the Liberation of the Peoples of Russia
Kork, Avgust: Head of the Military Academy 153
Korolev, Sergei Pavlovich 189–190
Kosarev, Alexander: execution of 206
Kossior, Stanislav 187; "enemy of the people" 187; execution of 206; Near East Committee of the Ukrainian Academy of Sciences, head of 187

Kosygin, Alexei: appointment to premier 67
Krasnov, Piotr (Lieutenant General): Brotherhood of the Russian Truth, founder of 174; repatriation to Soviet Union 174; trial and execution of 174
Kresti prison, Leningrad *193*
Krestinsky, Nikolai 137–138
Kronstadt rebellion 42–43
Kropotkin, Piotr 40
Krupskaya, Nadezhda Konstantinovna 79, 82, 85
Krylenko, Nikolai: prosecuting attorney in show trials 101–102
Kuibyshev, Valerian 94, 137, 141, 142
kulaks *117,* 118; counterrevolutionary kulak-activists 99; deportations 99–100, 114; "enemies of the people" 97; liquidation as a class 99–100; rich kulaks 99; subkulaks (*podkulachniki*) 97
Kulik, [Grigori] Marshall 178
Kun, Bela (Comintern member): career of 159–160; Revolutionary Committee in the Crimea, head of 160
Kuomintang 211
Kuroedov, Vladimir: Russian Orthodox Church, repression of 65–66
Kutuzov, Mikhail Harionovich 59
Kuznetsov, Andrei 198

LaGuardia, Florio (Mayor) 197
Landau, Lev Davidovich (Professor) 188
Larina, Anna 145
Latsis, Martyn 7; arrest by Left SRs 36
Latvia (as part of USSR) 162
Lavoisier, Antoine (chemist): execution during French Revolution 4
Lavrenyov, Boris 25
Law of Seven-eights 114
League of Nations: expulsion of USSR 162
The League of the Militant Godless 57, 58
Lefortovo prison, Moscow 156–157
Left Opposition 24, 96; condemnation by Central Committee 81; formation of 81
Left Socialist Revolutionaries: rebellion against Lenin's domestic policies, 28; *see also* Left SRs
Left SRs: Bolsheviks, relationship with 35; uprising by 35–36
legal system under Bolshevik regime: new courts, types of 14–15
Lenin, Vladimir Ilich 159; assassination attempts on 6, 20, 37; attacks on 36–37; confrontation with Russian Orthodox Church 52–55; death of 8, 55, 82; *The Development of Capitalism in Russia* 71; dictatorship of the proletariat 13; domestic economic policies 17–20; early Marxist leanings 7–8; eradication of the capitalist basis of society 13; exile for anti-tsarist activities 8; history, scientific interpretation of 15–16; imperial family, role in murder of 28–29; industrialists and entrepreneurs, use in building socialism 17–18; leader of Bolshevik Party 3; mummification of 56–57; socialist approach to economy 12–13; "The Socialist Fatherland in Danger" 6, 16; *The State and Revolution* 5; terror and capital punishment as agents of change 7–8, 15–17; Testament 79–80, 82–83; Trotsky, reliance on 80
Lenin All-Union Academy of Agricultural Sciences: Trofim Lysenko as head 191
Leningrad (journal) 178
Leningrad Terrorist Center 121
Lenin's Testament 79–80, 82–83, 84–85, 87; *New York Times,* published in 86
Leonov, Alexei (Soviet cosmonaut) 190
"The Lessons of October" (Trotsky) 83
Levin, Vladimir (Dr.) 141
Lipshitz, Yakov 133
Literaturnaya Gazeta (journal) 95
Lithuania (as part of USSR) 162
Litvinov, Maxim Maximovich 198; People's Commissar for Foreign Affairs 194
Lozgachev, Piotr 199
Lubyanka prison, Moscow 6, 136, 154
Luke (Archbishop) 64
Luke (Metropolitan): appointment as Archbishop of the Crimea 64; appointment to Tashkent and Turkistan 62
Lurye, Moissei 126
Lurye, Nathan 126
Lysenko, Trofim 190–192; halt in work in genetics 192; Lenin All-Union Academy of Agricultural Sciences, president of 191

Machado, Gerardo 222
Magnitogorsk 119; deportees as unskilled labor 111; Ernest May, German architect 108; iron ore mining enterprise 108–112; Jack Scott, American welder 109–112; wrecking incidents at 111–112
Mahogany (Pilniak) 185
Makhno, Uestor Ivanovich: "enemy of the people" 40; Insurgent Army of Ukraine, leader of 39–41
Makhnovitsy see Insurgent Army of Ukraine
Malenkov, Georgii 197, 199
Mandelstam, Osip Emilevich 183–184
Marie Nicholaevna (Grand Duchess) 27, *28*; murder by the Ural Regional Soviet 30–31
Marin, Humberto Sori 225
Marshall Plan 193
Marx, Karl 12; religion as "opiate of the people" 49
Marxism: history, scientific interpretation of 11
Marxism and the National Colonial Question (Stalin) 73
Märzaktion (March Action) 160
May, Ernest: Magnitogorsk mine architect 108
Mayakovsky, Vladimir 179–180; *The Stern October Has Deceived Me* 179; *The Unfinished Poem* 180
Medvedev, Filip 121

Meir, Golda 195
Menshevik Party 3, 34, 78
Menzhinsky, V. R. 141, 142
Mercader, Ramon: assassination of Trotsky 93–94
Mershcherski, Alexei Pavlovich 17–18
Metro-Vickers: public wrecking trial 106, 108
Meyerhold, Vsevolod Emilovich 149, 181, *182, 183*; arrest and execution 183
Michael, Grand Duke: murder by Cheka 29–30
Mikhoels, Solomon Borisovich *196,* 196–197
military colonies: failures of 177; as a means of improving the lot of the serf 177
Mirbach, Wilhelm (Count): assassination by Left SRs 36
Moldavian Soviet Socialist Republic 162
Molotov, Vyacheslav Mikhailovich 133, 163, 205
Mornard, Jacques see Mercader, Ramon
Morozov, Feodor 146
Morozov, Pavlik 146
Morozov, Trofim 146
Moscow Commercial Bank 18
Moscow Metro 122
Moscow-Volga Canal 203
Moskalenko, Kirill Semyonovich (General) 202
Moussavi, Mir Hossein 244
Mrachkovsky, Sergei 125, 127
Muklevich, R. A. 157
Munich Conference (1938) 161
Muralov, N. I. 133
Muralov, Nikolai 88
Museum of the History of Religion and Atheism, Leningrad 59
Myasnikov, Gabriel (murderer of Grand Duke Michael) 29–30

Nansen, Fridtjof (head of League of Nations' High Commission for Refugees) 55
Nassiri, Nematollah (General): head of Savak 239–240
NATO 204
Nazi-Soviet Non-Aggression Pact (1939) 92, 157, 161–162
Near East Committee of the Ukrainian Academy of Sciences 187
NEP see New Economic Policy
Nepmen: demise of 24–25; economic rebuilding program, participants in 22–25; "new bourgeoisie" 24
Neumann, Heinz (Comintern member) 158
Nevelson, Nina 88
"new bourgeoisie" see Nepmen
New Economic Policy 8, 20, 70, 97; Civil Code of the USSR 22; economic rebuilding program 22–24, 43–44; see also Nepmen
New York Times: Lenin's Testament, publishing of 86
Nicholas I (Tsar): creation of the Third Section 177
Nicholas II (Tsar): abdication of 8, 19; ascendancy to throne (1894) 26; murder by the Ural Regional Soviet 30–31; Russo-Japanese War (1904–1905) 26; World War I (1914–1917) 26
Nikolaev, Leonid 120; execution of 121
Nikolai (Metropolitan): Office of Foreign Religious Affairs, removal as head of 67; retirement of 67
Nikon (Patriarch): influence on Tsar Alexei to change liturgy and ritual in Russian Orthodox Church 49
Nixon, Richard (President): Cambodia, bombing of 228; Nixon Doctrine 237
NKVD 89, 130, 135; Administration of Special Tasks 131; arrest of intelligentsia 189; investigation of 147; Kirov's murder, investigation of 121; Leningrad, mining of 165; Polish army officers, arrest of 162; purge of historians 186; special settlement camps 169; Trotsky, assassination of 93–94; Yezhov appointed as head of 131
Nol, Lon (General): King Sihanouk, overthrow by 228
North Caucasus: famine 116
Norway: invasion by Germany 163
Novaya Zhizyn (newspaper) 181

October Coup 42, 73
October Hall of the Trade Union House: show trial venue 124, 131, 136
Odessa Tales (Babel) 181
OGPU 87, 101, 113; in Ukraine 115
Olberg, Valentin 126
Old Bolsheviks: "enemies of the people" 123; show trials of 124–145
Old Bolsheviks, first show trial of: Bakayev, Ivan 125; Berman-Yurin, K. B. 126; David, Fritz 126; Dreitzer, E. A. 126; Dreitzer, Efim 125; Evdokimov, Efim 125, 127; Gaven, Yuri 128; Holtzman, E. S. 126; Kamenev, Lev 124–127, *129*; Lurye, Moissei 126; Lurye, Nathan 126; Mrachkovsky, Sergei 125, 127; Olberg, Valentin 126; Pikel, Richard 125; Putna, Vitovt 126–127; Smigla, Ivar 126; Smirnov, Ivan 126, 127; Zinoviev, Grigori 124–127, *129*
Old Bolsheviks, second show trial of: Arnold, Valentin 133, 135; Drobnis, Y. N. 135; Knyazev, I. A. 133; Lipshitz, Yakov 133; Muralov, N. I. 133; Pyatakov, Georgii 131; Radek, Karl 131, *134*; Rataichak, S. A. 134; Serebryakov, Leonid 131; Sokolnikov, Grigori 131, 135; Stroilov, M. S. 135
Old Bolsheviks, third show trial of: Bessonov, Sergei 137, 143, 145; Bukharin, Nikolai 139–141, 144; Chernov, M. A. 138; Grinko, G. V. 138; Ikramov, Akmal 145; Ivanov, V. I. 138; Karelin, Vladimir 140; Kerensky, Isaak 139; Krestinsky, Nikolai 137–138; Levin, Dr. Vladimir 141; Pletnev, Dr. Dimitri 142–143, 145; Rakovsky, Christian 137, 143, 145; Rosengolts, Arkady 144; Rykov, Alexei 139–

140, 144; Sharangovich, V. F. 139, 140;
Yagoda, Ginrikh 141–142, 144, 147, *148*;
Zubarov, P. T. 139
Olga Nicholaevna (Grand Duchess) 27, *28*;
murder by the Ural Regional Soviet 30–31
Operation Eagle Claw: American hostages in
Iran, attempted rescue of 241–242
Ordzhonikidze, Papuliya 135
Ordzhonikidze, Sergo 78–79, 87, 132, 135, 139;
suicide of 136
Orlov, Vladimir 157
Osipov, Alexander A. 65
Ostarbeitern 174

Pahlavi, Mohammad Reza (Shah of Iran) 235–
238; death of 238; departure from Iran 238;
Muslims, affronts to 238
Pahlavi, Reza (Shah of Iran): British and Soviet
governments, overthrown by 235–236
Palestine Liberation Organization 241
Pasternak, Boris 149
Pavlov, Dmitri (General) 163
People's Commissariat for Internal Affairs *see*
NKVD
People's Courts 15
People's Republic of Kampuchea: civil war
(1970–1975) 234
People's Will (revolutionary group): Tsar
Alexander II, assassination of 26
perestroika 69
Perm Soviet: Grand Duke Michael, murder of
29–30
Peru: "enemies of the people," use of concept 10
Peshkov, Maxim 137, 141, 142
Peter the Great (Tsar): Holy Synod, creation of
49; Russian Orthodox Church, interference
with 49
Peters, Yakov 59
Petrograd Soviet of Soldiers and Workers 3
Petrovsky, Grigorii 38
Pikel, Richard 125
Pilniak, Boris 185–186; All Russian Union of
Writers, president of 185; *Mahogany* 185; *Tale
of the Unextinguished Moon* 185; trial and exe-
cution of 186; *The Volga Flows into the
Caspian Sea* 186
Pimen (Metropolitan): appointment as Patri-
arch 68
Pimen (Patriarch) 69
Pius XI (Pope) 55
Platten, Fritz (Comintern member) 158
Plehve, Vyacheslav (Minister of the Interior):
assassination of (1902) 26
Pletnev, Dimitri (Dr.) 142–143, 145
Pokrovsky, Mikhail Nikolayevich 186; *A Brief
History of Russia* 186
Poland: invasion by Germany 162, 163; mem-
ber of Warsaw Pact 204
Poliansky, Piotr: arrest and execution 57
Politburo 77, 78, 124; Party democracy, resolu-
tion in support of 81

Political Bureau *see* Politburo
Port Arthur: returned to the Peoples' Republic
of China 204
Pospelov, Piotr Nikolaevich: commission to
investigate Lenin's excesses 205
Pot, Pol [*or* Pol Pot] 235; Four Year Plan 229;
Party members, purging of 230
Pravda 4, 21, 65, 81, 96; "The Death of an
International Spy" 94; "Murderers in White
Gowns" 199
Presidium of the Central Committee 205
Primakov, Vitaly: First Deputy Commander of
the Leningrad Military District 153
prisoner research unit 188, 189
prisoners of war, Soviet: amnesty by
Khrushchev 175; "enemies of the people" 174;
fate of 174–175; forced repatriation of 173–
174
prisons, Soviet: Butyrka 140, 145, 167, 184;
Kresti, Leningrad *193*; Lefortovo, Moscow
156–157; Lubyanka, Moscow 6, 136, 154;
Saratov, Saratov City 191
Proletarian Cultural and Enlightenment Organizations 179
Proletkult see Proletarian Cultural and Enlightenment Organizations
Proveshchenye (Enlightenment) (journal) 73
Provisional Government 4, 8, 33, 35, 71, 73,
130; incarceration of the imperial family 26–
27; overthrow by Bolsheviks 3, 27
Pu Yi (Chinese emperor) 211
purges, Soviet: Army high-command 152–154;
citizens of new territories 162–163; Comintern members 157–161; effect on Red Army
morale in World War II 164–165; lessening of
161; military officer corps 155–157; Soviet
advisors to Spanish Republicans 154–155
"The Purpose of Our Differences" (Trotsky) 84
Putna, Vitovt Kazimirovich 126–127; former
Military Attaché in London 153
Pyatakov, Georgii 131–132, 133, 135; "enemy of
the people" 132
Pyatakov, Yuri 86, 127

Radek, Karl Bernardovich 127, 132, *134*, 135
Raikh, Zinaida 183
Rakovsky, Christian 92, 137, 143, 145
Ramzin, Leonid 105–106, *106*
Ranaariddh, Nordum (Prince) 234–235
Rataichak, S. A. 134
Rayfield, Donald 198, 201
Reagan, Ronald (President) 242
Red Army: civil war battles 38, 39; death
penalty for retreating or surrendering in battle
164; Finland, invasion of 162; General
Tukhashevsky 41; prisoners of war, repatria-
tion of 173–175
Red Cavalry (Babel) 181
Red Guards 14
Red Terror 8; Sovnarkom's Decree on the Red
Terror (1918) 7

Regional Congress of Peasants, Workers and Insurgents 40
religion, persecution for practitioners of 59
renovationists 54–55
repatriation, forced: of prisoners of war 173–174; of Soviet nationals 173–174
Republic of China 211; Kuomintang 211
The Revolution Betrayed (Trotsky) 90
Revolutionary Tribunal, French 4
Revolutionary Tribunal, Russian 15
Revolutionary War Council 75
revolutions: common traits of 210
Riabushinsky, Dmitri 19–20
Riabushinsky, Pavel Pavlovich 18–19; *Utro Rossii* (Morn of Russia) 18
Right Communist bloc 139
Right Communists 96
Riutin, Marteman 120–121
Rivera, Diego 90, 91, 92
Robeson, Paul 197
Robespierre, Maximillian 210; death of 5; leader of the Jacobins 4
Rodos, Boris 206
The Role and Tasks of the Trade Unions (Trotsky) 76
Romania (member of Warsaw Pact) 204
Romanian Secret Police 160
Romanov dynasty: Bolshevik hatred of 25
Romanov imperial family **28**; "enemies of the people" 27; imprisonment in the Ipatiev House, Yekaterinburg, by Ural Regional Soviet 27–28; incarceration by Provisional Government 26–27; members of 27; murder by Ural Regional Soviet 30–31
Rosengolts, Arkady 144
Rozenberg, Marsel (Soviet ambassador to Spain) 154
Russia: civil war (1917–1922) 8, 28, 33, 35–46; Russo-Japanese War (1904–1905) 26; Union of Soviet Socialist Republics, member of 47
Russian Association of Proletarian Writers 180
Russian Imperial Academy of Sciences: Soviet scholars denounced 192
Russian Liberation Army 167–169, 170
Russian Orthodox Church: Archbishop Andrei of Chernigov 67; Archbishop Iov (Job) of Kazan 67; Archpriest Alexander Vvendensky 54; Bishop Antonin Granovsky 54–55; Metropolitan Alexei of Leningrad 62–64; Metropolitan Luke 62, 64; Metropolitan Nikolai 67; Metropolitan Sergei 57, 62–63; Metropolitan Tikhon 50–55, **51**; Old Believers 49; Patriarch Adrian 49; Patriarch Nikon 49; Patriarch Pimen 68, 69; Piotr Poliansky as temporary head 57; renovationist movement 54; resurrection under Gorbachev regime 69
Russian Orthodox Church, repression of: anti-religion demonstrations **66**; Black Hundred clergy, extermination of 53; under Bolshevik regime 48–69; under Brezhnev regime 67–68; destruction of churches by Soviet government 58–59, **60, 61, 63**; as "enemies of the people" 53; by Ivan the Terrible 48; under Krushchev regime 64–67; lessening of during World War II 62; by Peter the Great 49; post–World War II 64; tyranny of tsars *vs.* Bolsheviks 49–50
The Russian Revolution (Fitzpatrick) 210
Russo-Japanese War (1904–1905) 26
Ryabov, Yuri (discoverer of Romanov family remains) 32
Rykov, Alexei Ivanovich 23, 97, 120, 127, **138**; arrest of 136; opposition to Stalin's Five Year plan 97–98; Premier of the Sovnarkom 98; trial of 139–140, 143, 144

St. Petersburg Soviet of Workers' Deputies 71
Salt II 240
San Martin, Ramon Grau 222
Saratov prison, Saratov City 191
Savak: Iranian secret police force 236, 237–238
Schubert, Hermann (Comintern member) 161
Scott, Jack (American welder at Magnitorgorsk) 109–112
Secret Speech: denunciation of Stalin at Twentieth Party Congress 205–208, 209
Sedov, Lev 125, 133; death of 91–92
Sedov, Sergei 126; murder of 91
Sedova, Natalya 88
Sen, Hun 234–235
Serebryakov, Leonid 127, 131
Serge, Victor 22
Sergei (Grand Duke) 26; assassination (1907) 26
Sergei (Metropolitan) 57, 58; election as Patriarch 63–64
Sergei (Patriarch) 63–64; death of 64, 68
Seventeenth Party Congress 119–120, 205–206
Shakhty show trial 101–102, **102, 103,** 125
Shanghai, China: Left faction, purge of (1927) 86
Shaoqi, Liu: leader of People's Republic of China 218
Sharangovich, V. F. 139, 140
sharashka see prisoner research unit
Shcherbakov, Alexander 199
Shikai, Yuan (President of China) 211
Shlyapinkov, Alexander (chairman of All-Russian Metalworkers' Union) 76
Sholokhov, Mikhail Aleksandrovich: *Fate of a Man* 175
Shostakovich, Dmitri Dmitrievich 192; *Testimony* 192
show trials *see* show trials, public; wrecking trials, public
show trials, public 122
Shteppa, Konstantine 187
Shtern, Lina 198
Sihamoni, Norodum (King of Cambodia) 235
Sihanouk, Norodum (King of Cambodia) 228, 234
Since Lenin Died (Eastman) 84

Siqueiros, David Alfaro: attempt to assassinate Trotsky 93
Sixteenth Party Congress: "The Five Year Plan in Four" 100–101
slave labor camps 99–100; *see also* corrective labor colonies; special settlement camps
Smigla, Ivar 126
Smirnov, Ivan 126, 127
Smirnov, Piotr (Commander) 157
Smolensk Declaration (1942) 168
Smolny Institute, Leningrad 121
Social Democratic Labor Party 8, 12
Social Realism: Andrei Aleksandrovich Zhdanov 187–188
Social Revolutionaries 34
socialism: in post–Russian Revolution era 5
Socialist Realism: official policy of Stalinist regime 179, 181
Socialist Revolutionaries: assassination attempt on Lenin 20; assassination of Moisei Uritsky 20; Bolsheviks, uprising against 6
Socialist Revolutionary Party 3, 35
Sokolnikov, Grigori Yakovlovich 127, 131, 135
Sokolovskaya, Alexandra 70
Solzhenitsyn, Alexander Isaeevich 167; *A Day in the Life of Ivan Denisovich* 175
Soviet advisors to Spanish Communists, purge of: Marsel Rozenberg 154; Vladimir Antonov-Ovseenko 154; Vladimir Gorev 154–155
Soviet Army high command, purge of: Boris Feldman 153; General Avgust Kork 153; General I. E. Yakir 152; General Yan Gamarnik 153, 154; I. P. Uborevich 152; Marshall Mikhail Tukhachevsky 152–153, 155, *155*; Vitaly Primakov 153; Votovt Putna 153
Soviet military officer corps, purge of: Commander Ivan Belov 156; Commander Mikhail Viktorov 157; Commander Piotr Smirnov 157; Commander Vasily Bliukher 156; General I. I. Vasetsis 155–156; R. A. Muklevich, Director of Naval Construction 157; Vladimir Orlov, Deputy Minister of Defense 157
Soviet Republic of Hungary 159
Soviet Union: incorporation of eastern Europe 162; non-aggression pact (1939) with Germany 92, 157–158, 161–162
sovkhozes 97
Sovnarkom 38, 74; Alexei Rykov as Premier 98; All-Russian Extraordinary Commission for Combating Counter-revolution and Sabotage (Cheka), creation of 5; counter-revolutionary economic programs 21–22; Decree on the Red Terror (1918) 7; Table of Ranks, abolishment of 13
Spain: Catholic Church, power curtailed 151; civil war 150–152; Communist Party 152; Spanish Confederation of Autonomous Rightist Parties 151
Spanish civil war (1936–1939): Nationalists, support for 151; Republicans, rifts within 152; Republicans, support for 151–152
Spanish Confederation of Autonomous Rightist Parties 151
special settlement camps: Central Asia 169; in Kazakhstan 163; in Russia 163; Siberia 169
Spiridonova, Maria Alexandrovna: assassination of German ambassador, involvement in 35, 37
Stalin, Josef 23, 24, 69, 72–75, 77–80, 119, **138**; China policy 86; Commissar of Nationalities 9, 74, 75; Constitution of 1936 128; control of literary establishment 178–179; death of 199–200; denounciation by Khrushchev 9, 94, 205–208, 209; Five Year Plan 97–98; funeral of 201; General Secretary of the Communist Party 9, 44, 77; grain requisitioning plan 97–98; Kirov, investigation into murder of 121; Lenin's funeral, organization of 56–57; *Marxism and the National Colonial Question* 73; military high command, purge of 152–154; "On the Reconstruction of Literary and Art Organizations" 179; Order No. 227 164; Order No. 270 164; successor to Vladimir Lenin 9, 56; Trotsky, power struggle with 74–88; Tsaritsyn (Volgograd) food shortages 74
Stalin, Vasily 77; arrest by Beria 202
Stalin: The Man and His Era (Ulam) 148
"The State and Revolution" (Lenin): "dictatorship of the proletariat" 8
The State and Revolution (Lenin) 5
State Political Administration (*Gosudarstvennoe Politicheskoe Upravlenie*) *see* GPU
state security agencies: Cheka 5–8, 9; GPU 9, 47; KGB 68, 208; NKVD 89, 93–94, 146, 147; OGPU 87, 141, 146
The Stern October Has Deceived Me (poem) (Mayakovsky) 179
Sternberg, Isaac: Minister of Justice 16
Stolypin, Piotr: assassination of (1911) 26; Prime Minister of the Imperial Duma 26
The Story of My Imprisonment (Zabolotsky) 193
Strik-Strikfeldt, Wilfried (Captain) 167–168
Stroilov, M. S. 135
subbotniki 45
Sverdlov, Jakob 28, 73

Table of Ranks 13
Taiwan: Chinese Nationalist Party escape to 214
Tale of the Unextinguished Moon (Pilniak) 185
Tatiana Nicholaevna (Grand Duchess) 27, **28**; murder by Ural Regional Soviet 30–31
Tenth Party Congress, Moscow 8, 42–43, 77
Testimony (Shostakovich) 192
Thailand: Cambodia, occupation of 228
Thatcher, Margaret (British prime minister) 240
Third Section: political security under Tsar Nicholas I 177
Thirteenth Comintern plenum 126

Index

Thirteenth Party Congress 82–83; Trotsky, attacks on 83–84
Tikhon (Metropolitan): Cheka, arrest by 54; death of 55; election to Patriarch 50–55, *51*
Tikhon (Patriarch) 50–55, *51*
Tito, Josip Broz (Marshall of Yugoslavia) 204; differences with Stalin 193
Tomsky, Mikhail 96, 97, 120, 127; opposition to Stalin's Five Year Plan 97; suicide of 127
torture techniques: the conveyer 123
trade unions: banning of 77; Trotsky's policies about 76–77
Transcaucasian Federation: Georgia, pressure by Bolsheviks to join 78–79; member of Union of Soviet Socialist Republics 47
Transcaucasian Social Democrats 73
Treaty of Brest Litovsk 16, 28, 33, 35, 36, 140, 159; nullification by Bolsheviks 38
Treaty of Versailles (1919) 159
Triumvirate *see troika*
troika: dissolution of 85; formation of by Kamenev, Zinoviev & Stalin 78; role in diminishing Trotsky's military leadership 80
Trotsky, Lev Davidovich *72*, 79, 128, 137; accusations against during purge trials 125, 126; children, death of 88, 90, 91–92; Commissar of Foreign Affairs 9, 23, 71; Commissar of Transport 75–76; Commissar of War 9, 13, 71, 164; credentials as a revolutionary leader 70–71; "enemy of the people" 71; exile during Tsarist regime 88–95; exile to Siberia 70, 71; expulsion from Communist Party 9, 72, 88; *History of the Russian Revolution* 89–90; "The Lessons of October" 83; "The Purpose of this Explanation: Our Differences" 84; *The Revolution Betrayed* 90; *The Role and Tasks of the Trade Unions* 76; St. Petersburg Soviet of Workers' Deputies, chairman of 71; Stalin, power struggle with 74–88; Supreme Council of the National Economy, assignment to 85
Trotskyism 93, 95, 127, 132; defined by Stalin 84
Trotskyist-Zinovievite Center 125, 126
Truman, Harry S. (President) 199; aid package for Greece and Turkey 193
Trupp, Alexei (imperial family footman) 27; murder by Ural Regional Soviet 31
Tsektran (transportation agency) 75–76
Tsvetaeva, Marina Ivanovna 184–185; *Evening Album* 184
Tuchkov, Evgenii 54
Tukhachevsky, Mikhail (General) 43, 132, *155*
Tukhachevsky, Mikhail (Marshall) 153–154, 155, 156; Deputy People's Commissar of Defense 152; trial and execution of 153–154
Tupolov, Andrei Nikolaevich 188–189; "enemy of the people" 188
Turksib Railway 119
Twelfth Party Congress, Moscow 80
Twelve Stools (Fadeev) 197

Twentieth Party Congress 9; denounciation of Stalin by Khrushchev 205–208
Twenty-Second Party Congress 67

Uborevich, I. P. (Head of Osoaviakim) 152
Uglanov, N. A. 127
Ukraine: collectivization 114–115; deportation of kulaks 114; member of Union of Soviet Socialist Republics, 47; 1932–1933 famine 115–116; occupation by Germany 164; Polish invasion of 41; requisition of grain by Soviets 113–114; Ukrainian-Trotskyist Center 132
Ulam, Adam: *Stalin: The Man and His Era* 148
Ulianov, Alexander 7; *see also* Ulianov, Alexander Ilich
Ulianov, Alexander Ilich: Tsar Alexander III, assassination attempt 25
Ulrikh, Vasily: judge at Old Bolshevik trials 125; judge in Metro-Vickers show trial 106
The Unfinished Poem (poem) (Mayakovsky) 180
Union of Soviet Socialist Republics: Belorussia 47; creation of 47; Russia 47; Transcaucasian Federation (Georgia, Armenia and Azerbaijan) 47; Ukraine 47
United Opposition 96, 124; formation of 85–86
Ural Regional Soviet: imperial family, imprisonment of 27–28; imperial family and retainers, murder of 30–31
Uritsky, M. S. (head of Petrograd Cheka): murder by Leonid Kannegiser 37
Uritsky, Moisei: assassination by Socialist Revolutionaries 20; head of Cheka 20
Utro Rossii (newspaper) 18

Vasetsis, I. I. (General): "enemy of the people" 155–156
Vatsetis, Joakim (General) 75
Vavilov, Nikolai Ivanovich 191
Viktorov, Mikhail (Commander) 157
Vinogradov (Dr.) 198
Vlasov, Andrei Andreevich (Lieutenant General) *166*; American Army, in custody of 171; capture by German Wehrmacht 167; capture by Red Army 171; "enemy of the people" 167, 172; Red Army career during World War II 165–167; Russian Liberation Army 167–171; trial and execution of 171–172
Voino-Yasenetsky, Valentin Felixovich: and anti-religious policies of Soviet government, 59, 62; imprisonment, 62; Metropolitan of Tashkent and Turkistan, 62; name change to Luke, 62; *see also* Luke (Metropolitan)
The Volga Flows into the Caspian Sea (Pilniak) 186
Volga Germans: deportation ordered by Stalin 169
Volkhova, Zinaida 90
Volodarsky, Moisei: assassination by Left SRs 35

Voroshilov, Klimenti 74–75, 125, 126, 156, 200
Voznesensky, Nikolai 198
Vvendensky, Alexander (Archpriest) 54
Vyshinsky, Andrei Yanuaryevich *140*; chief prosecutor in Metro-Vickers show trial 106; judge in wrecker show trials 101, 104, *104, 107*; prosecutor at Old Bolshevik trials 125, 127, 132, 134–135, 137, 138, 139–141, 143

Warsaw Pact 204
The Whisperers (Figes) 149
White Army: Admiral Alexander Kolchak (Supreme Commander) 39; anti-Soviet army 28; battles against Red Army 39–40; defeat of 42; Evgenii Miller, General (Archangel) 39; General Anton Denikin (Ukraine) 39; General Nicholai Yudenich (Estonia) 39; General Piotr Wrangel (Crimea) 41; Russian civil war, participation in 33–41
White Guard 7, 38
White Sea Canal project 113
Wilhelm (Deutsches Reich, Kaiser, II) 29
World War I (1914–1918) 3, 26
wreckers 91; bourgeois specialists 101; as "enemies of the people" 102, 110–112
wrecking trials, public 101–106, 108

Xiaoping, Deng: "enemy of the people" 219; leader of People's Republic of China 218; political comeback 220–221

Yagoda, Genrikh 121, *203*; arrest of 136; NKVD, head of 120; OGPU, head of 113; trial of 139–140, 141–142, 144, 147
Yakir, I. E. (Commander of the Kiev Military District) 152
Yakunin, Gleb (Father): imprisonment of 68
Yalta Conference (1945) 173
Yarosalvsky, Emelian: *Bible for Believers and Non-Believers* 58
Yat-sen, Sun (Dr.) 156; Chinese Nationalist Party, leader of 211; death of 213
Yezhov, Nikolai Ivanovich ("Bloody Dwarf") 136, *148,* 154, 181, 186; arrest and execution of 147; as a Bolshevik 130; Central Committee, election to 130; NKVD, head of 130–131, 141; Organizational Bureau, membership in 131; Party Control Commission, membership in 131; removed as head of NKVD 147, 187; Russian Central Executive Committee, membership in 131
Yezhovshchina (terrible time of Yezhov) 131, 148
Yurovksy, Jacob: assassination of imperial family 30–31

Zabarsky, Boris (Dr.): Lenin, mummification of 197; Mikhoels' corpse, cosmetic surgery on 197
Zabolotsky, Nikolay: *The Story of My Imprisonment* 193
Zedong, Mao 211, 212; Chinese civil war (1927–1950) 213–214; Chinese Communist Party, leader of 213; death of 219, 220; five year plans 215, 216; Great Leap Forward 216–218; Long March 213; president, resignation as 218; purge of perceived enemies 216, 218
zeks 202, 203
Zelensky, Isaak Abramovich 139, 143
Zhdanov, Andrei Aleksandrovich 126, 192; death of 197, 199; Party boss of Leningrad 188
Zheludkov, Sergei (Father): imprisonment of 68
Zherebkov, Yuri Sergeevich 170
Zhilenkov, Georgii (General) 170
Zhukov, Georgy Konstantinovich (General) 161, 178, 202
Zinoviev, Grigori Yevseyvich 23, 78, 82–83, 86, 87, 120, *129, 138,* 160; Communist Party, expulsion from 88; execution as "enemy of the people" 96, 127, 128; imprisonment 121–122; Leningrad Terrorist Center 121; Party posts, expulsion from 85; show trial of 124–127
Zinoviev, Stefan 128
Zoshchenko, Mikhail (writer) 178, 179
Zubarov, P. T. 139
Zvezda (journal) 178

www.ingramcontent.com/pod-product-compliance
Lightning Source LLC
Chambersburg PA
CBHW030612230426
43661CB00053B/1953